2/19

FROM HITLER'S GERMANY TO SADDAM'S IRAQ

FROM HITLER'S GERMANY TO SADDAM'S IRAQ

The Enduring False Promise of Preventive War

Scott A. Silverstone

ROWMAN & LITTLEFIELD
Lanham • Boulder • New York • London

Published by Rowman & Littlefield
An imprint of The Rowman & Littlefield Publishing Group, Inc.
4501 Forbes Boulevard, Suite 200, Lanham, Maryland 20706
www.rowman.com

6 Tinworth Street, London SE11 5AL, United Kingdom

British Library Cataloguing in Publication Information Available

Library of Congress Cataloging-in-Publication Data
Names: Silverstone, Scott A., author.
Title: From Hitler's Germany to Saddam's Iraq : the enduring false promise of preventive war / Scott A. Silverstone.
Other titles: Enduring false promise of preventive war
Description: Lanham, MD : Rowman & Littlefield, [2019] | Includes bibliographical references and index.
Identifiers: LCCN 2018023182 (print) | LCCN 2018026514 (ebook) | ISBN 9781442274464 (ebook) | ISBN 9781442274457 (cloth : alk. paper)
Subjects: LCSH: Preemptive attack (Military science)—Case studies. | International relations—Case studies. | World War, 1939–1945—Causes. | Rhineland (Germany)—Strategic aspects. | World War, 1939–1945—Diplomatic history. | International security—Case studies.
Classification: LCC U163 (ebook) | LCC U163 .S545 2018 (print) | DDC 355.02—dc23
LC record available at https://lccn.loc.gov/2018023182

♾™ The paper used in this publication meets the minimum requirements of American National Standard for Information Sciences—Permanence of Paper for Printed Library Materials, ANSI/NISO Z39.48-1992.

Printed in the United States of America

CONTENTS

ACKNOWLEDGMENTS

I owe immense gratitude to friends and colleagues who supported this project in various ways. Brigadier General Tim Trainor and Brigadier General Cindy Jebb, successive deans of the Academic Board at the United States Military Academy, supported sabbatical leave that made it possible for me to complete the book. Colonel Suzanne Nielsen, head of the Department of Social Sciences at West Point, has been a great champion of this work, and I'm so grateful to my colleagues in the department who picked up a heavier load in my absence.

Much of the research for this book was made possible by a fellowship with New America from 2015 to 2017. Peter Bergen, vice president of New America, has been a source of energy and insight, and I would like to thank Anne-Marie Slaughter, president and CEO of New America, for welcoming me to this fantastic community. My New America colleagues have been an amazing source of inspiration, advice, and feedback on my work. The Carnegie Corporation of New York sponsored the first year of this fellowship, and the Center on the Future of War at Arizona State University provided sponsorship in the second year.

A number of scholars that I admire greatly have been kind enough to provide feedback on various renditions of this work: Jack Levy, Norrin Ripsman, Robert Art, Daniel Rothenberg, Dale Copeland, Tim Crawford, Rosa Brooks, Peter Jackson, Jeffrey Taliaferro, Seth Johnston, Michael Lind, Talbot Imlay, and Sam Mustafa—many thanks to this distinguished group. A workshop on grand strategy between the world wars, hosted by Steven Lobell at the University of Utah, provided a fertile environment for the early development of the ideas at the heart of this book. My agent, Kristina Moore at the Wylie Agency, has been a great advocate for this project.

Finally, I would like to thank my wife, Lisa Silverstone, who plowed through rough drafts of the manuscript, chapter by chapter, to give me outstanding feedback on every aspect of my writing.

This book is dedicated to my students, the cadets at the United States Military Academy at West Point. I've been teaching at West Point since 2001, a period that has gravely tested the operational skills, the endurance, and the creativity of the Army's leaders and its soldiers. Converting battlefield victories into real strategic success is the enduring object of war, and a challenge that every generation has to confront for itself, with insight and inspiration from those who have gone before.

Scott A. Silverstone
West Point, New York

I

THE FALSE PROMISE OF
LOST OPPORTUNITIES

Last time I saw it all coming and I cried aloud to my own fellow-countrymen and to the world, but no one paid any attention.

—Winston Churchill, 1946

Life is lived forward, but only understood backwards.

—Søren Kierkegaard, 1843

On the morning of June 28, 1940, Adolf Hitler stood on the wide stone terrace above the Jardins du Trocadéro in Paris, the conqueror surveying his prize. With the Eiffel Tower as a backdrop, Hitler and his companions posed casually for photographs, like common tourists enjoying one of the world's most iconic views. They admired the gardens and the Seine River below, the Champ de Mars beyond. Just six days earlier, in the small French town of Compiègne north of Paris, the Führer had accepted French capitulation with a show of theatrical contempt. The simple ceremony lasted a mere fifteen minutes, yet Hitler had prepared a poignant stage for this moment, ripe with historic meaning. In a clearing in the Compiègne forest sat the same train car used by French general Ferdinand Foch, commander in chief of Allied Forces, for the armistice meeting of November 11, 1918. It was this ceremony, over twenty years earlier, that signaled Germany's capitulation and the end of World War I. On Hitler's orders,

Foch's train car had been plucked from the Glade of the Armistice museum and moved just meters away to this precise spot, exactly where it stood in 1918. The inscription on a large stone monument in the clearing proudly declared that this was where the "criminal pride of the German Empire" was vanquished. But on this day, the leader of the Third Reich was in Compiègne to erase Germany's earlier humiliation. As Hitler surveyed the scene, one eyewitness, the journalist William Shirer, described his face as "afire with scorn, anger, hate, revenge, triumph."[1] Minutes later, German officers escorted the French delegation to Foch's train car to sign their own surrender agreement.

This was Hitler's first visit to Paris, and it was a victory tour to be sure. He entered the city in the wake of his conquering army, but the episode had none of the bombast that traditionally marked Nazi Germany's most important moments. Hitler's small entourage traveled in a modest three-car motorcade along the deserted Champs-Élysées and circled the Arc de Triomphe. They marveled at the Paris Opera House and the grandeur of the Panthéon. The Führer brooded over Napoleon Bonaparte's tomb under the dome of the chapel at Les Invalides, and he walked the grounds of the ornate Sacré-Coeur cathedral while Parisian congregants tried to ignore the sacrilege. Hitler confided to Albert Speer, his favorite architect and the most important guest on this tour: "It was the dream of my life to be permitted to see Paris. I cannot say how happy I am to have that dream fulfilled today."

Despite his ebullient mood, Hitler had ruled out a show of military triumph as part of the event. His restraint may seem odd; by the summer of 1940 the Third Reich certainly had much to celebrate. It had already absorbed Austria into a Greater Germany, bullied Czechoslovakia into submission and occupation, and violently split Poland with the Soviet Union nine months before. Denmark and much of Norway were under the control of the Wehrmacht, the Third Reich's armed forces. The blitzkrieg armor attack that overpowered France began in mid-May with the rapid conquest of the Netherlands and Belgium. Along the way, the invasion forced nearly 200,000 British soldiers and 140,000 French, Belgian, Polish, and Dutch troops, trapped by advancing German forces in the French port city of Dunkirk, into a desperate flight across the English Channel to avoid capture. The German Luftwaffe was preparing a campaign to destroy the Royal Air Force Fighter Command and terrorize London with nighttime bombing to compel British acceptance of armistice or surrender. Hitler had neutralized the USSR with a nonaggression pact ten months earlier, while the United States remained aloof from the conflict with unilateral Neutrality Acts of its own. Despite everything he had accomplished along this road to Paris, on that late June morning Hitler was looking to the future. To his adjutants he declared, "I am not in the mood for a victory parade. We aren't at the end yet."[2]

Five years later, when Nazi Germany ultimately reached its end in utter defeat, the final tally in the terror and bloodletting was unprecedented. There are so many ways to measure the misery. It was global in scope; war burned from the Atlantic Ocean across Europe and North Africa to East Asia and the western Pacific. Estimates for the death toll in World War II typically range from fifty million to seventy million.[3] Many more civilians died than actual combatants. If we ignore the Asian-Pacific conflict and focus only on the costs imposed by German aggression and the Allied response, the picture is still staggering. In the Western Theater there were an estimated fifteen million combatant deaths between 1939 and 1945, with approximately eighteen million civilians dead as a direct result of hostilities. Poland lost 20 percent of its prewar population. Twenty thousand were killed by the German bombing of London between September 1940 and May 1941, while twenty-five thousand died in Berlin on a single night during the Allied air raid of February 3, 1945. Five million prisoners of war died in captivity. Thirty thousand merchant seamen lost their lives in the Atlantic, mainly to German submarine wolf packs. Nazi death camps in occupied Poland, which churned away simultaneously with the broader war, consumed two million prisoners at Auschwitz and Treblinka alone, the same number of Soviet soldiers and civilians that died during the Siege of Leningrad, which became a death camp in its own right. The systematic genocide of millions more in the Holocaust strains belief.

These numbers are striking indeed, yet the enduring memory of this war doesn't depend on precise statistics. In the popular mind it remains fixed as a grotesquely painful period in human history, driven by a vicious regime and its Führer, who for generations has remained the absolute paragon of aggression and terror. And for each successive generation, World War II has held an enduring fascination that hasn't faded with time.

THE GUILTY MEN

There are two faces to this conflict, and they help to explain our lasting interest. While it's a story that presents the most evil of villains and the most brutal human suffering, it's also a righteous tale in which the "Greatest Generation" strikes back after early losses, ultimately offering us total victory at the end of a valiant struggle. But there is something else at work in this history that gives it such enduring meaning over so many years. Looking back, many see the Second World War as doubly tragic, the horror of its titanic proportions compounded by a profound postwar judgment: that the bloodletting was *avoidable*. The venerable Winston Churchill himself, the prime minister that led Britain through the darkest days of the Nazi onslaught, fed this view in the first volume of his wartime memoirs. Churchill called it "The Unnecessary War," proclaiming "there never was a war more easy to stop than that which has just wrecked what was left of the world from the previous struggle."[4] If valid, this claim is shocking—that the most costly war in history was also a war that could have easily been prevented. And the common judgment of history holds French and British—but mainly British—leaders of the 1930s culpable for this catastrophe.

The impulse to lay blame didn't rest until the war was finally won. The day after the last of the Allied soldiers were pulled off the beaches of Dunkirk, three British journalists met secretly on the roof of the *Evening Standard* building in London. In anger and despair, they mapped out a plan for a book that would point an accusing finger at fifteen British cabinet members and government officials they blamed for Hitler's triumph. *The Guilty Men*, published anonymously just weeks after the Führer enjoyed his victor's grand tour of Paris, quickly sold more than two hundred thousand copies in early July 1940, and went through twelve printings as German bombs fell on London through the fall. The "guilty men" thesis has been a persistent theme ever since.[5] In a narrative that's been repeated endlessly, they were too naive or blind to recognize the dangers building year after year. They were too feckless or cowardly to take urgent and decisive action against the rising power of Nazi Germany before the regime was ready to unleash its fury across Europe. The verdict rendered in this case, so often expressed with disgust, draws from a ubiquitous cry: How could they have missed the clear signs of Hitler's aggressive intentions? And why didn't they act to blunt this vicious threat before it was too late?

Building on this indictment, the tragedy of the 1930s seems to echo and amplify the words of French foreign minister Pierre-Étienne Flandin, who in 1936 called for "urgent, brutal, decisive measures" in response to Hitler's sudden remilitarization of the German Rhineland.[6] Flandin was calling for *preventive war* against Nazi Germany. And this call for preventive war brings us to the troubling strategic questions about rising threats at the heart of this book. Among the options states have for countering potential danger, none are as bold or brutal as preventive war. In the simplest terms, the goal of preventive war is to seize the initiative and physically beat back the rising power of a rival with military force. This is not about defense against actual aggression, or even a first strike to *preempt* an adversary's imminent attack. It is the choice to lash out as a rival grows stronger, to avoid the mere possibility that it might one day be strong enough to pose a great danger.

This is an audacious choice that certainly carries risk, but the allure of preventive war, as the political scientist Robert Gilpin once observed, is found in its promise to *eliminate* the looming security problem at its source.[7] This is what Flandin hoped to achieve when he called for "decisive measures" against the reconstruction of German power that Rhineland remilitarization would support. And given the grave threat we know France faced in the coming years, the wisdom of turning to the preventive war option to solve the problem seems obvious and beyond dispute. But British leaders refused to support the French call for preventive attack, so the proposal died. To this day, the British decision is condemned as a grave mistake, as a lost opportunity to eliminate the German threat before the brutality of Nazi aggression erupted. And as important, this judgment on history is treated as rich with lessons for the future. The 1930s serve as a rallying cry, prodding future generations into mustering the courage and the forces necessary to take similarly "urgent, brutal, decisive" preventive measures and suppress rising threats in our own time before it's too late to stop new catastrophes. With this rallying cry in mind, this book revisits these postwar conclusions about preventive war and the tragic history of the 1930s, but it does so with a critical eye.

What does this history really have to teach us? A central objective of this book is to demonstrate that preventive war offered a *false promise* as a solution to the dangers that were building. No matter how appealing, the claim that preventive war held the key to solving the European security dilemma simply does not hold up to close scrutiny. In fact, the decision to reject preventive war in 1936 was a sensible strategic choice, and British leaders have been unfairly maligned for making this decision ever since. They faced a genuinely tragic situation with no simple fix. While the chapters that follow will tell this tragic story, the objective is not limited to a reassessment of this history alone.

In broader terms, this book is about a perennial problem that spans all of recorded human history, a problem as old as the ancient Greeks and as contemporary as the daily nightmare of living alongside a nuclear-armed North Korea seeking intercontinental reach. It is about the problem of a shifting threat environment as a potential rival grows stronger, and the temptation to solve this problem through preventive military attacks. Interest in the promise of preventive war has surged in the twenty-first century, kick-started by the Bush Doctrine of "preemption" first announced in the summer of 2002 and put into action by America's subsequent march toward war with Iraq in 2003. Preventive war, in various forms, continues to find favor across the American political spectrum. Preventive war has its champions among those who believe military strikes could successfully blunt whatever nuclear ambitions Iran's leaders might cling to. And as this book goes to press, the Trump administration continues to study the preventive attack option to neutralize North Korea's growing nuclear weapon and missile capabilities.

The goal of the book is to cut through the cacophony of daily headlines and offer the reader a fresh way of thinking about this age-old dilemma, both in terms of the strategic logic of preventive war and the history of the preventive war temptation in practice. Along the way it will focus on the strategic flaws inherent to preventive war, which have as much relevance today as they did in the 1930s. As it stands, preventive war as a tool to "stop" World War II, and the pervasive moral condemnation of those who failed to grasp it in 1936, obscures our ability to extract the cautionary lessons this history actually offers. This book seeks to clear away the misleading conclusions that reverberate to this day, and in the process, offer ways of thinking critically about the promise of preventive war that will prove useful as we grapple with our own security challenges in the years to come.

URGENT, BRUTAL, DECISIVE MEASURES

The great British strategic thinker B. H. Liddell Hart, writing less than a decade after the war, captured this common frustration with the unimpeded rise of German power in the 1930s. "Nothing may seem more strange to the future historian," he observed, "than the way the governments of the democracies failed to anticipate the course which Hitler would pursue."[8] Liddell Hart was right. Scholars and casual observers alike perpetuate the impulse to pass judgment on the leadership of the 1930s for its lack of foresight and action. In fact, it's hard to find any recent work of history or international relations on the subject that doesn't point to missed opportunities to fundamentally alter the course of this terrible story. Not satisfied with simply explaining events as they occurred, we tend to ask the counterfactual question: Why weren't alternative decisions made? What went wrong? Surely *something* could have been done to knock the Nazi regime back on its heels, to deliver a potent defeat early in Germany's rise that would have torn through its self-confidence and deflated its aggressive plans. There must have been pivotal moments along the path to war when Nazi Germany's mounting power could have been suppressed. If only different decisions had been made, an alternative future might have emerged in which the suffering imposed by Nazi Germany was contained—or perhaps avoided altogether.

This verdict turns the 1930s into a story of heroes and goats. Winston Churchill is remembered as one of the heroes, among that small group of allegedly prescient leaders who recognized that each move Hitler made was one more step in a methodical plan of resurrection and conquest. The heroes recognized that confrontation was unavoidable, and they "cried aloud" to warn of the danger and insist on action to stop it. The goats in this common story are those leaders, like Prime Minister Neville Chamberlain, who lacked the wisdom to see the future or listen to those like Churchill, who could. And if they did recognize the firestorm approaching, the goats lacked the nerve to take the forceful action demanded of the moment to strangle Germany's aspirations before it was too late. The goats believed Hitler could be placated and pacified; the heroes were the "anti-appeasers" who publicly broke with their own government over the folly of running from confrontation with the Third Reich.

If these conclusions were treated as isolated in time—merely tragic stories we were told, and we repeated, about the distinctive experiences and mistakes of that distant generation—they would have little real consequence today. But when it comes to the story of the guilty men and the rise of German power, this isn't the case. To this day the Second World War seems to call out a warning to the future against repeating the folly of this earlier generation. And this is exactly how Winston Churchill would have it. In a speech to the House of Commons in 1936, Churchill insisted that we place blame on the past in order to avoid similar mistakes going forward. "It is no use recriminating about the past simply for the purpose of censuring and punishing neglect and culpability," he said. Instead, "the use of recriminating about the past is to enforce effective action at the present."[9] In other words, the past is a tool for political mobilization around action today.

So what relevance does the 1930s have for future generations?

There is a timelessness to the 1930s that can be traced to a problem inherent to international politics—the fundamental and inescapable problem of finding security in an often dangerous world. The 1930s experience reinforces what seems to be a truism: that physical power is central to life in the international system. Power shapes the hierarchy of political influence among the states that populate the system; it determines whether states can defend their territory and people from predators, secure dependable access to critical resources and trading partners, and pursue their own goals free from coercion. Power determines relative vulnerability and safety. In the extreme, power determines whether states survive.

International history offers an endless train of stories about violent death and destruction delivered by armies on the march, stories of territorial conquest and brutal struggles over scarce resources, stories of populations suffering and enslaved. This is a world driven by fear of the future. Who knows when the next dark cloud will appear over the horizon in the form of a marauding army, an armada of hostile warships, or ballistic missiles tipped with the most sinister weapons ever produced? If power determines safety and vulnerability, then the most dangerous situation is to find yourself—like Britain and France in the late 1930s—in relative decline as a potential rival grows stronger. Shifting power, and the fear of the future this dynamic generates, are among the most important engines of change and conflict throughout history.

The earliest example we have of this dynamic was offered by the ancient Greek writer Thucydides in his epic *History of the Peloponnesian War*, the most important work on strategy and war to emerge from the classical world. In his account of the brutal multigenerational clash between the great city-states of Athens and Sparta in the fifth century BC, Thucydides distills the essence of the problem that drove them to war. It was the continuing rise of Athenian power, he said, and Sparta's fear of its aggressive potential for the future. In the third and second centuries BC—years after the independent Greek city-states had been eclipsed and subdued by the Macedonian Empire, which saw its own strength peak and collapse—the cities of Rome and Carthage dominated the great power politics of the Mediterranean Basin. The conflict was kept alive by mutual fear of the other's expanding power and the potential threat each rival posed to their own survival and imperial ambitions.

The rise of the modern state system in Europe many centuries later, and the expansion of this political order to the global level in the nineteenth and twentieth centuries, didn't change the essential character of this engine of competition and conflict. Consider the early twentieth century, which was consumed by fear of shifting power and future threats. Russian and French leaders were afraid of Imperial Germany's expansionist ambitions, ambitions that were made possible by its blockbuster economy and proven martial prowess that gave it an offensive edge over its European rivals. Instead of taking comfort from its strength, German leaders were terrified that one day they would be swallowed up by the colossal power potential of a growing Russian Empire.

China, weakened by decades of economic and military decline and domestic political turbulence, became an object lesson for the Japanese, who recognized the dangers of falling behind in the power struggle. Called as a witness for the prosecution during the Tokyo war crimes trials in 1946, Japanese lieutenant general Kanji Ishiwara pointed an accusing finger at the treacherous world Japan was pulled into during the nineteenth century and the threat of expanding American and Russian power. This future danger, he explained to the surprise of his American interrogators, is what drove Japan's violent push for supremacy in East Asia. "When Japan did open its doors and tried dealing with other countries, it learned that all those countries were a fearfully aggressive lot. And so for its own defense," Ishiwara argued, "it took your country as its teacher and set about learning how to be aggressive."

The second half of the twentieth century introduced new technologies of unprecedented destructive capability, which simply accelerated the competitive frenzy at the heart of the relationship between the new superpowers. Less than a year after the USSR detonated its first atomic bomb in August 1949, American strategic thinkers expressed that timeless fear of shifting power in blunt language: "With the development of increasingly terrifying weapons of mass destruction, every individual faces the ever-present possibility of annihilation should the conflict enter the phase of total war."[10] While both the Russians and the Americans survived this precarious power shift during the 1950s, for the next forty years their Cold War was defined by a relentless fear of the existential dangers of losing ground. Despite the fact that America's Cold War adversary is in the dustbin of history, the United States has not found relief from that gnawing anxiety over what the future holds. From the continuing ascent of Chinese economic power and its rapid military modernization to the dark shadows cast by North Korea's nuclear arsenal and fear of a resurgent Russia, American foreign policy continues to fixate on this enduring dynamic.

Profound changes certainly distinguish the world of the ancient Greeks from the modern era, with changes in the geographic scale of political organization and reach, the identity of the key protagonists in the system, the productivity of national economies, the rate of technological innovation, and the destructive potential of weapons of war. Despite these changes, the core problem of international politics has remained the same over the millennia. And it's this problem of power shifts and fear of the future that makes the crises of the 1930s so familiar. In a way, the rise of German power in the 1930s is just one more example of this international phenomenon drawn from a long historical record. But the European security dilemma of the 1930s is rarely treated as just one more historical case. Instead, it carries special meaning for action in the face of shifting power and rising fear. The story of the "guilty men" persists, not merely as a retrospective assessment of the decisions made, or the decisions avoided, at a particular point on the timeline, by a particular set of leaders long since dead. It's been preserved as an iconic analogy, an unambiguous symbol of the terrible consequences of failing to anticipate the gravity of emerging threats and avoiding the bold action necessary to prevent these threats from becoming future disaster. This is a heavy burden for one historical period to carry. But the lingering emotional weight of World War II and the irresistible draw of that profound claim—that there were lost opportunities to stop the mass murderers who engineered this catastrophe—sustain the outsized role of this particular crisis and the appeal of the preventive war solution as we wrestle with the power-shift problems of our own day.

It takes little imagination to conjure up scenarios in which a rival translates increasing military capabilities into increasingly aggressive behavior. The more time that goes by, the stronger the rival grows, and the more dangerous the future appears, whether armed strength is measured by phalanxes of soldiers wielding thrusting spears and short swords or by nuclear-tipped missiles that could shatter continents. The implications of this fear of the future are obvious: State leaders face a potent incentive to take action while they still enjoy a window of opportunity. In most cases through history we find some form of counterbalancing against rising power: declining states buy more weapons, conscript more soldiers, invest in research and development of more-advanced military technologies, stage military exercises to improve combat readiness, or join forces with new allies to rapidly offset this erosion in security. Each of these options is motivated by the same goal—to reverse the declining state's slide in power.

In some cases we find states taking this impulse to its logical extreme. Why merely *balance* when you can *dominate*? Instead of just racing ahead to outpace a rival's growth by amassing your own physical power—building weapons, expanding armies, collecting allies—why not provoke a fight or launch an attack to physically destroy those growing military capabilities that haunt your visions of the future? When merely balancing, you *live* with the danger. Your safety rests precariously on your rival's decisions, on its ambitions, on the risks it is willing to run, and, ultimately, on your ability to fight and defend if the rival lashes out. Preventive war promises *deliverance* from that danger. The impulse to launch preventive attacks has an ancient lineage. Repeatedly through history we find its three key ingredients stirring a temptation to fight: shifting power, fear of the future, and strong voices warning of the terrible fate that lies ahead unless the growing threat is neutralized with preventive military action. For modern readers, this logic will sound familiar.

In fact, the allure of preventive war has actually grown since the early 1990s and retains its appeal well into the twenty-first century.[11] In recent decades the prospect of states such as Iraq, North Korea, and Iran developing nuclear weapons has become a core fear defining Americans' perception of the threat environment. And as in earlier eras, anxiety about a more dangerous future has been followed by calls for preventive military action to eliminate the problem. Consider the George W. Bush administration's fixation on Iraqi weapons of mass destruction (WMDs): here we find fear of the future most decisively moving the United States toward war, with strong support from Congress and the American public. In a televised speech on the night of March 19, 2003, President Bush declared that "the people of the United States and our friends and allies will not live at the mercy of an outlaw regime that threatens the peace with weapons of mass murder." Bush administration officials never claimed to have evidence that Iraq was actually preparing to use chemical, biological, or nuclear weapons against the United States or its allies, or that Iraq intended to provide them to any terrorist group. It was simply the *potential* for an attack by Iraq or its surrogates that was at the core of the strategic logic. In a speech at the US Military Academy at West Point nine months earlier, the president signaled what was to come, and he put the logic of war in familiar terms. "If we wait for threats to fully materialize, we will have waited too long . . . We must take the battle to the enemy, disrupt his plans, and confront the worst threats before they materialize."[12] Twenty-one days after the American-led attack began, coalition forces occupied the Iraqi capital and Saddam Hussein's outlaw regime was on the run.

In April 2003, as American forces were getting settled in Baghdad and 1,400 inspectors were organizing the search for phantom Iraqi WMDs, North Korea's previously announced withdrawal from the Nuclear Nonproliferation Treaty (NPT) became a new reality. It was the first time any state had pulled out of the global agreement to cap the spread of nuclear weapons, and in response, President Bush staked out an uncompromising position. During a summit meeting with Japanese prime minister Junichiro Koizumi in June, he insisted that "we will not tolerate nuclear weapons in North Korea." While he held out hope that diplomacy could keep North Korea nuclear weapons–free, the president warned that "further escalation of the situation . . . will require tougher measures."

Over the next three years, North Korea worked away on an explosive nuclear device as well as long-range missiles that could carry nuclear warheads to distant targets. To former secretary of defense William Perry, who had served in President Clinton's cabinet, and his former assistant secretary of defense for international security policy, Ashton Carter (who would later serve as secretary of defense in President Obama's cabinet), the Bush administration's failure to take some form of decisive action was intolerable. In opinion pieces that appeared in the *Washington Post* in June 2006 and *Time* magazine in July, they chastised the president for his preoccupation with the war in the Middle East while the North Korean threat grew. Using the same preventive logic that had been mobilized for war against Iraq, Perry and Carter called for military strikes "to destroy [North Korea's] missiles at their test sites."

Secretary Perry took this same position in 1994. As the Clinton administration debated its options for responding to North Korea's earlier threat to withdraw from the NPT in 1993, Perry urged the president to order air strikes against its nuclear facilities at Yongbyon. He justified this bold recommendation with a warning: "[W]hatever dangers there are in" the preventive attack option, he argued, "these dangers are going to be compounded two to three years from now when . . . they're producing bombs at the rate of a dozen a year."[13] As the pace of North Korea's missile testing continued through 2017, President Trump's National Security Advisor laid out the administration's position bluntly in a television interview: "What you're asking is are we preparing plans for a preventive war, right? If they have nuclear weapons that can threaten the United States," Lt. Gen. H. R. McMaster continued, that's "intolerable from the president's perspective. So of course we have to provide all options. And that includes a military option."[14]

Iran, the third member of Bush's "axis of evil," generates similar anxiety about the future, and this anxiety has produced a similar allure for the preventive war option. In late 2002 and early 2003, as excitement was building over the idea of war with Iraq, a joke circulating among policy wonks captured the enthusiasm in certain political circles for the transformative potential of preventive war: "Everyone wants to go to Baghdad," the joke went. But "real men want to go to Tehran."[15] Clearly, some have been more enthusiastic than others, but it's become axiomatic across the American political landscape to insist that "all options are on the table" to keep Iran from producing nuclear weapons. This included President Obama and many of the political rivals who were vying to replace him after the 2016 presidential elections. Obama went beyond President Bush's language in the case of North Korea. Bush declared that nuclear weapons were "intolerable" (which implies that the United States will continue to oppose the fact that North Korea has a nuclear arsenal, without saying America will actually take forceful action to eliminate it). President Obama adopted more-definitive terms for Iran: "We are determined *to prevent* Iran from acquiring nuclear weapons [emphasis added]," a phrase he approved for a speech Vice President Joe Biden delivered in Israel in March 2010. Obama ordered military leaders to update preventive attack options against Iran and to share these military options with Israeli leaders to convince America's nervous ally that the United States was serious in its intent.[16] As a presidential candidate, former secretary of state Hillary Clinton took this one step further, declaring unequivocally in September 2015, "I will not hesitate to take military action if Iran attempts to obtain a nuclear weapon."[17]

This language should not be dismissed as mere campaign rhetoric or a deterrent bluff. *I will not hesitate* paints a bright red line that should trigger American action. Most important, this language—and the broader reaction to her declaration—unambiguously demonstrate the confidence reserved for the preventive war option in American security policy. While Clinton's assertion was widely covered in the press, the idea itself was largely met with collective silence from other political leaders and presidential candidates from both parties, as well as virtual silence from media commentators. There was no debate over the merits of preventive war against Iran, no discussion of its viability to actually solve the security problems driving American fears. As of this writing, President Trump has not issued such definitive promises, but after tearing up the nuclear agreement designed to keep a cap on Iran's nuclear capabilities, we must ask: Is war a plausible alternative if suspicions over its nuclear programs grow during the coming years?

It's in these contemporary cases that the story of Europe in the 1930s can have its biggest impact on the way we think about changing threats and the decisions leaders make in response. Given its powerful emotional appeal, it's unsurprising to discover that modern advocates of preventive war have repeatedly mobilized the specter of Germany in the 1930s as an analogy to warn and cajole others into accepting decisive action to eliminate modern threats. There are two basic camps among scholars that study how historical analogies affect policy choice. One camp argues that policymakers actually turn to history as a decision tool. A more-cynical camp asserts that policymakers and opinion leaders mobilize specific analogies to justify decisions they've already reached and to convince others they are right. There are plenty of examples demonstrating both uses of historical analogies at work, so there's no need to treat these as rival views on the question. For our purposes, it's enough to recognize that claims about the alleged lessons of history are regularly deployed as part of the decision-making process and in consensus building around policy.

Analogies help decision-makers think through four basic questions (or shape how others think about these questions): What is the nature of the current problem we face? What are the stakes involved? What policy options do we have to deal with it? And what is the likelihood of success of the various options available?[18] In the case of Europe in the 1930s as an analogy for contemporary security problems, the answers it provides to these questions seem blunt yet compelling. What was the nature of the problem? An inherently expansionist state was determined to achieve its ambitions through aggressive military force. What were the stakes? They were total. The regime's genocidal inclinations would drive it to extreme levels of violence that put the lives of tens of millions at risk. What options were available to respond to this threat? Military confrontation to deter or destroy the aggressor state, early in its rise to full power, was the only option that could have stopped the approaching disaster. What was the likelihood of success? Since the *failure* to confront the rising aggressor allowed the disaster to happen, we tend to assume that early military confrontation would have *definitely* worked better as a solution to the problem.

It is this final conclusion that needs to be explored most closely before we can confidently adopt this as an analogous answer to our own fears. To do so, we must drill down into the 1930s and find specific moments for confrontation. If Winston Churchill is right—that World War II was an unnecessary war—where and when could Germany's adversaries have taken a decisive stand against the building threat? What specific decisions, if corrected, might have produced a different course of events that would have spared the Western world this pain? And how would confrontation, at a particular point in time, have actually eliminated the German threat?

Several key moments stand out. There was Hitler's ascent to power in January 1933, or perhaps when Germany withdrew from ongoing disarmament talks and bolted from the League of Nations in October. What about March 1935, when Nazi Germany unveiled its reconstituted air force, the Luftwaffe, and announced that conscription of young German soldiers would once again fill the ranks of its depleted army? How about the following year, when Germany reclaimed full sovereign control over the Rhineland and a small military force crossed into western Germany for the first time since 1918? Maybe March 1938, when the Nazi regime engineered the annexation of Austria? The final opportunity seems to be in the late summer of 1938, when Hitler's demand for the return of the Sudetenland of western Czechoslovakia brought the Third Reich and the Western allies closer to war than at any previous point.

By far, the most common moment plucked from this list is the Sudeten crisis in 1938 and British prime minister Neville Chamberlain's decision to negotiate with Hitler in Munich to keep the peace. The word "Munich" itself carries immense meaning, hardly requiring an explanation when invoked as a shorthand criticism of appeasing dictators. As the common story goes, Chamberlain was blind to Nazi Germany's truly aggressive character and naive to the point of gross negligence in thinking that he could secure peace by feeding—and thus satisfying—Germany's expansionist appetites. Had Chamberlain refused to concede the Sudetenland through the Munich Agreement of September 1938, the Führer would have realized he was running a grave risk in the face of international opposition. In the sunniest versions of this counterfactual scenario, British opposition would have rallied members of a homegrown conspiracy being organized by Lt. Col. Hans Oster, the deputy commander of the Abwehr, Germany's counterintelligence agency. Even if Oster's plot to overthrow the Nazi regime had fallen apart, this demonstration of international resistance might have deterred Hitler from following through on the aggressive acts he had planned for the coming years, those stepping-stones leading to domination in Europe.

As important as the Sudetenland is as a symbol of lost opportunities to derail Hitler's murderous plans, the moment that truly captures the imagination of many postwar observers occurred two and a half years before Munich: the Rhineland crisis of 1936. According to countless sources, this was *the* golden opportunity to stop Hitler. Just as important, it's seen as an opportunity to stop him at little cost. It's through the Rhineland story that we're offered the promise of deliverance through preventive war; the Sudetenland demand doesn't fit as a proper analogy for preventive war. The Munich conference was a reaction to a direct threat levied against a sovereign state, a French ally. If British and French resistance had led to war with Germany in 1938, it would have been clearly defined as defense of an ally against raw German aggression, no different than the Allied declaration of war following Germany's invasion of Poland in September 1939. A fight over the Rhineland, however, would have been pure preventive war.

TO THE RHINE

The Rhineland crisis had its roots in the 1919 Treaty of Versailles that ended the Great War. Standing in the rubble of this conflict, French leaders looked to the future with an almost "obsessive" fear of the inevitable resurgence of German industrial and military might.[19] Several years after the war French premier Raymond Poincaré observed, "Germany's population

was increasing, her industries were intact, she had no factories to recon-
struct, she had no flooded mines. Her resources were intact . . . In fifteen or
twenty years Germany would be mistress of Europe. In front of her would
be France with a population scarcely increased."[20] The French solution
to this vulnerability was to avoid the power-shift problem altogether, and
from the start, by imposing a wide range of artificial restraints on German
power for the indefinite future. During tough negotiations in 1919 with
his own skeptical allies, French premier Georges Clemenceau described
his country's position in simple but persuasive terms. "America is far away,
protected by the ocean. Not even Napoleon himself could touch England.
You are both sheltered; we are not."[21]

The full list of Versailles restrictions in the treaty's Military, Naval, and
Air Clauses is truly staggering in scope and detail. Versailles capped Germany's army at one hundred thousand personnel (when France could still
mobilize a million and a half men for war); it prohibited conscription of new
recruits each year, the creation of an air force, tanks, submarines, a general
staff—even professional academies for military officers, noncommissioned
officers, and cadets. But the centerpiece of the Versailles regime is found
in Articles 42 and 43, which stripped Germany of the right to full sovereign
control over its own Rhineland territory. Germany was barred from maintaining or assembling armed forces and constructing fortifications or bases
for mobilization in all German territory west of the Rhine River, and within
a fifty-kilometer strip running along its east bank.[22]

A quick look at a map of Western Europe shows that in simple geographic terms, a Rhineland demilitarized zone (DMZ) provided France (as
well as Belgium and Luxembourg) with a deep territorial buffer against the
rapid thrust of a German invasion force. It widened the distance that German bombers, attack, and reconnaissance aircraft would have to cover before crossing into France or reaching the British coast, and it kept French
cities and fortifications beyond the range of German artillery.

The DMZ had an equally potent effect on the other side of the strategic
equation. Because Germany had no ready defense along its entire western
frontier, it was perpetually vulnerable to French incursions against the
heart of its industrial power, which was concentrated in the Ruhr River
valley, a northern tributary of the Rhine. The DMZ also gave credibility to
France's alliance commitments with Poland, Czechoslovakia, Romania, and
Yugoslavia. In the event of German aggression to the east, French military
assistance depended on its ability to execute a rapid offensive push deep
into German territory from the west. Taken together, the strategic objective
of Rhineland demilitarization was to help sustain a broader political order

defined by indefinite suppression of German power as the means to sustain security and peace.

For Hitler, this was intolerable, and on March 7, 1936, he swiped the DMZ aside. In one of his trademark "Saturday surprises," the Führer announced that German military forces were, at that very moment, rolling into the Rhineland, overturning in one deft move a feature of the post–Great War European order designed to bottle up Germany's aggressive potential into the distant future.

For the French leadership, Germany's sudden shift was intolerable. Twenty-four hours after German soldiers rumbled westward across Rhine River bridges, the French cabinet agreed that preventive attack into the Rhineland was necessary to push German forces back out and maintain the desperate squeeze on its power. France would fight for this strategic objective, but its leaders imposed one condition on their own decisive measures: Military action must be supported, at least politically, by Great Britain. As it turned out, this condition was enough to block the preventive war option outright. During the first Monday-morning cabinet meeting in London after Hitler's Saturday surprise, fewer than forty-eight hours into the crisis, the British government firmly and without hesitation refused to sanction military action. And it was a decision the British cabinet made without debate, dissent, or serious discussion. France had given Britain veto power, and this is exactly what Britain exercised.

This is the decision remembered most commonly as the great lost opportunity to prevent World War II. Among the many observers drawn to counterfactual musings on the promise of 1936, Winston Churchill, who was not in the cabinet at the time, is the most prominent voice shaping postwar regret over the Allied failure to force the German military into retreat. In his memoirs he declared 1936 the "last chance [for] arresting Hitler's ambitions without a serious war." France alone, he contends, was powerful enough "to drive the Germans out of the Rhineland."[23] In Churchill's view, a military response would have achieved more than mere preservation of the Rhineland status quo. This single crisis, he wrote in 1948, held the key to the very survival of the Nazi government. Churchill even believed that it wasn't necessary to launch an actual invasion to have this effect. From his postwar vantage point, Britain's wartime leader confidently made this bold counterfactual prediction: If the French government had merely mobilized its army and air force in preparation for a preventive attack, "there is *no doubt* that Hitler would have been compelled by his own General Staff to withdraw, and a check would have been given to his pretensions, which might well have proved fatal to his rule."[24]

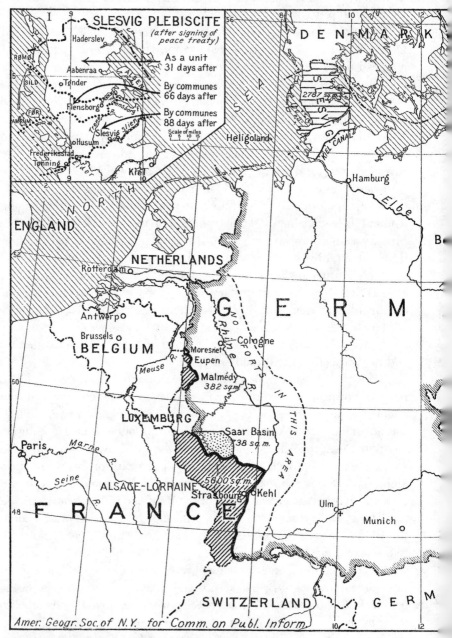

German Territorial Changes following World War I

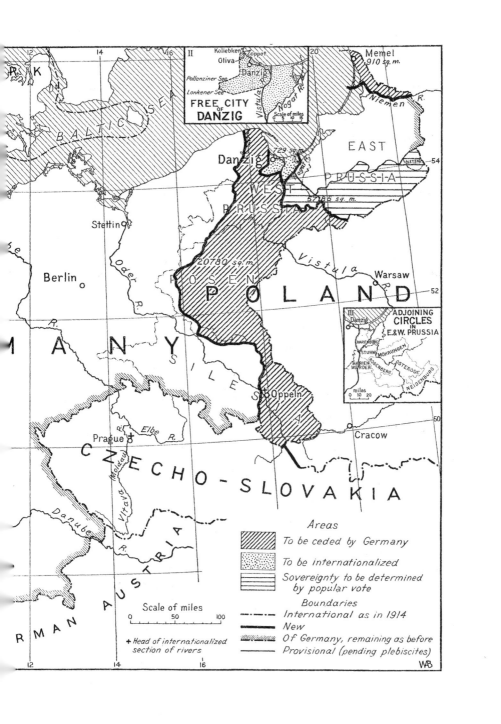

II

Koliebken
Oliva
Zoppot
Danzig

Pollenziner See
Lonkener See
Nogat R.

FREE CITY
of
DANZIG

Scale of miles

Memel
910 sq. m.

BALTIC SEA

Niemen R.

P
K

Stettin

Berlin

Oder R.

Danzig

729 sq. m

EAST

P·R·U·S·S·I·A

BLETZEN

54

WEST
PRUSSIA

5785 sq. m.

20780 sq. m.

P·O·S·E·N

Vistula

Warsaw

52

P·O·L·A·N·D

III ADJOINING
CIRCLES
IN
E.&W. PRUSSIA

Danzig

MARIENBURG
STUHM
MOHRUNGEN
MARIEN- ROSENBERG
WERDER
OSTERODE
NEIDENBURG

miles
0   10   20

R.

M A N Y

S·I·L·E·S·I·A

Oppeln

50

Elbe R.

Prague

Moldau
Vltava

C·Z·E·C·H·O - S·L·O·V·A·K·I·A

Cracow

Danube R.

R M A N

A U S T R I A

Areas

To be ceded by Germany

To be internationalized

Sovereignty to be determined
by popular vote

Boundaries

International as in 1914

New

Of Germany, remaining as before

Provisional (pending plebiscites)

Scale of miles
0   50   100

+ Head of internationalized
section of rivers

WB

If Churchill is right, this would have been a stunning strategic outcome, the ultimate prize in great power jockeying, achieved at virtually no cost. The American journalist William Shirer, an eyewitness to the consolidation of Nazi rule and the regime's drive to reassert German power in the 1930s, advanced this same postwar claim. In his best-selling history, *The Rise and Fall of the Third Reich*, Shirer described the crisis as the "last chance to halt, without the risk of a serious war, the rise of a militarized, aggressive, totalitarian Germany and . . . bring the Nazi dictatorship and [Hitler's] regime tumbling down." According to Shirer, a French military parry "would have been nothing more than a police action."[25] In the award-winning book *Munich: The Price of Peace*, Telford Taylor, who served as chief counsel for the prosecution at the Nuremberg war crimes trials, vented similar frustrations. Looking back to 1936, Taylor concluded that "French commanders should . . . have loaded their men into trucks and sent them across the border. They would have had no difficulty in driving out the small German contingents."[26]

We can find similar assessments on the German side. Gen. Alfred Jodl, chief of the operations staff during the war, recalled in testimony at Nuremberg that the small Wehrmacht units on the Rhineland frontier were so vulnerable that the French defensive force "could have blown us to pieces."[27] And much has been made of something Hitler himself reportedly said about the military risk he was running at this point in Germany's recovery. According to his interpreter Paul Schmidt, the Führer acknowledged that "the military resources at our disposal would have been wholly inadequate for even a moderate resistance" if French troops had "marched into the Rhineland."[28]

Many decades after these reflections on the Rhineland crisis were first published, this moment in time continues to serve as an iconic symbol of "lost opportunities." For example, the popular German newsmagazine *Der Spiegel*, in its 2009 edition commemorating the seventieth anniversary of the outbreak of war, asked plaintively, "Why Wasn't Hitler Stopped?" In its brief discussion of 1936, *Der Spiegel*'s article breezily repeats Churchill's conclusion that "there never was a war in all history easier to prevent by timely action."[29] Even the British National Archives, that great repository of official documents from British history, declares on its website that the "failure of Britain and France to act" during the Rhineland crisis "encouraged Hitler's aggressive policy." And the further one searches for references to the Rhineland crisis, the more one comes across a seemingly endless stream of claims decrying the failure to act, and thus halt a conflict that turned out to be among the greatest outrages in human history.

With the horrors of World War II looming over the Rhineland question, it's easy to understand the allure of preventive war as a retrospective solution to this tragic event. But there's a question that begs to be asked: Did preventive military action truly hold the key to stopping Hitler and World War II? Is Winston Churchill's confidence in the preventive war option justified? And, most seriously, should we mobilize the lessons of the Rhineland to push political leaders toward the preventive war option to confront our own fears of the future?

The simple answer to these questions, developed over the course of this book, is no. The grand pronouncements about this missed opportunity, repeated so many times over the decades since the Second World War, are driven more by wishful thinking than careful study of its details. And the impulse to turn this conclusion into an analogy that can guide decision-making today reflects little more than a futile search for a silver bullet solution to a profoundly complex problem. These silver bullet claims about the virtues of preventive war produce a distorted impression of the strategic dilemma confronting Britain and France in the mid-1930s and how difficult it would have been to actually fix this problem. This criticism does not mean that the study of this history will lead to dead ends. Just the opposite. A fresh look at the 1930s and the Rhineland crisis is valuable precisely because it opens a window onto the most important and enduring questions of international security, questions about power, and the strategic dimensions of war. Along the way, it will help us to understand two challenges that make preventive war an exceedingly problematic option for decision-makers seeking to neutralize threat. First, the inherent uncertainty of the future makes the decision to initiate preventive war a leap into the dark. Second, the very act of launching preventive war can have the paradoxical effect of making the threats you face even worse instead of eliminating them.

Consider the first problem. The Rhineland crisis shines a glaring light on the limited human capacity for seeing the future with real clarity. The ancient Greeks recognized these limitations, and in turn they revered the gift of "prognosis," that ability to accurately anticipate the future that few individuals seemed to possess. In their mythology, the Greeks told stories of the Titan named Prometheus, whose foresight was the source of his wisdom; his twin brother Epimetheus, in tragic contrast, was a rash fool who could only understand the world through hindsight. Unfortunately, Prometheans are a rare breed. Like Epimetheus, it's easy for mere mortals to look back in time and pass judgment on the decisions made in an earlier era. In fact, we are all susceptible to the "hindsight bias" trap—the assumption that those making decisions in the past should have understood the problems they faced in the same way those in the future understand them, even though future observers have information that simply was not available when earlier decisions were made. As the great Danish philosopher Søren Kierkegaard eloquently reminds us, life is only "understood backwards," but it's "lived forward."[30] This simple observation captures a tragic reality. Every leader who has had responsibility for making decisions today about how to deal with potential threats of the future has been caught in that unavoidable condition of having little real insight into how the future will unfold. Modern scholars have discovered that even experts in the field of international relations have a terrible track record for predicting the future with precision; they are no more successful at anticipating future events than non-experts or random chance guesses as to what lies ahead.[31]

This is a particularly serious limitation when it comes to shifting power and preventive war. By definition, the preventive war temptation bubbles up from fear of the future, and the intensity of the temptation to pull the trigger will spike when leaders grab on to worst-case predictions about the aggressive behavior of rivals as their offensive capabilities grow. Clearly, fear is an essential survival mechanism, provoking the action necessary to escape or neutralize threats before the damage is done. But fear is a two-edged sword. While this emotional response to the dangers lurking in your environment can improve the odds of survival, it can also lead to overreaction, misjudgment, and tragedy. The difference hinges on how accurately we anticipate the future. But can leaders see the future clearly enough to justify launching such wars with true confidence that the risks are essential for long-term self-defense? Are they actually preventing future aggression and more costly armed conflict by ordering military attacks against rivals that appear to be rising in power? Or are they simply bringing on the costs of war unnecessarily? Are they actually improving their future security by eliminating threats before they materialize? Or are they jeopardizing future security by setting in motion forces that spin off new and more-dangerous threats they will come to regret?

Was Secretary of Defense William Perry a hero for taking a bold stance in favor of preventive attacks against North Korea in 1994? Was President Clinton a goat for rejecting his advice? If North Korea ends up lobbing nuclear weapons against the American homeland, against the islands of Guam or Okinawa, or against Tokyo or Seoul in some future war, there will be a deafening outcry about Clinton's horrible mistake, rendered in the same terms used to condemn British leaders of 1936. If North Korea agrees to complete nuclear disarmament through negotiations, or collapses peacefully someday, and we escape such a conflagration, we will look back with relief and gratitude for Clinton's restraint in the face of rising fear. But today, it's impossible to state with finality what the future judgment on this decision will be.

We face the same problem in the case of Iran. In 2007, Israeli prime minister Ehud Barak asked President Bush for a green light to conduct preventive air strikes against key nodes in Iran's nuclear infrastructure to avoid what he saw as a nightmarish future just over the horizon. While Vice President Dick Cheney argued in favor of backing Israel, President Bush refused. Who are the heroes and goats in this case? As with the case of North Korea, it's too soon to say. At this point in time, it's impossible to predict whether Iran will actually pursue a nuclear arsenal, and if it does, whether it will lash out in an aggressive way across the region or against Israel, emboldened by the power it has developed. In the meantime, the dilemma remains, sustained by an inherently murky future.

The dilemma was no different for those trying to predict the future in 1936 while wrestling with their options for responding to the steady recovery of German power. In the pages that follow, we will burrow into the tragic circumstances of the 1930s. We will discover—at least in the time frame of the Rhineland crisis, that allegedly golden moment for preventive war—that there were no heroes, there were no goats. No one of stature in Great Britain joined French leaders in this call for preventive military action to suppress German power. This includes Winston Churchill and his fellow anti-appeasers who took a tougher stand against Germany as the years went by and the dangers of the near future began to truly crystallize. In 1946, in his famous "Iron Curtain" speech on the challenge of meeting rising Soviet power, Churchill claimed that in the 1930s he "saw it all coming." But in fact, Churchill too was struggling with the unavoidably cloudy future, a future that was too obscure in its details to justify embracing another great war with Germany. Like Prometheus, Churchill is revered for his foresight, but it's hindsight that led him to his confident postwar assertions about this particular mistake.

While the inherent uncertainty of the future was a key variable behind Britain's refusal to support preventive military action against Germany in 1936, the second major problem noted above was a potent restraint as well: British leaders believed that preventive war would make the German threat even worse. They recognized what is called in this book the "preventive war paradox." Simply put, this phenomenon is the cautionary twin to the preventive war temptation, warning leaders about a potentially perverse outcome in which preventive war sets in motion strategic blowback that actually makes the state's future less secure, even if it wins an operational battlefield victory against its rival. Today, this rationale might sound nonsensical. Rising German power was in fact leading to another great catastrophe. But as the British government saw it, pushing German soldiers back across the Rhine River would not solve the underlying security problems presented by Nazi Germany. Hitler would not be cowed. The Nazi regime would not crumble. The German military would not rise up and compel the Third Reich to accept a more-modest vision of Germany's place in the great power system. Instead, an Allied preventive attack would generate, with time, a guaranteed counterstrike by an aggrieved German nation seeking revenge. And in turn, this German counterstrike would lead to an even darker future than British leaders imagined looking forward from 1936.

By the end of the book we'll be able to consider, with the advantage of hindsight, a seemingly counterintuitive argument—that the British were right to conclude that preventive war in 1936 could not solve the European security dilemma. In the end, this remains a tragic tale. It's hard to spin out an ending that would have been happier if only more enlightened and more courageous leaders were at the helm. This is a frustrating conclusion, particularly if the story fails to serve as a tidy analogy that might be useful for solving our present-day security problems. But the story is rich in lessons, nonetheless, and worth another look to help us think critically about the promise of preventive war and the options for confronting our own fears of the future.

To get there, the coming chapters will roam far beyond Europe in the 1930s. We will examine the logic of preventive war and the strategic pitfalls in greater detail, and explore the consequences of preventive war in practice across a diverse historical landscape, from the ancient world to the modern, from the nineteenth century to the twenty-first century, which will bring the preventive war dilemma to life.

But first, to the Rhineland crisis.

2

ANOTHER FAIT ACCOMPLI

Adolf Hitler would not negotiate. He would not ask permission or appeal to the League of Nations. He refused to lay his case before international jurists at The Hague court like a common prisoner seeking parole. He would not propose, discuss, or even announce his intentions in advance. The Führer would simply act. And this next act would come as a single blinding flash. Hitler had no interest in executing a covert, slow-moving military buildup in the Rhineland that might escape detection for a while, merely to be "discovered" by foreign journalists or military attachés when it reached some critical mass. He would not execute remilitarization as if it were some shameful secret to be managed quietly under a cloud of fear. Besides, there was no drama in subterfuge. Secrecy would rob the Third Reich of this opportunity to showcase the power of the new Germany, the Nazi Party, and the daring of its leader. This would be a decisive hour in history, a moment to proclaim with pride, an event marked in time by a date on the calendar. The goal went beyond a reassertion of sovereign rights; it was meant to trumpet the end of the humiliation and the weakness that had defined Germany's expected place in the post–Great War order.

Once the French, the British, the Russians, Poles, Czechs, Italians, Belgians—the German people themselves—discovered that a change was coming in the Rhineland, remilitarization would be a fait accompli; literally, an *accomplished fact*. At whatever moment Hitler chose to reveal his bold stroke to the world, he wanted the Wehrmacht to be a proud reality on the ground, crossing Rhine River bridges, parading along streets crowded with jubilant citizens, moving into barracks for permanent garrison duty, touching down at airfields across the western territory of the Reich. The timing—and logistical choreography—had to be perfect to stage this piece of political theater with tens of thousands in its cast: from the Führer in Berlin, surrounded by hundreds of his loyal Reichstag deputies, and the thousands of German soldiers converging by train, truck, and horse column on cities and towns that stretched for hundreds of miles across the Rhineland, to the throngs of stunned Germans that poured into the streets to greet them. Over a single weekend in early March 1936, Hitler had his fait accompli. And it was an accomplished fact that no outside power would turn back.

IN THIS HISTORIC HOUR . . .

Just minutes before noon on Saturday, March 7, Adolf Hitler's open-air Mercedes limousine turned into Königsplatz square in central Berlin and rolled to a stop in front of the Kroll Opera House.[1] Tucked into the eastern edge of Berlin's Tiergarten park, the opera house had been the home of the German parliament since February 1933, when fire gutted the Reichstag building just a month after Hitler was appointed chancellor. It was an act of political arson the Nazis blamed on the Communists, the opening Hitler needed to extract emergency powers from an aging President Hindenburg, and to push Germany toward dictatorship. On the street outside the opera house, a cluster of uniformed officials met the Führer with rigid Nazi salutes, echoed by the crowd of curious Berliners who filled the sidewalk behind him. Three long columns of black-coated SS guards, Hitler's security force, lined the far side of the street, bayoneted rifles held erect in salute as their leader stepped from the car. There was no time for leisurely curbside greetings as the Führer moved quickly through the front doors and into the hall.

Inside the opera house, 660 Reichstag delegates waited with nervous excitement. They could sense something important was about to happen. The night before, the Reich Chancellery had announced that the Reichstag meeting scheduled for the following week was being moved abruptly to noon the very next day. While the purpose of this hasty meeting was left unclear, an intriguing detail in that Friday-night announcement offered an important clue: German foreign minister Konstantin von Neurath had called for an urgent meeting with the ambassadors from France, Great Britain,

Italy, and Belgium—the other signatories of the 1925 Locarno treaty—at precisely ten o'clock on Saturday morning. It was through Locarno, German officials were frequently reminded, that Germany herself had agreed to respect Rhineland demilitarization.

Diplomats and the foreign press quickly deduced that Locarno was Hitler's target, and this prediction found its way into the early-morning editions of the Paris newspapers and was shot abroad by the international wire services. The American correspondent Sigrid Schultz, reporting for the *Chicago Tribune* on March 6, added to the intrigue with an eyewitness report: "generals and admirals" were "converging at the war office for a big meeting" that night.[2] As predicted, the Locarno ambassadors walked away from their morning meeting at the Foreign Ministry with a blunt message: Germany "no longer considers herself bound to this now defunct pact."[3] But the Führer and his inner circle were holding back on one critical detail, safeguarding a secret about the unfolding fait accompli that no diplomat, journalist, or eager Reichstag delegate had foreseen.

Hitler crossed the opera house lobby and marched down the wide center aisle toward the front of the hall and climbed six low steps to the second level of a crowded three-tiered stage. Hitler shook hands with members of his cabinet: There was von Neurath, his foreign minister, an unflappable champion of Rhineland remilitarization; Joseph Goebbels, his propaganda minister, responsible for orchestrating the burst of nationalist pride that would envelop the Reich in the weeks to come; Dr. Hjalmar Schacht, his economics minister, who worried daily about the financial strain of the Führer's rearmament program; and Gen. Werner von Blomberg, war minister and commander in chief of the armed forces, who shouldered responsibility for executing the Rhineland military operation, and the most nervous man in the house. On the top tier of the stage, sitting immediately behind and high above the Führer as he stood at the center podium, was the hulking figure of Gen. Hermann Göring, commander of the German air force, the Luftwaffe, and president of the Reichstag. Above his head, three long red banners hung from the high ceiling to the floor, the center banner emblazoned with a blocky art deco Third Reich imperial eagle, the side banners with giant black swastikas.

From his perch under the imperial eagle, Göring could see hundreds of German and foreign reporters and a large contingent of foreign ambassadors crowding the balconies that ringed the hall. Missing from the diplomatic corps, if Göring bothered to notice, were the ambassadors from France, Britain, Belgium, Poland, and the Soviet Union.[4] Göring looked out over row after row of Reichstag deputies in the audience. To the American journalist William Shirer, the deputies appeared as "little men with big bodies and bulging necks and cropped hair and pouched bellies and brown uniforms and heavy boots." This Reichstag had been a legislature in name only since the day it had conceded dictatorial powers to Adolf Hitler three years earlier, in this very hall. It was nothing more than a boisterous backdrop for some of the Führer's most dramatic official moments. Reichstag delegates were handpicked members of the Nazi Party who would faithfully rally at every high point in Hitler's oration, a perfect setting for the propaganda films and radio broadcasts that showcased party discipline and the regime's iron will. Hitler would use the Reichstag to good effect at several critical moments for the Third Reich: to publicly announce the *Anschluss* uniting Germany and Austria in 1938; and to mark the end of the military campaign against Poland in 1939, the capitulation of France in 1940, and to declare war against the United States in 1941.

Today was no different. At 12:01 p.m., as live radio microphones waited to carry Hitler's speech nationwide, General Göring called the meeting to order. For nearly an hour, Hitler built his case by hammering away at grievances the Nazi regime had repeated endlessly over the past three years. In a low, hoarse voice the Führer growled about the "spirit of hatred inherent" in the 1919 Treaty of Versailles, with its privileges for the victors and oppression for the defeated. As long as Germany remained shackled by its punitive terms, the treaty would "sow dragon's seed for new struggles," Hitler warned, and long-term peace in Europe would be impossible.

When he turned to the threat of Soviet Bolshevism, Hitler's voice "rose to a shrill, hysterical scream."[5] "I will not have the gruesome Communist international dictatorship of hate descend upon the German people," he cried. On this point, the Führer knew he was stoking the sympathies of conservative opinion across Western Europe. "I tremble for Europe in what would happen . . . if the chaos of a Bolshevistic revolution should be successful across the Continent." Finally, the Führer ripped into the new defense pact linking France and the Soviet Union against an unnamed menace. Everyone knew that Germany was the target. Hitler ignored the fact that his own rearmament announcement one year earlier had inspired the agreement. But this alliance, he charged, had shattered the multilateral promise of support and nonaggression at the heart of the Locarno treaty. Germany was already vulnerable on its western flank; now it faced "the threatening military power of gigantic empire" to the east. The Reichstag roared in approval. "This discrimination," Hitler said, "is unbearable."[6]

Hitler now had the Reichstag stirred into a proper state of agitation, but so far, the audience had heard nothing new in any of these themes. There was only one relevant question his listeners could ask at that moment: What will Hitler actually do about these grievances?

Hitler's tone shifted and the cavernous hall fell silent as the deputies waited for his answer. The Führer had reached the moment of revelation. "Men of the German Reichstag," he continued. "In this historic hour, when in the Reich's western provinces *German troops are at this minute marching* into their future peace-time garrisons, we all unite . . ." The Reichstag exploded with cheers. One reporter watching from the balcony described it as a "cyclone of rejoicing" that drowned out the end of the Führer's sentence.[7] William Shirer captured the scene: Hitler "can go no further . . . They spring, yelling and crying, to their feet. The audience in the galleries does the same . . . Their hands are raised in slavish salute, their faces now contorted with hysteria, their mouths wide open, shouting, shouting, their eyes, burning with fanaticism, glued on" their Führer.[8] Hitler hung his head and let the roar fill the opera house.

Here was the surprise—the fait accompli—that Hitler and his inner circle had worked so hard to organize, execute, and keep secret until the Führer was ready to reveal it in one dazzling burst. This wasn't one more rhetorical denunciation of Versailles and Locarno. It was no simple call for diplomacy and *discussions* of Germany's rights. It wasn't an expression of future intent, an aspiration the Führer was laying before his wider audience. It was an accomplished fact. German troops were, at that very moment, marching in the Rhineland for the first time since 1918, when they had straggled home from the Western Front in disgrace and disarray. When the cheers and chants finally died down, he continued his speech with glassy eyes and a voice choked with emotion. After just five days of frantic planning, Operation *Winterübung* was in full motion.

Three hundred miles west of Berlin, three thousand soldiers of the German Wehrmacht waited in staging areas in the Rhine River town of Deutz. They had been rousted from bed early that morning to board troop trains, with no advance notice and no idea where they were headed. Even the officers commanding the Rhineland-bound units had no information about their final destination or purpose until they arrived.[9] Across the river from Deutz they could see the city of Cologne, an industrial powerhouse, historically the military center of western Germany, and still the largest and most important German city west of the Rhine River.

At precisely 12:50 p.m. the soldiers stepped off for the short march toward the Hohenzollern Bridge, which would carry them farther west. The arches of the bridge framed one of the most recognizable landmarks in Germany: Cologne Cathedral, the largest Gothic church in northern Europe, which loomed over the city. Its twin spires, at that time the second tallest in the world, soared to 515 feet. An hour and a half earlier, people on the streets of Cologne had witnessed a strange sight: nine Luftwaffe fighters circling the spires of the great cathedral. This early signal of German forces on the move simply caused confusion. But that afternoon the sound of an army band and the cheerfully singing soldiers that made their way across the bridge was like a cannon shot to the stunned Rhinelanders. There were columns of infantry in the field-gray uniforms of the regular army, motorized infantry detachments on motorcycles, horse-mounted cavalry riding two abreast, camouflaged supply trucks, communications soldiers on bicycles packing field telephones and radio gear, and horse-drawn service wagons hauling machine guns, antitank mortars, and steaming field kitchens.

At 1:00 p.m. the German army entered Cologne, timed perfectly with the climax of the Führer's Reichstag speech.[10] A growing stream of excited locals pushed out along the pedestrian walkways from the far end of the bridge to greet their soldiers, the first Germans to parade through the city in nearly twenty years.

A crowd of several thousand was already waiting on the far bank of the river and along the streets to Cathedral Square, while motion-picture cameramen captured the scene from multiple points along the parade route. When the end of the column finally reached the city, a formation of old German veterans, wearing the uniforms of past wars, joined the march. Thousands in the city center poured out of shops, apartments, and offices to swell the throngs that packed the sidewalks; windows on every block were crowded with faces watching the scene below. Flags sprouted on every building—Nazi swastikas and the red, white, and black of the German imperial colors. Some were hung out of impromptu enthusiasm, others because Joseph Goebbels, the propaganda minister, had ordered it. German flags were now flying nationwide, as Goebbels's proclamation read, to honor the World War dead, "whose sacrifice now no longer is in vain." Local Nazi officials went to work throughout the city to enforce this patriotic decree.

The police had trouble keeping the path clear for the approaching columns as eager spectators ran into the streets to march alongside the soldiers or shake their hands. Members of the League of German Girls tossed flowers, and boys from the Hitler Youth weaved among the troops handing out packs of cigarettes. In the middle of this carnival spirit, the young soldiers worked hard to maintain their military bearing; some gave in to the joy of celebration, waving, saluting, laughing, and shouting greetings as they tramped along.

Just after 2:00 p.m., Lt. Gen. Günter von Kluge, commander of VI Army Corps, entered Cologne in a black staff car and drove directly to his new headquarters at the Excelsior Hotel. The choice of the Excelsior, which stood on the edge of Domplatz (Cathedral Square), carried deep symbolism. Ten years earlier it had served as the headquarters of the British post-war occupation force in this sector of the Rhineland. The only reminder of that shameful era was a long groove that had been worn into the pavement along the front entrance by the boots of British sentries who had paced back and forth, around the clock, from 1918 until 1926. Today, two large swastika flags hung from the front of the hotel, where Cologne's lord mayor, dressed in the black uniform of the SS, and a pack of dignitaries from the city, stood ready to greet the Wehrmacht commander.

For the soldiers parading into town, the well-organized reception came as a great surprise. They didn't realize that the Propaganda Ministry in Berlin could take credit for orchestrating the spectacle. Goebbels didn't trust in spontaneous public enthusiasm to create the right scene for this historic moment. Two planes filled with journalists had flown to Cologne that morning to cover the bridge crossing, and Goebbels needed the right backdrop for the newsreel crews to capture on film, and a joyous public mood for newspaper reporters to describe in their dispatches.[11] Local officials were told of the coming deployment just hours before, and they had worked frantically to generate the kind of crowd that would satisfy Goebbels's vision. Happy citizens in the streets would show the world that this fait accompli was not some wild act of Adolf Hitler alone. And jubilation in cities and towns throughout the Rhineland would showcase the nobility of this cause for Germans across the larger Reich; it would stoke a nationalist impulse to accept whatever risks remilitarization held, and harden the political will necessary to defend Germany's sovereign rights in the West.

As Goebbels planned, the day ended with a jubilee across Germany, from the Rhineland to Berlin. St. Peter's bell tolled from Cologne Cathedral that night, ringing in celebration for the first time since the day British soldiers had marched out of the city a decade before. A giant torchlight parade wound through the city streets to toast the future. A torchlight parade illuminated Berlin that night, too, as fifteen thousand Nazi SS guards and SA storm troopers marched and sang through streets packed with wildly cheering spectators. Row after row they marched, rifles fixed with long bayonets, swastika banners and bronze imperial eagles held high, flaming torches and Nazi flags in each rank. They marched through the Brandenburg Gate onto Unter den Linden, the historic boulevard running eastward through central Berlin, then turned right and paraded down Wilhelmstrasse into the heart of official Germany, to pass in review for Adolf Hitler. The Führer, wearing a plain storm-trooper uniform, stood on a low second-floor balcony of the Reich president's palace, saluting the Nazi colors as unit after unit passed below. A rotating cast of Nazi officials, special guests, and military officers shared the balcony that night.

At 8:00 p.m., the airwaves once again carried Hitler's Rhineland speech through every radio station in the Reich, for those who had missed the live broadcast, or who simply wanted to relive this electrifying moment. Twenty-four hours later, *Winterübung* was complete.

BRITTLE NERVES AND FORCE OF WILL

The images of sublime national confidence that Adolf Hitler and his propagandists crafted that day were masterful—on the streets of Berlin, under the spires of Cologne Cathedral, within the Kroll Opera House, on newsreels, in the lively step of tens of thousands of German soldiers fanning out across the Rhineland. But these images masked a different reality. Within that small pack of top leaders responsible for planning and executing the operation, the mood was saturated with nervous pessimism and discord. Hitler never wavered. Once he reached the decision on March 2 to make his move, the Führer pushed the political and military machinery of the Third Reich toward that goal, unburdened by self-doubt or reservations. His strongest supporter within the inner circle was Foreign Minister Neurath, whose steadfast confidence reinforced Hitler's gut sense that he could pull off this maneuver without provoking a serious international backlash.[12]

The highest ranks of the German military, however, were deeply shaken by his orders. Just hours after Hitler's triumphant Reichstag speech, William Shirer crossed paths with General Blomberg in the Tiergarten park. It was a bizarre and unexpected sight, the Reich Minister of War, the commander in chief of German armed forces, alone on a nervous stroll, two dogs his only companions, so soon after Hitler's bold public defiance of the Versailles order. Blocks away the Wehrmacht leadership was braced for reports of French mobilization for war. Blomberg's "face was still white," as Shirer had observed earlier in the Kroll Opera House, "his cheeks twitching."[13] For the German military, the problem was not the Führer's objective. Senior leaders shared his deep conviction that restrictions on Germany's sovereign rights in the Rhineland were an outrage that had to be overturned.[14] Their resistance to Hitler's plan was simply a matter of its scale and timing. Germany needed more time to rebuild its military power before making such provocative moves; Hitler was stepping out too far, too soon.

Rumors of the German military's opposition to Hitler's plan appeared in the foreign press in the days that followed; years later, during the Nuremberg war crimes trials, these rumors were confirmed. The commander in chief of the army, Gen. Werner von Fritsch, had warned against running the risk of a French counterstrike. General Blomberg advised Hitler to pull back if the French mobilized. Perhaps, he suggested, Germany could offer to withdraw its Rhine forces if the French agreed to remove four to five times as many of their own soldiers from the border region. Gen. Ludwig Beck, the chief of the General Staff, advised the Führer not to send the Wehrmacht across the river, but if he did, his Reichstag speech should explicitly rule out German fortification as a way to soften the apparent magnitude of remilitarization.[15] One alternative floated was simply to convert paramilitary forces already operating openly in the Rhineland into active-duty Wehrmacht troops. The most capable paramilitary force was the *Landespolizei*, a state police organization with close to twenty thousand members in the Rhineland routinely trained in infantry tactics. Elsewhere the *Landespolizei* had been integrated into the regular German army in August 1935, so there was a precedent for this method of rapidly increasing the size of the armed forces.[16]

Hitler was disgusted by what he saw as poor judgment and weakness among his military leaders. He emphatically dismissed every protest and every alternative. A simple change of uniforms for the *Landespolizei*? No. He wanted men on the march, Luftwaffe fighters aloft, German trains and trucks moving regular Wehrmacht forces westward.[17] In fact, the army didn't have enough field-gray uniforms for the fourteen thousand *Landespolizei* that were converted into regular soldiers on March 10. It was enough of an embarrassment for Gen. Friedrich Dollmann, commander of the IX Army Corps, to review the parading army units in Frankfurt that day while nearly three-quarters of the soldiers were still wearing their green state police uniforms. Offer to compromise German sovereignty right from the start of the operation? Abandon German rights at the mere sight of French mobilization? The very purpose of remilitarization was to demolish an oppressive political order; any half-measures or retreat, Hitler said, would simply acknowledge the legitimacy of Germany's postwar humiliation.

Hitler pressed forward against this headwind of fear, warnings, and second thoughts, undeterred by the phalanx of senior officers that argued against his plan, the same leaders he was depending on to execute the fait accompli. And he did so with remarkable speed and secrecy. After the war it was rumored that Hitler, too, though unwavering, had been a bundle of nerves during the early stages of *Winterübung*. His main fear was that Germany would lose the benefit of surprise.[18] It's likely that no more than nine individuals were aware that Hitler was closing in on a Rhineland decision between mid-February and the early days of March.[19] Dirk Forster, the German chargé d'affaires in the Paris embassy, was one of only two government officials outside Hitler's immediate circle brought into early discussions. Hitler threatened Forster with execution if he didn't keep quiet about the meeting's subject.[20]

There were two questions on Hitler's mind during the weeks leading up to March 7. First, would France and Italy respond with military force? Forster warned Hitler on February 12 that no French government could tolerate a sudden upending of the demilitarized zone. Hitler sarcastically dismissed Forster's prediction about a muscular French response. And on February 22 the German ambassador in Rome sent good news to Berlin: Italy's Fascist leader Benito Mussolini would not join any international action to punish Germany for a Rhineland violation. Hitler's second question was purely political. Could he leverage the Franco-Soviet Mutual Assistance agreement, signed by both governments in May 1935, as a tool to legitimize German repudiation of its own pledge in the Locarno treaty to respect the Rhineland DMZ? On February 27, Hitler had his answer when the French Chamber of Deputies voted in favor of the pact. For Hitler, this was good enough to make the case that France had shattered Locarno by sealing this nefarious new security agreement with the USSR.[21] A political window of opportunity had opened, and within two days Hitler knew it was time to act.

The Führer announced his decision during a meeting at the Reich Chancellery on Monday, March 2, with just a few key leaders in the room: Göring, Blomberg, Fritch, and Goebbels; Joachim von Ribbentrop, Hitler's ambassador-at-large; and Adm. Erich Raeder, chief of the German navy. Later that day, General Blomberg issued operational orders to the three military services; their operations departments had just one day to develop plans, but staff officers were not told when the operation would be executed. All they knew were the two conditions General Blomberg set down to govern operational timing. First, the operations staff had to keep a tight timeline between the beginning of planning and the movement of German troops. Second, the operation had to be completed within two days.[22]

Hitler's cabinet wasn't informed until Tuesday, March 3, but when briefed, individual cabinet members were briefed alone. Hitler wanted to block any collective cabinet opposition that might disrupt the momentum of operational planning, while private notification would make it easier to enforce strict secrecy from cabinet officials who knew that leaks could be easily traced to the source. On Thursday, March 5, fewer than forty-eight hours before Rhineland-bound soldiers would begin moving westward, operations staffs were finally notified that forces would roll on Saturday, but they were forbidden to arrange troop transportation until Friday night.[23]

For all the discord and anxiety within the German government, for all the secrecy cloaking operational planning, for all of Hitler's bluster in the Kroll Opera House and the wild celebrations in German cities, it's hard to ignore how modest the scale of Rhineland remilitarization actually was over that one weekend. By Sunday night, the Wehrmacht had an order of battle that included twenty-two thousand soldiers in the Rhine zone. As one observer wryly noted, this was about "the size of an average soccer crowd in a big German city."[24] Two days later the number grew to thirty-six thousand when the Rhineland *Landespolizei* joined the ranks of the regular army. The Wehrmacht brought just 156 field artillery pieces and assigned 2 anti-aircraft artillery groups to defend bridges at Cologne and Mannheim. No tanks were deployed into the former DMZ. The Luftwaffe sent 54 fighter aircraft and 500 support personnel to airfields in Cologne, Coblenz, Frankfurt, Mannheim, and Düsseldorf, but bombers were held back.[25] Small garrisons of just a few hundred troops each popped up in four towns along the southern Rhine—in Freiberg, Kehl, Baden-Baden, and Rastatt—where the river forms the actual border between France and Germany. They were really no more than a novelty. In Kehl a cluster of German guards appeared, manning their post on the bridgehead opposite the French city of Strasbourg, under the watchful eye of thousands of curious French citizens who gathered at their end of the bridge to witness something that hadn't been seen from Strasbourg in more than a generation.

At four o'clock on Saturday, just a few hours after the Führer hit the climactic moment in his Reichstag speech, a train arrived in the city of Saarbrucken to deposit a thousand soldiers a mere three kilometers from French territory. A bugle corps announced their arrival and army bands played patriotic and martial songs on street corners throughout the city as residents cheered the spontaneous parade that snaked through the crowds. The train pulled out of Saarbrucken and worked its way northwest along the Saar River for forty miles to deliver another thousand soldiers to their new garrison in Trier, tucked up against the Luxembourg frontier. And further north, in the historic city of Aachen, where the borders of Germany, Belgium, and the Netherlands meet, a thousand soldiers arrived that day from their previous garrisons in the Ruhr River valley, to round out the new border outposts. These three thousand soldiers now in Saarbrucken, Trier, and Aachen, on the far western fringes of Germany, woke up that Saturday morning many miles from enemy territory, behind the comforting defensive barrier of the Rhine River, nested within large and powerful units of a growing Wehrmacht. That night they bedded down in makeshift barracks— old schoolhouses, abandoned factories, warehouses—within range of the heavy guns of French fortifications, on a frontier with no natural defensive barriers, with no ready support from their fellow soldiers.

While their arrival was a sensation, it was clear that these forces were not oriented for offensive operations beyond Germany's borders. Of the forty infantry battalions now in the Rhine zone, twenty-eight battalions remained *behind* the Rhine River. Technically they were within the fifty-kilometer strip running along the river's eastern bank, part of the prohibited zone defined by the Versailles and Locarno treaties. But they never crossed to the west. Seven more infantry battalions were stationed to the west of the Rhine, but they remained within a few kilometers of its west bank. The equivalent of two battalions was distributed among various small garrisons within the western Rhine zone.[26] Only three full battalions, those in Saarbrucken, Trier, and Aachen, were deployed to the far western border with France, Luxembourg, Belgium, and the Netherlands. These frontier garrisons were heavy on symbolism, but light on military muscle.

The broader deployment pattern of Rhineland forces, however, was not merely a symbolic effort to wave the Wehrmacht flag; there was a clear operational logic to their distribution. General Blomberg and his staff set up the most effective defense possible for two key areas Germany had to protect. Their first priority was the heart of German industry, that "unbroken forest of smokestacks" that stretched from Cologne northward along the Rhine to the city of Duisburg, then northeast along the Ruhr River to the city of Essen.[27] Essen was home to the largest iron and steel works in Germany, including the Krupp corporation, which fed German rearmament with tanks, artillery, munitions, and parts for warships and submarines. The Ruhr region produced vital strategic metals for the German chemical industry, and it was Germany's primary source of coking coal to fuel steel production. It's no surprise that the military forces stationed in the northern Rhine region were concentrated around the city of Düsseldorf, a virtual gateway to the Ruhr River valley. The western garrison at Aachen and the larger garrison at Cologne forty miles east of Aachen anchored a defensive line meant to block any French offensive drive toward the Ruhr in the northeast.

Their second priority was to defend the mid-Rhine region, centered on the city of Mainz, which sits near a sharp bend in the Rhine and directly across from the mouth of the Main River, where the Main flows into the Rhine. The French and Germans alike recognized the strategic value of Mainz, both as a vulnerability for Germany and an opportunity for France. It was here that in some future war an invading French force planned to cross the Rhine for a drive eastward into the Main River valley as it stretched across southern Germany. The Wehrmacht sent three thousand soldiers to Mainz to defend the river crossing. Goebbels's Propaganda Ministry apparently didn't work as hard to stir up a jubilant crowd for the arriving Wehrmacht in Mainz as it had for Cologne. Soldiers filed out of the troop train and wandered around the station and nearby streets on Saturday afternoon, but local citizens seemed either oblivious to their arrival or just confused when they spotted growing numbers of soldiers milling about. Once news of the Führer's announcement spread, the streets from the train station to the city center were lined with celebrants, and the cafés filled with locals hungry for news and gossip about remilitarization. To defend the Main River valley, the Wehrmacht concentrated forces within a triangle anchored on the west by the Rhine River cities of Coblenz, thirty-eight miles northwest of Mainz, and Karlsruhe, seventy miles to the south. The third point of the triangle was Frankfurt, which sat less than twenty miles to the east, upriver on the Main.[28] Within this defensive triangle, small garrisons appeared in Heidelberg, Ludwigshafen, and Speyer.

The new garrison at Coblenz was strategically located to support both the defense of German industry to the north and the river crossing at Mainz to the south. For more than one hundred years Coblenz had been the defensive center of the mid-Rhine region and the capital of Prussia's Rhine Province, while its population prospered from the barge traffic that gathered at this confluence of the Rhine and Moselle Rivers. The Ehrenbreitstein Fortress, built in the early nineteenth century, sat on a long bluff hundreds of feet above the Rhine's eastern bank, in a commanding position for defending this critical river juncture. In the years after World War I, Coblenz had become a sad shell of its former prominence and prosperity. An American occupation force of over 240,000 had been headquartered in the city between 1918 and January 1923, which pumped a healthy stream of US dollars into the local economy. After the American withdrawal from Germany, the city began a steep slide into economic decay. Anne O'Hare McCormick, the Pulitzer Prize–winning columnist for the *New York Times*, noted its pathetic state in 1936: "Coblenz in winter is a dull and shrunken place, as dark at night as a country village because it is too poor to pay for adequate lighting."[29] But on March 7, the Führer's announcement gave hope to the citizens of Coblenz that the city would recapture its former stature and good fortune in the new Germany. In a scene that resembled the celebrations under way in Cologne, the residents of Coblenz, "mad with joy" according to one observer, decorated the main Rhine bridge with evergreens as if it were Christmas, to honor the three thousand soldiers the bridge carried into their city.[30] And just like in Cologne, Berlin, and Mainz that night, Coblenz welcomed the Wehrmacht with a torchlight parade of its own.

It took just five days to plan, and two days to execute, but through this operation Hitler had managed to shred a defining feature of the post–World War I European order. The political drama and the military logistics had meshed seamlessly, just as he had imagined. Once the celebrations had quieted down, it would be time to stabilize this new status quo. Elated and relaxed, the Führer left Berlin by train on Sunday night for a rest in the Bavarian Alps.[31]

But in France, the crisis was just beginning. Before Hitler even arrived at the Kroll Opera House on Saturday morning to announce his fait accompli, nearly fifty thousand French soldiers were on the move toward the German frontier, and the preventive war temptation was beginning to boil.

FIRE KILLS

Just hours after early-morning reports reached Paris that German troops were on the move, dozens of trains pulled out of depots across northeastern France to rush soldiers from their peacetime garrisons into defensive fortifications that stretched for over 220 miles along the Franco-German border. It was a reflex reaction, a rapid thrust of men and materiel into the famed Maginot Line, that seemingly impregnable wall standing ready to deflect and destroy whatever aggressive punch the Third Reich might dare throw against France. Convoys of trucks, armored cars, commandeered buses, and private cars rumbled for hours down highways, through French villages, and along quiet country roads to deliver reinforcements for the one hundred thousand soldiers ordered into the Maginot Line two weeks earlier.

At dusk that day, thousands of French infantry paraded through the eastern gate of the ancient military city of Metz to begin the long march north, trudging through the night and much of the next day to reach their assigned positions along the line. Overhead, French pursuit planes maintained continuous daylight patrols after a German reconnaissance plane had been chased northward from the fortress city of Thionville and back across the border. Further east in Forbach, a city less than ten miles south of the Ger-

man battalion now in Saarbrucken, the French army rounded up taxicabs
and horse-drawn wagons to push the flow of soldiers and supplies into the
Saar River Gap, that weak spot in the line that the invading Prussian army
had poured through in 1870. An armada of requisitioned trucks rolled out
of the eastern city of Strasbourg carrying infantry reinforcements for the
city of Bitche forty-five miles to the north. North and south of Strasbourg,
frontier guards cut pontoon bridges that spanned the Rhine, linking France
and Germany, and constructed machine-gun outposts in their place to defend roads that now dead-ended at the river. By Sunday afternoon, when
the streets of Metz and Strasbourg were normally crowded with French
soldiers, not a single uniform was seen. By Monday morning the defensive
rush was complete. Nearly two hundred thousand soldiers now manned the
Maginot Line; "the fortifications," said the military governor of Strasbourg,
"are already jammed."[32]

The Maginot Line—named after André Maginot, the French war minister when construction began in 1929—was the most sophisticated fortification system ever developed, by any society, in any period of history. It's fair
to say that the Maginot Line was a material symbol, cast in concrete, of an
understandable national paranoia. It was the by-product of bitter history,
the suffering of successive generations that lived through two devastating
German invasions. In 1870, Prussia, the militant core of the northern German states, led an attack that smashed through the French Army of the
Rhine with such offensive power and speed that the French Second Empire and the reign of Emperor Napoleon III collapsed within a month. Two
weeks after the emperor's surrender, Paris was under siege. The invading
German armies of 1914 rolled back French forces once again; over one million French soldiers died in combat, and over four million were wounded
defending their homeland, while German territory was unscathed.

Allied victory in 1918 did nothing to temper French fears of German
recovery and future aggression. French leaders seemed resigned to an inescapable future clash, but the experience of trench warfare in the Great
War provided an answer to this problem: defense, they concluded, trumps
offense. While the offensive of 1914 brought the German army within thirty
miles of Paris and dangerously close to another victory, once the contend-
ing forces dug in along a front several hundred miles long and protected
themselves with heavy artillery, machine guns, and barbed wire, the defenders on both sides were able to throw back the enemy's offensive thrusts
repeatedly in a hail of metal and concussive shock. The key to saving France
when the next round of German aggression burst, French leaders came to
believe, was to build a permanent fortification system so ferocious in its

defensive power that any German army foolish enough to test it would be torn apart within a few miles of its own frontier. "Fire kills." This was the unofficial motto of the French army, and once the Maginot Line was ready to deliver on this promise, a near mystical faith in its defensive strength inspired the reflexive impulse to man its ramparts when the Wehrmacht moved across the Rhine River.

The Maginot Line of 1936 was no mere network of muddy field trenches protected by barbed wire and machine guns. Along the northern border with Luxembourg and Germany, the line was anchored by two Fortified Regions. On the western end it centered on Metz, where sixteen large forts and thirty-one intermediate and small forts covered a twenty-five-mile front protecting the industrial region of Lorraine. In the east, the six large forts and five intermediate and small forts of the Lauter Fortified Region stretched for over forty miles from the east bank of the Saar River to the Rhine. What made these forts distinct is that they were sunk deep into the earth, like a fleet of reinforced concrete battleships submerged twenty-five to thirty meters below the surface, protected from the heaviest enemy guns. Only their gun turrets and observation posts stuck up above the ground, and many of these could retract like a turtle's head into its shell to reduce exposure to enemy fire.

While the forts would provide the crippling firepower to safeguard the nation, they were not equipped with heavy guns. The operational concept for the Maginot Line was to engage the enemy in close combat just south of the German border, so the heaviest artillery in the line was a modified version of the 75mm guns made famous twenty years earlier in the Great War. The forts were set back from the German border between five and ten miles, and trees and brush were cut back for a clear field of fire, allowing the 75mm pieces, with a range of about seven miles, to target exposed German forces rushing toward the French line for an offensive breakthrough.

While these subterranean forts supplied the most potent punch, the Maginot Line was a system with multiple mutually supportive layers that began right on the German frontier. Some of the troops that rushed north on March 7 moved forward of the forts to reinforce the mobile guards manning a chain of fortified houses designed to blend in with the civilian homes on the border. When the Germans attacked, the defenders in these border outposts would sound the alarm and then go into action, blowing up railroad tracks, blockading roads, and destroying bridges to slow the Germans' advance. Two miles behind the frontier stood a line of concrete outposts, each with a permanent garrison that would engage the invading Wehrmacht with defensive fire for as long as they could hold out, allowing more time for the crews deep inside the forts to fully man and supply their combat stations. Antitank barriers—ditches and mines, and long lines of steel rails protruding from the earth, affectionately known as "asparagus beds"—laced the ground in front of and between the forts. Strands of tightly woven barbed wire filled the spaces between the steel rails to catch the advancing German infantry long enough to allow French machine gunners to cut them down. All along the line, across that vulnerable terrain that opened up between the underground forts, thousands of soldiers were manning hundreds of square concrete casements, ready to block German attackers that threatened to break through. Additional "interval" troops waited to the rear as a reserve force that could push into weak sections of the line. The final layer in this complex system was heavy artillery, which could be moved into firing positions behind the forts to provide additional cover for the French defenders and to direct long-range fire against enemy forces.[33]

The men who descended into the Maginot Line that weekend were organized like crews on a warship, rotating through four-hour shifts manning weapons and observation posts on the upper level or performing general duties or resting deep underground in the main level. Soldiers complained that the lack of central heating kept the forts cold and damp, except in the cramped bunk rooms where body heat made it hard to sleep. They enjoyed food prepared in modern kitchens, with a wine supply meant to sustain the entire crew for at least thirty days. Recreation rooms, theaters, and canteens helped make life underground a bit more tolerable. By the second week of the crisis, a "regional aid service for fortification troops," headquartered in Strasbourg, led a national collection drive that supplied 20,000 books, 100 phonographs, 5,000 phonograph records, and 150 radios to help their soldiers pass the endless hours of waiting for whatever came next.

THE SHADOW OF THE FUTURE GROWS DARKER

What would come next? Despite the uncertainty, foreign observers traveling through the region knew one thing: The French people had little to fear from the German forces planted in the Rhineland. The gross mismatch in military muscle deployed across the Franco-German frontier was impossible to ignore. Two weeks after Hitler's opera house speech, the *New York Times* carried Anne O'Hare McCormick's report of the stunning contrast between the crisis atmosphere sweeping Europe and the pathetic state of German preparedness in the western Reich.

For all you saw of military activity that week after the troops marched in, the Rhine might have remained demilitarized. I had to trail soldiers to their inconspicuous unfurnished barracks to convince myself of the reality of an army that had set the world quaking. Once found they did not look very formidable. The soldiers were pleasant boys in rumpled field gray . . . This is not the Kaiser's army. As yet it is not an instrument either bent on war or sharpened for attack. It looks like an improvisation of Adolf Hitler's, an idea hurriedly and carelessly executed under the stress of emergency.[34]

A correspondent for the London *Observer* had the same experience, reporting that he "traveled by car to Aachen from Cologne, then through the country districts to Coblenz, and back along the Rhine to Bonn. The only soldier I saw on the whole trip was a man on a bicycle who was making his way in a great hurry to the station yard at Coblenz."[35] No one doubted that France was well protected from German aggression that weekend; close to 200,000 soldiers were now settled into a heavily armed defensive crouch along a 220-mile fortified stretch of the frontier. Those "pleasant boys in rumpled field gray" were not even a shadow of the German armies that rolled through France in earlier generations.

So why did Hitler's decision to remilitarize the Rhineland generate such a frenzied crisis in the weeks that followed? As the French saw it, this was not a problem of security for the immediate future; the Maginot Line guaranteed that. The defiant slogan embroidered across the berets of the fortress troops—*Ils ne passeront pas*—"They will not pass"—said it all. Instead, this crisis was about dark clouds gathering over the future. The Rhineland DMZ was the keystone in a French postwar strategy that rested on a simple premise: A secure future depended on a European political order defined by German weakness. French leaders took little comfort from the collapse of the German Empire in 1918, the Kaiser's abdication and escape into exile, the revolution that upended the German political order, or the emergence of democracy after the fall of the Hohenzollern dynasty. They simply could not put aside a deeply rooted belief that Germany remained inherently aggressive, no matter who governed the state, or the fear that Germany would once again make a violent play for hegemony if it ever recovered the physical strength necessary to subdue its neighbors.[36] In this vision of the future, the Rhineland was material power. Hitler's move, as modest as it was in early 1936, set the conditions that would enable a long-term power shift in the years to come.

When the architects of the Versailles peace developed the treaty's long list of restrictions on German military hardware, they imagined a force responsible simply for internal security and local border protection. These limited missions could be executed without combat aircraft, tanks, heavy artillery, submarines, or a general staff to coordinate complex military operations, so each of these was banned. As long as Germany remained faithful to this cap on armed strength, to include a 100,000 personnel force limit, it would be decisively outgunned by its primary rivals to the east and the west. In the 1920s, Poland alone maintained an active force of 300,000 soldiers and could mobilize another 1.2 million for general war.

Instead of drawing confidence from the abundance of material security this postwar reality made possible, the past haunted French visions of the future. Particularly worrisome was an operational concept French military thinkers called the *attaque brusque*, or "surprise attack," a term describing the operational doctrine developed by Gen. Hans von Seeckt, the commander of the German army in the decade after the Great War. While surprise attack was one element of General von Seeckt's thinking, the essence of his doctrine was maneuver warfare. The Great War taught the French general staff that defensive firepower kills, and that in the age of combat between mass armies, victory would be found in attrition—the ability to sustain your fighting forces while grinding down the enemy until he was too exhausted to hold the battlefield. After all, exhaustion is what brought an end to Germany's fight on the Western Front.

Looking at this same experience from the losing end of the struggle, World War I taught von Seeckt a very different lesson. Attrition warfare on the Western Front was unproductive bloodshed that merely wasted the combatants. Germany's victories over Imperial Russia on the Eastern Front, however, illustrated an alternative way of war that would make it possible for a smaller, better-trained, better-led force to defeat a mass army fighting from static defensive positions. The key was a mobile force that could maneuver around a static enemy, find and punch through weak spots in the defensive line, and attack the enemy's flanks and supply lines to the rear. Under normal conditions, General von Seeckt said he would construct Germany's maneuver force with 200,000 to 300,000 soldiers. While Versailles made this force level impossible, he went to work nonetheless, organizing, equipping, and training a maneuver army that in no way resembled the modest internal security force the Allies had imagined would emerge in Germany.

French military leaders watched this process closely, and as one student of military strategy observed in the 1940s, there was a "verbal avalanche" of references to the *attaque brusque* in French military journals and speeches during the 1920s. To make the perceived threat even more serious, French officials didn't believe that von Seeckt's army was merely 100,000 strong; the assumption was that Germany could mobilize a highly effective professional force of 400,000 soldiers to execute the attack, with millions of veterans from World War I available to reinforce the German army once a conflict erupted.[37]

French leaders trusted defensive firepower and a fully mobilized army to stop a German advance and eventually prevail in total war. But everything hinged on *time*. While France had the largest army on the European continent into the mid-1930s, French strategists could not escape the limitations imposed by one brutal reality in the years after the Great War: the problem of insufficient manpower. France simply could not sustain an active-duty army large enough to repel a German onslaught at any point along what they called the *front continu*, that continuous defensive front— from Switzerland to the western coast—that had to be protected. The bulk of the army resided in a reserve force that required weeks to mobilize and deploy. In the early phase of a spiraling crisis, the French military had to set up *couverture*, a defensive "covering force" that would provide time for the full army to swell to wartime strength. So the defense of France came down to a race against the clock; the more time available, the stronger the fighting force in place. With this in mind, the demilitarized Rhineland was more than physical space providing a buffer zone between German armed forces and the French border. Through the DMZ, distance was converted into time. And, in turn, France would convert time into power.

Until 1930, France enjoyed what we might call "deep" *couverture*, or in the words of historian Jon Jacobson, *couverture par excellence*.[38] For more than a decade after World War I, Allied forces occupied the Rhineland and even controlled the bridgeheads on the eastern bank of the river in the cities of Cologne, Coblenz, Mainz, and Karlsruhe. While Versailles gave the victors the right to stay in the Rhineland until 1935, Britain, France, and Belgium agreed to withdraw their armies five years early to reward Germany for signing the Locarno treaty and agreeing to adhere to its rules governing perpetual demilitarization. The DMZ would remain, of course, so the Germans would be forced to launch an *attaque brusque* from the far side of the Rhine. But for many French leaders, losing the occupation force and the deep *couverture* it provided was unsettling; it was a loss of relative power that demanded some scheme to compensate for the erosion of defensive cover. The Maginot Line was the solution. Once encamped within their subterranean battleships, a relatively small force of rapidly deployed fortification troops could buy back the time France needed for general mobilization that occupation of the Rhineland once provided.[39]

But as formidable as the Maginot Line was, it had a potentially fatal flaw. And in 1936, the flow of German forces back into the Rhineland became a stark reminder of the remaining weaknesses in French defenses. By the second weekend of the crisis, Parisian movie houses were showing a short government film explaining what was at stake: While the Maginot Line itself could not be breached, the western end of the fortifications stopped two hundred miles short of the French coast, leaving its entire border with Belgium exposed. A remilitarized Rhineland could once again serve as the staging area for Germany to hurl its forces along a westward arc through Belgium into western France in a replay of the offensive of 1914. In a surprisingly frank reminder of the dangers, the government film used animated, stabbing black arrows on the map to depict a mechanized Wehrmacht force slicing west and southward from the Rhineland, cutting off relief from English Channel ports and encircling Paris from the west.[40] To prevent this nightmare, the *front continu* would pivot west of the Maginot Line and run to the northwest, across Belgium, until it reached the southwestern corner of the Netherlands and the North Sea coast. Along this line there was no system of interlocking heavy fortifications, merely units of defensive troops standing ready to deliver enough firepower to kill the German assault. As always, this strategy would crumble without sufficient time to mobilize and rush heavy French forces into the defensive line, which is exactly what the loss of the DMZ put at risk.[41]

This alone was enough to generate a sense of crisis in March 1936. But the loss of the Rhineland DMZ would deliver an additional blow to France's broader security strategy. Simply stated, it would undermine, and perhaps neutralize, France's ability to hold Germany itself hostage in exchange for its own good behavior. As long as the Rhineland was undefended and vulnerable to attack, it would serve as Germany's Achilles' heel. As the French saw it, German leaders would live under the dark cloud of superior French power. The mere threat of French invasion would force German leaders to abandon any tempting aggressive schemes they might pursue anywhere on the European continent. And if Germany succumbed to its aggressive inclinations, a retaliatory French attack would be punishing enough to compel a German retreat.

There were two basic avenues for French military action through the Rhineland. Most dangerous for Germany was the fact that demilitarization exposed its industrial power base along the Ruhr River in the north to French attack and seizure.[42] The second avenue of attack was linked to what both the French and British saw as the most likely targets of future German aggression: the states of central Europe that had been carved out of the old German Empire and its Austro-Hungarian ally after defeat in World War I, primarily Poland and Czechoslovakia. From the beginning of the post–Great

War period, Germans were seething over territorial losses in central Europe. Its revisionist impulses were particularly intense in the case of Poland, which had not existed as a sovereign state since 1795. Poland was reconstructed at Versailles, brought back to life for the first time in over 120 years after it was consumed in the late eighteenth century by a series of partitions among Prussia, Russia, and Austria. Even moderate German leaders of the 1920s considered this an outrage. A memorandum written by General von Seeckt in 1922 captured the common German belief in blunt terms: "Poland's existence is intolerable," he said, "incompatible with the survival of Germany. It must disappear."[43]

France, on the other hand, was not going to let that happen. Containment of German revisionism was the goal, and classic alliance building was the only vehicle French leaders fully trusted to keep Germany in check. In 1925 France linked arms with both Poland and Czechoslovakia, promising military support against aggression, and in 1926 and 1927 France partnered with Romania and Yugoslavia through military consultation agreements.[44] France's commitments, however, depended on its ability to deliver an offensive blow powerful enough to help its allies fend off coercion or turn back a German attack. For a brief period in 1935, France and Italy explored the option of turning Italy into a land bridge to carry French forces to Yugoslavia and a fight against Germany in the east. These talks collapsed in the fall of 1935.[45] The only realistic option for a French attack was the most obvious: an offensive drive across the Franco-German border to the city of Mainz, over the Rhine River and up the Main River valley through southern Germany, to link up with the Czechoslovakian army invading from the east.

Remilitarization of the Rhineland delivered a hammer blow to this option. Just two months before Hitler's Kroll Opera House cannon shot, General Maurice Gamelin, commander of the French army, warned the High Military Committee about this very problem. German fortification of its western frontier would "neutralize the French Army," he said. As a result, "free from any fear of an offensive from us, Germany would be completely at liberty to settle the fate of the states in central and east Europe."[46]

TO WAR FOR PEACE?

As this cornerstone of the postwar security structure was collapsing, the central question on that March weekend in 1936—the question debated within the French cabinet, among French citizens, in the French and international press, and in capitals around the world, including Berlin—was

what will France do *next*? Was the defensive reflex along the Maginot Line
just the beginning of a crisis that would escalate to general war? Would
the French military now drive across the German border to roll back the
Wehrmacht forces spread across the Rhineland? Would France pull the
preventive war trigger to restore the postwar order that kept German
power bottled up behind the Rhine River?

As early press reports relayed the news, it appeared that war was inevitable. Anonymous French officials, getting well ahead of actual government
decisions, were feeding journalists stories of French resolve and plans for a
punitive military expedition. Readers of American newspapers woke up on
Sunday and Monday mornings to headlines announcing "France Moves to
Oust Nazis"; its army was on a "War Footing . . . Ready to Employ Force
to Drive German Soldiers Out of Rhine"; France was "Moving to Combat
Hitler." On Tuesday a banner headline in the *Atlanta Constitution* declared
"British Agree to Back Paris with Army"; on Thursday the *Boston Globe*'s
headline virtually jumped off the page: "French Talk Preventive War." According to one unnamed French official, whose words found their way into
newspapers across Europe and America, "we know war is coming in two
years anyhow. We might as well have it now, while we are prepared. The
only way in which Hitler's troops will leave the Rhineland is for the Locarno
signatories to drive them out."[47]

The French government's uncompromising position on the Rhineland
question fed predictions of war, making these sensational newspaper headlines seem reasonable. But uncertainty prevailed. While observers noticed
an "unnatural calm" on the streets of Paris and in towns and villages on
both sides of the border, there were clear signs of nervous speculation
about the likelihood of war.[48] Many were hungry for information, to be
sure; newspapers across Paris sold out as quickly as new copies could be
printed and rushed into the streets. The Bank of France reported a brief
run on gold by panicky depositors who "lined up with suitcases and traveling bags," but the insurance giant Lloyd's of London downplayed the
likelihood of war in the rates it charged clients (Lloyd's figured the odds
of a European war in six months to be nine and a half to one against, and
the odds that French soldiers would invade the Rhineland to be forty-eight
and a half to one against).

Wall Street shared Lloyd's of London's optimism.[49] While the financial
community remained calm, a number of American students studying in
Paris received cables from nervous parents ordering them home. Parisians
with country homes left the city in larger numbers than usual that first crisis
weekend, and air-raid sirens were tested throughout the city. Officials in

the city of Nancy launched a crash program to build air-raid shelters. The government made no move toward general military or industrial mobilization during these uncertain first weeks, yet the French Senate unanimously approved a bill increasing military conscription from one year of service in uniform to two years, and on March 12 it voted overwhelmingly to ratify the Franco-Soviet military pact. In Metz on Sunday an international soccer match between the French city's team and Germans from Stuttgart went on as planned, with heavy police presence to prevent violence in the stands. The stadium, however, was empty as French fans boycotted this demonstration of neighborly goodwill. Nearby, artillery practice sparked a flood of worried phone calls to police and newspapers. Entrepreneurial motion picture studio heads at Warner Brothers and Paramount Pictures deployed dozens of camera crews into the Rhineland to record as much stock film footage as possible. They wanted scenes of German and French soldiers on the march—not for newsreels, but for what producers hoped would be the next Hollywood blockbusters in the event of European war.

While international expectations were mixed, German diplomats in the London embassy were becoming more pessimistic by the day. They were frantically collecting information on the evolving politics of the crisis from a variety of sources, mainly government officials from France, Britain, Belgium, and Italy, who were in London for an emergency meeting of the Locarno signatory states. By the end of the first crisis week, Ambassador Leopold von Hoesch and the embassy's military attachés were cabling warnings to Berlin that attitudes on the Rhineland fait accompli could harden in a matter of days and tilt toward some form of retaliatory military action. For Ambassador Hoesch, the crisis felt too much like 1914, with its tightening alliances, escalating demands and counterdemands, its spiraling fears and military maneuvering. On the receiving end of these warnings was General Blomberg, who suffered a complete loss of nerve. Overcome by fear that France might actually launch a preventive attack, Blomberg was desperate to reduce the odds of such a calamitous turn. He reached out repeatedly for a meeting with the Führer so he could make his case for an evacuation of the border garrisons, but Hitler simply ignored him.

Hitler was receptive to minor recommendations from the Foreign Ministry meant to avoid overt and unnecessary provocation. He agreed to cancel military parades scheduled for March 16 in Frankfurt, Cologne, and Coblenz, and the German press corps was ordered to dial down the severity of its rhetoric in stories about the Rhineland. Hitler authorized the Foreign Ministry to release official figures on the number of Wehrmacht troops now in the Rhineland—36,500, according to the press release, including former

Landespolizei—to emphasize that this force posed no threat to France. He also agreed to a four-month moratorium on the construction of fortifications. Aside from these few insignificant or temporary concessions, Hitler refused to back down in any way that would provide France with some measure of relief from the building pressure.[50]

Within days it was obvious that France and Germany had staked out irreconcilable positions; only one could prevail. From the start, French premier Albert Sarraut made sure the French political position was clear and uncompromising: Germany was guilty of a violent rebuke to the Versailles and Locarno treaties, guilty of a hostile return to the rule of brute force and an outrageous affront to the rule of law. Demilitarization was the key to peace for future generations, and Germany must not be allowed to tear this apart. On Sunday night, in his first radio address to the nation on the crisis, Sarraut bluntly declared that France would not "allow Strasbourg to be under the fire of German cannon."[51] If Hitler wanted to discuss an alternative future for the Rhineland, he said, that's fine, but France would never negotiate while Wehrmacht boots were planted in the forbidden zone. And if Germany refused to withdraw, in the words of Foreign Minister Pierre-Étienne Flandin, France claimed the legal right to take "urgent, brutal, decisive measures" to compel German compliance.[52] Germany must withdraw its forces, period. Hitler's reply came on March 12 during a fiery speech in the city of Karlsruhe, just six miles from the northeastern corner of France: "Nothing, absolutely nothing, will induce us to renounce our regained sovereignty over the Rhineland."[53] The problem of turning back remilitarization, then, was thrown back to the French government.

Twenty-four hours into the crisis the French cabinet decided that if preventive war was necessary to compel a German retreat, France would fight. What the bold public statements by French officials did not reveal, however, was the level of rancor within the cabinet on Sunday morning over this specific question. The great champion of preventive war in this debate was Georges Mandel, a cabinet member who carried the unassuming title of minister of posts and telegraphs. His title was not only unassuming, it was deceptively innocuous, because Mandel had been among the most influential members of the French governing class since World War I, when he served as Premier Georges Clemenceau's chief personal assistant. Most recently, Mandel took the lead in pulling together the Sarraut government at the end of January 1936, and despite his official title, the press routinely assumed that he was the cabinet's true mainspring.[54]

Perhaps Mandel's position on preventive war was predictable; it certainly was consistent with his traditional hard line on the German question, as well as his personal history. His parents had fled the eastern province of Alsace in 1871 to escape life under the new German Empire after it annexed the region at the end of the Franco-Prussian War. In early 1936, Mandel was also proudly serving as the high commissioner for Alsace and Lorraine, which France recovered after World War I. During the Great War he was at Clemenceau's side, helping "the Tiger" reinvigorate the nation's dangerously flagging commitment to total war against Germany, and again at the Paris Peace Conference in 1919, supporting the construction of a peace that would hold Germany down. Not only was Mandel a fervent opponent of early Allied withdrawal from the Rhineland in 1930, he also believed France should hold on to deep *couverture* for as long as possible. After all, he argued, the Versailles Treaty gave the Allies the right to extend Rhineland occupation beyond 1935, until the day the Allies declared Germany in full compliance with the treaty's long list of demands. Germany would always fall short of full compliance in some way, Mandel reasoned, which in turn would allow the Allies to push the evacuation date further and further into the future. With French forces on the Rhine River, German leaders would have to fight the next war on their own soil, and for Mandel, this was the best deterrent imaginable to German aggression.[55] Mandel lost that particular argument, and France lost its deep *couverture*, but in 1936 he was determined to push his colleagues toward immediate preventive war to keep France from losing one of the few surviving remnants of the Versailles order.

Sarraut and France's permanent delegate to the League of Nations, Joseph Paul-Boncour, were sympathetic to this position. But Mandel confronted a fierce opponent during this cabinet debate when Gen. Maurice Gamelin, commander of the French army, took the lead in throwing the cold water of military pessimism on the idea of immediate war. To be sure, Gamelin would bristle at any suggestion that the military leadership lacked courage in the thick of the crisis. During the cabinet debate Gamelin was greatly offended when Foreign Minister Flandin called Gen. Louis Maurin, the war minister, "timorous." Several weeks later rumors ricocheted around Paris that Gamelin and Maurin were to blame for the lack of bold action. In late April, the vice chief of staff of the army recorded in his diary that General Gamelin "considers it intolerable that they should say that the soldiers would not march on 7 March." On the other hand, Gamelin was proud to report to the High War Council that "the soldiers had been forced to restrain the politicians."

It wasn't that the French army was unfit to confront the Wehrmacht in war. In a meeting with the British military attaché on April 11, General

Gamelin confidently reported that the army was "in excellent shape," and he acknowledged the preventive logic of fighting Germany in the near term, if war was bound to come, rather than suffering heavier costs at some future date.[56] But offensive action against Germany, Gamelin and Maurin insisted, had to wait until France mobilized full *couverture*—a minimum of one million soldiers drawn from the regular army, and reservists from the three most recent classes of conscripts—and started down the road to general mobilization, a process that would take at least two weeks and carry a high price tag.[57]

The military's warnings about the dangers of an impulsive strike were serious, but at the end of the contentious debate their caution could not derail a consensus from crystallizing around action to compel a German retreat. Agreement came with a heavy caveat, however: A sizable cabinet majority rejected *unilateral* action outright.[58] France was going to face down Germany, but it must do so within the reassuring embrace of its Locarno treaty partners—particularly Great Britain—and with the backing of a League of Nations resolution finding Germany guilty of Versailles Treaty violations. For Georges Mandel, this caveat would not stand in the way of ultimate success. As he left the cabinet meeting that Sunday, he made this prediction: "We are going to act," he said. "Sarraut is going to speak over the radio tonight in terms we have agreed on together, and after which there will be no going back."[59]

No going back, perhaps, but what was the path forward? The army was on notice that it might be called on to play its own role in this evolving coercive drama. But from this point forward the real burden would fall on Foreign Minister Flandin, because the only path to a demilitarized Rhineland that French leaders were willing to tread ran straight through London. And in turn, this put Great Britain's new and untested foreign minister, Anthony Eden, squarely in Flandin's diplomatic crosshairs.

A MAN WITH A MISSION

The first step in Flandin's plan of attack was to engineer a guilty verdict against Germany. Here he scored two quick victories: On March 12, diplomats from France, Britain, Belgium, and Italy (the Germans were left off the invitation list) concluded a meeting in London by agreeing unanimously that Germany had in fact violated the Locarno treaty's rules on the Rhineland DMZ, and on March 19, at the end of a special League of Nations session held at St. James Palace in central London, the League council voted unanimously to condemn Germany for its blatant breach of Articles 42 and 43 of the Versailles Treaty. The second step was much trickier: To constrain the Reich's growing power, Flandin had to draw his European partners into a scheme of escalating coercive steps that he hoped would force Hitler into retreat.

Flandin found two ready partners for this mission in Belgium and the Soviet Union. Belgian prime minister Paul van Zeeland enlisted in Flandin's cause without hesitation. France and Belgium had suffered so much together during the last round of German aggression, and they would share the same fate once again if Nazi Germany turned its swelling offensive capabilities against its western neighbors. So with grim resignation, van Zeeland accepted the possibility that escalating pressure might lead to preventive war. The Soviets brought the greatest fireworks to the proceedings. Hitler's rise to power forced a radical shift in German–Soviet relations that swept away the strange yet mutually supportive relationship of the 1920s, when the new Soviet government hosted secret production facilities for German combat aircraft and tanks and training sites for their crews. Hitler's hate-filled tirades against the Bolshevik virus and the Soviet menace to Western civilization clarified any lingering ambiguities about the character of German hostility. With Hitler's verbal abuse in mind, Soviet foreign minister Maxim Litvinov tore into the Third Reich with abandon during the special League of Nations meeting in London. Litvinov shouted and threw his arms around wildly as he warned his counterparts about Germany's violent plans for hegemony over Europe. Rhineland remilitarization was nothing but a "smokescreen for aggression," he said. And with the USSR on Hitler's target list, Litvinov promised that his country would go to the "limit authorized by the League in inflicting punishment."[60] On the final day of the League meetings, as Hitler's special envoy Joachim von Ribbentrop addressed the assembled diplomats, Litvinov turned his back and made a show of his contemptuous disregard by reading his newspaper with noisy flourishes throughout the German's speech.

Belgian and Soviet support was valuable, but if France was to ratchet up the coercive pressure and force Germany to climb back down in the Rhineland, the only partner that really mattered was Great Britain. It was a relationship that British leaders accepted from the start. The most important link between them was Britain's unambiguous promise to throw itself into the fight if Germany actually attacked France. And while France stepped into a leadership role to cobble together a firm international response, British leaders agreed to host both the Locarno meetings and the special League of Nations session to demonstrate their commitment to the common cause—and, most important, to ensure that Britain had a strong voice shaping the action plans that emerged. While Britain stepped up in this way, Flandin remained frustrated throughout by what was at best a limited partnership, and from a British perspective, a partnership meant to constrain muscular French actions as much as it was to constrain the expansion of German power. This crisis wasn't merely a contest between the West European allies and Germany; it was also a contest between France and Britain, driven by rival visions of the path forward and the strategic outcomes to pursue. As a result, the crisis became a contest between two foreign secretaries—Flandin and Eden—to shape the future.

Appointed at the age of thirty-eight, Anthony Eden was the youngest British foreign secretary since 1851. Frequently described as handsome, dashing, and a fashionable dresser, he carried the honorific "Captain Eden" well, as a respectful nod to his service in the British infantry during the Great War. A year earlier, during a lunch meeting at the British embassy in Berlin, Eden and Hitler discovered that during the war they had faced each other in opposing trench lines near Ypres, Belgium. By the time German soldiers rolled across the Rhine River in March 1936, Eden had held the post of foreign secretary for little more than two months. The crisis was immediately seen as his first major test. Like Eden, Flandin was a political conservative; he did not serve in uniform during the World War, but Flandin was a veteran politician who had served in the French Chamber of Deputies since 1914. While just eight years older than Eden, he had already held numerous cabinet posts before becoming foreign secretary, to include commerce and industry, finance, and public works, and from November 1934 to June 1935 he served as French prime minister.

Just three days into the crisis, the foreign secretaries squared off in Paris to work through options for a collective response. They were joined by Prime Minister van Zeeland, as well as by Lord Halifax, a seasoned political figure who held the post of privy seal in the British cabinet, sent as a chaperone to keep a watchful eye on his protégé and ensure that the new foreign secretary didn't promise Flandin more than Eden's colleagues were willing to deliver. Flandin wasted no time dancing around the nature of the problem and its solution. He hit Eden with a plan that involved escalating coercive steps and the optimistic prediction that the Locarno partners would not have to climb very far toward preventive war before Germany caved. The first step, Flandin said, would be to hammer an economically vulnerable Germany with sanctions against critical trade goods and foreign capital. The German economy would certainly collapse, he argued, and Hitler's rearmament program would grind down. Best of all, he mused, the Nazi regime might actually crumble under the strain of rising unemployment, agitation in the military stoked by shriveling defense budgets, and the loss of political support from German industrialists no longer willing to tolerate the financial consequences of Hitler's risk-prone impulses and menacing bluster. Besides, Flandin reminded his Locarno partners, a year earlier, when Hitler announced his rearmament plans, unveiled the Luftwaffe, and reintroduced conscription, the League of Nations authorized economic sanctions against states that unilaterally violated international treaties.[61]

And what if these economic sanctions fail? That's unlikely, Flandin insisted, but the second step would be military mobilization; the mere threat of invasion might be enough to cow the German government and force a conciliatory retreat. What if Hitler stands firm, hoping that Allied mobilization is just a bluff? Then the third step up the coercive ladder, Flandin explained, would be an actual military advance into German territory by the Locarno powers. Not to wrest control of the entire Rhineland, he emphasized, but to secure a *prise de gages*—a more-limited territorial guarantee—held hostage until Germany succumbed to international demands for complete withdrawal from the Rhineland. The day before, Prime Minister Sarraut had demanded a plan for this operation. That morning General Gamelin and the French General Staff reluctantly presented two alternatives: First, France could occupy the neutral principality of Luxembourg to demonstrate its ability to maneuver and seize territory. (Civilian leaders found this option puzzling and counterproductive, however, and dismissed it outright.)

Second, the French army could push northward through the Saar Gap, the section of the Maginot Line facing the German industrial city of Saarbrucken, following in reverse the same invasion route used by Prussian forces in 1870. Once in Germany the French army would occupy a twenty-five-mile-long stretch of the border between Saarbrucken and the town of Merzig. If the German army offered little resistance, French forces could then push out to the east and west, expanding their hold on a wider front, or even cross the Rhine River to the east to occupy the German end of key bridges that would open routes for a larger follow-on invasion force. Perhaps, Flandin speculated, if economic sanctions were not threatening enough to bring down the regime, then the shock and danger of foreign troops on German soil would set in motion political effects far beyond German capitulation on the Rhineland. If this blow inspired the German military to take down Adolf Hitler and the Nazi regime in a coup d'état, it would bring a decisive end to the Third Reich's aggressive agenda.

And if these steps produced nothing but continued defiance? Well, Flandin admitted, if these lower steps on the escalatory ladder failed to compel German withdrawal, the Allies must be ready to mount the kind of preventive attack that would "liberate" the Rhineland from Wehrmacht occupation for the indefinite future. Remember, he insisted, we will most likely achieve victory before ever reaching this ultimate preventive option. But, he warned, once the Allies set out on this coercive path, falling short of full demilitarization would hand a great victory to Hitler and a disastrous defeat to France. This turn of events would inevitably swell the Third Reich's confidence as its masters plotted the next steps toward dominance in Europe.[62] Of course, both Flandin and Zeeland admitted, war against the Wehrmacht on German territory was a risky solution. But from their perspective, the risks and costs of war today were not the real problem. The problem, they argued—drawing on fear of the future and the allure of preventive war—is that German power will simply grow more fearsome as the years go by, and peace in Europe depends on keeping Germany physically constrained.

The next day Eden and Halifax were back in London to report on these conversations. In frank terms, Eden laid out the French position to the cabinet. He told them Flandin was "infuriated" by Eden's speech in Parliament on Monday night that suggested a willingness to treat Hitler's peace overtures seriously. And "if the German challenge was not taken up now," the French say, "a much more formidable situation would arise in two years' time. At the moment," Eden said, Flandin and van Zeeland "believe that the risk of war being precipitated by firm action was remote, but that if Germany was allowed to remain unmolested in military occupation of the Rhineland, war in two years' time was a certainty and would be fought under very unfavorable conditions."[63] The only option, they insisted, was to compel Germany, by force, if necessary, to accept its place in the European order as a truncated great power.

Flandin's warning and his appeal for bold action fell flat. Going into these consultations, French leaders had implicitly offered Britain veto power over the coercive strategy they envisaged, and British leaders slapped it down without hesitation. The British had a different approach to the problem, emphasizing compromise and a process of reconciliation with Germany that might blunt the strategic significance of Rhineland remilitarization. While France insisted on total withdrawal of Wehrmacht troops from the forbidden zone, Britain tried to coax Hitler into drawing down his forces to a "symbolic" level, perhaps no more than ten thousand soldiers; this would signal a restoration of German sovereignty over the Rhine without posing an actual threat to France or Belgium. While France pushed for escalation that might lead to Allied preventive attack, Britain proposed an international peacekeeping force that could buffer rival forces along the Franco-German border and build confidence in a stable future. When French leaders stood fast behind a table-pounding demand prohibiting German fortifications in the Rhineland, Britain pressed the German government to accept this position.[64] Hitler would only promise a four-month moratorium on fortification while a new political order was negotiated among the Locarno signatories. While French leaders refused to negotiate over Hitler's proposals for this new political order, the British government reached out to Hitler with a questionnaire that might clarify exactly what he had in mind, resolve the ambiguities in Germany's proposals, and offer a way forward toward a negotiated settlement on the broader German role in Europe.[65]

It's impossible to find a definitive end point to the Rhineland crisis. Britain failed to move Germany toward a mutually acceptable compromise, just as France failed to move Britain toward a coercive solution to the problem. For those European statesmen working day in, day out, to stabilize or turn back this challenge, the crisis simply fizzled with time as new problems distracted leaders across the Continent in a crisis-filled year. Looking back, one specific moment signals that the prospects of negotiated settlement were stillborn from the beginning. On March 24, seventeen days after German soldiers deployed to their western outposts, the Third Reich delivered a double blow against the Allied effort to hold German power in check. That morning the Reich formally notified London that it rejected a compromise plan the other Locarno powers had offered to resolve the dispute. More important was a defiant pageant staged that night by Joseph Goebbels and his Führer. According to Sigrid Schultz's account in the *Chicago Tribune*, one million German citizens lined a five-mile "triumphal road" in Berlin that ran from the Reich Chancellery to Deutschland Hall, the grand arena built for the 1936 Summer Olympics, to cheer on Adolf Hitler as he made his way to deliver the most fiery speech of the past few weeks. Twenty thousand Germans in the arena, and millions tuning in by radio, listened that night as the Führer declared that Germany would never surrender to the inequalities at the heart of the Locarno powers' demands. "We are through with being humiliated slaves," he said. "It is the most beautiful thing in the world to be able to fight for a people who were wronged and tortured, and to drive them into action."[66] A few days earlier, during a speech in the city of Hamburg, Hitler affirmed that Germany "won't retreat a centimeter."[67]

From this point forward, Hitler never budged from his "no surrender" position. There would be no withdrawal of German forces from the Rhineland to some symbolic level. Germany would never allow an international

military force to set up peacekeeping stations on its territory. Any demilitarized zone on the German side of the frontier must be matched by demilitarization on the French side, which Hitler knew France would never
accept. A four-month moratorium on fortification was acceptable, Hitler
agreed, but after that Germany could never accept perpetual vulnerability.

While Hitler's defiant stance was set less than three weeks into the crisis,
it took a while for the futility of negotiated compromise to become clear.
On July 6 Eden conceded in the House of Commons that Hitler would
never answer their questionnaire, that good-faith effort to clarify Hitler's vision for a new Locarno order. Reich officials had politely asked for patience
as the weeks turned into months, until British leaders stopped asking for a
reply. Hopes for a new Locarno conference to settle a range of outstanding
questions were kept alive in London through the summer and early fall of
1936. Germany and Italy initially accepted an invitation for a meeting to be
held in September, but then asked for a postponement until late October.
By early October it was clear that the Locarno process was dead; the conference never met.[68]

In the intervening months, other issues pulled French and British leaders away from the Rhineland question, until it was just one more variable
in a rapidly changing European security environment. The date for new
parliamentary elections was bearing down on the Sarraut government
in France at the end of April. In early June a new left-leaning Popular
Front government was formed under Socialist prime minister Leon Blum,
who was suddenly absorbed in a crippling domestic crisis when industrial
workers, hoping to spur true revolution, staged violent strikes and factory
seizures. In the spring and early summer Great Britain and France were
also struggling through bitter antagonism over how to treat Italy's brutal
drive to conquer Ethiopia. Britain worked hard to push this problem to the
top of the League of Nations' agenda and to tighten international sanctions
against Italy.

For Britain, this was another power-shift problem that demanded preventive action to keep Italy from consolidating a North African foothold
that could threaten Britain's Suez Canal lifeline to India. France, on the
other hand, insisted that the League drop economic sanctions to ensure
that Italy remained a reliable partner in a joint effort to hold German ambitions in check. Great Britain had been Ethiopia's greatest champion since
the fall of 1935, which set Britain up for a humiliating blow to its prestige
in the summer of 1936 when the government was forced to concede that
sanctions had failed to stop Italian aggression. It was a concession that
signaled Britain's unwillingness to do anything further to liberate this poor

North African state, a member of the League of Nations, from the grip of its new colonial master. The League of Nations dropped sanctions against Italy on July 15.

That summer, civil war ripped through Spain's political system and divided European nations against one another as most lined up to support and supply either the republican government or the Spanish military's right-wing rebellion. Britain waged a futile campaign to generate a Europe-wide pledge of nonintervention. In October, Belgium abandoned its alliance with France, and British ruling circles were rocked by a growing crisis at home when King Edward VIII announced his intention to marry the American divorcée Wallace Simpson. The king abdicated the throne in December. In the meantime, Hitler's promised four-month moratorium on new troops in the Rhineland expired on August 1. Three weeks later the German government issued a surprise decree increasing the term of service for conscripts from one year to two years in uniform. The rapidly swelling ranks of the Wehrmacht allowed the army to create eight new divisions that fall. Six were sent into the Rhineland, bringing total official strength in the former demilitarized zone to at least ninety thousand soldiers.[69] The Rhineland DMZ was now a relic of postwar history.

For French and British leaders caught up in these events, battered by domestic political crises, by Italy and Ethiopia, and by Spain, Hitler's fait accompli in the Rhineland became just one more item on a complicated and confounding roster of challenges they could not control. But in retrospect, Rhineland remilitarization takes on special significance in this tumultuous year; Ethiopia, Italy, Spain, fallen monarchs, and workers' revolutions seem insignificant in contrast. With the clarity of hindsight, Rhineland remilitarization emerges from the clutter of daily distractions and rapid change as one of those turning points in the tragic story of this increasingly violent era. To be blunt, it's impossible to ignore the link between Hitler's bold moment in 1936, the Allies' decision to let Rhineland remilitarization stand, and the explosive punch of the German blitzkrieg that broke France's back less than four years later. The road to victory ran through the Rhineland.

1940: THE ROAD TO VICTORY

Just a month after he led Army Group South in the lightning offensive that crushed Poland in September 1939, Gen. Gerd von Rundstedt found himself on the western frontier in command of Army Group A. Here General Rundstedt held the central section of a German front that stretched for six hundred heavily armed miles, northward from Switzerland along the Rhine River border with France, westward across the heavily fortified section of the Maginot Line, then northward again along the common frontier with Luxembourg, Belgium, and the Netherlands. By the time Rundstedt arrived to take his new command, Germany was already at war with France and Great Britain. But the opening of this war looked nothing like 1914, when mobilization and cascading declarations of war tore open the floodgates holding back the rival armies that quickly met in full-scale armed combat on the West European front.

A few days after war was declared on September 3, 1939, a French force moved out of the Maginot Line and executed a halfhearted offensive through the Saar Gap, but it advanced no more than five miles into German territory. They held twenty-four square miles of the Saarland for three weeks, hoping the image of the French army on the move would give its Polish ally courage as the Poles struggled for survival against the German blitzkrieg. But the French invasion was merely symbolic; French leaders never intended to execute operational plans developed years earlier to halt German aggression in the east by driving deep into German territory from the west. Once Poland capitulated three weeks later, there seemed to be no point to this modest occupation. Czechoslovakia had been swallowed up six months earlier. The French army withdrew and settled into a tense and uncertain standoff with the Third Reich that stretched through the fall of 1939 and into the winter of 1940.

The Führer's plan was to build momentum with his victory in Poland to propel the Wehrmacht to a quick blitzkrieg victory against France and Great Britain, but momentum was fouled by persistent bad weather. As the standoff on the Western Front stretched into the spring, the German force deployed to the Rhineland during this "sitzkrieg" grew to massive proportions: 114 infantry divisions, 10 armored Panzer tank divisions, 4 motorized infantry divisions, 2 motorized SS divisions, a cavalry division, and a parachute division. Hitler's fait accompli force of 1936 was meaningless in comparison. In March 1936, a mere 2,000 German soldiers, organized into two battalions, covered the border sector between the cities of Trier and Aachen, part of the total official force of 36,500 men, organized into 40 battalions.

In the opening months of World War II, through the false starts and postponements, General Rundstedt waited with forty-five and a half Wehrmacht *divisions*—each division manned by 16,500 soldiers organized into nine battalions—covering that same section of the German border. This number doesn't include the additional seven armored divisions assigned to Army

Group A in the central sector. When the blitzkrieg was unleashed, General Rundstedt alone commanded over 700,000 troops. While not a single tank was deployed into the Rhine zone in the spring of 1936, four years later General Rundstedt commanded 1,800 Panzers, standing ready to charge across the frontier as part of a forty-five-mile-wide "giant phalanx."[70] To the north of Aachen stood another twenty-nine and a half divisions of Army Group B, under the command of Gen. Fedor von Bock, to include roughly 600 Panzers in three armored divisions. South of Trier was Army Group C, commanded by Gen. Wilhelm von Leeb, whose nineteen infantry divisions waited along a front that stretched across the Maginot Line and down the Rhine River to the Swiss border. Dozens of additional divisions waited in reserve. In March 1936, 54 fighter aircraft, but no bombers, were deployed to Rhineland airfields. In May 1940, the Luftwaffe had approximately 1,000 fighters and 1,400 bombers committed to the coming offensive against the Western Allies.[71]

As General Rundstedt waited he refined his plans and exercised his forces to fine-tune the coordinated tank and aircraft maneuvers that were key to rapid victory in the impending blitzkrieg attack. While Rundstedt held the shortest of the three sections of the German front, he was handed the decisive operational role: to tear through the weakest portion of the enemy's defensive line in the northern French city of Sedan, then drive toward the English Channel to envelop and smash the Allied forces caught in a pocket further north in Belgium. Before dawn on May 10, this is exactly what Rundstedt put in motion. By May 13 French defenses at Sedan were collapsing as the Wehrmacht fought its way across the Meuse River. On May 14, the first of the Panzer divisions in the breakthrough were racing west toward the English Channel at a pace that shocked Hitler himself. One month later, German tanks rolled unopposed through the streets of Paris. On June 22, France surrendered. One year later, the Wehrmacht stormed across the plains of the western Soviet Union, and the world faced four more years of ghastly war and suffering.

Rhineland remilitarization set the stage for this chain of events. The success of the entire offensive depended on two basic conditions: the secrecy and speed of the Panzer divisions' rush toward the Sedan breakthrough, and a flashy diversionary invasion of the Netherlands farther north.[72] On May 9, at 1:15 p.m., the lead Panzer division, under the command of Gen. Heinz Guderian and his XIX Panzer Corps, received orders to begin movement toward the Luxembourg border. Guderian was a visionary apostle of armored warfare and the victorious commander of one of the pincers that broke the Polish defense eight months before. He stood at the sharp end of an invasion force that within hours was able to move into position for a race down three highways through Luxembourg and southeastern Belgium, through the Ardennes Forest, toward the breakthrough point in the French line. At nine o'clock that night the Wehrmacht command sent a coded signal notifying all units in the Rhineland, which had been kept on a twenty-four-hour alert since January, that the blitzkrieg would launch at 5:30 the next morning. According to plan, as General Guderian's Panzers rolled unhindered through Luxembourg, a bit farther north Gen. Erwin Rommel led the VII Panzer Corps in a parallel rush into southern Belgium.

To the north, the Luftwaffe was tearing apart Dutch airfields and army barracks and strafing the streets of The Hague. Four thousand parachute troops were dropping deep in Dutch territory to capture important airfields for thousands of follow-on airborne infantry. Along the border, hundreds of Panzers from General Bock's Army Group B stormed into the Netherlands and northern Belgium. The northern attack was a feint, designed to convince the Allies that the main German thrust was coming down through the Netherlands and central Belgium for a hook into western France. Like the "matador's cloak" that draws the bull safely to the bullfighter's side,[73] the Netherlands diversion would draw French and British forces deep into Belgium, away from Germany's sword arm, and hold them there in a defensive line north of the French border, like a breakwater waiting for the approaching German onslaught.

In the meantime, much farther south, Rundstedt's Army Group A would swing in for the kill. With full control of the Rhineland since 1936, the Wehrmacht could avoid large-scale force movements in the weeks prior to the invasion—force movements that might have tipped off the Allies to the fact that the main German push was coming through the Ardennes Forest toward Sedan. If Germany's real intentions had been detected earlier, the Allied armies might have been able to push reserve forces into the weakest part of their line to block the rapid Panzer breakthrough that led to German victory.

The French were willing dupes in the German war plan. In 1934, Marshal Henri Petain, the French war minister, scoffed at the idea of a German invasion through the Ardennes, saying that it was "impenetrable" for a large mechanized force. Even if German Panzers made it through the forest, Petain asserted, it would be impossible for them to cross the Meuse River, with its steep and twisting cliff banks that offered the defenders a strong advantage. The French military remained convinced in 1940 that with the Maginot Line and the Ardennes Forest protecting the long eastern stretch of France's northern border, the only reasonable invasion route was through central and western Belgium, just as in 1914.[74] On May 10, the Wehrmacht set out to prove them wrong, from Germany's Rhineland launch pad.

The fall of France brings us back to our original question: Why did the Allies allow the Germans to recover the Rhineland in the first place? It's impossible to deny that each of the predicted consequences of losing the DMZ was realized between 1938 and 1940. Hitler's Rhineland fait accompli delivered a mighty boost to the Nazi regime's prestige at home, elevating Hitler's reputation as a political and military strategist. The fortified Rhineland deprived France of an unimpeded invasion route deep into German territory, the only threat that many believed would deter German aggression in the east. And Rhineland remilitarization deprived France of the deep buffer zone that might have protected it from a German *attaque brusque*. The so-called Phony War—the eight-month lag between the declaration of war in September 1939 and Germany's western blitzkrieg in May 1940—certainly provided France with plenty of time to mobilize for defensive *couverture*; but Rhineland remilitarization also offered Germany the operational conditions necessary for maximizing its offensive punch against France's most vulnerable defenders.

The conquest of Czechoslovakia, Poland, and France; the neutering of Great Britain; the brutal drive to grind down the Soviet Union; the titanic Allied struggle to turn the aggressive German wave and bring this evil regime to an end—all could be traced back to that fateful weekend in March 1936. Few moments in history offer such an emotionally poignant focal point for lamenting the decisions not made, the actions not taken. Few moments in the 1930s seem to stand out so clearly as a lost opportunity to bottle up the shift in power that produced such devastating effects, a lost opportunity to "stop Hitler," to "prevent World War II." It's hardly surprising that the Rhineland crisis remains an iconic case among champions of preventive war who are drawn by its promise to strangle emerging threats before horrible futures emerge.

So why did British leaders let this window of opportunity pass them by? Because they recognized that preventive war offered false promise, there was no silver-bullet solution to the European security dilemma. And they recognized a paradox embedded within the preventive war option: that even if French forces successfully pushed the Wehrmacht back across the Rhine River, this would not fix the strategic problems they faced, and would likely make these problems worse. Looking at this assessment in hindsight, with full knowledge of the heartbreaking story that unfolded, it still seems to be a sensible judgment. This is a bold claim, admittedly, and runs contrary to conventional wisdom on what many say France and Britain should have done in 1936 to counter rising German power. On its face, this claim sounds absurd, so it requires some explanation. How can victory on the battlefield have the paradoxical effect of producing strategic failure?

The next several chapters take a step back from 1936 to answer this question, to dig deeper into the preventive war temptation and its cautionary twin, the preventive war paradox, to explore the broader history of preventive war, including those decades before 1936 that shaped beliefs about security, power, and preventive war in profound ways. It is only with a more-nuanced appreciation for the pitfalls of preventive war and a deeper background to the European security dilemma of the mid-1930s that we can understand why Britain did not jump through the window of opportunity of the Rhineland crisis.

3

THE PREVENTIVE WAR TEMPTATION MEETS THE PREVENTIVE WAR PARADOX

In war the result is never final.

—Carl von Clausewitz, *On War*

The three least-uttered words in Washington—"and then what?"

—Secretary of Defense Robert Gates

FEAR AND THE PREVENTIVE WAR TEMPTATION

The English philosopher Thomas Hobbes, one of the most important intellectual figures in the history of Western political thought, lived in a horrifically violent world. Hobbes wrote his masterwork, *Leviathan*, while the Thirty Years' War churned across Germany and Central Europe, accumulating deaths from combat, disease, and pillage that ultimately killed a greater percentage of the European population than either of the world wars of the twentieth century. And for nearly a decade before *Leviathan* appeared in 1651, his own country was consumed by a civil war that cost the lives of King Charles I, found guilty of high treason and beheaded, and up to two hundred thousand of the king's former subjects. It should be no surprise, then, that embedded within this great work on political order are

Hobbes's reflections on what he called the "causes of quarrel"; in other words, why humans engage in competition and violent conflict. To this day, Hobbes's simple yet profound explanation remains at the heart of the study of international relations and war. Without Hobbes's basic insights, it would be impossible to explain the preventive war temptation and the European security dilemma of the 1930s.

The allure of preventive war is rooted in fear; and fear, according to Hobbes, is the essence of life in an anarchic world.[1] By "anarchy" he did not mean chaos or disorder. Instead, anarchy captures the character of the world that individual states inhabit. It points to the fact that they coexist with no higher political authority to adjudicate disputes or provide protection from predators and violent assault. In the anarchic world Hobbes described, states live in constant fear of what others *might do* with the power they possess. This dark cloud of fear and uncertainty creates what he called a perpetual "state of war." It's not that states are actually engaged in continuous warfare; this simply means that war could break out at any time, given that there is nothing to stop it. As a result, leaders live in dread of the mere potential for war. The uncertainty of an anarchic system is enough to generate deep anxiety over the possibility of coercion and violence that threaten the state's population, its territory, or broader interests. Under these conditions, Hobbes said, a state's own physical power—and its constant readiness for armed conflict—is the only source of security against whatever barbarian might appear at your gates.

Uncertainty and fear may be a constant condition in the international system, but students of international relations have long recognized that fear is most acute when power is shifting among states. This is particularly true for those that see their relative power in decline as a rising challenger enjoys increasing strength—strength that comes from a more rapidly growing economy that can underwrite military investment, an expanding population that can be mobilized for wealth and war, technological innovation that improves a rival's military punch, the swelling ranks of an army that can march and conquer, or expanding control over strategic territory that improves economic or offensive potential. And as the declining state watches its power erode, fear of the future grows. As the months tick by, as the years slip away, pressure builds while relative strength wanes. A day of reckoning seems to draw closer; the expected costs of a potential future clash grow. The passage of time itself becomes an adversary, stirring an impulse for urgent action to arrest this alarming trend before it's too late. Hobbes would have understood French anxieties in the years after World War I.

So what should the prudently paranoid leader do? Historically, the most common options for stopping a dangerous loss of relative power have been drawn from the classic instruments of balance-of-power politics: amped-up military spending, and the negotiation of alliances to counter the challenger's increasing strength. Swelling arsenals and capable allies might deter the challenger from using its new aggressive potential, or at least make it possible to muster a more-potent defense should war come. But merely "balancing" a rival carries risk. A seemingly never-ending push to keep pace over time, or to maintain your superior edge in the distribution of power, can be exhausting.[2] Spiraling arms races absorb limited resources, drive up public debt, and divert national treasure and talent from more-productive outlets. A balancing state might overextend its power as it takes on strategic commitments to regions or allies that are actually impossible to defend. And, in the end, you may be no safer from the potential threat than when the competitive spiral began, as your rival races along, too, amassing its own arms and allies. Perhaps most worrisome, despite heavy investment in an expanding power base, deterrence might fail, defenses collapse, allies defect. Your rival's ambitions, its confidence, its willingness to challenge the status quo, to make threatening demands, may all expand along with its power. And if war comes, the longer it is delayed, the heavier the blow your rival can deliver.

Out of the clawing apprehension and perpetual uncertainty produced by this dynamic comes the potential to see *domination* as the only viable solution to the problem. Here we find the origins of the preventive war temptation, its promise most seductive when leaders see it as a way to eliminate their fears at the source. The strategic logic of preventive military action is simple: The objective is to physically destroy or neutralize the rival's growing offensive capabilities with a first strike or by coaxing war, at an early stage in the power shift, before the rival is potent enough to pose the threat that haunts your visions of the future.

It is important to recognize that "preventive" attack is not synonymous with "preemption." The term *preemption* has been widely adopted since it was popularized by the Bush administration to characterize the rationale behind the invasion that toppled Saddam Hussein in 2003. Preventive war and preemption do share one important feature: Each constitutes a first strike motivated by fear of future danger. But preemption, specifically, is a response to the "imminent" danger of an adversary's attack. Historically, preemption has been treated as an act of true self-defense. No state is obligated to absorb an enemy's aggressive first blow when there are clear indicators that an attack is coming. International custom, law, and long-standing ethical standards have all sanctioned a state's inherent right to hit first when the tactical advantages of making the first move will help to deflect or stop the enemy's assault. The Arab-Israeli Six-Day War in June 1967 is the classic example. Israel struck first and scored a punishing victory over Egypt, Syria, and Jordan. But it did so in response to a rapid sequence of threatening moves indicating that Israel's adversaries were setting the stage for war. Within a matter of days, Egyptian president Gamal Abdel Nasser mobilized military forces on the Sinai Peninsula, demanded the withdrawal of the United Nations peacekeeping force that had been on the Egyptian–Israeli border for the past decade, and closed the Straits of Tiran, blocking Israel's southern route to the Indian Ocean in a move Israel had long warned would be cause for war. Jordan and Iraq soon joined the Egyptian–Syrian coalition, and Nasser turned up the threatening rhetoric with public claims that "our basic objective will be to destroy Israel." To Israeli leaders, and most outside observers, the threat seemed imminent indeed, so they turned to the preemption option to strike it down.

Preventive attack, on the other hand, is about the *possibility* of future danger as a rival's capabilities grow. There is no imminent attack in this scenario, just the fear of what *might* happen and a determination to avoid the mere *potential* of future aggression and the higher costs of war this aggression would bring. The Bush administration's most frequently repeated and politically effective explanation for the invasion of Iraq was drawn directly from preventive war logic. The president's 2002 State of the Union address noted that the "Iraqi regime has plotted to develop anthrax, and nerve gas, and nuclear weapons for over a decade." These efforts, he said, "pose a grave and growing danger" and the possibility that Iraq "*could* provide these arms to terrorists" and "*could* attack our allies or attempt to blackmail the United States." As the president's national security advisor Condoleezza Rice famously put it, "The problem here is that there will always be some uncertainty about how quickly [Saddam Hussein] can acquire nuclear weapons. But we don't want the smoking gun to be a mushroom cloud." The National Security Strategy of 2002, released just a few days after Rice offered her frightening imagery, echoed the administration's motive for war: "America will act against such emerging threats before they are fully formed . . . even if uncertainty remains as to the time and place of the enemy's attack."[3] More precisely, the strategy should have said, even if uncertainty remains as to whether a future Iraqi attack would occur at all.

While true preemption has been rare,[4] preventive logic has been much more common as a motive for military conflict. Leaders across thousands of years of history—from the ancient Greeks and Romans to the twenty-first-century American superpower—have been tempted by the promise of preventive war as an escape from the uncertainty and fear generated by a shifting threat environment. In the twentieth century, shifting power and fear were central to the origins of World War I and World War II. In popular memory, however, the preventive motivation in each of these conflicts is typically overshadowed by the moral damnation that shapes how we think about Germany and Japan and the horrific wars they launched. This is understandable. Germany and Japan—for good reason—remain icons of aggression, of brutal warfare waged in the service of rapacious territorial conquest, of extreme violence inflamed by hyper-nationalism and beliefs in racial superiority. Their villainous rulers subjected millions of ordinary people to misery and ruin and their great power rivals to what seemed like a death struggle through total war. Article 231 of the Treaty of Versailles, the so-called "war guilt clause," blamed German aggression for "all the losses and damage" suffered during the First World War. The first legal charge leveled against Nazi officials and top Japanese leaders during the war crimes trials of 1945 and 1946 was "crimes against peace," described as the "planning, preparation, initiation or waging of a war of aggression."[5] In so many ways, Germany and Japan of the early twentieth century seem like grotesque outliers in the broader history of international politics. The moral burden they earned by launching these wars is easy to justify.

Nevertheless, we should not let the ethical character of these events obscure an important fact about their wars of conquest and domination: They were driven in large measure by the same kind of uncertainty and fear of the future that sparked that long parade of preventive conflicts we can observe over thousands of years of history. To say that German and Japanese leaders were drawn to war out of fear and uncertainty in no way justifies their decisions; it merely helps to explain why they chose war, and makes it possible to link these seemingly exceptional modern cases with other wars driven by similar insecurities and temptations.

The character of the German government went through radical changes across the first four decades of the twentieth century, yet successive generations of German leaders fixated on a common nightmare: the looming, swelling power of the Russian empire to the east that might one day dwarf—and then cripple—Germany in a fight over dominance in central Europe. The leadership of both Imperial Germany before World War I and Nazi Germany before World War II believed this fight would not be a contest simply for spheres of influence; it would be a fight for national survival. Russian military reforms launched after a humiliating defeat in the Russo-Japanese War in 1905, and its accelerating railroad construction in the west, meant that with each passing year Russia could more rapidly mobilize an increasingly larger and more capable military force that could be unleashed against the German army. As Russia's alliance with France tightened in the early years of the new century, perceptions of German vulnerability spiked. According to the General Staff, Germany would finally lose its military edge in 1917, making victory in a future war against its rivals doubtful. As the crisis of July 1914 spiraled toward war, German chancellor Theobald von Bethmann Hollweg reflected on what appeared to be the underlying stakes: "In a few years, Russia will be supreme and Germany, her first, lonely victim."[6] Preventive war, as an outgrowth of the July crisis, seemed to offer Imperial Germany the only viable way to crack this looming threat before Russian power became unbeatable.

This same fear was at the core of Adolf Hitler's obsession with the Soviet Union as Germany's greatest threat, and it drove his determination to cripple Soviet power through war and wholesale annexation of massive chunks of Soviet territory. When we strip away the Third Reich's genocidal visions of Aryan dominance, of securing the Reich through violent conquest of "inferior races" like the Russian Slavs, we find one core belief that many Germans—Nazis and non-Nazis alike—would rally behind in the 1930s and early 1940s. It was that the steady growth of Soviet industrial and military power was an increasingly deadly threat to German survival. And preventive war, before German power went into irretrievable relative decline, was the only escape from a future in which Germany would be virtually helpless in the face of overwhelming enemy capabilities.[7] There is, of course, a long list of important distinctions between the Imperial German government of 1914 and Nazi leaders a generation later, their attitudes toward war clearly among the key differences. Kaiser Wilhelm II and Chancellor Bethmann Hollweg accepted war with Russia in 1914 with a mixture of grim fatalism and trepidation that at times bordered on near panic when they thought through the grave risks of fighting not only Russia and France, but Great Britain as well.[8] Adolf Hitler, on the other hand, was bolstered by his earlier conquest of France, the virtual paralysis of Britain, and the ideological and emotional thrill of living out his own Wagnerian opera. He embraced his window of opportunity to smash the Soviet Union in 1941 with gusto. Despite these differences, the fear and uncertainty of a future dominated by growing Russian might runs as a common thread through the German pattern of grasping at the promise of preventive war to solve the power-shift problem.

Half a world away, Japanese leaders also felt the tug of the preventive war temptation as a solution to decline and vulnerability; the attack on American naval forces at Pearl Harbor in December 1941 fits neatly into this preventive war framework. In the summer of 1941, the German army was driving hundreds of kilometers deep into Soviet territory. Japan, on the other hand, was struggling with the seemingly fatal implications of America's efforts to turn back Japan's own drive to dominate its part of the globe. For most of the previous year, the United States and Japan had been locked in a largely diplomatic struggle over the future power structure of Asia. Japan's vision of a Greater East Asia Co-Prosperity Sphere was announced in August 1940 as an initiative to liberate Asian people from Western colonialism. In the United States it was seen as simply a vehicle for Japanese imperialism and hegemonic control over a rich natural resource base and large labor population. The struggle over the fate of Japanese power in East Asia took a dangerous turn in July 1941, when the United States embargoed oil exports in reaction to Japan's military occupation of the southern portion of French Indochina in Southeast Asia. America's price for resuming oil shipments—which accounted for 80 percent of the oil flow into Japan—was an end to its three-year fight to subdue China.

For the Japanese Imperial Army, this was an intolerable demand. But according to Imperial Navy estimates, an American petroleum embargo meant that the war in China could not be sustained for more than four months. As Japanese leaders saw it, the two basic choices before them—concede to America's demands by giving up much of their growing empire, or holding firm in the face of American coercion—would produce the same result: a disastrous downward slide in national power. Japan would inevitably fall from the ranks of the great states, its military capabilities and its industrial potential would shrivel, and for the indefinite future Japan would be vulnerable to the whims of those states that remained among the first-tier major powers. The consensus view of this crisis was captured in a report developed under the leadership of Prime Minister Fumimaro Konoe:

> Even if we should make concessions to the United States by giving up part of our national policy for the sake of temporary peace, the United States, its military position strengthened, is sure to demand more and more concessions on our part, and ultimately our empire will lie prostrate at the feet of the United States.[9]

Fear of this future led Japanese leaders to what they fully acknowledged was a high-risk, even desperate, solution: the seizure of the oil-rich Dutch East Indies, preceded by a surprise preventive attack against US forces at Pearl Harbor, Wake Island, and the Philippines to destroy those American military assets that could physically stop Japan's audacious expansionist move before it was too late to save its declining power base.

THINKING STRATEGICALLY ABOUT
PREVENTIVE WAR

As we see in each of these cases, the strategic logic of preventive war is simple. It seems intuitive in terms of the way we think about power and security. It is timeless, propelled by fear, one of the most potent human emotions to stir bold action. And the historic record confirms its enduring appeal, from the ancient world to the nuclear era. Its appeal, however, cannot gloss over the most important question facing any leader tempted to pull the preventive war trigger. Will it work? *Will preventive war really solve the long-term security problem?* The preventive wars of Germany and Japan clearly did not solve the security problems that darkened their visions of the future; they ended in disaster. But these cases do not get to the unique strategic problem with the preventive war option. When we ask *Will it work?*, we are not interested in the risk of battlefield defeat, a risk inherent to any war, regardless of the motivation that compels it. It sounds counterintuitive, but preventive war is uniquely susceptible to producing *strategic failure*, in which security is eroded rather than bolstered, even if the war itself is judged as a *victory* in *operational* military terms.

This is what we can call the "preventive war paradox," the temptation's cautionary twin. This paradox is precisely what British leaders could not get past in 1936 during the Rhineland crisis; and frankly, they were not alone. A number of leaders throughout history have recognized these distinctive security risks, and with good reason rejected preventive war as a solution to the changing threat environments they faced. But just as we find moments in history in which states pulled back from the preventive war temptation because of its strategic pitfalls, we also find examples of states that launched preventive wars only to suffer from an erosion of security that the paradox warns about. To fully understand how British leaders saw the Rhineland problem and the broader European security dilemma of the 1930s, we must go beyond the preventive war temptation side of the equation.

As we have seen, the preventive war temptation emerges from changes in relative power, new capabilities that make a rising state a greater military threat that is expected to grow ever more menacing as time goes on. It's not surprising, then, that most observers approach the key question posed above—*Will preventive war solve this security problem?*—from a purely military perspective. As a first cut at the question, this seems reasonable. No sensible leader will rush into this decision without first evaluating the hard facts imposed by the relative distribution of military power between the combatants. Simply put, Which state is most likely to stand victorious on the battlefield when the smoke clears? Can the state that pulls the preventive war trigger deliver a sufficiently crushing blow to free itself from its rival's rising power? Or is it taking a foolish gamble that could just as easily end in disaster on the battlefield?[10] Warfare waged for any reason inevitably brings with it serious risks: the risk of simple failure to achieve operational objectives, the risk of outright defeat, the risk of heavy costs paid in blood and treasure, and risks to other interests put in jeopardy by war. "Victory," from this perspective, is measured by target destruction, terrain seized, an army defeated in the field, relative to the physical costs of achieving these military effects. Asking hard questions about the operational dimensions of military conflict is clearly a critical step in any discussion of whether preventive war is a viable solution to developing threats.

When most observers look back at historical cases to evaluate whether preventive war was a viable option, to include the question of war against Nazi Germany in the 1930s, they judge the likelihood of victory with the same type of calculus. How many soldiers could each side mobilize? How rapidly could they move? What kinds of weapons did they carry into combat? How many tanks? How many ships and submarines? Of what size and operational capabilities? How many fighter aircraft and bombers? Who held a technological edge in key weapons systems? What defensive tools could the target state use to disrupt offensive action? How many soldiers, aircraft, and ships could each side deploy at one point in time compared to the forces they were expected to deploy several years in the future? The assumption behind each of these questions is simple: that the likelihood of success in war is a function of the balance of military power—that preventive war will generate greater security if the attacker has sufficient military means to deliver successful destruction of the threatening capabilities in the enemy's hands.

Unfortunately, the assumption that a purely military calculus is sufficient to judge whether or not preventive war will enhance a state's security is fundamentally flawed. The problem lies in the fact that it confuses *operational success* with *strategic success* in war. As strange as this might sound, war is not about winning battlefield victories. War is about the *political objectives* that states seek through military means. And as many leaders throughout history have painfully discovered, brilliant operational success on the battlefield will not automatically produce the strategic political outcomes they desired. This often debilitating disconnect between operational and strategic success is captured perfectly by an exchange between envoys of two wartime adversaries, Col. Harry Summers of the US Army and Col. Nguyen Don Tu of North Vietnam. Just days before North Vietnamese forces rolled into Saigon in 1975 to secure their defeat of South Vietnam, Colonel Summers was in Hanoi leading a delegation of American officials sent to the adversary's capital city to discuss the war's impending end. During a quiet moment, reflecting on a fact that frustrated many American soldiers, Colonel Summers pointed out to Colonel Nguyen, "You know you never defeated us on the battlefield." Colonel Nguyen simply replied, "That may be so, but it is also irrelevant."[11]

Despite the repeated operational military success enjoyed by US combat forces over the duration of the American war in Vietnam, the United States failed to achieve strategic success. Strategic success had been defined as a postwar political order in which America's South Vietnamese ally survived as an independent state, a South Vietnam that enjoyed sufficient legitimacy and support from its own population to escape the mortal dangers of domestic insurgency. Strategic success would be a political order in which North Vietnam's ambitions were tamed and America's reputation as a reliable and effective leader in the global struggle to contain Communist expansion was upheld. Despite the massive amount of firepower applied in this thin slice of Southeast Asia, America simply did not have the right kind of power to reshape the domestic politics of South Vietnam or to sap the fervent nationalist political will of North Vietnam, and thus achieve the strategic outcomes the United States pursued at such great cost.

Carl von Clausewitz, the great nineteenth-century Prussian strategic thinker, is best known for this precise point. While his classic treatise *On War* emerged from his experience of warfare during Napoleon's rampage across Europe in the early 1800s, Clausewitz is still read today because of his reflections on the enduring character of war. And as he famously declared, the purpose of war is defined by the political objectives that states seek; these political objectives matter most in how we think about armed conflict. So, as Clausewitz observed, there are limits to what purely military effects on the adversary can tell us about success or failure: "[T]here can be no question of a *purely military* evaluation of a great strategic issue," he said, "nor of a purely military scheme to solve it."[12] Drawing from this key insight, Colin Gray, a modern student of Clausewitz, has provided a useful way of thinking about strategic effects and preventive war. Gray said warfare is about the "character of the subsequent peace" it produces.[13] Along similar lines, Sir Basil Liddell Hart, one of the most influential writers on war in the mid-twentieth century, echoed Clausewitz when he observed that the "objective in war is a better state of peace."[14]

From this strategic vantage point we must then ask, what "better state of peace" is preventive war meant to serve? How can we conceptualize its objectives in terms of political end states that provide greater security? The operational objective of any preventive war is easy to define: to deliver a physical blow against a rising adversary potent enough to yield destructive effects that weaken its military capabilities to some degree, to some point in the future. Yet even if preventive war were to produce these immediate military effects, Clausewitz would insist on asking whether it had the strategic effect desired. Did these military effects against the adversary produce a more-secure future? Did successful target destruction create a less-threatening postwar environment?

America's experience in Iraq after the 2003 invasion nicely demonstrates this stubborn Clausewitzian distinction between operational military success and political end states, and how this distinction might be relevant to the preventive war temptation. As a preventive war the invasion had two primary operational military goals: to destroy Iraq's alleged weapons of mass destruction (WMD) programs, and to depose the vile government said to be willing to use these weapons, or to secretly supply them to its terrorist allies to carry out devastating attacks. As for strategic outcomes, a better state of peace was expected simply because America would no longer face an adversary suspected of nurturing dreams of regional dominance and revenge, and the weapons that might make these dreams possible.

These specific goals for the war were ambitious indeed, but the strategic political effects the Bush administration hoped to achieve were much grander than merely squelching the fear of Saddam's growing power. Supporters of this war predicted that American military power would achieve nothing less than a complete political transformation of the Middle East, solving a range of security problems for the United States and its allies. Once Saddam Hussein's regime—this barbaric roadblock to freedom—was wrenched from power, democracy would flower in a largely secular and stable Iraq, while its well-educated population, strong middle class, and oil wealth would put this liberated state on the road to economic prosperity. The new Iraq would be a pro-Western partner in the quest for regional security, and with its emergent democratic character Iraq's animosity toward Israel would fade. Once Saddam's regime was gone, the United States could remove the military forces it maintained in Saudi Arabia as a deterrent to Iraqi aggression, which would ease the anti-American anger among Muslims who were offended by the presence of US forces in an area sacred to Islam. It was predicted that Iraq would become a model for political change throughout the region, as other autocratic regimes came to recognize that stability and prosperity would flow from political and economic reforms. Most important, these reforms were expected to "drain the swamp" that bred the frustration, radicalization, and nihilistic violence of terrorism.[15] Now that certainly would be a better state of peace.

The defeat of Saddam Hussein's regime merely three weeks after the start of the invasion on March 20, with relatively few casualties suffered by American and coalition combatants, was an unambiguous measure of America's battlefield prowess. By mid-April occupation headquarters had been established in Saddam's Republican Palace, and American inspection teams ranged across Iraq in an unhindered search for nuclear, chemical, and biological weapons depots, manufacturing sites, and research facilities. At first blush, this looks like overwhelming victory. But did military victory over the Iraqi government, and the overwhelming battlefield advantage that American forces continued to enjoy after the regime fell from power, produce the strategic effects that were promised before the war?

Fourteen months after the initial invasion, Gen. Richard Myers, the chairman of the Joint Chiefs of Staff, bluntly acknowledged there was a gross disconnect between military dominance on the battlefield and America's goals in this increasingly costly operation. In Senate testimony General Myers asserted there was "no way to militarily win" this conflict. This was a stunning turnaround when compared to the confident prewar predictions about the grand political objectives that would be achieved once Hussein was deposed with military force. Not only was the United States facing a diverse and brutal insurgency fighting over the future political order within Iraq, the "state of peace" created in the wake of America's invasion was hard to characterize as more secure for the United States' broader interests. The invasion and occupation stoked anti-American sentiment around the world, among allies, partners, and competitor states alike. Most worrisome, it fueled anger in the Islamic world and a surge of support for violent opposition and terrorism against American and allied targets. The challenge of adapting to a counterinsurgency fight and the roiling instability of post-Saddam Iraqi politics diverted military forces, money, and leadership attention away from the smoldering conflict in Afghanistan and its dangerous spillover into northwest Pakistan.[16] By 2010, estimates of the financial costs of the Iraq War ranged from $806 billion to over $3 trillion, driving up the national debt just as America entered an economic crisis that shook the foundations of its power and raised questions about faltering global leadership.[17] Perhaps the most profound regional consequence of the Iraq War was the empowerment of Iran. The downfall of Saddam Hussein not only freed Iran from the counterbalancing role that Iraq had played under his regime, but the Iranian government now enjoyed deep influence with the new Shiite-dominated government of

Iraq and the wide field of play this offered to magnify Iranian power across the increasingly chaotic Middle East.

So did the United States "win" the Iraq War? It certainly achieved the operational military objectives linked to the preventive motivation for this conflict. An Iraqi regime under Saddam Hussein's rule, in possession of weapons of mass destruction, is no longer a future scenario the United States must fret about. But did preventive war actually save the United States from a future in which this threat materialized? Given the fact that Iraq had no active WMD programs in 2003, and no evidence was found that Iraq had maintained a research and development infrastructure that would have allowed rapid regeneration of these dangerous capabilities in the coming years,[18] it is impossible to conclude that the United States really achieved the strategic goals set for this preventive war. When put in the context of the broader political order left in this war's wake, the "state of peace" the United States faced as the post-invasion years slipped by seems worse than the state of peace America endured while Saddam Hussein was still alive, in power, and subdued.[19]

The Iraq case opens an interesting window on the potential strategic consequences of preventive war, and, like the Vietnam War, it certainly helps to illustrate Clausewitz's essential point about the difference between battlefield victory and true strategic success. But at this point we need to refine the concept of the preventive war paradox and explain how it might play out as a general phenomenon in world history. The question is, how might an operationally successful preventive attack actually produce a political order that is less secure? As we will see, the answer emerges from how we define the concept of "threat," and how the political dynamics set in motion by preventive war shape the intensity of the threat environment over time.

AND THEN WHAT?

The problem with the logic of preventive war begins with a truncated understanding of what determines threat. Its central logic fixates on the relationship between power and political order, treating this relationship as though there is a straight line linking an increase in power to an increase in security. To revise Chairman Mao's famous aphorism, the unstated assumption behind the preventive war temptation is that security "grows out of the barrel of a gun." This seems like a commonsense proposition, and as a first stab at understanding your threat environment, it's an important place to start. The material capabilities of a potential adversary—those offensive tools in its arsenal—are what provide it with the means to inflict varying degrees of harm through aggressive behavior. The more relative power this potential adversary has, the more of a threat it becomes. So if a preventive attack physically destroys key assets in the target's offensive toolkit, it seems logical to conclude that the threat it poses declines—that the security problem is solved.

But this assumption grossly simplifies the problem of security in international politics. Thinking beyond the military dimensions of war to its political effects, Clausewitz explains how. "In war the result is never final," he said. "The defeated state often considers the outcome merely as a *transitory evil,* for which a remedy may still be found . . . at some later date."[20] This seemingly simple observation points to a profound insight about international politics. While military operations can have a definite end point, the political process among states never ends.[21] Which begs the question, what happens the day after the preventive attack? What political reactions does it set in motion? How will the target of the attack respond over time? What will other states do? And what do these political reactions mean for the threats the preventive war was meant to neutralize?

As a number of international relations scholars have argued, security is not merely a function of the distribution of power; it is also a function of the political relationships among states. Threat is determined by offensive capabilities *and* the degree of hostility or aggressive intentions you face from potential adversaries. Hostile intent will shape whether the offensive military capabilities others hold actually pose a danger; it also determines the severity of these threats, and the likelihood of future armed conflict.[22] A quick scan of history shows that the character of the political relationships among particular states will range across a wide continuum defined by the degree of hostility between them. On one end of the continuum we can find committed enemies locked in a seemingly unbreakable cycle of violence, while on the other end are states that cannot even imagine resorting to violent coercion or armed conflict against the other. And for any particular set of states, the degree of hostility and the likelihood of armed conflict can shift along this continuum, rising or falling over time. Kenneth Waltz, one of the most important international relations scholars of the twentieth century, was best known for insisting that physical power is the dominant factor shaping world politics. Yet he also observed during the Cold War that the United States and the Soviet Union were "learning gradually how to cope with each other," and that "the quality of their relations" changed in the 1960s and 1970s, making "peaceful coexistence" easier. They continued wrangling over power across the globe, modernizing and expanding their conventional military forces, pursuing technologies that would increase the offensive potential of their nuclear arsenals. Yet within this essentially competitive relationship the superpowers also shared a deepening belief that actual armed conflict between them was unlikely, which increased the stability of sustained peace over time.[23]

A key variable shaping these political relationships, and thus perceptions of threat, is behavior, observed through the choices states make as they pursue security, and how this behavior is interpreted by others. This ties into one of those enduring problems of international relations: the security dilemma—or, what can be more accurately called the "security paradox."[24] While the fear and uncertainty generated by international anarchy provide a compelling incentive for any state to seek security through increasing power, the drive for power itself can have the perverse effect of undermining security. Other states, attuned to their own security needs, will likely see the other's rising power as rising threat, and will respond with counterbalancing power plays of their own. This process becomes self-defeating when all it produces is a competitive cycle in which rivals lock horns in an ongoing power struggle, expending more resources and accepting greater commitments to allies, with nothing to show for it in actual added security.[25] As Waltz put it, while power is essential for defending yourself in an anarchic world, it is possible to provoke even greater dangers than you currently face by "pressing too hard" against your rivals.[26] John Herz coined the term *security dilemma* when he articulated the logic of this paradox in 1950. Like Waltz, Herz remained skeptical that power competition could ever be eliminated from world politics; yet he also warned about the potential for violent disaster that would surely follow from "gladiatorial" behavior.[27] Strategies meant to gain dominance over others run the risk of pushing states into a spiral of increasingly hostile relations, into long-term militarized rivalries marked by deeper and deeper antagonism, perceptions of the other's implacable aggressive intent, and revisionist demands that dramatically increase the risk of major war.[28]

Preventive war is particularly susceptible to the risks produced by the security paradox. The political character of preventive war sets it apart as a radical alternative to the traditional balancing options of alliance building and arms races. While these traditional approaches might provoke the security dilemma, they do not entail direct offensive military action against other states, so it is easier to cast your policy choices as purely defensive initiatives to safeguard against a rival's potential aggression. Advocates of preventive war typically wrap this option within the morally comforting patina of self-defense.[29] Yet it is hard to ignore the fact that it is, by definition, an act of *war initiation*, an unprovoked violent blow against another state in reaction to fear of a *possible* future, not a response to actual acts of aggression or preemption of imminent attack.[30] As a result, preventive war has long been classified in political, legal, and moral terms as an act of aggression itself.[31]

So think about this in strategic terms. While you may win victory on the battlefield or destroy a rival's key power assets through preventive war, you might also sow "dragon's teeth" that yield a political order stewing with hostility and ripe for further violent challenges. Unless this war leads to the complete annihilation of your adversary, it will likely intensify security competition and push rivalries to extremes.[32] The target of this attack might be seized with determination not only to recover from this blow, but to push even harder for military capabilities that it never intended to pursue, all the while nurturing passionate demands for revenge. Other states may find new incentives to link arms in a hostile alliance meant to hold down the aggressive state in their midst. In time, the perverse feedback loop of preventive attack could make an even worse armed conflict more likely than it otherwise would have been. With this in mind, any leader contemplating preventive war would be wise to consider whether the "character of the peace" left in its wake would undermine the value of launching the attack in the first place. State leaders that recognize these dangers might then reject preventive war not merely to avoid the risks of the armed conflict itself, but to avoid its destabilizing effects on the political order left behind—a political order likely to be dominated by deep hostility and the heightened dangers of violent coercion among entrenched rivals. A few choice examples from the past—some ancient, some more recent—will help bring this paradox to life.

THE PREVENTIVE WAR PARADOX AT WORK

The best way to begin any exploration of the preventive war dilemma through history is to roll the timeline back 2,400 years to the Peloponnesian War, which tore apart the world of the ancient Greeks for nearly three decades in the fifth century BC. According to Thucydides, an Athenian who lived through these violent years, this was "the greatest disturbance in the history" of Greek civilization, and perhaps, he was bold enough to proclaim, "the whole of mankind."[33] Thucydides began this war as an Athenian general, but his fellow citizens had no tolerance for military commanders that suffered defeat on the battlefield, so he was banished after a failed effort to defend the city of Amphipolis against Spartan attack a few years into the war. While this was a terrible personal blow to Thucydides, his banishment was a great gift for posterity. Exile gave him the freedom to travel widely, to collect information on the terrible events that churned through the Greek world, and to think through and record the enduring lessons this war offered.

For contemporary students of international relations, Thucydides's history of the Peloponnesian War remains the most widely studied work from the ancient world, thousands of years after his death. In fact, few modern books on international relations rival Thucydides's readership and influence. The reason for its enduring appeal is simple: It is no mere historical narrative of the great clash between Athens and Sparta. Instead, it is rich with general lessons about politics, power, strategy, leadership, and the causes and consequences of war that echo loudly in our own era. Thucydides tells us explicitly in his introduction that he was not interested in writing an account merely "designed to meet the taste of an immediate public"; he aspired to create something that would "last forever." And "human nature being what it is," he says, the "events which happened in the past . . . will, at some time or other and in much the same ways, be repeated in the future."[34] Thucydides would be very happy indeed to know that for the past several hundred years, each generation has turned to his work to explore the great themes woven throughout the gripping history he left behind. The English philosopher Thomas Hobbes was the first to translate Thucydides from ancient Greek into the English language in 1628, and he then borrowed heavily from Thucydides's insights while writing *Leviathan*. Thomas Jefferson wrote to John Adams in 1812 that reading Thucydides was a refuge from the dismal accounts of current affairs found in newspapers. During the Cold War it was common for scholars and students to see parallels between the Athenian–Spartan rivalry and the power game between America and the Soviet Union. And at the center of this timeless account is the interplay between the preventive war temptation and the preventive war paradox.

In one of the most widely quoted passages from his history, Thucydides points directly to the core logic of preventive war to explain the mechanisms driving the Greeks into conflict. While specific grievances sparked the fight, he emphasizes that the "real reason for the war," what he concludes made war "inevitable," "was the *growth* of Athenian *power* and the *fear* which this caused in Sparta."[35] Following Thucydides's lead, modern students of the Peloponnesian War treat this case as exactly that—a Spartan preventive war to stop Athens's continued rise. But what is typically downplayed in this interpretation is what Athens was actually doing with its rising power, and the chain of events that led to Sparta's decision. It was not an abstract fear of a rising Athens that pushed Sparta to war; it was fear and anger sparked by Athens's own preventive use of force in a localized conflict between the rival Greek city-states of Corcyra and Corinth.

Thucydides begins his account of the Peloponnesian War with this local conflict, and he does so with good reason. It is the pivotal event that sets in motion the political changes that led to the great power clash. The Athenians did not care about the details of the dispute spurring the fight between Corcyra and Corinth, but Athens jumped into this regional war nonetheless because of its own fear of a dark future that might emerge if this local clash led to a broader power shift that undermined Athens's naval superiority within the Greek world. In other words, Athens succumbed to the preventive war temptation to safeguard its power, and thus its security, only to find that its use of force had pushed the Greek political order to such levels of hostility toward Athens and fears of its aggressive character that Sparta abandoned its long-running tolerance, or blasé disregard, of Athens's expanding empire and led its allies in what became a twenty-seven-year war to "break" the "hostile power."

The Athenians had been warned. In fact, they fully understood the strategic risks of preventive war before launching their warships to the scene of the approaching fight. Thucydides tells us that when the citizens of Athens first debated over whether or not to intervene, there was wide recognition of the dangers of preventive military action—not the danger of military defeat; that was not a concern—but the paradoxical danger of successful preventive war that would upend the stable state of peace between Athens and the other major city-states. But the preventive war temptation was too potent, stirred up by envoys from the city of Corcyra who were desperate to draw Athens into an alliance to help them fend off an impending Corinthian attack. And to make their case, the envoys presented a full-throated preventive war argument in a speech before the Athenian assembly.

The Corcyraeans recognized that the best way to coax the Athenians into this alliance was to stoke their fear of the future, and they did so by warning the Athenians about two things. First, they warned that the conflict between Corcyra and Corinth had moved Athens toward the edge of a dangerous and sudden power shift that cut directly at its core strength: its dominant naval power. Corinth and Corcyra were the second- and third-largest maritime powers of the day. If Corinth defeated and absorbed the Corcyraean navy into its own, Athens might fall to the second rank in naval power. Second, they warned that Athens faced a clear threat of future war with Corinth and its most important ally, Sparta. Without offering any evidence, the Corcyraean spokesman proclaimed three "facts" that he argued must guide Athens's decision: "that Sparta is frightened of you and wants war, that Corinth is your enemy and is also influential at Sparta," and that "Corinth has attacked us first in order to attack you afterwards."[36] The only sensible response to this dangerous future, he argued, is to stop the power shift that would inevitably come with a Corinthian victory.

An envoy from Corinth moved to the speaker's platform next to deliver his retort. His goal was to convince the Athenian citizens standing before him that this dark image of a future threat was absurd and unfounded—and, most important, to warn the Athenians that their future security was at risk only if they were pulled into the conflict by the preventive war temptation. His point was simple: Whatever power advantages you gain from joining Corcyra in this conflict, the decision will surely backlash by inevitably making "open enemies of us now." As the Corinthian delegate insisted, "we are not enemies who are going to attack you . . . *There is no certainty that a war will come.*" Corcyra, he rightly pointed out, "is trying to frighten you into doing wrong by this idea of a coming war." Instead of falling for this hyped fear, "a much wiser course would be to remove the suspicions which we already feel toward you. [. . .] You should be conscious," he continued, "that we are in one of those critical situations where real friendship is to be gained from helping us and real hostility from opposing us."

When the Athenians turned to debate this question among themselves, the Corinthian's warning dominated public opinion in the assembly. But the next day, this warning was brushed aside and the citizens voted to form a defensive alliance with Corcyra. Thucydides gives no details on the deliberations among the Athenians—a frustrating gap in the evidence left behind on this pivotal moment—but his explanation for the final decision is clear: "[T]he general belief was that, whatever happened, war with the [Spartan alliance] was bound to come. Athens had no wish to see the strong navy of Corcyra pass into the hands of Corinth."[37] As simple as that.

But the Athenians could not escape the truth of the preventive war paradox the Corinthians had predicted with such clarity. The spiral of escalating hostility began when Athens was called on to make good its promise to defend Corcyra against a Corinthian offensive. Ten Athenian warships were on the scene when a massive Corinthian naval force arrived at Corcyra to take their revenge for an earlier defeat. Under orders to avoid combat unless Corcyra was at risk of defeat, the commander of the Athenian force tried to hang back from the fight. But as the day unfolded, in what Thucydides tells us became the "biggest [naval] battle that had ever taken place between two [Greek] states,"[38] the Athenians were drawn into a direct clash with Corinthian forces. The next morning, facing this fresh fleet of Athenian ships, and worried that more were over the horizon, the Corinthians abandoned the fight altogether.

For the Athenians, this was clearly an operational victory. The relatively small naval force Athens had committed to the engagement proved decisive in defending its Corcyraean allies—at the scene of battle—against crushing Corinthian retribution. But was this a strategic victory as well? The Athenians certainly achieved their stated political objectives. They prevented the negative shift in naval power that would certainly have followed a Corinthian victory. But did the preventive use of force against Corinth, and these specific gains, really make Athens more secure? Athens's own response to this tactical victory provides the answer. As Thucydides observed, "Athens had no illusions about the hatred felt for her by Corinth," which now had "her first cause for war against Athens." Most worrisome, the Athenians knew that "Corinth was searching for means of retaliation."[39] After one more collision with Athens over the distant city of Potidaea, Corinth turned to Sparta, and the preventive war paradox kicked in hard.

Despite the Athenian belief that war with Sparta was just a matter of time, Thucydides gives us no reason to trust this judgment. In fact, Thucydides finds Sparta's strategic behavior odd. For fourteen years, Sparta had remained detached as Athens's rise continued. On one level, Thucydides understands this was just part of the conservative Spartan character; Spartans were "traditionally slow to go to war," he explains, "unless they were forced into it." Yet on another level, even though he was an Athenian himself, Thucydides was puzzled by the fact that Sparta did not meet Athens's challenge earlier, as power among the Greeks progressively shifted in Athens's favor. The Spartans, he marvels, "though they saw what was happening, did little or nothing to prevent it."[40] It took merciless shaming and badgering by their Corinthian allies—after the Corinthians had suffered the blows inflicted by Athenian military power—to shake Spartan leaders out of their complacency; to get them to look closely at the rise of Athens, its character, and its aggressive conduct; and, eventually, to debate whether or not to wage war to stop this active threat. A direct path leads from Athens's preventive war decision at Corcyra to the Corinthian demand for an allied assembly at Sparta to put an end to Athens's aggression.

Another Corinthian spokesman summed up the argument that a majority of the Spartan allies found persuasive: "[L]et us make up our minds that" Athens has established its power throughout Greece "to dominate all alike, and is planning to subdue what has not been subdued already. Let us then go forward against it and destroy it, let us be able to live our own lives in the future without fear."[41] This is the preventive war paradox at work. Athens's quest for greater security through greater power, and greater power through preventive war, led Athens to cross a strategic threshold that pushed Sparta toward a fundamentally different political relationship—from detachment to total war. And after nearly three decades of conflict and "unprecedented suffering,"[42] total war ended with the collapse of Athens's empire.

Two centuries later, the cities of Rome and Carthage came to define the power structure and the most important security dilemma of the ancient Western world. These ambitious, expanding city-states first fought for control over the central Mediterranean islands of Sicily and Sardinia in the First Punic War, between 264 and 241 BC. A generation later, the Carthaginian Hannibal Barca launched his legendary invasion of Italy with a harrowing trek across the Alps. From one perspective, Hannibal's invasion of Italy in 218 BC, which ignited the Second Punic War, seems to be a simple act of revenge. Among the stories passed down through the centuries about the Barca clan of Carthage, we find an episode in which Hannibal's father, Hamilcar Barca, before setting out to establish a Carthaginian empire in Spain, asked his nine-year-old son to pledge eternal hatred of Rome. Perhaps Hannibal's war was motivated by nothing more than personal animus and a desire for vengeance against Rome for defeating his father more than twenty years earlier.

While Hannibal's hatred of Rome might certainly have played a role in his decision making, the specific circumstances that led to the decision to go on the offensive at that time point to a different explanation. Hannibal was afraid of Roman power, which was spreading westward across the northern Mediterranean, threatening to weaken Carthaginian control over towns in its Spanish empire. The danger reached a breaking point for Hannibal with the revolt of the town of Sagantum in 219 BC. Several years earlier Rome had formally recognized Carthaginian control of the region in which Sagantum was located, yet Rome maintained close diplomatic ties with the town's largely Greek population. For Hannibal, the assassination of the pro-Carthage faction within Sagantum, and the town's subsequent turn to Rome for help against the Carthaginian siege that followed, meant that Roman influence and ambitions in the western Mediterranean had become too dangerous to tolerate (even though Rome ignored Sagantum's call for help). His response was no mere local defense of Carthaginian territory against Roman encroachment. The preventive war temptation led Hannibal to seek a total solution; he wanted to break Roman power at its source by securing a decisive military victory on Rome's home turf and by fracturing

Rome's network of allied and satellite cities which sustained its broad geographic influence across the Mediterranean.

In the long run, Hannibal's bold preventive war against Rome was a gross strategic failure. In fact, we can draw a direct line—albeit, a line that stretches over seven decades—between Hannibal's invasion in 218 BC and Rome's final decimation of Carthage in 146 BC. But this is not merely a case of a military commander taking a risk on war yet failing on the battlefield. Hannibal was an operational military genius who won a string of overwhelming tactical victories against Roman forces in the field, and he maintained a foothold in Italy for ten years. His most spectacular victory came early in the war at the battle of Cannae. In a single day, August 2, 216 BC, Hannibal's army enveloped and systematically cut down and killed nearly fifty thousand Roman soldiers, to include almost one-third of the members of the Roman Senate. To this day Cannae remains the site of the single greatest number of battle deaths suffered by any army in one day in all of Western history. But as Clausewitz would suggest, this brutal battlefield win would mean nothing if it did not produce the political objectives—a better state of peace—that the war was intended to serve. Hannibal's political objective was to crush Rome's will and ability to rival Carthage as a Mediterranean power, to create a postwar order in which Carthage could extend its commercial ties and consolidate its empire free from interference by a powerful rival. Despite his repeated tactical success, and nearly ten years with an army on the Italian peninsula, Hannibal could not break Rome's will. The Second Punic War ultimately ended in 201 BC with a Roman win at the Battle of Zama on the North African coast.

If the story ended here, we might conclude that the strategic effects of Hannibal's preventive war were dictated by the long-term military contest between Rome and Carthage. Perhaps Hannibal simply miscalculated the relative ability of these two great cities to sustain a fight for dominance. We might even propose that Hannibal's miscalculation, despite the costs of the war itself, did not really undercut Carthaginian security. The Carthaginians accepted Rome's peace terms and moved forward in luxurious enjoyment of growing commercial success. But the preventive war paradox had much more sinister implications for the unsuspecting Carthaginians: Their military prowess had a strategic political effect that backfired terribly in the decades to come. Hannibal's preventive war and the near-miss disaster it brought to Rome's doorstep planted the seeds of a long-running fear of Carthage that would not die.

The peace terms that Rome imposed were remarkably similar to the punitive conditions demanded from Germany in 1919. While the Versailles

Treaty stripped Germany of the right to maintain an air force, submarines, and tanks, Rome's peace forced Carthage to surrender its entire navy except for a small number of coastal defense craft, to destroy all of its war elephants, and pledge to never again train these bizarre cavalry forces. Carthage was stripped of its imperial territory along the northern Mediterranean, and Rome demanded a war indemnity to be paid over a fifty-year period. Carthage also lost the right to wage war on its own initiative; assigned the formal subordinate status as a "friend and ally" of Rome, Carthage could only resort to force if given explicit permission by the Roman Senate.

But unlike Germany after World War I, Carthage accepted its new place in the Mediterranean power structure after the Second Punic War. Its leaders and citizens turned with enthusiasm to the pursuit of wealth, while remaining faithful to the military constraints demanded by Rome. Carthage offered to pay off its war indemnity years ahead of schedule and to provide free grain to the Roman army; Rome refused both offers in order to sustain its tight grip. Among the various political factions in postwar Carthage, none were hostile to Rome or challenged the political order it was cultivating. Despite all signs that Carthage would remain compliant with the Roman-dominated political and military status quo, fear of the future continued to grip prominent Roman leaders who obsessed over the mere potential that Carthage would one day turn its accumulating wealth into military revival. Dangerous future scenarios were easy to imagine: Carthage could certainly convert its economic might into military power projection that would once again threaten Rome's expanding imperium; even if Carthage chose not to rebuild its own military forces to challenge Rome directly, its growing wealth could be used to hire mercenaries on short notice—a common practice at the time—to rampage against Rome.

For one Roman politician, Cato the Elder, the only lasting solution to this amorphous yet gripping fear was obvious, and he ended every Senate speech by reminding his fellow Romans of this solution with one simple phrase: "Carthage must be destroyed." And in the end, this is exactly how Rome solved its nagging security dilemma. In 150 BC Carthage violated its peace treaty with Rome by taking up arms in a local dispute with the neighboring kingdom of Numidia, without the Roman Senate's approval. There was nothing about this localized North African border conflict that directly threatened Rome or its increasingly far-flung interests. There was nothing about this treaty violation that demanded more than a sharp yet proportionate reminder that as a "friend and ally" of Rome, Carthage must respect its rules. Yet for Rome, this was an opportunity to unleash the preventive war temptation that had festered for decades, along with Carthage's growing latent power. The Third Punic War ended four years later with the utter annihilation of the city and the enslavement of its surviving population, an end that would ensure that the Carthaginians' resilience would remain just a memory.[43] Through preventive war, Rome eliminated its Carthage problem forever. Here we have the preventive war paradox taken to its terrible extreme: In the long run, Hannibal's preventive war, launched to sustain Carthaginian security by knocking down its main rival, undercut its security by generating such hostility and fear that the city of Carthage suffered the equivalent of death.

Perhaps the most interesting, and the most controversial, example of the preventive war paradox comes from recent history, one we can draw out of the tortuous security dilemma of Middle East politics. It involves a familiar cast of key players and reverberates more than thirty-five years later as world leaders continue to grapple with nuclear weapons proliferation and regional rivalries that drive contemporary security debates. On June 7, 1981, near sunset on a Sunday afternoon, eight Israeli F-16s raced across the northern desert of Saudi Arabia, hugging the terrain, below the sweep of air-search radars. They crossed into central Iraq, aiming for a target twelve miles southeast of Baghdad. Israeli F-15s loitered high overhead, ready to engage any Iraqi fighters scrambled to intercept the inbound enemy aircraft. One by one, the F-16s popped up to five thousand feet before nose-diving to hurl a pair of two-thousand-pound bombs through the dome of the Osirak nuclear reactor.

When the attack was over, the Iraqi Nuclear Research Center was a shattered ruin. From an operational military perspective, the raid was a brilliant success, despite the immense challenges that could have led the mission to disaster. The American-supplied F-16s were new to the Israeli air force, which had no previous experience conducting or even training for long-range bombing missions. The nearly six-hundred-mile round-trip flight exceeded the F-16's normal operating range without in-flight refueling, so Israeli engineers and pilots had worked for months to find a fuel tank and flight configuration that would give the strike aircraft the necessary endurance. Between extra fuel and their explosive payload, the planes were carrying twice the weight they were designed to bear. The Israeli jets would be streaking through Iraqi airspace to bomb a heavily defended target close to the enemy's capital city, while Iraq was already at war with Iran. A pair of Iranian F-4 Phantoms had bombed this same nuclear facility just eight months before. In response, the Iraqis had surrounded the site with batteries of antiaircraft artillery and Soviet-supplied SA-6 surface-to-air missiles, and tethered antiaircraft balloons around the perimeter to obstruct incoming bombers. By the time the third Israeli jet was popping up for its bombing run, the skies were saturated with antiaircraft fire. When it was over, seven of the eight F-16s had delivered their ordnance right on target, the Osirak reactor was in flames, and all aircraft made it safely home to the Eitan air base in the southern Sinai Peninsula.[44]

Israeli prime minister Menachem Begin, the political force driving the decision to attack, knew this was an audacious act—not only for the pilots that would risk their lives to pull it off, but audacious as well for both domestic politics and the likely international reaction. Begin had been warned by members of his own cabinet, and by senior opposition politicians who knew of the plan, that a surprise attack against a sovereign state, with no immediate threat to justify it, would stir up a potent global backlash.

As predicted, international condemnation was sharp and nearly universal. The most stinging rebuke came from Israel's superpower patron. While President Ronald Reagan had warm personal views on the Jewish state and was sympathetic to Israeli fears about Iraq,[45] the White House described his reaction to the Osirak attack as "shocked," "distressed," and "disturbed."[46] The Reagan administration could have issued a simple public statement of disapproval and moved on, but they took the rebuke a big step further with a decision that rings with historical irony: The United States teamed up with Iraq in the United Nations to craft a Security Council resolution that "strongly condemns the military attack by Israel," calling it a "clear violation of the United Nations Charter and the norms of international conduct." The UN Security Council approved the resolution with a unanimous vote.[47] In her Security Council speech before the vote, US ambassador Jeane Kirkpatrick, a hawk among hawks, declared that the United States remained committed to dealing with "the dangers of nuclear proliferation." "Nevertheless," she said, "we believe the means Israel chose to quiet its fears about the purposes of Iraq's nuclear program have hurt, and not helped, the peace and security of the area."[48] For more than two months following the raid, the United States suspended delivery of the additional F-16s Israel had purchased, while reviewing whether Israel's use of American-built equipment violated the Arms Export Control Act and its stipulation that military equipment sold to foreign countries must be used only in self-defense, and not for aggressive purposes.[49]

Throughout this barrage of international criticism, Prime Minister Begin remained defiant. Drawing directly from the logic of the preventive war temptation, Begin painted a stark picture of Saddam Hussein's aggressive intentions against Israel, his commitment to increasing Iraq's military power with a nuclear arsenal, and the short-term window of opportunity

Israel enjoyed to destroy this nascent capability while Saddam's nuclear program was still under construction. The alternative future for Israel, as Begin saw it, was too dark to tolerate. Israeli government fears focused on two possible routes from the Osirak reactor complex to nuclear weapons. First, France had promised to deliver, over time, up to seventy kilograms of highly enriched uranium to fuel the reactor; if Iraqi scientists diverted this fuel into a weapons program, it conceivably could provide the explosive core of three atomic bombs. Second, if properly reconfigured, the reactor would have the technical means to generate plutonium as an alternative supply of explosive material.[50] According to internal Israeli calculations, Iraq could have a nuclear weapon by 1985. The weight of this timetable and the magnitude of this power shift's security implications pressed heavily on the prime minister. In October 1980, during the first full cabinet meeting called to discuss the problem, Begin quickly got to the point:

> [A] great clock is hanging over our heads, and it is ticking. Somewhere on the banks of the Tigris and the Euphrates, there are men plotting to annihilate us . . . Every passing day brings them closer to their goal . . . In another five years, or maybe just three years, the Iraqis will have two or three atomic bombs . . . Saddam Hussein is a bloodthirsty tyrant who . . . will not hesitate to employ weapons of mass destruction against us. We must take that as our point of departure.[51]

Two days after destroying Osirak, the prime minister took his case public with a uniquely Israeli framework for understanding the threat and explaining his decision: "[I]n this case, it was an act of supreme, morally supreme act of national self-defense. Israel has nothing to apologize for. Ours is a just cause . . . There won't be another Holocaust in history. . . . We shall defend our people with all the means at our disposal." And to make sure his audience—at home, in the neighborhood, and around the world—understood that this preventive attack was not about Iraq uniquely, Begin converted the case into an example of an emergent Israeli security doctrine: "We shall not allow any enemy to develop weapons of mass destruction against us."[52]

Israel was not completely isolated in its claim to have both morality and strategic wisdom on its side. Prominent members of the US Congress spoke out on Israel's behalf, condemning the Reagan administration's treatment of the attack in the process. A *Wall Street Journal* editorial captured an assessment of this preventive attack that eventually came to reflect conventional wisdom on its value; it declared we now had a model of "at least one effective anti-proliferation policy in the world."[53] The key word here is *effective*. The blunt conclusion was that preventive attack worked—that it produced a more-secure future through bold, timely action. According to Senator Alan Cranston of California, the inherent danger of nuclear proliferation in the Middle East made Israel's preventive strike "arguably defensive and not offensive," just as an American strike on Soviet missiles in Cuba would have been in 1962. Senator Daniel Patrick Moynihan of New York accepted this position: "Anything that takes out a nuclear installation, I'm in favor of." Senator Edward Kennedy of Massachusetts blamed the crisis on failures in the existing international technology control mechanisms. Until these failures are fixed, Kennedy argued that others "should not second-guess Israel" if it believes force is necessary to meet the same nonproliferation goal so critical to Israel's security. *New York Times* columnist William Safire joined the chorus, arguing that Israel's strike "has denied an aggressive dictator the ability to inflict atomic terror."[54] Eventually, the Reagan administration lifted the embargo on future F-16 deliveries. Secretary of State Alexander Haig, whose initial reaction was to label the attack "aggression," now complained about the inherent ambiguity between offensive and defensive action to justify the turnabout in US policy.[55]

From the vantage point of 1991, ten years after the raid, this same conclusion about its effectiveness was reflected in a gift presented to Gen. David Ivry, commander of the Israeli Air Force in 1981. American secretary of defense Dick Cheney gave General Ivry an enlarged satellite photograph of the Osirak reactor taken days after the F-16 strike. At the bottom was a handwritten note: "With thanks and appreciation. You made our job easier in Desert Storm." The implication was clear: Israel's destruction of the Osirak reactor delayed Iraq's nuclear weapons program long enough to prevent Saddam Hussein from having the bomb when Iraq invaded Kuwait in August 1990, and then fought the international coalition that drove him out again beginning in January 1991. The ceasefire agreement that ended the Gulf War demanded access to suspect Iraqi unconventional weapons sites. International inspectors were shocked to discover how close Iraq had come during the 1980s to reaching the technical means to begin churning out nuclear weapons fuel through uranium enrichment. A common interpretation of this discovery was that the Osirak raid forced Iraq to pursue a more technologically difficult and time-consuming covert route to the bomb, and luck was with the international community when Saddam launched his Kuwaiti adventure while his scientists were still struggling to reach their atomic goals.

But there is a more convincing interpretation of the inspectors' nuclear discoveries in Iraq that undermines this optimistic assessment. The best evidence available today, only accessible after the American-led invasion of

Iraq in 2003, shows that instead of disrupting a coherent and determined Iraqi plan to develop nuclear weapons, Israel's preventive attack actually was a decisive moment that spurred Iraq's efforts along this dangerous path, making it more likely that Iraq would become a nuclear power with time. In other words, while the raid was a smashing success in terms of target destruction, it inadvertently energized the kind of political backlash the preventive war paradox warns about, arguably putting Israel at greater risk in the coming years. And this was not a conclusion drawn merely in hindsight; key leaders in Israel had predicted just such an outcome in the months leading up to the strike.

Prime Minister Begin was confident and resolute, but important government officials had serious reservations that persisted over months of intense debate, right until the final cabinet vote when ten members supported the mission and six members opposed it. And these were not marginal members of the government. The opponents included a deputy prime minister, the deputy defense minister, the chief of Mossad (Israel's intelligence agency), the intelligence director of the Israeli Defense Force, the minister of Internal Affairs, and the director general of the Israel Atomic Energy Commission. Begin's first defense minister (a former commander of the Israeli Air Force), Ezer Weizman, remained an active opponent of preventive attack, persistently pressuring the prime minister and other key leaders to drop plans to strike Osirak, even after he resigned from the government in May 1980.[56] There were a number of arguments motivating this opposition, but there was one essential question they did not bother to debate: the feasibility of the military operation. While all recognized the complexities of this raid and worried about the pilots executing it, political leaders did not challenge the Israeli Air Force plan or oppose the raid because it might fail to destroy the nuclear reactor. The opponents were thinking beyond the immediate military questions, focusing on the political consequences and how the raid might undermine Israeli security from a broader strategic perspective, even if the air force succeeded in destroying Osirak.

There were a range of predictions offered. Some worried the attack would undercut American political and military support, which was a well of seemingly limitless power Israel could draw from to help ensure its survival. Some predicted the attack would serve as a rallying cry for Arab states, helping them plaster over the deep cracks in their own relations and reenergize the anti-Israel cause. Perhaps the Soviet Union would find new incentives and opportunities to support Arab solidarity and the more-threatening anti-Israeli initiatives this support would make possible. An attack against Iraq might compel Egypt, the one Arab state that was decisively moving away from the violent hostility of the past, to break from the peace process and slip back into old patterns of confrontation with Israel as an enemy state.

Each of these scenarios would undermine Israeli security, in terms of both hostile intent and relative physical power. Nevertheless, Prime Minister Begin was willing to accept these effects as a reasonable strategic trade-off if it meant Israel could avoid the much graver threat of Saddam Hussein in possession of a nuclear arsenal. But was Begin's assumption about the strategic effects of destroying the Osirak reactor valid? Would Osirak put Iraq on track to develop the bomb? Would its destruction eliminate this threat? Several of the prime minister's opponents challenged his assessment on these questions directly. Not only would the destruction of Osirak be merely a temporary setback for the Iraqis; more worrisome yet, they argued, was the fact that it would goad Israel's enemies into pursuing nuclear weapons with a determination they did not yet have. As the Israeli deputy defense minister saw it, "[O]ur overweening ambition is liable to induce the Arabs to manufacture bombs at remote sites."[57] Shimon Peres, the leader of the opposition Labor Party and a former prime minister and defense minister, shared this view. He had been tipped off secretly about the attack and tried to stop Begin with a memo on May 10 outlining the strategic risks: "[W]hat is intended to prevent," Peres warned, "can become a catalyst."[58] With the benefit of hindsight, the toppling of Saddam Hussein, and subsequent access to secrets held by senior officials and scientists in his nuclear program, we now can see how prescient these warnings were.

The best evidence now available clearly shows that the Israeli preventive attack "triggered a nuclear weapons program where one did not previously exist."[59] These are the findings of an enterprising Norwegian researcher who carefully reconstructed the history of Iraq's nuclear program, drawing from memoirs and interviews with the program's key personnel, to include the scientific head of the program, the director of the uranium enrichment centrifuge program, the individual responsible for documenting program activities, and the chief of the Iraqi Atomic Energy Commission.[60] There is no doubt that when Saddam Hussein ordered the development of a nuclear program in 1975, his goal was to acquire the infrastructure that would give him the option to develop the bomb. In fact, he said so publicly. While pointing an accusing finger at Israel during a 1975 interview, Saddam said, "The search for technology with military potential was a reaction to Israel's nuclear armament, and the" contract with France to build the Osirak plant "was the first actual step in the production of an Arab atomic weapon."[61]

But until the early fall of 1981, this "first step" toward an Arab atomic bomb was unimpressive. The program was "directionless and disorganized"; it had no explicit mandate from Iraqi leaders to pursue a weapon, it was poorly structured, and it had a meager budget and limited staff.[62] Saddam himself had hobbled the program in December 1979 when he ordered the arrest of Hussain al-Shahristani, the chief science adviser to the Iraqi Atomic Energy Commission, and one month later had Jafar Dhia Jafar, the preeminent nuclear physicist in Iraq, confined to house arrest for his persistent agitation to get Shahristani released. This directionless and disorganized program was in no position to exploit Osirak for a secret bomb project, particularly with French engineers on-site every day, and monitoring by the International Atomic Energy Agency. Iraq was dependent on French engineers to construct and operate the plant, and it would be for years to come. France would only supply the reactor with highly enriched uranium fuel in small quantities, and refuel the reactor only after spent fuel was fully accounted for and returned. These safeguards would prevent Iraq from diverting the uranium into the explosive core of a weapon. The production of bomb-ready plutonium would require a major reconfiguration of the reactor, something that could not escape detection. And if Iraq withdrew from the Nuclear Nonproliferation Treaty and expelled French engineers and international inspectors, it simply did not have the home-grown expertise or equipment to operate the reactor independently.[63]

Saddam's halfhearted focus on nuclear weapons and the haphazard nature of his nuclear program changed decisively after the Israeli attack. Iraq's post-Osirak nuclear program would remain effectively concealed for the next decade, but in the months that followed the attack Saddam put the international community on notice with barely veiled language in a series of public statements. Israel's strike, he said, "will not stop the course of scientific and technical progress in Iraq. Rather, it is an additional strong stimulus to develop this course . . . with even greater resources and with more effective protection." In a press conference Saddam talked about the "side effects of this attack" which "might not have occurred to the Israelis when they launched their aggression," the side effects that Iraqis would learn from as they moved forward. In an interview he went further, explaining that "when we feel an imminent danger posed by Israel to the Arab nation, we will let the Iraqis' minds operate to the maximum, and try by every possible means to protect ourselves."[64]

Saddam's agitation over the Osirak attack changed the fortunes of Jafar Dhia Jafar, who suddenly found himself freed from house arrest and in private consultations with the Iraqi president as he looked to the future. During a meeting in September 1981, Saddam was blunt about his intentions. "How is it that Israel is allowed to develop nuclear technology and nuclear weapons, while we aren't? In the future, we will not be able to keep the Israelis' aggression at bay without something to deter them with!" Saddam made it clear that Jafar's mission was to move past the destruction of Osirak and get serious about building an actual weapon in a revamped clandestine program. "From today, that's our goal," the Iraqi leader insisted.[65] This was not empty rhetoric; Saddam made good on his pledge. Jafar returned to the Nuclear Research Center with this mandate and created a new directorate that would spearhead Iraq's first serious nuclear weapons effort. Over the next decade the program staff grew by 60 percent each year, from four hundred scientists to seven thousand scientists, while program funding expanded from $400 million to $10 billion.[66] In 1987 Saddam's scientists reported they were ready to move toward weaponization, and estimated that they could produce the first bomb in the mid-1990s. Saddam enthusiastically agreed. In 1990 and 1991, with the help of a desperate drive fired by the war over Kuwait, Saddam came astonishingly close to the nuclear weapons threshold.

In that same year, Saddam's nuclear dreams collapsed under the weight of American air strikes and defeat in the Gulf War, through the work of international inspectors scouring his country to uncover and destroy its nuclear facilities, and the pressure of economic sanctions that added heavy incentives for Saddam to quietly dismantle his weapons of mass destruction programs. In the end, the potential Iraqi threat to Israel was indeed neutralized through military force. But it is hard to give much credence to the argument that Israel's preventive attack in 1981 helped to make this possible. The Israeli attack is what the Iraqis needed to focus, reorganize, and get serious about actually producing nuclear weapons with an independent, secret program that could do its work completely free from international scrutiny. Israel's brilliantly executed and operationally successful raid on Osirak produced a terrible burst of the preventive war paradox. It did not set the Iraqis back; rather, it spurred them on, setting in motion the kind of political change necessary to make Iraq a true danger over time. What saved Israel from facing the grave threat of Saddam Hussein with an atomic bomb was a pure historical fluke. It was Saddam's unrelated decision to invade Kuwait and confront the overwhelming power of the coalition that turned against him, before Iraq had a nuclear deterrent to help Saddam stand his ground.

The same tragic dynamic is at the heart of the debate over how to confront Iran's nuclear ambitions and the fear that its spinning centrifuges will spit out enough highly enriched uranium to fuel an atomic arsenal for the Islamic Republic. It's no secret that Israeli leaders feel the same temptation to launch preventive attacks against Iranian facilities, in a replay of 1981. This temptation swelled in 2007, and again between 2010 and 2012. It also seems that the question of attacking Iran generated the same kind of internal divisions within the Israeli national security community that caused such stress in 1980 and 1981, with two former Mossad chiefs, a deputy prime minister, a foreign minister, a former defense minister, and a director of internal security, all publicly protesting that an attack would have damaging strategic effects on Israel's safety. And the preventive war paradox is the strategic logic many point to.

We also find key leaders in the United States opposing preventive attack in the same terms. Former secretary of defense Robert Gates provides an excellent example. Gates is perhaps the most forthright American public official to weigh in on the strategic logic of preventive war in decades. It is impossible, in fact, to find a senior leader as willing as Secretary Gates to engage in an honest and open discussion of his skepticism. He frequently went on record to suggest that he actively opposed a preventive attack against Iran's nuclear infrastructure because it would set back Iran's program by no more than one to two years. But most important, Gates recognized its paradoxical effects, worrying that a preventive attack would give Iran an incentive it might not otherwise have to actually produce nuclear weapons.

In a private memorandum for President Bush in 2007, as the Israeli government was looking for American support to hit Iran, Gates argued that an American or Israeli attack would "guarantee that the Iranians will develop nuclear weapons, and seek revenge."[67] "They would just bury the program deeper," he said, when the question surged again in 2012, "and make it more covert."[68] According to Gen. Michael Hayden, former director of the Central Intelligence Agency and the National Security Agency, Gates was not alone in this view: "When we talked about this in the government, the consensus was that [attacking Iran] would guarantee that which we are trying to prevent—an Iran that will spare nothing to build a nuclear weapon and that would build it in secret."[69]

Here General Hayden distills the essence of the problem to its most elementary form. Preventive war "would guarantee that which we are trying to prevent." From the ancient to the modern world, across the profound changes that over time have altered political systems, military technology, and economic orders, across cultures, in different geographic settings, and with changes in leadership, the general phenomenon is the same. Instead of eliminating future threat, preventive war brings the risk of generating greater threat, stimulating dangerous power shifts, intensifying hostility, and increasing the likelihood of future armed conflict. And this paradox is at the heart of the story of the 1936 Rhineland crisis.

Before we put it to work to explore the tragic dilemma of the 1930s, the next several chapters roll the timeline back to trace the evolution of the European security dilemma from the late nineteenth century through World War I, and the years that followed the Great War and the Treaty of Versailles. While this might seem like a detour from the crisis of 1936, it is impossible to understand how European leaders thought about the recovery of German power under the Third Reich and the strategic alternatives available to confront this changing security environment without an account of what came before. The Great War and the tumultuous political order of the 1920s cast a heavy shadow on the future. British and French leaders of the mid-1930s were not working in a historical vacuum, as if Nazi Germany had so fundamentally changed world politics that the recent past was irrelevant. The recent past was alive, framing what they believed about the causes of war and how to avoid it.

The next chapter will pick up the European story in the second half of the nineteenth century. It was a period dominated by the tussle between the preventive war temptation and the preventive war paradox, and at its center is German chancellor Otto von Bismarck, an outsized figure from history. Bismarck was perhaps the most skilled practitioner of power politics in the modern era, certainly the most skilled in German history. He engineered a massive increase in German power in the 1860s and 1870s, and he secured Germany against the most serious threats that might have emerged in the late nineteenth century, all while holding the line in a series of internal policy battles against the champions of preventive war in his own government. Bismarck had a keen appreciation for the preventive war paradox, which he knew could destroy everything he had achieved. Bismarck not only offers the best example we have of a major world leader fighting against the preventive war temptation; his experience will also help to set the stage for the tragedy suffered by the generations that followed, as the European drama unfolded after he passed from the scene.

4

HAUNTED BY THE
PREVENTIVE WAR PARADOX

I have the thankless task of pouring water into the sparkling wine and
trying to make it plain that we are not alone in Europe.

—Otto von Bismarck, 1866

Otto von Bismarck, the "Iron Chancellor" of Prussia and Imperial Germany for nearly three decades in the late nineteenth century, is among
the giants of modern history. In just six years, Bismarck engineered the
most dramatic shift in the European power structure since Napoleon
Bonaparte's *Grande Armée* swept across the continent at the beginning
of the century. Bismarck catapulted Prussia from its long-standing position as the least influential and most vulnerable of the European great
powers, to its new place in 1871 at the core of a unified German empire.
For the first time in history, a politically consolidated Germany stretched
across the entire northern tier of Central and Western Europe, from the
Russian empire in the east, to the Netherlands, Belgium, and France in
the west. And in the process of forging this new Prussian-centric German
state, Bismarck knocked Austria from its perch as the most important
power in the center of the Continent. Bismarck then delivered a blow to
French power and prestige from which it never truly recovered. Bismarck
certainly understood the value of state power, that indispensable ingredi-
ent for securing a vulnerable Prussia. He dreamed about state power for
years; it was central to his worldview. He pursued it with unflagging drive,

and took serious risks along the way to achieve it. And in the end, Otto von Bismarck's struggle to amass Prussian power fundamentally transformed the European political landscape.

Given this legacy, it might seem natural to treat Bismarck as the spiritual godfather to the German empire builders of the twentieth century, those who believed that the brightest future for Germany could only come through wars that won uncontested domination over the entire great power order. Bismarck's mastery of power politics might lead us to assume that he would have championed the logic of preventive war that set Imperial Germany on an offensive path in 1914 and swirled through the poisonous brew of violent ideologies that spurred on the Third Reich a generation later. But this reading of the Iron Chancellor's legacy is fundamentally wrong. Bismarck has an important role in this broader study of preventive war and the tragic story of the 1930s, but not because his beliefs about security and war blazed a path for the preventive wars waged by his successors. Quite the opposite. Bismarck was haunted by the preventive war paradox. He lived with an unshakable fear that if German leaders overreached in the pursuit of power—particularly through preventive war—Germany would surely suffer a terrible Europe-wide backlash, creating external threats that simply did not yet exist. One of the great tragedies of European history is that while those German leaders who followed in his wake would glorify Bismarck's success in constructing a powerful unified Germany, they never understood what he understood: that true security depended on German self-restraint in how its power was actually used.

German leaders, from Bismarck to Hitler, all had to grapple with the hard reality of Germany's central geographic position in Europe and the potential danger of Russian and French armies on Germany's wings. They all believed that power would remain an essential variable in any German security scheme. But they parted most severely on the question of preventive war. The preventive war temptation had its day with Kaiser Wilhelm II and his senior leaders in 1914, and with the Führer's invasion of the USSR in 1941. It ultimately led to disaster in both cases. For Chancellor Bismarck, on the other hand, preventive war was a grossly flawed approach to the enduring problem of national security, and he stood virtually alone in the German government during this era, holding firm against well-positioned rivals who had succumbed to the preventive war temptation. We hear an echo of Bismarck's experience in the strategic dilemma British leaders faced sixty years later, so his story serves as important background to the struggle over the Rhineland that continued several generations after Bismarck's death. This is clearly among Bismarck's most important legacies in the history of strategic thought, and it deserves a closer look before we turn to Europe after World War I.

Bismarck did not shrink from war as a political tool. Under his leadership Prussia's rise was made possible by war: Victories over Denmark in 1864, Austria in 1866, and France in 1870 showcased the power Prussia could now mobilize to stunning effect. The Iron Chancellor himself was not a military man. As a young adult he served in the Prussian army for a year and as an officer in the Landwehr reserve forces, but throughout his career Bismarck was a civilian servant of the Prussian state and the Hohenzollern dynasty that had ruled the kingdom since it was formed in 1701. While he followed his king to the battlefield on horseback in 1866 and 1870, Bismarck can take no credit for Prussia's martial prowess or the string of victories that put Prussia in a position to master the great power game. Credit for Prussia's rapid growth in offensive power belongs to Gen. Helmuth von Moltke, appointed chief of the Prussian general staff in 1857. The victories he engineered over Denmark, Austria, and France testify to the fact that Moltke was an organizational genius who could mobilize, deploy, and supply his army better than any of his rivals.[1]

Yet still, it was Bismarck who played the decisive role, leveraging these battlefield victories to propel Prussia into a position of political dominance and to unify the German states within the new empire. Military triumph alone could not revolutionize the security landscape of the European continent. Bismarck's political genius for turning operational military success into a strategic win was the key to the epoch-making changes of this period. For another twenty years after German unification, the Imperial Chancellor seemed to "hold Europe in his palm," safeguarding Germany by deftly manipulating his counterparts across the European system. After leaving office in 1890, Bismarck was lionized, held up as a strategic prodigy, a diplomatic puppeteer who could intrigue, charm, or saber-rattle his way through any looming threat. These epithets have found their way into countless histories and biographies that paint Bismarck in shades of admiration that border on hero worship.

This image of Bismarck as heroic genius is certainly not universally shared. Some scholars scoff at the notion of Bismarck as the master puppeteer of Europe, arguing that German interests actually suffered from his many mistakes. Some have vilified Bismarck for setting Germany on the path that led to the titanic power struggles and catastrophic wars of the early twentieth century.[2] Many of Bismarck's traits and much of his behavior make it hard to admire him on a personal level. Bismarck was bullying and contemptuous of most people he encountered. He was arrogant, deceitful, and domineering, even with his own king. He was prone to emotional tantrums, frequent threats of resignation to win debates over state policy, even tears when faced with frustration. Bismarck was grossly overweight, he ate and drank heavily every day, often late into the night, and would complain regularly of sleepless nights, a long list of physical ailments, and emotional stress. Bismarck suffered from depression, and a number of times during his tenure the Iron Chancellor retreated from the pressures of his office by spending months at a stretch away from Berlin at his country estate near the Baltic Sea. This is hardly the image one would expect of a Teutonic hero. The fact that he survived so long in office is a testament to his indomitable political skills. King Wilhelm no doubt considered him truly indispensable, and Bismarck got results.

But for our purposes, it really doesn't matter whether we find Bismarck admirable as a person, a noble hero or a wretch. What really matters is that Otto von Bismarck remains the single best example we have of an important historical figure who wrestled self-consciously and overtly with the dueling pressures of the preventive war temptation and the preventive war paradox. Bismarck pops up frequently in contemporary studies of preventive war, widely cited as one of the most serious critics of the preventive war option. It certainly helps that Bismarck is so eminently quotable on the subject, having provided us with a number of colorful metaphors to explain his opposition. He worried that launching preventive war could "break eggs out of which very dangerous chickens might hatch." It is, he said, "tantamount to committing suicide for fear of death."[3] Bismarck did flirt with the preventive war temptation at times, and he certainly was not alone. He was surrounded by high-level, outspoken advocates of the preventive war option, in the German military as well as the foreign ministry, who felt the allure of its promise to eliminate alleged threats to the west and the east in the 1870s and 1880s. But it was Bismarck's realistic understanding of power politics that led him to reject what many of his contemporaries found so seductive. He saw the preventive war temptation as a siren song that would lead to strategic disaster; *victory* in preventive war, he believed, would destroy the carefully crafted political relationships he had built across Europe's strategic terrain that offered the soundest footing for German security.

When we look closely at Bismarck's career, we find two reasons for his opposition. First, he was highly sensitive to the inherent uncertainty of the future. At three crisis points—on the eve of the Franco-Prussian War in 1870, during the "War in Sight" crisis of 1875, and during the war scare of 1886–1888—Bismarck was surrounded by talk of the inevitability of war and colleagues who demanded that Germany take the offensive before it was too late. But he refused to accept this "better now than later" logic. In his memoirs he explained it this way: "I have always opposed the theory . . . as regards a war which we should probably have to face sooner or later, to bring it on . . . before the adversary could improve his preparations." The problem is that "one cannot see the cards of Providence far enough ahead to anticipate historical developments according to one's own calculation."[4] As he knew from experience, "from one moment to the other an unexpected circumstance might arise which would" prove that launching a war of anticipation was "a precipitate decision."[5] In other words, those who have predicted the inevitability of war at specific points in time have been wrong far more often than they have been right. The twists and turns of events, diplomatic interventions, perceptions that are proven erroneous, the withering of grievances with time, have all diverted rivals from what seemed like an inevitable collision before they met in violent conflict. In fact, to Bismarck, the future was something to be shaped and directed, not something that threw inevitabilities in a statesman's path. If a future war was something that Germany was going to face, it was because Bismarck himself had concluded that war was truly the best means to accomplish his political objectives.

Which brings us to the second, and most important, reason for Bismarck's opposition to preventive war: He understood what Carl von Clausewitz meant when he insisted on a strategic assessment of war. Bismarck once said, "To my shame I have to confess that I have never read Clausewitz."[6] Nonetheless, Bismarck clearly shared his fellow Prussian's most important views on the relationship between war and the political objectives of the state.[7] Bismarck, in fact, was the perfect Clausewitzian. As we saw earlier, Clausewitz insisted that war is not merely about winning battlefield victories. Success in war cannot be measured by the amount of pain inflicted on your adversary. As Bismarck wrote, while "the task of the commander of the army is to annihilate the hostile forces," this must never be confused with the actual "object of war," which is "to conquer peace under conditions which are conformable to the policy pursued by the state."[8] This was the responsibility of political leaders who must never be satisfied with merely asking "Can we beat our adversary in the fight?"; instead, they must focus on the strategic question, "Will war actually produce the political results we seek?"

Bismarck never lost sight of this first principle of war. While he was surrounded by military enthusiasts looking to score brilliant victories in a series of armed contests, Bismarck remained the stubborn Clausewitzian over the course of his career, pushing back hard against those who didn't understand Clausewitz's most important strategic insights. And when it came to preventive war, Bismarck knew it was hobbled as a strategic option by the security paradox—the insidious effect of stirring up greater dangers than you faced before, even in the wake of operational victory. We find this contest between the preventive war temptation and the preventive war paradox play out in bitter policy debates among German officials in the mid-1870s and late 1880s. But Bismarck's appreciation for the preventive war paradox is first revealed in 1870, not through an effort to stop Germany from falling into this trap, but through his manipulation of a brewing crisis with France. It was a crisis that tempted French leaders to knock back Prussia's growing power through preventive war, but which trapped France in its own preventive war paradox, thus helping Bismarck secure the most important strategic goal of his lifetime.

TRAPPED BY THE PREVENTIVE WAR PARADOX

In early March 1871, Otto von Bismarck found himself on the outskirts of Paris alongside the German emperor, the Prussian crown prince, and General Moltke, watching thousands of soldiers from the allied German states pass in review as they entered the French capital for occupation duty. The occupation was purely symbolic, a condition the new French government accepted to end a four-month siege and the heavy artillery barrage that had battered Paris during the last days of the Franco-Prussian War. Germany's victory over France was total; this parade through the enemy's capital was hardly necessary to prove the point. Within a month of the first major clash, the French army had collapsed as an effective defensive force. On September 2, 1870, French emperor Napoleon III personally surrendered after the disaster of the Battle of Sedan, bringing the French Second Empire to a pathetic end. Four months later, Prussia's King Wilhelm was crowned German Kaiser in the Hall of Mirrors at the Palace of Versailles, the home of French kings since the reign of Louis XIV in the late seventeenth century. In defeat, the only real form of resistance left for the new French Third Republic was to deny the German emperor himself a chance to parade through the Arc de Triomphe. According to the armistice terms, thirty thousand German soldiers could occupy Paris until the French government ratified the agreement. Kaiser Wilhelm waited eagerly for his chance to lead the final contingent of troops scheduled to march into the city on the third day of occupation. Given the chaos that riddled the French Third Republic, German leaders were looking forward to settling in for a satisfying stay. But the National Assembly spoiled the emperor's plan by rushing through the ratification process on the second day, so German soldiers marched right back out again on the day meant for the Kaiser's grand entrance.[9]

For Bismarck, now carrying the heavy title of "Imperial Chancellor," this was irrelevant; all that mattered was that this war achieved its primary political goal. The French declaration of war against Prussia on July 19, 1870, was enough to rally the southern German states to Prussia's defense and catalyze the constitutional unification of the German states. This is all Bismarck wanted from this war, and it was a political goal that didn't hinge on this display of total victory. But as the war took its course, unfolding according to its own unpredictable logic, this is where the road to French surrender ended. With the German unification project successfully under his belt, we find Bismarck wrestling with the same question he confronted in 1866 at the victorious conclusion of Prussia's war with Austria: What state of peace will best secure Germany for the future? What should he actually do with this overwhelming victory? In 1866, during a bitter struggle with his king and the army chief of staff, Bismarck insisted on a moderate peace for Austria. His greatest fear was that Prussian ferocity in victory would create a much wider world of dangers, what came to be called the "nightmare" of an anti-Prussian coalition linking Austria, Russia, and France. "If Austria were severely injured," he argued, "she would become the ally of France and of every other opponent of ours; she would even sacrifice her anti-Russian interests for the sake of revenge on Prussia."[10]

In 1871, the Imperial Chancellor was once again in a position to dictate a punishing settlement or to show restraint. For France, however, Bismarck chose to dominate his defeated enemy. This raises an obvious question: Where was Bismarck's fear of the security paradox that led to his desperate call for moderation in 1866? Wouldn't this tremendous display of German military power, surprising even to the Prussian king and general staff,[11] generate the nightmare of an anti-German alliance that Bismarck dreaded after defeating Austria? Wouldn't the accretion of Prussian power through German unification and this stunning weakening of France rouse the other European powers out of their complacency in the face of this sudden power shift? In short, the answer is no. In an ironic twist, Bismarck knew that Germany could escape the security backlash in this case because France itself was suffering the consequences of the preventive war paradox. France paid a price—abandoned by any potential allies that might have helped keep Germany in check—for launching what European leaders across the Continent saw as an aggressive preventive war to stop the further growth of Prussian power and secure French hegemony. To tell this story properly, we need to return to the prewar period, before German unification, before German forces shredded French armies on the battlefield, to the years when the French army was still considered the most powerful land force in the world.

In the years before the Franco-Prussian War, Emperor Napoleon III and key French officials watched the steady growth of Prussian power with increasing agitation. To Napoleon III, Prussia's military victories in 1864 and 1866 seemed to demand some form of compensation for France. After all, he fumed, France remained neutral while Prussia roughed up the Austrian army; such restraint should be rewarded with some meaningful prize—Luxembourg, perhaps, or a slice of Belgium. Such a prize, awarded for merely standing aside, would signal to audiences at home and abroad that Prussia had been able to take this bold move only because France allowed it.

But to Napoleon III's great dismay, the war with Austria passed with nothing for the French Second Empire.[12] It was as though Bismarck wasn't grateful for French restraint, as though he had no need for French acquiescence. What Bismarck demonstrated was that Prussia in fact did not need French permission to alter the hierarchy of power and prestige on the Continent, and he certainly had no reason to placate France with compensations to balance out Prussia's rising position. As Napoleon III's indignation simmered in the years after 1866, yet another concrete sign of Prussia's expanding geographic influence—and its seemingly insolent disregard for French sensitivities—stirred the French government into spasms of outrage.

In the wake of revolution, Spain needed a new monarch. In the spring of 1869, while an emissary from the *Cortes*, the Spanish legislature, surveyed the royal houses of Europe in search of a suitable candidate to sit on its empty throne, Bismarck suggested that Prince Leopold, from the Prussian Hohenzollern dynasty, might make a worthy choice. Bismarck immediately recognized the opportunity created by the Spanish vacancy, and the political and military advantages of turning a Hohenzollern prince into Spanish royalty. Not only would it be, Bismarck said, "an excellent thing to have on the other side of France a country upon whose sympathies we could rely," but he also figured that in a crisis, the fear of Spanish support for Prussia would tie down two corps of the French army on its southern border.[13] Trouble emerged when Napoleon III and his foreign minister, the Duc de Gramont, came to see the implications of a Hohenzollern as king of Spain the same way Bismarck did.

At the beginning of July 1870, the French foreign minister delivered a ferocious warning to parliament—and, in the process, to Spain and to

Prussia—that the power implications of this proposal were intolerable. To fix this problem, Gramont warned, "We shall count on the friendship of the Spanish people and the clear-sightedness of the German people." But "If it should prove otherwise," if Spain and Prussia do not cancel this emerging link between them, then "fortified by your strength, gentlemen, and that of the nation, we know how to fulfill our duty without hesitation or weakness."[14] Across Europe, and in Berlin, this call to "duty" was interpreted as a call to war. Emperor Napoleon and the Duc de Gramont had fallen hard for the most seductive promise of preventive war: that it would *eliminate* the security problems they saw looming out of the future.

And then events took a strange turn. Prussia quietly conceded, but France refused to let the dispute die. As the crisis came to a full boil, Prince Leopold—the intended future sovereign of Spain and the object of French fury—was on holiday, hiking in the Swiss mountains. With Leopold unreachable, his father became the target for the growing dismay in capitals across Europe. Letters from Prussian King Wilhelm, Queen Victoria of Great Britain, Belgian King Leopold II, and envoys from Paris and Madrid, all urged him to bring this trouble to an end by withdrawing his son's name. Just six days after Gramont's inflammatory speech, he did just that.[15] The crisis should have ended here, but in Paris Gramont would not consider the matter closed. This was not a crisis to be averted; rather, it was an opportunity to be exploited, a chance to disrupt what was seen as relentless momentum behind growing Prussian power. To realize the potential of this moment, Prussia had to be publicly humiliated—if not through war, then at least through open diplomatic retreat in the face of bold French demands.

The same day Prince Leopold's name was withdrawn, Gramont telegraphed a new set of demands to French ambassador Vincent Benedetti, who was encamped in the Rhineland resort town of Bad Ems, where Prussian King Wilhelm himself was on holiday. The next morning Benedetti staged a diplomatic ambush, while the king was out for his morning walk. In a face-to-face exchange, polite but cool, Benedetti relayed French demands. Not only was King Wilhelm to publicly renounce the Hohenzollern candidacy for the Spanish throne, he was also to publicly promise France that Prussia would never pursue the Spanish throne at any time in the future.[16] The king dismissed Benedetti's request as impossible, the matter was closed, and with a tip of his hat, the king continued his stroll.

Back in Berlin, Otto von Bismarck was distraught. Prince Leopold's withdrawal, while France blustered and threatened, was a "slap in the face." Prussian weakness would surely push the southern German states away from unification, spoiling Bismarck's carefully cultivated dream. Later that day, the dark clouds seemed to give way; Bismarck had found a way to salvage Prussian pride. Over dinner with General Moltke, the Prussian chief of staff, and General Roon, the war minister, he produced a tautly worded version of the telegram the king had transmitted to the foreign ministry, reporting the exchange in Bad Ems. In its edited form—the notorious "Ems Telegram," which Bismarck released publicly—the French insult was crisp and Prussian defiance was sharp.[17] And this defiance had its intended effect: Just days later the French government declared war on Prussia, and both sides mobilized for the coming clash.

Napoleon III rolled the dice on the preventive war option. At the time, this decision didn't seem like a wild military gamble, given the widespread belief that the odds were in France's favor. Despite Prussia's victory over Austria four years earlier, France was still considered to have the best army in the world. Its soldiers were now supplied with a superior rifle, and France maintained a large standing force that—in theory—could be moved into combat positions in fourteen days, while the Prussian army, relying heavily on reserve forces, might need seven weeks to mobilize and move to the front.[18]

But the fight ended disastrously for both Napoleon III and his empire. The French movement to the front was a confused mess, its military leadership was incompetent and riddled with interpersonal rivalries, and once deployed to the frontier, the French Army of the Rhine went into a defensive crouch that gave Prussia the extra time it needed to fully prepare for war. General Moltke's genius for planning, mobilization, and the logistics of large-scale warfare proved decisive once again. Universal conscription gave Prussia the ability to mobilize a force twice as large as the French standing army, with better-disciplined and -trained soldiers. Prussia had the most advanced artillery in the field, with tactics that produced devastating effects on French formations. Within weeks of the opening shots of this war, Prussia and its German allies rolled through northeastern France, and the French Second Empire collapsed. Prussian power shattered expectations on the battlefield, but what's really important about this war is how it shattered expectations of the great power game.

A quick survey of the seismic shift in the European power structure between 1866 and 1871 has to lead to one critical question: How did Prussia get away with it without provoking a counterbalancing reaction from the other great states of Europe? Consider what had changed in just five years. Not only was the center of Germanic power torn from the Hapsburg Empire of Austria by an increasingly confident and capable Prussia, but the Kingdom of Prussia itself had morphed into the German Empire. In 1860, the Prussian population was less than half that of France; in 1866 it was half that of Austria. The Prussian-German population more than doubled between 1866 and 1871 when unification linked an additional twenty million Germans to the nineteen million populating the Prussian Kingdom. The thirty-nine million subjects of the new German Empire now topped the population of France at thirty-five million and Austria at thirty-three million. The territory under Prussian control swelled in size by over one-third. In the immediate aftermath of unification the German economy expanded faster than it had in the previous twenty years, decades already marked by rapid industrial and financial growth. Germany surpassed France in steel and coal production and railroad construction. Between 1866 and 1870 Prussia tripled the size of its armed forces by extending mandatory conscription across all states within the North German Confederation. Every German male was expected to serve three years on active duty, four years in the reserves, and an additional five years in the *Landwehr* national guard, giving Prussia the ability to mobilize an army of more than eight hundred thousand soldiers. In 1871, with universal conscription extended across the entire empire, which included the southern German states of Baden, Wurttemberg, and Bavaria, Germany could now field an army over one million strong.[19] And these were not just abstract numbers suggesting latent power potential. It took the Prussian army of 1866 less than three weeks after a declaration of war to strike the decisive blow at the Battle of Königgrätz that opened an easy path to Vienna. Just six weeks after the first major engagement against France in the summer of 1870, the German army had Paris under siege. And these were not close calls. Prussia dominated on the battlefield. Benjamin Disraeli, the Conservative opposition leader in the British House of Commons, bluntly summed up the meaning of these changes: "[T]he balance of power has been entirely destroyed."[20]

In the grand tradition of European power politics, such a sudden, massive, and vivid display of shifting strength should have set in motion a vigorous response by other European states, driven by an understandable fear of the aggressive potential of this new behemoth in the center of the Continent. We would expect Europe-wide rumblings about new alliance arrangements and military staff consultations, a shifting of armies alert and ready to defend against Germany's next moves. We might expect changes in conscription laws to make additional reserve manpower available in future wars, or investment in the kinds of force structure and military technology that would stand up to Germany's proven martial abilities. Surprisingly, this is not at all what we find. Admittedly, most European capitals were unhappy with certain German demands; perhaps Germany was digging too deeply as it extracted French concessions in the peace talks. But there was no tightening of alliances, no movement of countering armies, no military staff talks or panicked reassessments of military spending. No European state stepped in to help shore up France's teetering position in the balance of power or sustain its ability to keep the new German empire in check. The general European reaction to Germany's overwhelming victory, France's crushing defeat, and the power shift this enabled was simply to tolerate it. And this tolerance sprang directly from a consensus belief that Prussia was blameless, forced into war by reckless French belligerency. Perhaps, many proposed, France even deserved to suffer the consequences of its aggressive behavior.

Bismarck had long recognized that culpability for any future war had to fall in France's lap. In his memoirs Bismarck recalled his conversation the night he edited the Ems telegram, when he acknowledged that his version of the telegram, once it was released to the press and Prussian embassies around Europe, would "have the effect of a red rag upon the Gallic bull." There's no doubt that Bismarck wanted to goad the bull into a charge, in order to spur the southern German states into making a political home within Prussia's orbit. But strategic success in the coming war, he said, "essentially depends upon the impression which the origination of the war makes upon us and others; it is important that we should be the party attacked."[21] With the security paradox in mind, Bismarck knew that the question of war with France could not rest on military calculations alone. The most important variable would be the *political* reaction of other European states. The entire enterprise could fail—even if Prussia beat France in the anticipated duel—if Prussia were seen as the aggressor. As he told a confidant, Prussia must accept war with France only if "we appear to the rest of Europe as the injured party, acting in justified self-defense."[22]

And when that moment came, Bismarck's political instincts paid off exactly as he intended. At home, parliamentary deputies across the political spectrum, to include Social Democrats, voted for war credits to fund the conflict, while Socialist newspapers and labor associations rallied behind this war of self-defense.[23] At the pan-German level, the southern German states had made it clear that their alliance commitments to Prussia and the North German Confederation would only kick in if the Germans faced a defensive war. The French declaration of war on July 19 and the French army's brief penetration of German territory two weeks later neatly solved this alliance requirement. Not only did the southern states throw their fortunes in with Prussia, strengthening Prussia's military position for the coming fight, but their decision kept Austria on the sidelines of the war, unwilling to seek its revenge for Königgrätz while German states across Central Europe joined together to repulse French aggression. But most important from a strategic perspective, fighting for the common defense against France opened a door to German unification, the very political goal that motivated Bismarck's embrace of war.[24]

Finally, at the international level, in both London and Saint Petersburg the crisis was seen as a deliberate French effort to stoke preventive war, what British ambassador Lord Lyons said was the result of France's slow-burning determination to "have it out with Prussia sooner or later."[25] Just a week before France declared war, Lord Lyons had warned Paris about the dangers of this power shift showdown. Once the Prussian prince had turned away from the Spanish crown, it "wholly changed the position of France . . . I said that France would have public opinion throughout the world against her and her antagonist would have all the advantage of being manifestly forced into war, in self-defense, to repel attack."[26] What *advantage* did Prussia enjoy by being "forced" to fight a war of self-defense? The other great powers simply left it alone as German forces tore through the French Second Empire, as the French nation was broken and humiliated, as the new German empire scrambled the European power structure in a profound, sudden, and unambiguous way.[27]

A PERVERSE VICTORY

If the story of the Franco-Prussian War ended here, it would seem natural to conclude that it was simply a smashing military and political success for Prussia and its German allies. Victory allowed Otto von Bismarck to forge a unified German empire in the heart of Europe, and to do so without provoking any sort of backlash from the other great powers. But the story does not end here. By squeezing France in peace through annexation of the border regions of Alsace and Lorraine, Bismarck was planting the seeds of a grievance that left France burning for revenge. Deep hostility percolated for decades, sometimes more vividly in German fears than in actual French politics, saddling Germany with a persistent threat that would swell every time the enemy's military power expanded and its political will to act on these grievances intensified.

For many senior German leaders the solution to this nagging problem seemed obvious: Every time French capabilities grew, Germany must strike it down once again. This preventive war impulse became Bismarck's problem in the years after 1871. He was haunted by the consequences of this unstable peace, and for the next twenty years he struggled to manage both sides of the rivalry—the threat of a French war of revenge, and the threat of the preventive war paradox that would generate greater dangers in the future if he could not keep the champions of preventive war in his own government in check. Bismarck's persistent bureaucratic struggle to hold back this temptation is why we remember the Iron Chancellor as the great opponent of preventive war, and rightfully so. Yet in an ironic twist, Bismarck himself, as the architect of the peace imposed on France, was responsible for creating the political conditions that agitated France so severely, sowing the "dragon's teeth" that made future war seem even more likely than it would have been if Germany and France were mere rivals jockeying uneasily for power and influence in Europe.

Bismarck had been warned about the dangers of a punitive peace. French general Emmanuel Felix de Wimpffen, who had the sad duty of surrendering the French army after Napoleon III was captured, told Bismarck that a heavy peace would create perpetual insecurity. It "would throw back the slow civilization of Europe," he predicted, "and awaken all the dormant instincts of revenge. There would be wars without end."[28] Russian leaders were particularly vocal on this point; what really mattered was not the growth of German power but whether Germany would pursue a postwar political order that would yield sustainable peace.

In the first weeks of the Franco-Prussian War, Russian foreign minister Alexander Gorchakov argued that "the establishment of peace on a just and durable basis" depended on "arrangements which both parties could accept without an intention of disturbing them as soon as they might be strong enough to do so." Specifically, he worried that "if Prussia should commit so great an error as to annex territory," thinking that it would secure itself for the future against French aggression, it would inevitably discover that it had instead created "a constant source of weakness and embarrassment to Germany, and a germ of future wars." Echoing General Wimpffen, the Russian tsar warned King Wilhelm that future security would not come from crushing superiority over France, "only [in] an honorable and just peace." The Austrians too recognized the consequences of German annexations, but perhaps unsurprisingly Austrian leaders saw this as an advantage. As long as France harbored thoughts of revenge, Germany would be forced to look fearfully westward, and limit its ambitions to the east.[29]

But Bismarck knew this. He had articulated these exact points in the years leading up to this moment. Three years before victory at Sedan he asserted, "I shall avoid this war" with France for "as long as I can; for I know that once started, it will never cease."[30] Less than a year before war actually broke out, Bismarck forecast the very situation he later faced. "If Prussia were to gain the victory over France," he mused, "what would be the result?" "Supposing we did win in Alsace, we should have to maintain our conquest and to keep Strasbourg perpetually occupied. This would be an impossible position, for in the end the French would find new allies—and then we might have a bad time!"[31] And yet Bismarck made this "impossible position" a reality. So does this mean he had forgotten his long-standing fear that pursuing domination would create a swirl of anti-Prussian alliance formation and undermine everything else he had accomplished on behalf of Prussian power, prestige, and security?

Bismarck's speech to the newly created German Reichstag on May 2, 1871, reveals why he took this fateful step. Annexation was no mere opportunistic land-grab or war trophy for the victor. True to his Clausewitzian orientation, Bismarck justified this dangerous element of the peace as essential for securing the war's key political goal: unification of the southern German states within the German Empire. By war's end, he realized that the unification project made a defensive buffer imperative to meet the security demands of the new Germany's southern tier. Bismarck noted that geographically, Alsace and Lorraine created a wedge of French territory stabbing eastward, like the tip of a broad sword physically prying apart and separating the southern German states from the North German Confederation. He thought this wedge was a more dangerous geographic feature than the Main River, the traditional political border between northern and southern Germany.

Bismarck quoted at length from a conversation he had had fifteen years earlier with the king of Württemberg, who said, "Give us Strasbourg," the main city of Alsace, "and we will be united for all eventualities, but as long as Strasbourg is a sally port for a power which is continuously armed, I must fear that my country will be inundated by foreign troops . . . As long as [Strasbourg] is not German," he warned, "it will always be a hindrance to South Germany giving itself, without reservation, to German unity."[32] In a fascinating foreshadowing, in mirror image, of the strategic dilemma created in the Rhineland by the victorious powers after World War I, Bismarck argued that simply turning Alsace and Lorraine into a demilitarized zone, while allowing France to maintain sovereignty over these border regions, would be like kicking a hornet's nest without actually eliminating the threat. It would "stir up French passions" and guarantee a French challenge, because it "establishes an obligation on foreign ground and soil, a very oppressive and troublesome burden on the feelings of sovereignty, of independence."[33] The only option, as Bismarck saw it, with the vulnerabilities and fears of southern German states in mind, was to create a fully German-controlled buffer zone by ripping away Alsace and Lorraine forever.

STUNG BY THE PREVENTIVE WAR TEMPTATION

For the remainder of his life, Bismarck never spoke or wrote openly with regret about the annexation of French territory. But the consequences of this decision tormented him until he left office two decades later. By using war and territorial conquest to solve one problem Bismarck had created another one. From this point forward, the Iron Chancellor was afflicted by an unshakable fear of French revanchism. In a secret cable in 1874 he stated his vision of the future bluntly: "[N]o one can be under any illusion about the fact that when France is strong enough to break the peace, peace will be at an end."[34] There was nothing Bismarck could do to soothe French hostility, short of releasing Alsace and Lorraine. This option was impossible. Controlling the French threat then became a matter of suppressing French power. And France would not give Bismarck much time to figure out how to do this.

By 1873, German leaders could not ignore how rapidly their enemy was recovering from defeat—economically, politically, and militarily. General Moltke added a sense of urgency by circling a date on the calendar; in 1877, he predicted, Germany's window of opportunity for action would close, France would be ready for its war of revenge, and 100,000 more German soldiers would die in that later war than if Germany took the fight to France today.[35] By 1875 the pressure to break the momentum behind French recovery had reached a crisis point. And the strange scheme Bismarck devised to solve the problem—a scheme that violated his own strategic principles—led him into the worst foreign policy blunder of his long career.

The signs of growing French power were unmistakable. Its economy had rebounded from the war with remarkable speed, allowing the French government to pay off its five-billion-franc war indemnity ahead of schedule. In 1871 Bismarck had believed that the magnitude of this financial burden would be a drag on the French economy for many years to come, undermining its ability to reinvest in military power. Better yet, as long as France delayed payments, the peace treaty allowed German occupation troops to remain planted on French territory. On September 16, 1873, with the payments complete, Germany lost this coercive tool when the last of its troops marched out of the French fortress city of Verdun to begin the journey home.[36] Even more alarming was a military bill working its way through the French parliament that would reorganize the army by adding an extra battalion to each regiment. General Moltke's assessment for the Kaiser was that reorganization would quickly add 144,000 soldiers to the French army's ranks, allowing France to field nineteen army corps compared to Germany's eighteen corps, while each French corps would have eight more battalions than Germany's.[37]

The consensus in the German government was that the very purpose of French army expansion was to fight a war of revenge. It was impossible for France to sustain the high costs of these heavier forces for the indefinite future, they reasoned, so the only plausible rationale was to open a temporary window of superiority in the near term for launching an offensive.[38] In February 1875 the German government learned that France had agents abroad to purchase ten thousand saddle horses to equip its growing military. The specter of saddle horse proliferation might seem quaint today, when our fears of secret nuclear weapons programs can bring states to the brink of war. But to Otto von Bismarck, this intelligence fed his conclusion that France was preparing for conflict, so he ordered an embargo on German horses destined for France.[39]

With the clock ticking on their own shrinking window of opportunity, German military leaders talked of preventive war; the general staff had been developing plans for such a war since 1872. How else could Germany suppress the growth of French power? In April 1875, rumors reached the German ambassador in Paris, who dutifully reported back to Bismarck, that "high-placed [German] officers, including Minister of War Kameke, assert that Germany must attack France before being attacked by her and that, if war was not already unavoidable, the best course would be to begin it next year." Back in Berlin, this was no secret. In fact, General Moltke was advocating preventive war directly with the Kaiser and the chancellor, in the words of the crown prince, "urgently and insistently."[40] Around town, Moltke began to ask politicians how "the country [would] take it if he should start an offensive war before the year was over."[41]

With the military talking openly of war, Bismarck quietly poked the coals feeding the growing excitement over what Germany might be preparing for France; those rumors and questions spread among Berlin elites, within diplomatic circles and in foreign capitals. His objective was to stoke a perceived crisis intense enough that the French and other European leaders would come to *believe* Germany was at the tipping point of a preventive war decision, without ever intending to push for war within the German government. He worked to keep his personal role hidden, and whenever confronted on the question Bismarck flatly denied any interest in the preventive war option. He tipped his hand slightly to the Kaiser, knowing the Kaiser firmly opposed war and worried about Bismarck's intentions. While disavowing any preventive war temptation, Bismarck still insisted France must believe a German preventive war was possible. We must not "give an antagonist the assurance," he said, "that whatever happens one will wait for *his* attack."[42] It is fair to say that this part of Bismarck's plan was a success.

Bismarck's crisis came to a full boil in April and May, when European newspapers and diplomats buzzed about agitation at the highest levels over the promise of preventive war to solve its power-shift problem. On Bismarck's secret orders, a story appeared on April 8 in the Berlin newspaper *Die Post*—with a headline that screamed "Is War in Sight?"—laying out the dangers of rising French power and hostility and suggesting that a German preventive attack might be necessary in response.[43] The foreign diplomatic corps in Germany was convinced that Bismarck was preparing for war. British ambassador Odo Russell didn't need convincing. A year and a half earlier he had informed London about Bismarck's frustration with French recovery; according to his December 1873 report, the chancellor declared "he would greatly prefer to fight it out at once and declare war [on France] tomorrow than wait until they were prepared to attack."[44] Bismarck launched a well-coordinated campaign to spread this same message beyond Berlin and ensure that German ambassadors repeated it in London, Saint Petersburg, and Vienna.[45]

As rumors swirled, French anxiety over Germany's plans intensified after a conversation between Élie de Gontaut-Biron, the French ambassador to Germany, and Joseph Maria von Radowitz, a Bismarck confidant, during a dinner hosted by the British ambassador in Berlin on April 21. Radowitz was known for his candor after a few glasses of wine, and over this well-lubricated dinner he gave the French ambassador an earful on Germany's predicament. In a harangue Gontaut-Biron took as a direct reflection of Bismarck's personal attitude, Radowitz insisted that the resentment France "naturally feels at the loss of" Alsace and Lorraine would "drive her inexorably to declare war on Germany." And "if we have allowed France to revive, to expand," asked Radowitz, "have we not everything to fear?" "If France's inmost thoughts are bent on revenge—and it cannot be otherwise," Radowitz said, "why wait to attack her until she has gathered her forces and contracted alliances?"[46] The French ambassador faithfully reported these comments in detail to the French foreign ministry.

Bismarck's objective in promoting such talk was to achieve the same strategic goal that would be pursued through an actual preventive attack: to stifle improvements in French military capabilities and deflate its political will to launch a war of revenge. He expected the threat to have this effect along two axes: through the domestic politics of France and the international politics of Europe. Two years earlier, Bismarck saw political changes within the French government as a troubling sign of hardening French attitudes on war. In April 1873, French president Adolphe Theirs, a steadfast opponent of war with Prussia in 1870, resigned after losing a no-confidence vote in parliament. He was succeeded by Patrice de MacMahon, a distinguished French general who held deep affection for the royal Bourbon dynasty. In Bismarck's imagined future, should MacMahon and his monarchist supporters overthrow the republican government, France would once again become an attractive alliance partner among the conservative European states, Russia first among them. Bismarck also worried that as a devout Catholic, MacMahon would find sympathy in Italy and Spain.

Even without these allies, Bismarck predicted that a monarchic regime in France would be more prone to act on the desire for revenge than a moderate republican government.[47] Rumors of a possible German war, Bismarck hoped, would lead to MacMahon's ouster, sent packing for antagonizing Germany and risking attack. Internationally, Bismarck predicted that Britain and Russia would be so worried about the destabilizing consequences of another Franco-German conflict that they would put immense pressure on France to scale back its military growth and give up its plans for revenge.[48] Whatever led him to believe this audacious diplomatic gambit would work remains a mystery. What we do know is that this so-called War-in-Sight crisis was a test run of preventive war paradox logic—and that the scheme backfired badly. What Bismarck discovered is that the mere idea of a German preventive war was enough to provoke vigorous counterbalancing by the other great powers. Bismarck created the very threat he feared most—an anti-German coalition of great states that closed ranks to check German power.

Radowitz's dinner harangue was the tipping point in this crisis. With the French ambassador's report on the conversation in hand, the French foreign minister, Louis, duc Decazes, turned the tables on Bismarck. Decazes ordered his diplomatic corps to raise an alarm against German hostility, declaring it a fierce threat to French "national existence." He called for Russian diplomatic intervention to block Germany's aggressive intentions, and he fed the press with information to broadcast the threat of war more widely.[49] On May 6 the *Times* of London ran an exposé written by its Paris correspondent, but inspired by Decazes, which warned about a "powerful party" in Germany "comprising the whole military element, which thinks

Germany concluded a bad Treaty" in 1871, since it "only half crushed the enemy." The article captured Germany's dilemma perfectly: If it tried to maintain dominance over France through arms racing alone, to "defend for fifty years the conquests she made in six months," Germany "risks exhaustion." But the alternative—preventive war—would blacken its reputation and saddle Germany with all the political risks that aggression inevitably drags along with it.[50]

For its part, the British government—from Queen Victoria on down—heaped criticism on every hint of the preventive war temptation circulating within Germany, and Bismarck was left in no doubt about the damaging political effects an actual preventive war would generate. Over a year earlier, Queen Victoria wrote to Kaiser Wilhelm to remind him that as a largely Protestant nation, English "sympathies would be entirely with Germany in any difference with [Catholic] France, *unless*" it appeared that Germany was tempted to use its "greatly superior force to crush and annihilate a beaten foe, and thus to endanger the belief that a strong and united Germany was not, after all, the expected mainstay of European peace." "Be *magnanimous*," she beseeched him.[51] In the midst of the crisis Queen Victoria wrote to her daughter, the wife of the German crown prince, that despite her desire for a close relationship with Germany, she worried Chancellor Bismarck was becoming "so overbearing, violent, grasping and unprincipled" that this was impossible. "*All* agreed," she reported, "that he was becoming like the first Napoleon whom Europe had to join in putting down."[52]

Prime Minister Benjamin Disraeli concurred: "Bismarck is really another old Bonaparte again, and he must be bridled." The day the *Times* of London warned of preventive war agitation in Germany, Disraeli directed Lord Derby, his foreign secretary, to explore the prospects of an alliance with Russia, and perhaps Austria and Italy, to contain German ambitions.[53] In a letter to the queen, Lord Derby summed up the political danger Bismarck faced in stark terms. In 1870, he recalled, "France was the aggressor, and the opinion of Europe went with Germany." But if their roles are now reversed, "if France is to be attacked without provocation, merely in order that she may not have an opportunity of making herself troublesome hereafter, there will be in all countries, and in no country more strongly than in England, a protest against the abuse of force, and a common jealousy, inspired by the sense of a common danger."[54]

The crisis came to a humiliating end for Bismarck on May 10, during a previously scheduled visit to Berlin by Russian tsar Alexander II and Alexander Gorchakov, now the Russian chancellor. With France and Britain urging him on, Gorchakov seized this opportunity. Bismarck naturally denied he was responsible for the unnerving sound of war drums echoing through the German press. The crisis was a fiction, he insisted, promoted by stock market speculators and excitable newspaper editors, and he blamed Moltke for spreading rumors of war. Bismarck accused the French ambassador of inventing his dinner conversation with Radowitz, and if the story were true, his support for preventive war did not reflect Bismarck's own views on the problem. Most important, Bismarck denied Germany had any intention of disturbing European peace by launching a new war against its Gallic rival. To Bismarck's dismay, his Russian counterpart pounced on this simple statement, declaring to the world that it was a promise extracted from one great power by another, Russia—the arbiter of European peace—holding German power in check.[55] Three weeks later, with his pride bruised and his nerves frayed by stress, the Iron Chancellor retreated from Berlin to his country estate, where he remained in relative isolation for five months.

For Bismarck, the War-in-Sight crisis was a turning point on the question of preventive war. Whatever ambivalence he felt about its utility going into this crisis was broken by the European reaction, cementing his strategic opposition to preventive war for the rest of his career. Many years later, when he reflected on the War-in-Sight crisis in his memoirs, Bismarck dismissed the notion that he was ever tempted to lash out against France. From his account we hear that this decision had nothing to do with estimates of relative military capabilities, the battlefield risks Germany would face, or the likelihood of operational success. In fact, Bismarck acknowledged that the empire's military leaders had high confidence in their ability to dominate France once again in combat.[56]

But Bismarck also knew that Germany could not escape the political logic of this war. In a Reichstag speech on February 9, 1876, Bismarck asked, how could I

> come to the conclusion after my long political experience to commit the colossal political stupidity to come before you and say: it is possible that we will be attacked in a few years, so we should anticipate this move by attacking our neighbor and tear them to pieces before they are completely ready—if you will, commit suicide because I am worried about dying? I could not answer what observers would demand to know: what was the actual *casus belli*?[57]

His memoirs frame the German security problem and the preventive war temptation this way: Foreign states, Bismarck said, "tolerate the new development of German power, and . . . regard [it] with a benevolent eye," particularly "after the astonishing proofs of the nation's military strength" in 1866 and 1870, only because of the subsequent "peaceful character of German policy." War in 1875, "which could have had no other motive than preventing France from recovering her breath and her strength," would have destroyed this tolerance for Germany's new position. "A war of this kind," he explained,

> could not, in my opinion, have led to permanently tenable conditions in Europe, but might have brought about an agreement between Russia, Austria, and England, based upon mistrust of us, and leading eventually to active proceedings against the new and unconsolidated empire . . . Europe would have seen in our proceedings a misuse of our newly acquired power; and the hand of everyone . . . would have been permanently raised against Germany, or at any rate been ready to draw the sword.[58]

For Bismarck, the character of the peace that would follow preventive war, even with victory secured on the battlefield, would have been worse than what he expected from the peace that would follow the continued rise of French power. This was a problem he would just have to address with a different set of strategic options.

BISMARCK HOLDS THE LINE

As Bismarck's long odyssey at the highest rungs of political leadership was (unknowingly) drawing to a close, Germany faced one more great war scare between 1886 and 1888. It was an eerie preview of the strategic turbulence that underpinned the march to war in 1914, when German fears of being crushed between the colossal power of Russia and its French ally fed the preventive war temptation, with its promise of relief from future danger through decisive action. In the summer of 1886 all of the comfortable assumptions about the threat environment were swept away. No longer could German leaders find solace in the fact that France was isolated as a threat, that no matter how intensely the French revanchist spirit might flare, Germany could focus its crosshairs against an enemy that had no allies to mobilize for a fight. In 1886 it seemed that Russia was rethinking its relationships: Anti-German sentiment was on the rise, along with a burst of pan-Slavic ethnic pride; Russian empire-builders had an appetite for increasingly muscular methods to dominate the Balkans, even at the risk of war with Austria; and, most worrisome, the increasingly prominent Russian voices calling for alliance ties with France became impossible to ignore. The nightmare of a two-front war against the great powers on Germany's flanks no longer seemed to be the abstract worst-case scenario it had been for decades. As perceptions of future dangers intensified, the apostles of preventive war emerged once again within powerful circles of the German government, and they were looking to seize the moment to break the threat of encirclement. To Bismarck, his compatriots' perception of the threat and their fear of a coming war were not groundless or overblown. He did not need convincing that dangers were on the rise. Despite his own fears and his resolve to meet the challenge, the Iron Chancellor stood firm and virtually alone throughout this crisis, like a levy holding back the pressure of the preventive war temptation that rose up around him.

While rising German angst would eventually focus the preventive war gunsights on Russia, the catalyst for crisis was found in France—more precisely, with a man who became known as "General Revanche." Gen. Georges Boulanger was a Legion of Honor–winning French army officer, a dashing thirty-year veteran of wars that spanned the globe, from Indochina to the Mediterranean, from the desperate fight against Prussia in 1870 to the struggle at home to save the new Third Republic from the radicals of the Paris Commune following defeat in 1871. But most ominously, General Boulanger personified *revanche*, that smoldering determination to salvage French honor and repatriate its lost territory.

In January 1886, General Boulanger became French war minister; by the summer he was a sensation. "Almost absolute in power," the *New York Times* correspondent reported from Paris. "Idolized by the army, petted by the populace, and feared by his colleagues."[59] And what a season he had. The country was transfixed by his campaign to strip royalist army officers of their commissions and rid the republic of the monarchist threat. He dazzled the throngs gathered on July 14 for the Bastille Day parade, on his black horse in full dress uniform, leading columns of soldiers just returned from a victorious campaign against China to secure French colonial control of Tonkin in Southeast Asia. He fought a pistol duel to defend his honor against a senator's charge of cowardice, while a massive crowd waited at the War Ministry to celebrate his bravery. Boulanger fever spread through popular songs and Boulanger-themed memorabilia—five-franc notes, pins, ties, and carved wooden pipe bowls. His portrait appeared in shop windows throughout Paris, and even outsold pictures of Louis Pasteur, the reigning national hero. He boldly broke decorum by attending cabinet meetings in full uniform with a saber at his hip. And he gave French nationalists tough talk: "[P]lace me at the head of the army and France will subjugate the world," he promised. For the League of Patriots, which pushed fervently for war against Germany, this was gold. Its members secretly urged Boulanger to overthrow the cautious French government in a coup d'état to make this dream possible, while the newspapers were filled with speculation about Boulanger's Napoleonic aspirations.[60]

There was more to the Boulanger phenomenon than the carnival atmosphere that swirled around him. He initiated serious military reforms that observers agreed had a potent impact on the capabilities of the French army. He purchased 40,000 magazine-fed repeating rifles and pushed testing of a new chemical explosive with greater destructive power than the gunpowder used in artillery and mortar shells. He introduced a new recruitment bill that would add 44,000 soldiers to the army's ranks, brought home thousands of troops serving in colonial outposts to strengthen French forces on the Continent, and built new barracks on the eastern frontier to house the growing number of French soldiers sent to garrison duty near the German border. The military maneuvers he organized in the late summer were widely praised by foreign observers for their realism and sophisticated tactics. For the following year he planned to stage an ambitious test of the entire French army's readiness for war: a drill that would rehearse full mobilization with an entire corps, without revealing which corps would be selected or the date of mobilization until the moment the exercise was put in motion. General Boulanger happily reported that "at length we can abandon the miserable defensive policy and henceforth boldly assume the offensive."[61] Looking to the future, *La France Militaire*, a professional journal staffed by Boulangists, predicted that by 1891 General Revanche "will make the German princes tremble on their thrones."[62]

Bismarck, if he had replied directly, would likely have scoffed with indignation at such an insulting swipe at German courage. During one of his most memorable chest-thumping speeches to the Reichstag in early 1888 he declared famously, to a roar of approval, "We Germans fear God, but nothing else in the world." Nonetheless, the Iron Chancellor treated this revanchist flare-up as the most threatening turn in French politics in fifteen years. In one of Bismarck's most important speeches, delivered in the Reichstag on January 11, 1887, he drew from that timeless theme to explain the problem: Germany faced an inherently uncertain future, he said, and uncertainty alone demands bold steps to guarantee security against the threats that could emerge. The current French government has no stomach for a replay of the last great clash with Germany, Bismarck acknowledged, but French aggression could erupt with little warning. "Boulangists" were circling hungrily around the Third Republic, waiting for their man to seize power and pursue their collective dream through force of arms. Perhaps French leaders would turn to violent revanchism to distract their people from domestic troubles. Its military leaders might optimistically miscalculate their present strength and decide the time was right for a Rhineland rematch. What if French rulers exploited a faraway war between Russia and Austria as a ripe moment to liberate Alsace and Lorraine? The "epoch of frontier warfare with the French nation . . . is not at an end." We have no choice, he declared, but to fear war with France, "whether it be in ten days or in ten years." Less than three weeks later *Die Post*, the same Berlin newspaper that stoked the crisis of 1875, announced that Europe was "On the Razor-Blade" edge of war.[63] According to *Die Post*, General Boulanger's position "is becoming unassailable . . . He can only govern the situation by keeping up the warlike impetus he has given it."[64]

The German General Staff was less frantic in its assessment of the French threat, confident that military superiority would once again crush the French army in a clash limited to a Western battlefield.[65] But it was not a fight with France alone that German leaders now feared. The scenario that still plagued the German military and Otto von Bismarck was the dreaded two-front war that would force Germany to hold back a French attack to recover Alsace and Lorraine in the west while throwing a large force into combat with Russia in the east. For years, Bismarck successfully kept this scenario from crystallizing by nurturing a healthy relationship with the Russian empire. And he had plenty of common ground to build on. It had been nearly seventy years since Russia had joined forces with Prussia in the coalition that broke Napoleon's iron grip on Europe, but the warm glow of victory in a grand common cause had lingered for decades between these wartime partners.[66] Russia and Germany had an explicit common interest in suppressing the dangers of Polish nationalism, dating back nearly one hundred years to the day Russia and Prussia first sliced and absorbed large sections of Poland in 1793. Their conservative rulers stood shoulder to shoulder in defense of monarchy in an epic struggle to hold back liberal and radical political forces across Europe. When it came to disputes serious enough to spark a great power war, Russian sights were set on its southern flank, around the northern rim of the Black Sea, in the straits leading to the Mediterranean, and in the Balkans, specifically Bulgaria. This was Austria's problem, not Germany's. To make sure the Russians were clear on this point, Bismarck repeatedly said that Germany had no direct interest here, even throwing active German support into Russian expansionist schemes.[67] And Russian-German ties ran deeper than mere political interests: Until an assassin's bomb ended his life in 1881, Russia's Tsar Alexander II genuinely adored his uncle, Prussian king and German emperor Wilhelm I.

German support for Russian interests in the south came with one serious caveat: Russia could not pummel Austria in the process. While Germany did not care about Bulgaria, it did care about Austria as a great state potent enough to help contain Russian power in the broader European system. Now this became Russia's problem, because war with Austria was indeed where the contest over the Balkans might lead. And the Russians were not alone in this forecast; observers in capitals across Europe considered war virtually inevitable. Russia provided plenty of concrete support for this prediction by massing troops along a 140-mile fortified and entrenched section of Austria's Polish frontier.[68] With France in the grip of Boulanger fever and revisionist agitation, the moment seemed ripe for Russia to reach out for an eagerly waiting ally in the west that could draw off German combat power in the east.

Russian foreign minister Nicholas de Giers tried to assure Bismarck that the new Tsar, Alexander III, had no interest in an alliance with France. But the summer of 1886 offered plenty of evidence to make the Germans nervous. Anti-German attitudes were flowering in the Russian empire. What Bismarck saw was a "public emotion" within Russia throwing its affections toward "all things French" and "outspoken hostility . . . toward all things German." While General Boulanger was parading in Paris, Paul Déroulède, a celebrated French poet, cofounder of the League of Patriots, and a devoted champion of revanchist war, was the toast of Russian military circles in Saint Petersburg. Russian officers cheered his call for Russia and France to fight Germany as a common enemy, while Paris newspapers were "trembling" with the news that the German military attaché didn't receive an invitation from the Tsar to observe military maneuvers in Warsaw.[69] The Russian press widely advocated for an alliance with France, and key members of the Tsar's own government sympathized with this position.[70] How could Tsar Alexander III, who didn't share his late father's familial affections for the German Kaiser, his great-uncle, resist this widening enthusiasm for linking arms with France? Perhaps Bismarck was overstating the threat, but in a letter to Lord Salisbury in November 1887, he put it bluntly. "Given this state of affairs," he wrote to the British prime minister, "we must regard as permanent the danger that our peace will be disturbed by France and Russia."[71]

So the question now before the German government was this: How should Germany meet the "permanent" danger that would only grow worse with time? A remarkably large number of German leaders in both the foreign ministry and the military thought the answer was obvious: preventive war against Russia. Not only was war inevitable, military leaders concluded, but they had their eye on a narrow window of opportunity that would soon shut. Germany's relative military power would peak when they completed a rearmament program in 1888; by 1889 the military edge might be lost.[72] The top two military leaders, General Moltke and Gen. Alfred von Waldersee, Moltke's deputy and eventual successor as chief of the General Staff, disagreed on the character of the necessary fight with the Russian empire. As early as 1885 Waldersee had concluded that security would only be found "in a Great War in which we lastingly cripple an opponent, France or Russia."[73] He was saying the same thing in the summer of 1888 as chief of staff.[74] General Moltke, on the other hand, denied that a crippling war against Russia was possible. He was confident, however, that Germany could beat the Russians with a "series of hammer blows."[75]

Despite their differences over the operational character of the war, they coauthored a memorandum for the Kaiser in late 1887 calling explicitly for a German preventive attack during the coming winter. The memo showcased improvements in the Russian army since its war with the Ottoman Empire a decade earlier, and continuing Russian work on fortifications and railroads in Poland. Moltke and Waldersee insisted "there could be *no doubt* that Russia is arming for immediate war and is preparing the deployment of her army." In his cover letter to Chancellor Bismarck, General Moltke argued that "only if we take the aggressive in company with Austria and at an early date will our chances be favorable."[76] In early December 1887 Waldersee secretly traveled to Vienna to push this idea on the Austrian government; days later he and Moltke met with the Kaiser, without informing Bismarck, to push him in the same direction.[77]

When the official military assessment was phrased this way—that there was *no doubt* Russia was preparing for immediate war—it might seem foolhardy for Germany's political leadership to hold out hope for continued peace and to let the enemy choose the best moment for the clash. Bismarck didn't need convincing that the rising threat demanded an urgent response. But true to form, the Iron Chancellor once again saw the General Staff's call for preventive war as a gross mistake. His response was forceful and unwavering: "[S]o long as I am in office I will never give my consent to a prophylactic attack on Russia."[78] And if Austria launched an offensive against Russia on its own initiative, Germany would leave Austria to meet its fate alone. The chancellor was the only major figure in the entire German government that opposed war. At the age of ninety-one, and closing in on death, Kaiser Wilhelm was in no shape to actively engage in the decision.[79] Despite his isolation in this grand policy debate, Bismarck's opposition alone was enough to shut down the General Staff's urge to begin saber-sharpening for a winter campaign.

This decision was partially rooted in his traditional resistance to "inevitabilities." In fact, Bismarck actually warned the Reichstag that if he ever came before the body predicting an inevitable armed clash with France and Russia, and asked for financial support to pay for preventive war to blunt the threat, they should simply refuse to put their trust in the chancellor's judgment. "Well, gentlemen," he said, "I do not know whether you would have such confidence in me as to grant such a request. *I hope not.*"

On one level, the problem with being swept away by inevitabilities starts at home. How can you rally the nation when it's riddled with doubt and skepticism that the risks and pain of war were actually justified by predictions of a coming attack? "If we in Germany desire to wage a war with the full effect of our national power, it must be a war with which all who help to wage it, and all who make sacrifices for it . . . must be in sympathy. It must be a people's war; it must be a war that is carried on with the same enthusiasm as that of 1870, when we were wickedly attacked." But if the German government plunged into its own preventive attack, he said, "It will be very difficult . . . to make it clear to the provinces, to the federal states and to their people, that a war is inevitable, that it must come. It will be asked: 'Are you so sure of it? Who knows?'"

National unity in war could be the decisive variable on the field of battle. But Bismarck also knew that the preventive war paradox would generate a much deeper problem, even if the German army beat its rivals militarily. Would preventive war actually solve Germany's security problems? Would it leave a better state of peace in its wake? To Bismarck the answer was clear: absolutely not. What would Moltke's successive "hammer blows" yield? " 'Holy Russia' will be filled with indignation at the attack," he warned the Reichstag. "France will glisten with weapons to the Pyrenees. The same thing will happen everywhere."[80]

He made this point fervently to Crown Prince Wilhelm in the spring of 1888, just weeks before his father died and he ascended to the throne. "*Even after a successful war* Germany would *gain nothing*, for Russia would be filled with hatred and desire for revenge, and Germany would be in a hopeless position between two defeated states of great potential military strength."[81] What about Waldersee's "crippling blow"? What would that require? In December 1887, Bernhard von Bulow, the German chargé d'affaires in Saint Petersburg, sketched out an answer that Bismarck found compelling. Preventive war must

> bleed the Russians to such an extent that . . . they will be incapable of standing
> on their legs for twenty-five years. We must stop up Russia's economic sources

for years to come by devastating her black-earth provinces, bombarding her coastal towns, destroying her industry and commerce . . . we must drive Russia back from the two seas—the Baltic and the Black Sea . . . I can only picture to myself a Russia truly and permanently weakened . . . such a peace would only be enforced if we stood on the banks of the Volga,

with both Saint Petersburg and Moscow in Germany's hands. To Bismarck, such an absolute military outcome was absurd. But short of this outcome, Bulow argued, "from a purely political viewpoint, the prospects of war with Russia are not too brilliant . . . if they emerge from the conflict with a black eye, we should be burdened for a very long time with their unassuageable thirst for revenge which would be even stronger than that of the French . . . and in a few years it would start all over again." As a result, Bulow concluded, "it would . . . from a political standpoint certainly be best if we could get along with the Russians." In the margins of the memo Bismarck simply wrote "Yes!"[82]

Political fence-mending with the Russian empire to sooth its agitated nerves, and military strength oriented toward deterrence and defense— these were the two parts of Bismarck's alternative approach for generating real security in the face of legitimate threats from east and west. Bismarck pushed two military bills through the Reichstag in 1887 and 1888, predicting that this money would fund "a million good soldiers to defend each of our frontiers. At the same time we can keep in the rear reserves of half a million and more, or a million even, and we can push these forward as they are needed." But the greatest advantage of this defensive buildup, Bismarck said, is that it would deter any challenger. "The very strength at which we are aiming necessarily makes us peaceful. This sounds paradoxical, but it is true. With the powerful machine which we are making of the German army no aggression will be attempted."[83]

Bismarck's security strategy went one step further. In the spring of 1887, in the midst of the ongoing war scare and rising anti-German tremors in Russia, Bismarck launched a diplomatic initiative to convince the Tsar that there truly was no cause for quarrel between these great powers. In the "Reinsurance Treaty" they negotiated, Russia and Germany promised to remain neutral if the other went to war with a third great power, unless Germany attacked France, or Russia attacked Austria. Russia wouldn't tolerate another German thrashing of France, while in the east Austria would help keep Russian expansionist temptations in check. But the most important feature of the Reinsurance Treaty as a political instrument was explicit German support for Russia's most sensitive security interests on its southern flank. In a secret protocol to the treaty, Germany conceded a "free hand" for Russia to install a friendly government in Bulgaria and pledged military neutrality and diplomatic support should Russia take up arms to defend the entrance of the Black Sea.[84] In the end, the "inevitable" war that the bulk of the German government believed was approaching, the war the General Staff had predicted with "no doubt," simply failed to materialize.

EUROPE AFTER BISMARCK

As Bismarck held the line until this most recent wave of preventive war temptations passed in 1888, Germany was a great power on the edge of a new era, an era dominated by new leaders and a change in strategic direction that would channel Europe's fortunes toward that horribly tragic preventive war of 1914. The year 1888 was the "Year of the Three Emperors." Kaiser Wilhelm I, who had reigned through those miraculous years of military glory and political expansion, but who had resisted the idea of war at each of those decisive moments in his kingdom's history, died in March. His son and successor, the great hope of German and European liberals, would sit on the imperial throne as Kaiser Frederick III for just ninety-nine days, until he too was dead after high-risk surgery on his cancer-infected larynx. Kaiser Wilhelm II would now rule the German empire until defeat and revolution forced him to abdicate in November 1918. Wilhelm II did not share his grandfather's naturally restrained foreign policy instincts or his father's liberal sentiments. German military leadership was on the cusp of change too. Gen. Helmuth von Moltke, the organizational genius that delivered those successive victories for his sovereign, retired as chief of the General Staff in 1888, and he died in April 1891. But the most important signpost marking the end of this era came in March 1890, when Otto von Bismarck, the man at the helm of the Prussian state and Imperial Germany for nearly three decades, was forced into bitter retirement by the young Kaiser.

What did the loss of Bismarck mean for German foreign policy and the European political order? Germany lost his steady commitment to strategic restraint and his sensitivity to the security paradox. Germany lost his persistent voice reminding his colleagues that security depended on making Imperial Germany's power tolerable to the other great states. Germany lost the one leader that intuitively understood the dangers of the preventive war paradox when the preventive war temptation seized other members of the government. Germany lost his diplomatic finesse, that essential tool for maintaining the increasingly complicated political relationships he had crafted across the Continent, the finesse that kept Russia and France from linking arms in an anti-German alliance and Britain detached from Continental affairs. A new generation of political and military leadership brought new ideas about Germany's proper role in the world and a surge of confidence in what its growing economic power could achieve, while new social forces were emerging that championed militarism and imperialism with no understanding of the consequences for European order and German security. This is not an effort to romanticize Bismarck's leadership. But it's hard to deny that the new direction in German foreign policy introduced by this new generation fed a spiral of great-power competition that ended in the catastrophic duel for supremacy in Europe. Just six months before he became Kaiser, Crown Prince Wilhelm complained that "the Chancellor . . . doesn't want another war . . . I shall have to pay the interest on this delay later on," when we are forced to fight Russia after it has grown even more dangerous.[85] That was in 1888, twenty-six years before the Great War erupted in 1914. Bismarck's restraint saved Germany from that earlier, avoidable war. As one of Bismarck's most unrelenting modern critics has conceded, "it is inconceivable that had he been chancellor in 1914 he would have allowed Germany to be dragged into Armageddon."[86]

While there is no straight line linking Bismarck's downfall and World War I, we can map out five basic stages of the twenty-four-year period after Bismarck that are logically connected, in a roughly sequential process, that pushed the world toward war. First, the 1890s were marked by a surge in domestic political agitation over Germany's constrained position in the international system, and rising popular enthusiasm for a militarized foreign policy. Not only did Germany's rapidly expanding economic power seem to demand that the empire elbow its way into the global imperial game, but its growing industrial economy also created a severe political challenge for traditional elites who now had to contend with the demands of a rising labor force and middle class. Imperialism and militarism, key leaders reasoned, could provide a legitimizing national cause that might defuse pressures for reform.[87]

The second phase was a natural consequence of this enthusiasm for imperialism and militarism: concrete initiatives to expand Germany's international position. In 1897 Bernhard von Bulow, now German foreign minister, and on his way to an appointment as chancellor in 1900, announced the empire's aspirations for its "own place in the sun," the goal of Germany's new *Weltpolitik*, a "World Policy" of colonial expansion from China to Africa. To back up these expanding global ambitions, Germany launched a bold naval construction program in 1898 and pursued a provocative challenge to France's imperial claims over Morocco in 1905 and 1911.[88]

The third phase in this sequence is exactly what Bismarck feared most—the creation and tightening of an encircling counter-German alliance linking the Russians, French, and British. It was an outcome Bismarck predicted repeatedly, something he held to be so dangerous to German security that avoiding it became the centerpiece of Germany's foreign policy during his last twenty years in office. The first step toward this German nightmare occurred almost immediately after Bismarck resigned, when the new German government refused to renew the expiring Reinsurance Treaty with Russia. The historian Gordon Craig observes dramatically that with this one decision, "the Russian tie was irretrievably snapped," setting "in train the whole chain of calamity that led toward the catastrophe" of the First World War.[89] Within a year, jubilant Russians welcomed a French fleet in the port of Kronstadt, the seat of the Russian admiralty and the main port for the city of Saint Petersburg. Two years later a Russian fleet paid a visit to France's most important Mediterranean port at Toulon. By 1894 France and Russia were committed to a mutual defense agreement targeting German aggression. Germany's Moroccan adventure of 1905 and an acceleration of its naval construction program pushed Great Britain toward a new military commitment and staff talks with France and into a dogged race to sustain the Royal Navy's dominance against the German challenge. In 1907, Britain and Russia sealed the anti-German Triple Entente by signing a defense agreement of their own, while France was investing in Russia's military recovery, its strategic shift toward the west, and Russia's "Germany first" policy for defense prioritization. Germany's second Moroccan adventure in 1911 simply deepened this political alignment and the defense commitments at its core.[90]

As security dilemma logic would predict, the fourth phase of this process was rising German fear of hostile encirclement and an increasingly desperate search for a way to break the Entente's suffocating embrace. Which brings us to the fifth and final stage in the deadly evolution of German security policy: a resurgence of the preventive war temptation among German leaders seeking a way out of this precarious threat environment. Ironically, German chancellor Theobald von Bethmann Hollweg, putatively at the helm in the critical years leading into World War I, shared more in common with Otto von Bismarck on foreign policy than he did with Kaiser Wilhelm II and the military leadership of 1914. Like Bismarck, Bethmann Hollweg was highly sensitive to the security paradox, arguing that "We must drive forward quietly and patiently in order to regain that trust and

confidence without which we cannot consolidate politically and economically." He considered the naval arms race with Great Britain to be "costly
and self-defeating," and he was convinced that preventive war would not
solve Germany's underlying security problems. From his perspective, only a
political relationship with Britain, freed from suspicion and hostility, could
secure Germany from the triple threat it now faced and restrain the danger
of Russian adventurism.[91]

But unlike Bismarck, Bethmann Hollweg was powerless to check the
Kaiser and the military; his cautious instincts were drowned by the rising
tide of the preventive war temptation that inundated a broad swath of the
German leadership. As Russia shook off the shock of its defeat by Japan
in 1905, a new military spending program in 1912 and 1913 led to predictions that by 1917, Russia would have a reorganized and reequipped army
that could be quickly mobilized and transported westward on a rapidly
expanding network of strategic rail lines stretching toward the German and
Austrian borders.[92]

The logic of war under these conditions was summarized nicely by Gen.
Helmuth von Moltke "the Younger," chief of the General Staff and nephew
of General Moltke "the Elder." Just months before the Great War erupted,
as an aide recalled, Moltke argued that "In two [to] three years Russia
would have completed her armaments. The military superiority of our enemies would then be so great that he did not know how we could overcome
them. Today we would be a match for them. In his opinion there was no
alternative to making preventive war in order to defeat the enemy while we
still have the chance of victory." In time, Chancellor Bethmann Hollweg
himself seemed to accept the dark image of a "future [that] belongs to Russia which grows and grows and becomes an even greater nightmare to us."[93]
Given the defense commitments that linked France to Russia, a preventive blow against Russia alone was impossible. What began as an isolated
regional power play between the Austro-Hungarian empire and Serbia
quickly blew up into a Continent-wide great-power struggle. Germany's
preventive war and its play for security through hegemonic dominance
ended in defeat after four brutal years.

And it's with German defeat in 1918 that the story of the 1936 Rhineland
crisis really begins. Nearly a generation would pass before Adolf Hitler
defied the rules of the postwar order in the Rhineland, sending French
soldiers on a mad rush into the Maginot Line and their leaders into a
diplomatic flurry to build support for preventive war to turn back Hitler's
challenge. We know how this story ends: The crisis spins, it burns itself out,
absorbed within a chain of distracting events in a momentous year, and

Hitler's remilitarization of the Rhineland stands as a fait accompli. We also know of the heavy burden British leaders of the period have carried ever since, blamed for missing that golden moment to stop the horrors of World War II with decisive preventive action. To understand 1936, we must continue our exploration of the evolving European security dilemma; we must move the timeline to 1918 and 1919, to 1923 and 1925. These were years of postwar reconstruction—reconstruction of devastated societies and the political order holding the international system together. They were also years of revolution, occupation, economic chaos, coercion, and resistance. This history weighs heavily on the tragic events that spun into the next world war. This is where we find the roots of British strategic thinking—the belief that the Rhineland demilitarized zone was a time bomb built into the architecture of the postwar order, and that preventive war to preserve it was a strategic dead end.

5

THE ROOTS OF A BITTER PEACE

Neither [side] had won, nor could win, the War. The War had won, and would go on winning.

—Edmund Blunden, 1928

Germany and its allies lost the Great War, but the suffering was shared across the battle lines. Sixty-five million ordinary men were mobilized by their national armies for the fight on both sides. Ten million would be killed, twenty-one million wounded. Eight million civilians died as a direct result of armed conflict. The war was nothing like the rapid offense-driven clash leaders in both camps expected in 1914, who remembered the quick German victories of 1866 and 1870. This disaster was shocking in its ferocity, its scale and duration. What could the world possibly salvage from the horrors of this total war? American president Woodrow Wilson had an answer to this profound question.

No matter what you may think about the details of his plans for the postwar order, it's hard to deny that Wilson was thinking big. In his own memorable words, the president's strategic goal was to turn this tragedy into the "War to End All Wars." If the Great War had any value, Wilson reasoned, it would serve as an enduring showcase for the character of total war in the industrial age. It would convince leaders and their citizens that war could no longer serve as a rational tool of state policy; it would highlight the dangers of traditional balance-of-power politics that fed the conflict.

His vision of a new international political order demanded nothing less than a revolutionary break from this tradition, to save the world from going through such a terrible experience ever again.

To make this vision work, in January 1917 President Wilson appealed for a peculiar-sounding outcome to the war: "peace without victory." Easy for the American president to say, before the United States itself had joined the struggle, but the concept had a logic that Otto von Bismarck would have understood well. Victory, Wilson said, "would mean peace forced upon the loser, a victor's terms imposed upon the vanquished." The danger here is that these terms "would be accepted in humiliation, under duress, at an intolerable sacrifice, and would leave a sting, a resentment, a bitter memory upon which terms of peace would rest not permanently, but only as upon quicksand." British prime minister David Lloyd George saw the problem of peacemaking the same way. He worried about a peace dictated "in a spirit of a savage vendetta" that would produce "mutilation and the infliction of pain and humiliation." Stable peace, he argued, "will depend upon there being no causes of exasperation constantly stirring up either the spirit of patriotism, of justice, or of fair play," which would compel Germany, some-day, to pursue change through violent conflict.[1]

This high-minded concept for peace, no matter how logical, was too much for French leaders to swallow after the German army had chewed up northern France, after millions of young French men died in the trenches—by machine gun, artillery barrage, and poison gas—after Germany had seized 40 percent of French heavy industry that ended up behind the front lines. In the early months of 1919 the Allies wrangled over the details of the treaty among themselves at the Palace of Versailles, outside Paris. The Germans had no seat at the table. And as Woodrow Wilson had feared, it was indeed a "peace forced upon the loser." The German government rejected the treaty's punitive terms immediately, but was then slapped with an ultimatum: either pledge to sign by midnight on June 24, or face a new Allied offensive. Field Marshal Paul von Hindenburg, the German chief of staff, informed the new German president that military resistance was impossible, and the treaty was signed on June 28.

From this rocky start, a pernicious question hung like a dark cloud over Versailles: How long would any of its commands last before the sting, the resentment, the bitter memories pushed the loser to snap these restraints? How long would Germany respect the treaty's limitations on the size of its armed forces, on prohibited classes of weapons, or the new borders drawn by foreign statesmen who had lopped off chunks of its territory? How long would Germany tolerate the vulnerabilities created on its western flank through Rhineland demilitarization? Pessimism and fear of the future—a German challenge was just a matter of time—drove the typical response to these questions. Germans of all political stripes were revisionists hungry to break from this harness.

But then in January 1925, something remarkable happened. German foreign minister Gustav Stresemann launched what he called a "peace offensive" with the Reich's former enemies. In a note to the British government that spoke directly to their fears about this fragile European order, Stresemann said what they all wanted to hear: His goal was simply "to secure peace between Germany and France" with a new, more stable security pact for Western Europe. In October of that year, on the shores of Lake Maggiore in Locarno, Switzerland, the foreign ministers of Germany, France, and Great Britain hammered out a treaty that seemed poised to rescue Europe from the quicksand of Versailles. Most important, the Locarno treaty was constructed, it appeared, on voluntary German acceptance of its truncated position in the international system, a price it seemed the Germans were willing to pay to avoid the tragedies of another Great War. And one of its pillars was Germany's agreement to respect demilitarization of the Rhineland. A signing ceremony in London on December 1 sealed the deal, and British officials were ecstatic. Foreign Minister Austen Chamberlain crowed about the "spirit of Locarno," which, he said, was the "real dividing line between the years of war and the years of peace" in Europe.[2] France gets its Rhineland demilitarized zone, and Germany agrees to preserve it. Adolf Hitler himself, a decade later, reaffirmed Germany's commitment to Locarno and its Rhineland clause. Rhineland demilitarization, the Führer said in March 1935, was Germany's contribution to the "appeasement of Europe." So when Hitler announced, just one year later, that Wehrmacht forces were streaming across the Rhine River, it was the Locarno agreement that French officials shook about angrily, wielding both the spirit and the letter of this treaty as a diplomatic cudgel to rally international condemnation, to hold Hitler accountable for endangering European peace, and to hold Britain accountable for helping France to enforce the treaty's rules.

To this day, the legacy of Locarno has a powerful impact on how the story of the Rhineland crisis is typically told. We're reminded of its origins in a German proposal, that it was voluntarily signed. Its animating spirit would fix the dysfunctions of the dictated Versailles peace; its rules would stabilize the political order, particularly through the DMZ, now seemingly cast in stone as an indelible feature of the European landscape. Even though he promised to respect its rules, Adolf Hitler tore Locarno apart, bringing the world one big step closer to World War II. Many have then asked, what more did the British government need in 1936, both legally and strategically, to justify preventive action that would force the Wehrmacht into retreat and restore the DMZ as a cornerstone of peace and security? What more evidence did they need of Hitler's aggressive plans for the future than this upending of Rhineland restrictions? Why did Britain step back from this opportunity to deliver a heavy blow against German power, when the spirit of Locarno seemed to legitimize war to enforce this vital treaty?

To answer these questions, the coming chapters will linger in the 1920s to tell a story that covers essential details often ignored in the usual rendition of this history. Without them, Britain's choices in 1936 are hard to comprehend.

As we will see, behind the celebrations of 1925 British leaders were wrestling with a more sober assessment of Germany's motives for initiating the talks that led to Locarno and whether the Rhineland demilitarized zone was in fact a stable feature of the international order for the long haul. A stark reality nagged at British leaders from the beginning: Locarno was not the product of an enlightened German willingness to make sacrifices for the common good. Locarno was an act of desperation. While the spirit of Locarno electrified the political world, British leaders were quietly concluding in 1925 and 1926, with good reason, that the Rhineland pledge was impossible to sustain indefinitely, and that using military force to compel German compliance would be a fool's errand. The story of how the British came to this conclusion, and how it fed the belief that preventive war was a strategic dead end when the crisis of 1936 erupted, unfolds in the following pages. To tell this story properly, it's essential to first roll the timeline back by just a few years, to return to those brutal closing months of the Great War and the tortuous effort to construct a viable peace in its wake. Once we do, we'll be in a better position to explain why Germany proposed the "peace offensive" that led to Locarno, and, most important, why British leaders wrote off the viability of the DMZ and preventive war over a decade before Hitler's Rhineland coup.

VICTORY, DEFEAT, REVOLUTION

Within weeks of the opening shots of the Great War, Gen. Erich Ludendorff was on his way to becoming a legend in the German army. In the span of only thirteen days, he had the amazing good fortune to be at the center of the two most important battlefield breakthroughs of the early war, on both the Western and the Eastern Fronts. Ludendorff's fame was sealed in a moment of crisis just two days after the German invasion of Belgium on August 4, 1914.

Ludendorff was the deputy chief of staff for the German 2nd Army, the spearhead of the giant right wing of the invasion force. Its mission was to execute a sweeping envelopment of Paris from the west that, according to a meticulous battle plan, would bring France to its knees in six weeks. Quick victory in the west would then allow the bulk of the German army to pivot eastward and meet the massive Russian army mobilizing more slowly on the other wing of the German empire. But the 2nd Army had a serious problem: Its offensive drive had stalled on the main invasion route to France. A mere thirty-six miles from the German border, the Belgian forts that ringed the city of Liège and protected its roads and rail lines leading south had repulsed repeated German attacks. Ludendorff was on the scene as an observer when the commander of the 14th Infantry Brigade was killed in the fight. Without hesitating, Ludendorff took personal command of the brigade and led its soldiers in the first breakthrough into the city. The newspapers hailed his heroics; readers particularly loved the story of Ludendorff bringing down a Belgian fort by simply pounding on its giant wooden entrance and demanding surrender. The Kaiser awarded him the *Pour le Mérite*, the highest Prussian order for personal valor.

Just one week later, the hero of Liège found himself on the far eastern frontier, chief of staff to Gen. Paul von Hindenburg, who days before had been recalled from a three-year retirement. Their task was to prevent an unfolding disaster by saving the retreating German 8th Army and East Prussia from the advancing Russian 2nd Army. Five days after Hindenburg took command on August 23, the German 8th Army encircled and annihilated the Russian force in what became known as the Battle of Tannenberg, the most celebrated German victory from World War I. Kaiser Wilhelm II awarded General Ludendorff the Iron Cross, and Hindenburg and Ludendorff together rode the luster of these victories to the very pinnacle of wartime leadership, ultimately granted supreme authority over German military and political affairs in the second half of the war. Four years later, General Ludendorff's Great War ended where it began, on the Western Front. But in a terrible turnabout from its glorious start, Ludendorff's war ended in military defeat, psychological crisis, and exile.[3]

In the spring of 1918, Ludendorff was determined to break the stalemate in northern France, where the combatants were locked in a seemingly unmovable system of defensive trenches that scarred the landscape from the English Channel to Switzerland. The Germans had little time to work with. America was now in the fight; a light stream of poorly trained but healthy and enthusiastic American soldiers was now flowing to Europe. This stream would certainly become a flood of fresh troops that Germany could never match. The balance of forces would eventually tip so severely that a future German breakthrough against the Allied armies would become impossible. General Ludendorff opened the final act of this terrible war on March 21, 1918, with the first of five offensives that roared and collapsed in succession through the spring and into midsummer. In June, German forces actually pushed to within forty miles of Paris, which set the French government scrambling to prepare for evacuation. But on July 19, the final offensive was over. Ludendorff's army had suffered hundreds of thousands of casualties, which he could not replace. Nearly one million German soldiers had deserted. The army was grossly short of critical supplies of every type—food, ammunition, horses, weapons, fuel. Ludendorff himself was on the "verge of emotional collapse."[4]

With the German line so badly battered by these failed assaults, the Allied armies launched the final offensive of World War I on August 8. As French, British, American, and Belgian soldiers pushed forward along the entire front, Ludendorff's calculations swung wildly, along with his emotions. He reeled between despair over the reality of his disintegrating army and renewed confidence that Germany could hold a defensive line long enough to break the Allies' will. By early September, General Ludendorff's despair was overwhelming. Thousands of German soldiers were killed or severely wounded every day, but for what purpose? The army, he believed, was not only being torn apart by the enemy, it was also rotting from within the ranks—its fighting mettle was collapsing, mass desertions compounded losses from casualties, whole units were infected by Bolshevism and refused to fight. Ludendorff saw rot within the nation too—radicalism and an antiwar spirit were spreading; politicians were refusing to provide the number of new recruits and supplies he was demanding. While the Americans alone had millions of young men to throw into the conflict in the months to come, Ludendorff believed the German people were abandoning their army in the middle of his desperate stand to save the empire.

His despair ran deeper than the immediate crisis on the battlefield; the Allies' relentless advance threatened to shatter his beliefs about German security and the empire's future, beliefs that had given purpose and direction to Ludendorff's work through his entire career. General Hindenburg had retired in 1911 believing there would be no future war to justify continued service. Ludendorff, on the other hand, was convinced that conflict with Russia and France was inevitable. For years he was among the most fervent champions of preventive war and its promise to eliminate the enveloping threat and secure Imperial Germany by tearing away large chunks from the Russian empire and winning hegemonic dominance over Europe.[5] But now, General Ludendorff had to wonder whether he could save Germany itself from invasion. And what would stop the enemy's army from marching to Berlin? Emotional strain produced a fierce temper, and he lashed out angrily at subordinates and General Hindenburg alike. He issued nonsensical orders, he was gripped by paranoia, and suffered through sleepless nights and repeated bouts of weeping for his stepson recently killed in action. Staff officers quietly summoned an army psychiatrist, one of Ludendorff's trusted friends, to evaluate his mental state. Even though the Allied advance continued, the doctor pleaded with Ludendorff that the only way to beat this nervous exhaustion was to relocate his headquarters farther from the front, to Spa, Belgium, where he must commit to four weeks of daily therapy.[6] Surprisingly, Ludendorff agreed.

While the doctor was delighted to observe that therapy in Spa was restoring the tormented general's emotional balance, his army continued to disintegrate on the battlefield. As one historian describes the situation, it was not quite a rout; rather, the German army was suffering a "controlled deterioration."[7] On September 28, two days after the Allies opened a coordinated attack against Germany's last defensive line, Hindenburg and Ludendorff recognized that nothing short of an immediate armistice would stop foreign troops from crossing the German border. Just one day earlier, President Woodrow Wilson seemed to offer a way out of this nightmare. In a speech at the Metropolitan Opera House in New York, Wilson called for a peace based on "impartial justice" for all parties caught up in this war. The German government reached out for this lifeline. For German leaders, who sincerely believed they had been forced into a defensive war by the suffocating encirclement of the other great powers, "impartial justice" would mean a peace that preserved Imperial Germany with minimal concessions. On October 12, four days after Allied soldiers overran the Hindenburg defensive line, the imperial government accepted full withdrawal from France and Belgium as a condition for negotiations to reach this political end.

While the diplomatic window on peace was being pried open, the fight went on for four more horrendous weeks. The Germans were grappling with additional armistice demands, demands that called for nothing short of the end of Imperial Germany. President Wilson refused to negotiate peace with the militarist rulers that had set this tragic conflict in motion. If German leaders had read Wilson's opera house speech carefully, this would not have been a complete surprise. While calling for impartial justice, the American president also asserted that "there can be no peace obtained by any kind of bargain or compromise with the Governments of the Central Empires." In effect, he expected the obliteration of the Kaiser's reign along with his imperial government as a precondition for a truce. On October 25 an outraged Ludendorff made the outlandish claim that the German army could soldier on for months until the Allies retracted this impossible condition. Despite this show of loyalty, the Kaiser fired General Ludendorff the very next day in a futile effort to appease the Allies. The hero of Liège and Tannenberg, according to his own wife, was now "the most hated man in Germany." Soon after returning to Berlin, a city in turmoil, Ludendorff fled to Denmark in disguise to escape threats against his life.

By the beginning of November 1918, appeasing Woodrow Wilson was irrelevant; the Kaiser's rule was doomed by political crisis at home. A mass rebellion began in the northern port city of Kiel, where mutinous German sailors seized the garrison's armory and commandeered the Kaiser's warships to prevent Fleet Admiral Tirpitz from launching a desperate attack against the British navy. The sailors' revolt quickly spread to Hamburg and Cologne, and the mutineers seized bridges along the Rhine River. Revolutionary councils were soon in control of major cities throughout Germany; even soldiers posted to the army's headquarters in Spa were organizing a Bolshevik council. The Kaiser was tempted to order German soldiers to suppress the revolution with force, but General Hindenburg insisted that these sons of Germany would never fire on their countrymen. On November 10 the Kaiser yielded to the reality of defeat. With no other feasible endgame to his tragic failure, Wilhelm II fled into exile too, escaping to the Netherlands directly from Belgium, denied the small dignity of returning first to Germany by revolutionary soldiers in Liège that made the route home too dangerous. On November 11 the Great War was over.

PEACEMAKING: ANOTHER VICIOUS TURN OF THE WHEEL

Carl von Clausewitz, the Prussian strategic theorist of the early nineteenth century, compared war to a wrestling match. Each wrestler "strives by physical force to compel the other to submit to his will: each endeavors to throw his adversary, and thus render him incapable of further resistance." The Great War, in this sense, was indeed like a wrestling match among the world's major powers—a physical contest of brute strength and tactical finesse between their armies and navies, as well as their fully mobilized economies and populations. In the end, the Allies' hard-won battlefield victory settled this violent contest. Germany was exhausted as a society, its army had disintegrated, its imperial government was shattered, its political system wracked by revolutionary agitation, and its maritime trade was suf-focating under the pressure of enemy blockade. Germany was no longer capable of further resistance.

But wrestling is an imperfect metaphor for war. Unlike a wrestling match that ends with one combatant pinned to the mat, the simple object of the contest satisfied, war must serve a deeper purpose. Clausewitz pushed be-yond this wrestling imagery to define war as "an act of violence intended to compel our opponent *to fulfill our will.*"[8] While the military contest was settled, the *objective* of victory in this war could not be defined merely by defeat of the enemy's forces in the field. As we have seen, Clausewitz would insist that the *strategic purpose* of the war must be defined by the political goals pursued in its wake. Victory on the battlefield opened up political space for asking the most important question now facing the Allies: What do we do with the peace?

Military victory liberated Belgium, Luxembourg, and northern France from German occupation, liberated them from the trenches, the screaming artillery shells, the barbed wire, the rattling machine guns, the bayonets, the poison gas, and the millions of soldiers from multiple nations that suf-fered here. Military victory liberated Alsace and Lorraine from German rule, restoring the territorial limits that had defined French sovereignty, in spirit if not in fact, for a hundred years. And military victory saved the Eu-ropean continent from German hegemony. Achieving these political goals essentially *restored* key features of the prewar world. But as important as these specific political goals were, Allied leaders agreed that the magnitude of this conflict demanded more-ambitious political ends than mere restora-tion of the status quo. While they would clash viciously over many of the deep principles and details of the peace-building project they faced, there was strong consensus on one critical goal: to create a political order that could secure them against a horrible repetition of total war.

For nearly two decades after the Great War, the Rhineland demilita-rized zone was central to this effort. Its immediate origins, however—as a concept and as a material fact on the ground—are found in the termination phase of the war and the armistice conditions the victors imposed on the new German government. When the idea first surfaced during an Allied war council in October 1918, soldiers on both sides of the Front were still tearing into one another across a shifting battlefield. What Allied leaders feared most in these heady final weeks was that Germany would treat an armistice as simply a ceasefire, a chance to rest, reorganize, resupply, and rebuild morale, before throwing the army back into the fight in the spring of 1919. This was a sensible fear: General Hindenburg himself admitted in a letter to his wife in October that by accepting an armistice, "we have at least disengaged ourselves and won time, then we shall be more fit to fight than now."[9]

So the armistice could not be a mere ceasefire in place, nor could it simply demand that the German army pull back across its own border from occupied areas of France and Belgium. Germany had to be stripped of the physical assets and the geographic base that would make renewed conflict possible, truly neutralizing the enemy's ability to resist. The Allies demanded a heavy price: 25,000 guns, 1,700 airplanes, 3,000 trench mortars, 5,000 locomotives, 150,000 railcars, and 5,000 trucks would be surrendered and divided among each of the Allied armies. The German navy was ordered to surrender all of its submarines, six battle cruisers, ten battleships, eight light cruisers, and fifty destroyers, to safeguard the continuing seaborne flow of men and supplies from the United States. The German navy ultimately defied this last order in June 1919 by scuttling the entire fleet before the ships could be delivered to the Royal Navy.[10]

While losing this equipment would severely degrade Germany's war-making capabilities, the Allies' plans for the Rhineland hit the German armistice delegation the hardest. Opinion among Allied commanders varied widely on the territorial question. On one end of the spectrum was Field Marshal Douglas Haig, commander of the British Expeditionary Force, who simply wanted German evacuation of occupied French and Belgian territory, along with the provinces of Alsace and Lorraine. On the other end of the spectrum were the two ranking American military officers, Gen. John J. Pershing, commander of the American Expeditionary Force, and Gen. Tasker Bliss, the American Permanent Military Representative to the Supreme War Council. Generals Pershing and Bliss both argued for rejecting an armistice and pressing on with the war until Germany accepted unconditional surrender, even if this meant a march all the way to Berlin.

In the end, it was the Supreme Allied Commander, French general Ferdinand Foch, who won the debate on the territorial conditions for the armistice. In the months to come Foch would press hard for a peace treaty that crippled German power for the indefinite future, yet he refused to accept the American recommendation to carry the war toward an occupation of the enemy's capital. "To continue the struggle longer would incur great risk," he said. "It would mean that perhaps fifty or a hundred thousand more Frenchmen would be killed . . . Enough blood, alas! has already been shed."[11] Instead, Foch's nonnegotiable demand to end the fighting was Allied occupation of the Rhineland. This would provide a deep territorial buffer against a renewed German offensive, and it would serve as a hostage to ensure that Germany would actually pay whatever financial reparations were required by the peace treaty. Foch also insisted that the occupation force control a thirty-kilometer arc around three bridgeheads on the eastern bank of the Rhine; bridges spanning the river from the west bank cities of Cologne, Coblenz, and Mainz were eventually selected for this purpose. According to General Foch, these footholds to the east could serve as a "suitable military base of departure" for an offensive deep into Germany should the war flare up once again.

President Wilson and British prime minister David Lloyd George both worried that particularly harsh armistice terms could play into the hands of the German militarists by generating a severe backlash against peace, and ultimately undermine the Allies' most important strategic objective. Echoing Otto von Bismarck's 1866 warning about the dangers of punitive peace against Austria, Wilson warned against the paradoxical effects of "too much success or security on the part of the Allies [that] will make a genuine peace settlement exceedingly difficult, if not impossible."[12] Despite these fears of pushing too hard, by November 1 Allied leaders had accepted General Foch's position that Rhineland occupation was the best insurance against renewed German aggression. It was a bitter demand for members of the German armistice delegation—the German navy's representative was in tears when he learned that enemy soldiers would now raise their own flags in the Fatherland—but there was nothing their crisis-stricken nation could do to resist it.[13]

At 5:30 a.m. on November 17, 1918, six allied armies under General Foch's command moved out of their forward trenches in battle order, marching northeast toward staging areas along the entire German frontier. Retreating German forces had fifteen days to evacuate Belgium, France, Luxembourg, Alsace, and Lorraine, and another sixteen days to cross the Rhine River, leaving the Rhine zone open for the wave of enemy soldiers—750,000 in the occupation force—that followed just ten kilometers behind. As agreed, at 5:00 a.m. on December 1, Allied soldiers crossed into Germany. To the north, the British 2nd Army moved toward the city of Cologne, reaching its outskirts on December 6. To the strains of an army band playing "Dixie," the American 3rd Army entered the Moselle River city of Trier in the center of the Rhineland, just a few miles from the Luxembourg border. By December 11 the majority of the American occupation force had moved up the Moselle valley to reach their new headquarters in Coblenz, where the Moselle flows into the Rhine. Two days later, in a cold drizzle, American troops streamed across a pontoon bridge that linked the old city center to the Ehrenbreitstein fortress sitting on the far shore, on a cliff high above the Rhine. Farther north British troops moved from the center of Cologne across the heavy iron Hohenzollern bridge, and like the Americans, pushed the occupation of western Germany into those thirty-kilometer arcing bridgeheads on the eastern bank. To the south of the American zone, the French army became the master of the upper Rhine by pushing beyond liberated Alsace, across what had been France's north-eastern border before the German conquest of 1871, and into the vacuum created by their brutally hard-won victory.[14]

With the armistice settled and the task of crafting a stable postwar order before them, French leaders quickly converged on what they considered a first principle of European security: A secure future depends on perma-nently neutering Germany as a great power. But France faced a serious challenge, despite its victory in the Great War. Defeat would not alter the fact that Germany retained inherently greater power potential for the fu-ture. It would recover from collapse, its industrial might would revive, its population growth rate would continue to outpace France. In an interview with British journalist Ward Price in April 1919, Marshal Foch argued that the Germans had learned nothing from the bloodletting. "Remember, that these seventy millions of Germans will always be a menace to us . . . They are a people both envious and warlike . . . Fifty years hence they will be what they are today."[15]

With the future casting such a dark shadow back on the present, French leaders set out to construct a postwar order that would flip what seemed to be the natural distribution of power in Europe by locking in artificial constraints on Germany while propelling France into a dominant Conti-nental role. The new political order should drain Germany of the financial strength that could feed its militant tendencies, and physically squeeze its ability to launch a deadly repetition of the invasions of 1870 and 1914. The new order should magnify Germany's own vulnerabilities to collective pun-ishment, compelling good behavior with the perpetual threat of retaliation should they be tempted to misbehave in the years to come.

At the core of this strategic vision we find one of the great examples from history of the preventive war paradox at work. Germany gambled on pre-ventive war in 1914 as the solution to its own fears of the future. Smashing Russian power was Germany's most important strategic objective, to pro-vide relief from those nightmares in which the expanding Russian empire either crushed Germany through war and conquest or merely subjugated Germany within a Central European system defined by Russian hegemonic rule. France was simply an adversary that had to be dispatched in short order, a prerequisite for the main act—the epic showdown in the east—a first step made necessary by the existing alliance system. During the first three years of this fight the Allied armies in the west were able to pin down the German invasion force; war on two fronts rather than quick victory over France certainly prolonged the struggle against Russia. But in the end, France and Great Britain could not prevent Germany from achieving its hegemonic aspirations in Eastern Europe. While the costs were high—1.5 million German soldiers were killed, wounded, or captured on the Eastern Front—victory here allowed Germany to impose radical changes to the distribution of power and the political order in the east.

Revolution brought down the imperial government of Tsar Nicholas II in February 1917, and the Bolshevik regime that ultimately seized power presided over a broken country: drained economically, its social order in turmoil, its military shattered. The Brest-Litovsk peace treaty the Bolsheviks signed on March 3, 1918, stripped away 25 percent of the Russian empire's population and industry, as well as 90 percent of its coal mines. Latvia, Lithuania, Estonia, Ukraine, Belarus, and Russian Poland were lost, ceded to Germany as dependencies. Further north, Soviet Russia renounced the imperial claims in Finland.[16] By the summer of 1917 it seemed that this war had solved the problem of the Russian juggernaut for the indefinite future.

Ironically, Germany's preventive war gamble failed in the west, after it had already achieved its primary strategic goals against the Russian phantom. The hundreds of thousands of German soldiers transferred from the Russian theater to finish the job on the Western Front could not compensate for the logic of expanding hostility and war that its hegemonic drive had produced. The European political order of 1914 had forced Germany into a fight with France as a step toward crushing Russia, but the military logic of Germany's preventive war—with its wide offensive thrust through neutral Belgium to envelop Paris—forced an unintended fight with Britain as well. Two and a half years later, with the war stalemated along the trench lines, military logic produced the decision to launch unrestricted submarine warfare against neutral shipping. While German chancellor Theobald von Bethmann Hollweg assured the Reichstag that this decision would compel Britain to sue for peace,[17] it instead provoked an unintended fight with the United States, outraged by Germany's assault on the commercial rights of neutral countries and its aggression against civilian targets. The unstoppable flow of American soldiers sailing across the Atlantic and marching into the battle line by the spring of 1918 produced a decisive shift in the military fortunes of the combatants. Strategic victory in the east, Germany's real goal, was obliterated by the expanding war in the west.

But the real backlash came with the peace. Germany's violent play for European hegemony through preventive war was made possible by the raw military power it had amassed over previous generations. So it seems natural that the disarmament clauses of the Versailles Treaty would follow. Andre Tardieu, a leading French statesman during the peace negotiations, explained that it was "necessary to break" the three components of Germany's "instrument of aggression"—its organization, its manpower, and its armaments.[18] Versailles demanded a permanent cap on the size of Germany's army at one hundred thousand men, and it prohibited short-term conscription that over time would build a large reserve force that could be mobilized for war. Versailles barred Germany from creating an air force or building tanks and submarines. Germany was to abolish its famed General Staff, the heart of operational planning and expertise that had ensured Prussian and German dominance in war since the 1860s. The Versailles Treaty even outlawed professional academies for training German military officers, noncommissioned officers, and cadets. Even with such severe limits built into Versailles, French leaders worried about the effectiveness of disarmament alone to keep the nation safe. Marshal Foch, with characteristic bluntness, said that "disarmament, one cannot repeat too often, gives us only a temporary, precarious, fictitious security. It is almost impossible to prevent Germany from arming in secret . . . If [Germany] has the will to wage war, nothing will prevent it from finding the means."[19]

So French leaders turned to the Rhineland and alliance-building as the cornerstone of a new security structure for Western and Eastern Europe alike. Their initial goals were extremely ambitious, nothing short of cleaving the western Rhineland completely from German sovereign control.[20] Rumors swirled about wide support within France for outright annexation. This was a bit too provocative, French leaders conceded quietly, too close to raw conquest. So Foch's first official plan, advanced on December 1, 1918—the same day Allied soldiers crossed the German border for occupation duty—was to create one or more nominally independent states in the western Rhineland. While premier Georges Clemenceau would have been satisfied with an independent demilitarized buffer zone between France and Germany, Foch worried about the seventy-five million German speakers to the east of the Rhine River facing down the paltry fifty million citizens of France, Belgium, and Luxembourg to the west. Foch insisted on integrating the 5.4 million Rhinelanders in these newly independent republics into a tight political, economic, and military relationship with the western states to more effectively defend the west against future German aggression.[21] This particular scheme, however, didn't sit well with France's allies. Maj. Gen. Henry Allen, who commanded the American Rhineland occupation force, certainly understood this French impulse to neuter Germany; it was a natural reaction to recent history and fear of the future. But when the French military cultivated separatist movements in the Rhineland, Major General Allen recalled, it stirred up more "discord" with the British and the Americans "than all other causes combined."[22]

As serious as the Rhineland dispute was, it really reflected a deeper and more-serious divide between France and its Anglo-American allies over the principles that should guide the postwar peace. All agreed on the strategic goal: a durable, stable European political order that would prevent another ferocious great-power war. Yet the Allies had radically different conceptions for how to achieve it. At its core, this split over strategic principles reflected the fact that the Allies were looking to opposite ends of the classic security-dilemma spectrum for answers to this perennial problem in international affairs. France saw power as the key to a stable and secure peace; put simply, the best way to safeguard Europe was to suppress German power into the indefinite future. From a historical perspective, the French view reflected a tradition that reaches back thousands of years into the past, and it finds support in the realist school of international relations. There is an intuitive appeal in the assertion that if a state can sustain maximum power relative to other states, it's in the best position to impose the maximum amount of restraint on their dangerous behavior. Yet within the same realist school of thought, as noted in chapter 3, other scholars warn that the drive for maximum power will simply generate fear and hostility within those states on the losing end of this power game. As a result, one state's efforts to maximize security by maximizing power will increase the pressure on others to push back, perhaps aggressively, to overturn these moves toward dominance in the system. As Otto von Bismarck recognized, to avoid this perverse and potentially tragic paradox, the wisest move might be to reduce the other states' level of fear and hostility by exercising self-restraint in your own use of power.

This is how the British and the Americans alike saw the situation in the postwar years. The French solution, they believed, would produce the very instability and violence they all desperately wanted to avoid.[23] From this perspective, the key to stability and security was to decrease Germany's desire to upset the postwar order through violent revisionism. Germany was going to recover its strength, just as Clemenceau and Foch acknowledged. The only way to prevent this was to dismember Germany politically—break it into smaller Germanic states and re-create the divided political conditions of its earlier history, or tear away its industrial heartland in the Ruhr

River valley and fatally undermine its economic potential. But such drastic measures were impossible. Given this reality, the Anglo-American goal was to shape German intentions in the postwar world. As one member of the British delegation at Versailles put it, "We must either squeeze all we can out of Germany, or help her to her feet again. It is impossible to do both."[24] Permanently severing the Rhineland from Germany would be just such a painful, nationalist humiliation, planting the dragon's teeth of German revenge, just as the infuriating loss of Alsace and Lorraine had in France nearly fifty years earlier.

While British and American leaders refused to accept the risks that came with France's power-maximizing impulses, they did recognize two other key points about the security dilemma before them. First, French fears were legitimate. As Prime Minister Lloyd George put it, "Twice in living memory invasion of French soil had come from the same quarter. France was therefore entitled to consider her fears."[25] The postwar power structure had to provide physical safeguards against renewed German aggression. Second, unless it had reliable safeguards, France would continue to pursue power-maximizing schemes, inadvertently increasing the danger of war, rather than decreasing it. They had to find some way to get France to relax its perception of the threat and eventually ease up on coercive measures that would push Germany into a dangerous corner. So Wilson and Lloyd George promised at Versailles that the Great War alliance would live on in the postwar world; they were ready to join the fight once again if German forces stormed westward in unprovoked aggression.[26] According to the original plan, this de facto alliance would remain in place until the League of Nations offered robust collective security to protect its members. The Allies agreed to build a Rhineland DMZ into the peace settlement and to maintain a fifteen-year joint occupation of the Rhine zone to help institutionalize the DMZ for the long run. In exchange, France had to drop its schemes to tear the Rhineland away from Germany completely.[27] It was hard getting to this point in the negotiations, but with this compromise on future security, the Allies left Versailles with both hope and trepidation. Perhaps more trepidation than hope.

A NEW ERA?

German delegates signed the Versailles Treaty on June 28, 1919, with its force structure limitations, the territorial losses, the financial reparations, the occupation of the Rhineland by Allied armies for the next fifteen years, and Rhineland demilitarization for the indefinite future. On July 9, the German National Assembly ratified Versailles by a vote of 209 in favor and 116 against. The Germans had little choice: The threat of an offensive enemy push across the Rhine hung over the decision, and their impotent army offered no hope of organized resistance. In Clausewitzian terms, it was a ripe moment for the Allies to impose their will on the adversary, and Germany surrendered to the logic of brute force in this titanic wrestling match. Even so, as far as the British government was concerned, Allied victory had not solved the great-power security dilemma. By the mid-1920s leading British statesmen worried out loud about the system collapsing into war once again.

Winston Churchill, then Chancellor of the Exchequer, described the problem with his usual flair for vivid language. The problem, he said, is that the "quarrel between France and Germany" remains "unappeased." Fixing this ongoing political aggravation was the key to saving "ourselves from being involved in another Armageddon." Even victory in a second great war would bring "our ruin scarcely less surely than defeat."[28] Foreign Minister Austen Chamberlain saw the core strategic problem the same way Churchill did. If France and Germany "could not be reconciled fairly soon," he said, "it would be too late to mend matters and they would be involved in a catastrophe even worse than the Great War."[29]

But who had responsibility for breaking this "unending vicious circle," as Chamberlain called it? Britain's role, he said, was "preaching the gospel of reasonableness" to these rivals. For its part, Germany had obligations to its former enemies. It carried the burden of guilt for the Great War, according to Article 231 of the Versailles Treaty, and Chamberlain never flagged in his determination to see that Germany atoned. But while Austen Chamberlain was proud to be the most pro-French member of the British cabinet, and among the most distrustful of Germany,[30] he agreed with many of his compatriots that the onus was on France to solve this problem. And it must do so by relieving the pressure on Germany that made the problem worse. This pressure, Chamberlain said, simply "reproduces that very feeling of bitterness in Germany which is the cause of" French fears.[31] Now was the time to leverage French strength and German weakness—not to crush Germany, but to cultivate a healthy political relationship while the risks were as low as they ever would be.

With Britain looking to France to solve this problem in the early 1920s, and finding little reason for optimism, German foreign minister Gustav Stresemann jumped into the breach to renew hope. Stresemann, it seemed, shared the Western powers' fears of future war, and genuinely desired to

push past the dictated Versailles peace to create something more enduring. And what he proposed led to a diplomatic sensation, the most exciting
moment for war and peace of the decade. It seemed to promise a political
breakthrough that would deliver a fatal hammer blow to the vicious circle
of fear and anger that could drive the world into Churchill's Armageddon
once again. The diplomats would work through the details of the new security pact Stresemann had outlined, from his initial notes to foreign capitals in January and February 1925 to the celebrated meeting in Locarno,
Switzerland, in October. The revolutionary character of this moment,
however, did not spring from the details; it was the *spirit* of the moment
that captured the imagination and sparked hope for the future. The "spirit
of Locarno" was the spirit of reconciliation, embodied by the three leading
statesmen that pushed the negotiations forward.

There was Austen Chamberlain, son of a wealthy Birmingham industri-
alist and turn-of-the-century member of Parliament and statesman, whose
trademark monocle was an accessory adopted by his son while Austen was
still a student at Cambridge University. He was half-brother to Neville
Chamberlain, who would serve as prime minister in the late 1930s and
during the opening stages of World War II. Austen Chamberlain was the
honest broker whose calm mediation helped his French and German partners work through doubts and trouble spots. As a friend of France, he was
trusted to keep a critical eye on details that might genuinely put French
security at risk. As a friend of stable peace in Europe, he was trusted to
champion Germany's legitimate interests and fairness in the talks. Chamberlain was awarded the 1925 Nobel Peace Prize for his leadership. There
was French foreign minister Aristide Briand, one of the most seasoned
political figures of the Third Republic, who would serve eleven times as
French premier and hold twenty-six cabinet posts over his career. Briand
was a devoted internationalist who was eager to build sustainable peace
with Germany through law and a system of collective security in Europe.
Yet Briand also recognized the importance of preserving French power
while this internationalist system of peace developed.[32] And then there was
Foreign Minister Gustav Stresemann, a proud German patriot, a friend of
the exiled former crown prince after Germany's defeat, and staunch supporter of the Kaiser during the Great War. But Stresemann was also cos-
mopolitan, erudite, and committed to stability within the postwar German
republic. Most important, he was an intrepid champion of compromise who
would risk assassination and furious opposition at home from hardened nationalists looking to derail any hint of accommodation with France. Briand

and Stresemann together would win the 1926 Nobel Peace Prize for the diplomatic breakthrough at Locarno.

Chamberlain and Briand were actually astonished by the underlying meaning in Stresemann's initiative, and they characterized it in similar terms. Briand called the German approach a "courageous act."[33] Chamberlain said it was "an act of high courage and great wisdom." Courageous indeed, as one British army officer observed; things ended badly for every previous German statesman that cooperated with the Allies to fulfill the Versailles Treaty, when an assassin took aim at his back.[34] What they found most amazing, the aspect of his proposals they drew such hope from, was Stresemann's voluntary acceptance of a condition first demanded in the Versailles Treaty six years before: a permanent position of vulnerability for Germany in the great-power system. While Versailles had been a dictated peace, the principles of the Locarno order would be negotiated. Most of these principles, however, simply restated or supported many of the rules already built into the Treaty of Versailles. Germany promised to respect the new borderlines drawn across Western Europe in 1919. There was a mutual pledge among the Germans, the Belgians, and the French that they would "in no case attack or invade each other or resort to war with each other." Germany agreed to binding arbitration of future disputes. And, most important, Germany agreed to respect an unyielding component of French strategy: indefinite demilitarization of the Rhineland.[35] The only new promise in Locarno, and it was a major step in the security structure of Western Europe, was that Britain and Italy agreed to assist any party to the treaty, including Germany, if it was the victim of "an unprovoked act of aggression" by another signatory.

This last promise seemed to offer real value for Germany since it demonstrated balance in the rights of the parties and in theory offered protection from abusive French behavior. But the treaty of Locarno was not about creating equilibrium between France and Germany. The viability of this security scheme depended fully on German acceptance of its weakened position in the system. Stresemann created a bit of a stir before the conference opened when he asked the Allies to drop the war guilt clause from Versailles and for the return of a few prewar overseas German colonies. They rejected these requests firmly. In the end, all Versailles restrictions remained unchanged and unchallenged in the negotiations. Considering how bitter Germans were since the war over the demand that the Reich remain a second-tier power, such a turnaround in the German government's attitude was puzzling. To Chamberlain, Stresemann's voluntary submission to this order was "a most remarkable thing for him to have offered."[36] It's puzzling indeed, and we'll return to this question in the next chapter. But in 1925 British leaders did not dwell on this puzzle. They were elated.

The correspondent from the *New York Times* called Locarno a "sleepy, humdrum town in Italian Switzerland," while the London *Observer* said it was "the most beautiful and fascinating of all the glorious resorts on the shores of Lake Maggiore."[37] Differences in aesthetic tastes aside, it was an exciting time to be in the resort city. The crowds that gathered every day outside the Palace of Justice, where the German flag flew alongside those of all other delegations, knew something bold was happening inside. Strict secrecy was the rule, but the newspapers were still filled with rumors of the deals being struck on the conference hall's second floor, in private hotel suites, and during a Sunday-afternoon cruise on the lake. On October 16—Austen Chamberlain's sixty-second birthday—the loyal crowds and impatient journalists heard the news they had been waiting for. At 7:30 that night the second-floor windows opened suddenly and the diplomats shouted out that a new security pact had been approved. Fireworks burst from the driveway, nearly hitting the bodies hanging from the windows above, and the crowds cheered for Stresemann just as heartily as they did for Chamberlain and Briand. That night more fireworks shot over the lake and the music and dancing went on for hours. Chamberlain proclaimed this to be "the happiest birthday of my life." During the closing ceremony that brought negotiations to an end, Chamberlain emotionally choked out a short speech that many had trouble hearing, and Briand predicted that "from Locarno a new Europe must spring up." Chamberlain was the last to exit the conference hall as delegates departed for home. It was a scene we might consider a strange foreshadowing of his half-brother Neville's joyous, yet ultimately infamous "Peace for Our Time" moment in the fall of 1938, when he returned to London after signing the Munich Agreement with Adolf Hitler. A large crowd hailed Austen Chamberlain as he walked slowly down the steps to the street, clutching a bulky envelope with the text of the treaty. As the hopeful well-wishers pressed around the foreign minister's car, he held the treaty high and waved it in the air triumphantly as the car drove away.[38]

The British government hosted the signing ceremony for the new pact, formally titled the Treaty of Mutual Guarantee, in London on December 1. For its senior leaders, the moment was electric. The spirit of Locarno was treated publicly as nothing less than a decisive break from the coercive, explosive past. Prime Minister Stanley Baldwin looked back on the seven years since the Armistice of 1918 as a "purgatory to the world—an intermediate state, neither peace nor war." Locarno offered a progressive path forward. "If we could convert the Rhine from being what it had been in the past—a frontier, full of threat and menace—to a peaceful highway," he said, "we would have transformed the life of Western Europe for this generation and for the generations to come."[39] Winston Churchill hailed Locarno because it drew a "merciful veil across the lurid and tragic past and . . . because it affords . . . the only possible security for the maintenance of peace in the future."[40] Austen Chamberlain said it was a "decisive point in history for the peace of Europe and possibly for the whole world." And he meant this quite literally. Chamberlain drew his confidence in this assessment from the political atmosphere he experienced at Locarno. "We have come here," he said, "not to impose conditions or to make demands, but to get together with Germany as representatives of *free and equal nations* to seek for a solution to the troubles of Europe . . . to bury the dead past and look ahead to the future."[41] It was Gustav Stresemann's initiative that allowed Chamberlain to say this, and Stresemann himself proudly declared in his own opening remarks, "We are all here on an equal footing."

But Stresemann knew this was not true. And so did the British government. This claim about "free and equal" partners in peace obscured an uglier reality. Britain and its partners did not have to "make demands" or "impose conditions" across the table at Locarno for one reason: Germany had already cracked under the pressure of what Stresemann called the "Ruhr War." It was the punishing French and Belgian military occupation of Germany's industrial core in the Ruhr River valley, between 1923 and 1925, that pushed the Germans into these negotiations, after it had driven the German state into extreme crisis. As Stresemann explained in a letter to the former crown prince in September 1925, "We must get the stranglehold off our neck" or Germany will collapse in civil war or revolution, its economy broken, its territory eviscerated.[42] To Stresemann, the choice was either surrender to the subjugated status France had been demanding since 1918, or see Germany crumble as a nation-state. Stresemann's offer to negotiate a new security order for Europe, the celebrated initiative that led to Locarno, was an act of desperation, not reconciliation.

For the British, the good cheer and florid rhetoric of late 1925 could not erase the dark implications of the stranglehold that compelled Germany's promise. Did a truly voluntary spirit at Locarno actually replace the dictated peace of Versailles? Were the restrictions on German power in the Rhineland any more tolerable, and thus sustainable after 1925 than they had been after 1919? The British wanted to believe this was so, but they were honest enough to recognize their own doubts and acknowledge the serious flaws that swirled around this moment of peace-building. The ugly reality of the conditions that drove Germany to Locarno, they quickly came to believe, simply meant that the Rhineland demilitarization pledge embedded within the treaty was a time bomb. When the Rhineland time bomb finally detonated in 1936, French foreign minister Pierre-Étienne Flandin would point to the promises built into Locarno in order to justify preventive action to turn Germany back. British leaders, on the other hand, could not forget that Locarno was a product of coercion, just like Versailles.

The next chapter fills in the gaps of this largely neglected part of the story, an experience that rippled heavily into 1936.

6

THE RUHR WAR

On the day that France is indemnified for her ruin and sheltered from
attack, the whole continent will have a greater likelihood of regaining
tranquility.

—French premier Raymond Poincaré, February 1924

On the morning of January 11, 1923, at 3:45 a.m., thousands of French
troops in full combat kit moved out of the Rhine city of Düsseldorf and
crossed into unoccupied Germany to seize the Ruhr River valley, Germany's industrial heartland. With cavalry and infantry soldiers leading the
way, and tanks, armored cars, and motorized machine-gun units filling out
the column behind, the invading force dashed toward its primary target, the
city of Essen, twenty-five miles to the northeast.[1] Five French generals and
their staffs descended on Düsseldorf to command the unfolding operations,
ready to move into the Ruhr valley behind their advancing forces. One
hundred seventy-nine troop trains supported the move; some worked their
way north from the mid-Rhine city of Mainz, while others approached the
Ruhr valley from the western city of Trier. More soldiers were piled into an
armada of German automobiles, requisitioned from every citizen of Düsseldorf that owned one. Seventy special trains waited in the northern French
city of Nancy to load reinforcements for occupation duty in the Rhineland,
as their compatriots pushed deeper into Germany. Belgium joined the mission, its soldiers converging on Essen from the city of Duisburg, where the

Ruhr River flows into the Rhine. At 10:00 a.m. the Allied force reached Essen's central square, with six tanks in the vanguard. The infantry seized the rail station, posted sentries at the gates of the giant Krupp steelworks to control access, and organized patrols through the streets of Germany's most important manufacturing center. By the end of the day, eighteen thousand French and Belgian soldiers were in the Ruhr valley.

French leaders called it an "economic occupation," simply a bit of muscle to compel delivery of what rightfully belonged to the victorious Allies: every ton of coal demanded as part of the package of reparation payments imposed after the Great War. German officials had been asking for reparations relief, claiming they could not turn over more than 80 percent of the coal scheduled for delivery in 1922. For France, this was a serious problem, and it was more than a mere matter of principle. The Ruhr produced some of the best coking coal in the world, with the right chemical structure for reaching the extreme temperatures needed to smelt iron ore for industrial production. After Germany annexed the iron ore–rich region of Lorraine from France in 1871, German industrialists had integrated Ruhr coal and Lorrain iron ore in a tightly linked economic system. France reclaimed Lorraine in 1918, but the region remained dependent on Ruhr coal for steel manufacturing.[2] When the Allied Reparations Commission met to consider the German shortfall problem, the French and Belgian commissioners outvoted their British colleague, declaring the German shortage of 1.5 million tons to be an act of "willful default" on its war guilt debt. While the vote provided legal cover for the invasion, the French cabinet had been discussing the idea since late November 1922. The decision to execute the operation came nearly a week before the reparations commission voted. The military force spearheading the occupation was powerful, and it certainly seemed intimidating. But, French officials insisted, this force was there merely to provide basic security for the Allies' technical personnel at the heart of this economic mission, and if Allied bayonets and tanks kept the pressure on the Germans to ensure that the coal quota was delivered without delay, even better.[3]

The British and American governments wanted nothing to do with this operation. The British kept their distance by declaring "benevolent neutrality" as the affair unfolded. They were trying to thread a needle in this crisis, avoiding an open break with France while simultaneously refusing to add weight to this explosive move. British soldiers were still in command of Cologne, an important gateway city in the occupied Rhineland for French forces moving in and out of the Ruhr valley, but the British stood aside. The American reaction was easier to interpret. The very day French and

Belgian troops mobilized, the United States government announced that its wartime partnership with Allied forces, which had continued after the Great War through Rhineland occupation, was officially being severed. Four days earlier, as France was openly signaling its preparations for armed enforcement action, the American Senate voted 57 to 6 to bring their remaining 1,200 soldiers home. Two weeks later, the American flag flying over the Ehrenbreitstein fortress, high above Coblenz, was lowered for the final time in an early-morning ceremony. The French tricolor was raised in its place, and the last of the American troops in Europe boarded trains for Antwerp where a transport ship waited to carry them back across the Atlantic.

As the Franco-Belgian force pushed deeper into Germany on the first day of occupation, the French ambassador in Berlin delivered a note to the German foreign minister. "No trouble of any kind is anticipated," it read, "and no changes will be made in the normal life of the population." And on that first day, this seemed like a reasonable prediction. German and French leaders alike recognized that military opposition was impossible; while some naive nationalists rallied for war, most Germans had no doubt that French power could crush whatever armed resistance they might throw into a fight to defend the Ruhr valley. To avoid disaster, Gen. Hans von Seeckt, commander of the German army, ordered all military units to fall back if confronted by the invading force.[4] There was relative calm on the streets of Essen that day; it seemed that the locals would bow to the realities of power and weakness, just like the German military had, and accept French demands with grim resignation. That weekend, Parisian moviegoers cheered and laughed at newsreels showing the "stolid, astonished, speechless Germans watching" helplessly as French "armored cars, cyclists and cavalry [were] marching into Essen."[5]

It was a promising start, but as the French ambassador's note pointed out, the ultimate success of this economic mission would depend completely on the "goodwill of the German government and the German authorities."[6] And by goodwill, he meant active participation. The French thought the operation would resemble a business transaction. Their technical experts and engineers would oversee the syndicate of German mine owners that managed the coal industry, and the syndicate would execute the logistics of the coal shipments the French ordered—a simple commercial operation to collect on a debt. The occupiers understood their own limitations: that the engineers and workers they imported from home simply did not have the right kind of expertise or local knowledge to run the German mines, the machinery, or the railroads by themselves. This was meant to be a "supervisory" mission over Germans with the skills to make it happen, and these Germans would deliver the coal to France and Belgium.

But this was no mere technical limitation—it was the invaders' Achilles' heel. And on this point, the German authorities refused to acquiesce. French premier Raymond Poincaré would insist throughout the crisis that France's only objective was to collect on lawful reparations obligations. But the Germans saw the most sinister goals behind French policy. The occupation was not just a violation of the Versailles Treaty, said German chancellor Wilhelm Cuno, nor merely "criminal robbery," as Gustav Stresemann characterized it. According to Cuno, the "warlike" French occupation was an "act of violence against a defenseless people," a "state of siege" meant to bring about nothing less than the economic and territorial collapse of the German Reich.[7] While the French had not anticipated it, there was deep trouble indeed for all sides from the very first days, and life for the Ruhr population would not return to normal for years. This was not a war in the traditional European sense, with large armies maneuvering around battlefields torn apart by the fire of thousands of rifles and artillery pieces. It was an unconventional war, its magnitude and intensity best captured through the details of the conflict, the individual acts of resistance, protest, sabotage, and terror, and the retaliatory counterattacks that kept the conflict churning. The spiraling violence of this fight made life in the region a misery for Germans, French, and Belgians alike, but its legacy rippled far beyond the confines of the valley.

As the details of these individual stories accumulate, we can step back and see the broader impact on the fraught politics of European security. Most important, without the Ruhr War, it's impossible to understand British skepticism over the Rhineland demilitarization promises found in the Locarno treaty, and British resistance to preventive war over a decade later, when the Wehrmacht moved in to reclaim full sovereignty over the western Reich.

RESIST!

Two days after French and Belgian forces rolled into Essen, every political party in the Reichstag, from the Social Democrats to the hard-line nationalists, rallied around Cuno's response: Germany would defy the invaders with a campaign of passive resistance. Since the German military was powerless to defend the nation, civilian leadership would be issuing the orders for the struggle. The opening move was brilliant: The entire Ruhr coal syndicate—its directors and its advisory personnel, with their detailed files and archives on the coal industry—fled the region as the crisis percolated, taking refuge in the city of Hamburg before the Allies made their move on Essen. For everyone who remained—the industrial barons, the local government authorities, the public works personnel, the miners, the railroad engineers, and the factory workers—Berlin's orders were explicit. Cooperation with the occupying force was forbidden. They would not mine, process, load, or transport a single chunk of coal for France; and with the German government still paying their wages, the workers now idled by this resistance order rallied behind the cause just as fervently as the wealthy industrialists did.

Within days the occupiers realized that a terrible wrench had been jammed into the gears of their plan. There was no alternative to the supervisory model for the operation, no alternative to putting the Germans themselves to work to pry the reparations loose. The only way to make this "economic occupation" viable was to break the passive resistance campaign. If German authorities refused to cooperate with goodwill, they would be forced to cooperate through coercion. So the Allies turned up the pressure. Thousands of new French and Belgian troops poured into the Ruhr valley; five days after seizing Essen, the force had nearly tripled, from eighteen thousand to almost sixty thousand soldiers that fanned out to occupy new cities and towns.

As reinforcements flooded in, the German government declared Sunday, January 14, a national Day of Mourning. Five hundred thousand Germans took to the streets of Berlin to demonstrate unity with the cause; two hundred thousand filled Königsplatz square in front of the Reichstag building, where the German flag flew at half-staff. Protesters swarmed around the victory column and a larger-than-life statue of Otto von Bismarck, each monument a reminder of prouder days for Germany, singing patriotic songs and cheering a parade of speakers railing against French oppression. Four thousand Berliners rushed the barricades in front of the Brandenburg Gate, set up to protect the French embassy on the other side. Truckloads of German police rushed to the scene to reinforce the fifty mounted officers holding back the surging crowd with drawn swords. Two days later, thousands converged in front of the city hall in Bochum, the center of Ruhr mining, shouting in outrage at the French general whose headquarters were inside. A group of five hundred marched through the streets that evening singing songs from the Great War—which the French had outlawed—and they faced off against French troops guarding a public building. The protesters refused an order to disband, the soldiers fired into the crowd with rifles and machine guns, and the first German casualty fell dead on the pavement.

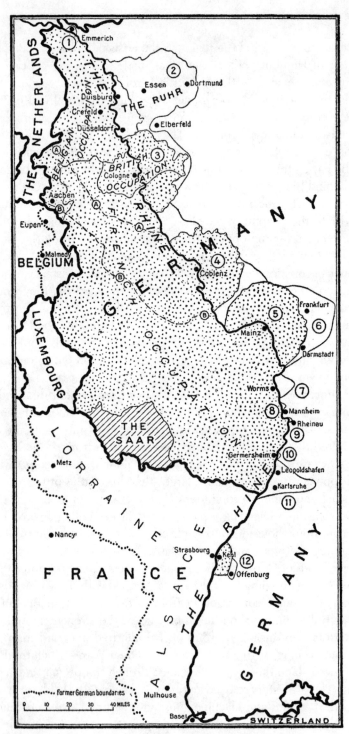

Occupied German Rhineland and the Ruhr Valley

This is where the real trouble started, as French pressure and German resistance spiraled into increasing chaos, retaliation, and deadly confrontations. Each side dug in with remarkable commitment and internal solidarity. Each side rejected compromise in any form and accepted the escalating costs that seemed essential to victory. Within these first days, the main elements of the Ruhr War took shape in the form of three grand ongoing battles: the battle of the mines, the battle of the railways, and the battle for the streets. What no one could predict in its early weeks was where this war would lead.

The passive resistance campaign was just that: the passive refusal to provide the expertise, the administrative support, the equipment, or the labor necessary to make good on reparations demands, and it focused on the mines that supplied industrial-grade coking coal and the rail system that delivered it. Coal was still being mined, but it was mined haphazardly across the Ruhr. Between mine closures, idled labor, and strikes to protest the occupation, coal production fell by 60 percent within two months. The coal that did make it to the surface was used to feed local factories only; the rest began to accumulate by the ton in huge piles at pitheads across the valley. But even this coal was virtually useless to the French and Belgians because the regional rail system was collapsing. Only 357 of 170,000 railway workers remained on the job,[8] and by the spring the demand for railcars would drop by over 80 percent. Forty-five hundred French engineers tried to fill the void, but this produced little more than a disastrous string of collisions, derailments, and mangled track junctions because the foreign rail workers didn't know how to operate German switches and signals. No coal was moving out of the Ruhr.

And no matter how much escalating pressure the French applied, the Germans would not crack. Occupation leaders made fist-pounding demands and threats that led to the arrest, imprisonment, and expulsion of tens of thousands of Germans—local government leaders; rail and mine officials; and police, postal, and customs officials, along with their families—as punishment for noncooperation. The French army tried to isolate the region economically with tank crews, cavalry, infantry, and artillery units at strategic points on the rail lines and canals to cut off all coal deliveries into unoccupied Germany. By mid-February the French realized that most of the coal was consumed within the Ruhr valley itself, so they expanded the trade embargo to prohibit shipment of all iron, steel, chemicals, dyes, and manufactured goods from Ruhr industries. The occupiers erected a customs barrier to seize duties and collect taxes on all other goods carried beyond the occupation zone. They imposed internal coal taxes and threatened to starve Ruhr valley factories if the taxes weren't paid. They tried to isolate the region politically, after Chancellor Cuno made a surprise visit to Essen and delivered a defiant speech to stiffen the population's spirit. After that stunt, the French banned all national-level government officials from the region.

The list of penalties kept growing. French general Jean Degoutte, commander of the Franco-Belgian force, ordered the confiscation of all coal stockpiles and threatened five-year prison sentences for anyone who interfered. His forces seized rolling stock and occupied mines. In June they shut down the rail lines used to deliver six hundred carloads of food a day to key Ruhr cities, just as a food crisis gripped the region, hoping to force German rail workers to return to the job on other lines. This too failed. They even offered to pay pensions if German officials would simply provide a helping hand; there were no takers. General Degoutte was mild-mannered by nature, short in stature, with small round glasses and a gentle smile that made him look like a kind schoolteacher. But when his frustration boiled over one day in February, he warned that France would stay planted in the Ruhr for one thousand years if that's what it took to force Germany's hand. As winter turned to spring, and spring turned to summer, nothing worked to break the Germans' will. As long as passive resistance continued, and German solidarity remained unshaken, France and Belgium would have to endure the repeated frustrations of this failing mission.

As frustrating as this impasse was, passive resistance was not the source of real trouble for the Allies. The real trouble came from what Geheimrat Kirdorf, who was known as the "dean of the Ruhr industrialists," called "the seeds of hate sown by the French in the Ruhr." In a "fiery speech" in Berlin on March 14, Kirdorf said that these "seeds of hate . . . have entered German hearts and sprouted the tree of national unity," and in turn, "hate of the enemy is the best means of mobilizing all the nation's force."[9] And true to this claim, Germans from all sectors of the Ruhr population mobilized for something much more serious than the government-sanctioned passive resistance campaign. They mobilized for *active* resistance that played out as a running battle for the streets of Ruhr cities and towns, through sabotage, through assassinations and terrorism. It was through active resistance and Franco-Belgian retaliation that the Ruhr conflict came to resemble a war that rolled on month after month, flaring spasmodically across the landscape, generating casualties on both sides.

In the battle for the railways, canals, and communication lines, Germans quickly went to work creating havoc for the occupiers through direct action. In the early weeks, as Allied technicians were still trying to figure out the complexities of the rail network, bold German engineers became blockade runners, secretly rushing as much coal as possible into unoccupied Germany on unguarded tracks or by racing through guarded checkpoints under fire. Once beyond the grasp of French forces, the liberated train cars would never return. The Allied cordon was tightening with each passing week, a task made easier by the continuing flow of reinforcements. One hundred thousand French soldiers were in the Ruhr by mid-March, and with the help of expanding air patrols, the force was sealing up the remaining escape routes. The French prohibited passenger-train locomotives from leaving the region until an engine of equivalent value returned; they were seizing train stations; and they even expanded the military occupation zones far to the south of the Ruhr, on the eastern bank of the Rhine River, in towns like Mannheim and Karlsruhe. This gave the French control of the rail lines linking the Ruhr with the cities of Frankfurt, Stuttgart, and Basel, Switzerland.

The Germans responded with the only form of direct action left in this battle of the railroads: sabotage and terror bombings that grew more violent and widespread as the scope of French control expanded. Week after week, sections of track across the Ruhr were attacked. Bolts were removed, stones and iron debris scattered on the rails, whole sections of track were pulled away or torn apart by bombs, bridges were disabled by explosives. In response, French authorities announced the death penalty for saboteurs and ordered their troops to shoot to kill, to stop sabotage in the act. French newspapers reported that sabotage orders came directly from the minister of transportation in Berlin; Berlin responded with orders for local officials to cut off water, gas, and electricity to all rail stations occupied by the French. Despite the death threats, Germans expanded their attacks to include the canal system. On February 14, the locks on the Rhine–Herne Canal were blown up, disabling the most important waterway carrying heavy barge traffic between the Ruhr and Rhine rivers. As soon as the locks were repaired, saboteurs sunk two one-thousand-ton barges between them.

By early March, Germans were attacking the train lines every day, and the fight escalated for weeks. On March 14, the French tried to raise the costs of sabotage further by using human shields. From that day forward, German mayors and municipal officials would ride every train operated by the French and Belgians, day and night. If saboteurs weren't deterred by threats to their own lives, maybe they would be by endangering their fellow citizens. The new policy did nothing to slow the Germans down. Two days later, three bomb attacks hit two separate trains and damaged track switches that sent an empty freight train into a head-on collision with a troop train coming from Trier, killing one French soldier and seriously injuring six. That same month, the locks on the Rhine–Herne Canal were blown up once again.

This battle of the railways seemed to peak that spring on April 27, when five separate bombs hit different targets, but it grew even more vicious in June. There was the usual smattering of sabotage bombings meant to disable railroad infrastructure, but two events were particularly shocking. On June 27 a bomb was thrown into the waiting room of the Wiesbaden train station, across the Rhine River from the city of Mainz, the first terror attack targeting Germans riding French trains. Two Germans were killed and ten severely wounded—a bloody warning to other Germans about the dangers of "collaboration" with the occupiers' rail operations.

The second event delivered the heaviest blow to Allied forces since the beginning of the conflict, but this time Belgian troops were in the crosshairs. The attack was seen as retaliation for a deadly confrontation in the city of Duisburg, when Belgian soldiers shot seven suspected German saboteurs, and for a death sentence handed down by a French military court against seven more Germans convicted of sabotage three days later. On the night of the death sentence convictions, a time bomb ripped through a passenger train car carrying Belgian soldiers home for leave, completely shredding its exterior, leaving only the twisted, smoking steel ribs that framed the train-car walls. The bomb killed ten soldiers and badly wounded forty-three. Belgian authorities shuttered the city's theaters, cafés, and restaurants, and banned all vehicle travel, including streetcars; they also seized the mayor of Duisburg and twelve leading citizens and held them as hostages against further attacks, and forced other hostages to ride all trains traveling through the Belgian occupation zone.

And then there was the battle for the streets, which burned nearly continuously within Ruhr valley cities and towns. Agitated Germans struck back at the occupiers in both covertly subversive and openly violent ways; the occupiers would retaliate to suppress the insurgency, and the cycle continued into the summer of 1923, racking up so many hostile confrontations that it's hard to paint a comprehensive picture of the struggle. One foreign correspondent described the "indelible impression of a country occupied by an enemy army under essentially warlike conditions . . . that if you only motor far enough you will run into the drumfire of a major battle or . . . trench warfare . . . as the French army tightens its grip on the Ruhr."[10] A few choice examples, where the battle for the streets flared brightest, help to capture the nature of the conflict and its intensity.

As we saw earlier, the first major clash of the Ruhr War was in Bochum on January 16, where hundreds of protesters singing war songs taunted French guards, the guards fired on the mob, and the first German casualty fell. This seemed like an isolated incident, until a wave of street violence swept northward from the mid-Rhine city of Mainz, where on January 24 a French military judge convicted and fined the six leading directors of Ruhr mines for refusing to supply reparations coal. The news was telegraphed across the Rhineland and into the Ruhr, followed by orders for a region-wide general strike that brought thousands into the streets in Mainz and Coblenz, in Düsseldorf and Dortmund, and then Essen. The railroads, barge traffic, telephones, and the telegraph were paralyzed by midnight, shops were shuttered, and throngs of Germans roamed about, looking to vent their anger. Rioters in Mainz marched on the hotels housing French officers, singing the wartime favorite "Victory over France," smashing windows and jeering at sentries, until cavalry forces broke up the crowds. In Coblenz, rioters tore apart the offices of a French-sponsored newspaper that had been agitating for Rhineland separatism. Further north in Düsseldorf a peaceful protest by hundreds of well-dressed middle-class Germans—bank clerks, shop owners, engineers, managers—turned violent, with French cavalry riding down the stone-throwing mob and soldiers firing volleys to drive them back. One German was shot and several French soldiers were pulled from the scene after being struck down by flying rocks. The next day the mayor and police chief were arrested for failing to stop the rioters; French tanks and machine-gun crews controlled all strategic points in the city; armored cars patrolled the streets, and the infantry locked down the rail station. In Essen a huge crowd was waiting for the convicted mine directors returning home from prison, and the crowd turned into a protest march. The protesters ringed the hotel where French engineers were billeted; a few threw stones and they all sang war songs until the sentries set up machine guns and a rifle shot rang out in warning. German police arrived to break up the march before the mob reached French military headquarters, while batteries of French artillery waited in firing positions outside the city to defend French formations.

For weeks, Essen remained a "small volcano," in the words of one witness. The streets each night were "surging with people and police dashing hither and thither and French patrols chasing . . . frightened crowds into side streets."[11] The volcano erupted again in mid-February when French authorities decided it was time to break a boycott by local restaurants, cafés, and shops that refused to serve French and Belgian customers. The plan was to suffocate these businesses by ordering them closed, but the order let loose an escalating whirlwind of mutual retaliation. The Kaiserhof Hotel, the French engineers' headquarters, went dark after its electricity was cut; in turn, French officials threatened to cut power to the entire city. Packs of young men rampaged through the streets chased by French patrols, and ordinary citizens filled the public squares to protest the shop closings. Essen's mayor, the vice mayor, the director of the electrical works, and the president of the Hotel Keepers' Union were all arrested for allowing things to spin out of control. French officials seized the two largest hotels in the city; their troops were arresting German police who refused to salute French army officers; and occupying soldiers were taking goods without payment from the shops that remained open. On February 16 a beer-hall brawl broke out after the barman refused to serve two French soldiers, who then jumped behind the bar and helped themselves to the beer taps. A gun battle with the German police left the French soldiers severely wounded and one German policeman dead. A battalion of French infantry stormed the Essen police barracks, where they arrested the police chief and disarmed all one thousand of the city's police officers. For days French cavalry and armored cars patrolled the streets, attacked sporadically by roaming gangs and making arrests in turn, while the local police refused to enforce the law from that day forward. On February 17 a bomb exploded in the alley outside the Kaiserhof Hotel, shattering its first-floor windows.

As Essen boiled, riots and counterattacks flared across the Ruhr and in Düsseldorf, Coblenz, Dorsten, and Recklinghausen, where fifty thousand were in the streets, supporting a citywide general strike and French tanks and infantry reinforcements rushed in to suppress the swelling violence. A German laborer was killed by a French sentry in Gunkenrath, a German policeman was killed and another wounded in Oberhausen, a local was killed when French soldiers fired into a mob in Witten. In the city of Gelsenkirchen, perhaps the most important coal-mining town in Europe, a fight between a German police patrol and two French gendarmes who refused to obey a traffic stop left one of the Germans dead and both of the gendarmes wounded. In response, a heavy French force surged into the city with cavalry and artillery; it disarmed all local police and made dozens of arrests, including the mayor, vice mayor, director of the local Reichsbank branch, and top police officials, who were all forced at gunpoint to goosestep their way into custody. French soldiers began a door-to-door collection forcing residents to turn over money and goods to help cover the fines levied against the entire town for the disturbances. The next day a French army officer was severely beaten by a German pack as he tried to board a train.

Bochum, where the battle for the streets began, was still "alive with uncowed humanity," as one reporter saw it.[12] Six hundred were arrested on the night of February 24 for violating the nine o'clock curfew; they were in the streets to protest the death of another German killed by a French patrol firing into a crowd. They were also furious over the ransacking of the local chamber of commerce headquarters by French troops earlier that day. The French explained that they simply needed furniture for their own offices, and that officials at the chamber had refused to cooperate. Bystanders watched the French make off with more than just the furniture. They took the carpets, the curtains, and the library; they stole money from the office safe, and looted the wine cellar. Two days later a heavily armed "punitive expedition," with ten tanks and machine-gun crews, moved in to enforce martial law. The French force cut off the business district completely, closing all of its hotels, restaurants, cafés, and theaters; the drugstores were the only businesses left open. The town was fined, the police force disbanded, and the mayor and the twenty-two members of the city council were arrested. By the end of February, the mayor of every city and town in the Ruhr valley except two had been arrested or expelled from the region.

March was no less violent; two incidents vividly capture the intensity of the ongoing clash. In the city of Buer, on the night of March 13, a hunt for the assassins that gunned down a French officer and a civilian administrator led a team of gendarmes to the home of a German policeman, where they found him hiding in a closet with his accomplice, a local official from the German railroad. During the arrest they made a run for it, but were killed by the French police before they could escape. As news of the deadly arrest spread, hundreds of angry men took to the streets, and in a frenzy they charged a French guard post. Eight of the attackers were shot down, leaving five dead and three wounded. The French army responded with a brutal threat: The mayor and four other town officials were seized as hostages, to be shot at once in retaliation for the next assassination or ambush of occupation troops.

Two weeks later, Essen was the site of another deadly flare-up. The spark this time was a French demand for more automobiles from the local population. When the call went out to individual owners and companies to turn over vehicles, the giant manufacturer Krupp was on the list. On the morning of March 31 a French officer and ten soldiers arrived to execute what they thought would be a routine requisition. But as they stood in the street in front of the Krupp garage, confined by the enormous factory buildings lining each side, the factory sirens blared and seven thousand workers streamed out, quickly filling the street and crowding around the small French team. As stones and coal flew from the mass of workers, the soldiers took cover in a smaller garage, where they were assaulted with jets of hot water from the steam hoses. Warning shots were fired, the crowd pressed forward, and the French detachment opened fire directly into the surging mob. French tanks and machine-gun crews raced to the scene, where the final tally revealed that thirteen Krupp workers were dead and fifty wounded. Gustav Krupp von Bohlen und Halbach, the director of Krupp Works, and three of his senior staff, were arrested, charged with orchestrating the assault, and held responsible for the deadly results.

THE WAR AT HOME

Throughout the Ruhr War, Chancellor Cuno's commitment to the passive resistance campaign never flagged. The stakes in this fight sustained his determination. This was not about reparations, he insisted; France aimed for nothing less than the destruction of the German Reich. If Germany held firm for just a bit longer, he believed, sheer frustration with the occupation's continuing failure would break the enemy's will and Germany would emerge victorious. But Cuno had a serious problem: By the summer of 1923, Germany, not France, was on the edge of political exhaustion. Economic collapse and revolutionary chaos threatened to consume Germany by the day. In an emergency meeting on August 8, Cuno stood before the members of the Reichstag with trembling hands as Communist Party delegates hooted, shook their fists, and called him a liar, a crook, a traitor, until he threatened to have them removed by force. This bruising confrontation within the German legislature reflected a more-severe civil conflict tearing across the Reich outside. Still, Cuno persevered in his plea for struggle against France: "Passive resistance . . . must be continued with all our strength," he said.[13]

But the chaos in Germany had reached a tipping point. Hyperinflation and turmoil in German industry, which Germans traced directly to the Franco-Belgian invasion, were feeding anger and desperation in the labor force, and it intensified by the month. Just weeks after foreign forces had rolled into the Ruhr, prices in Germany shot up 248 percent; in February they climbed another 136 percent. By July the cost of living was rising faster than at any time in recorded history, in any country. The value of wages plummeted, along with the value of the German mark. The Reichsbank could not print paper currency fast enough to meet the demand for banknotes across the economy, and employers and local banks found it impossible to keep enough currency on hand to pay workers their full wages. German government statisticians calculated that the price of food, rent, home heating, and clothing at the end of August 1923 was 1,183,434 times higher than it had been just a few years earlier, before the Great War.[14]

By springtime, this severe economic distress had a profound effect on the character of political violence in Germany. While Germans continued to target French and Belgian occupiers sporadically into the summer, in late April and May a new kind of political violence exploded across the Ruhr valley, when rioting workers—what some called "unemployed malcontents" and others saw as Communist revolutionaries—fought vicious street battles against German police and citizen groups mobilizing to protect their towns. The city of Mulheim was ravaged by three days of mob rule that left ten dead and seventy wounded. Two thousand unemployed workers in Düsseldorf fought German police, leaving seven workers and police seriously injured. Two casualties fell in a day of fighting over wages, food, and clothing in Katernberg. The next day the town's factory sirens rallied four thousand locals who rushed to block the main road into town as another four thousand rioters converged for a second assault, leaving one more dead in the fight. German police in Essen fended off attacks by Communist bands trying to seize the coal mines. In Dortmund, five rioters were killed and up to eighty wounded when German police fired into a crowd of protesters. Citizen "self-protection forces" joined the fray armed with clubs. Communist agitators in Gelsenkirchen jumped into the vacuum left by the expulsion of the local police force; they seized police headquarters and took control of the city, plundering shops and forcing shop owners to slash food prices until citizen brigades and the fire department counterattacked. Eight more Germans were dead and nearly one hundred wounded. In Bochum, rioters attacked German police with grenades in a fight that led to thirteen more deaths. A total of forty Germans died at the hands of other Germans in the last week of May. As the weeks rolled along, this new fight among the Germans themselves racked up a higher casualty count than was ever produced by the fight between Germans and foreign occupation forces. Throughout this struggle, the French and Belgians stood aside as Germans tore into one another.

At the end of May this fratricidal fight made a major geographic leap out of the Ruhr valley into eastern Germany when rioting workers fought police and right-wing nationalists in the city of Dresden, where Communists were shuttering shops and looting those that refused. The uprising expanded to Frankfurt in the west and to Leipzig in the eastern region of Saxony. Nearby in Breslau, where hundreds of shops were ransacked and more Germans died, shopkeepers were opening their doors for three hours a day to show off their bare shelves, hoping to keep the looters at bay. Cuno ordered the German army to take control of Potsdam, a political stronghold for the Communist Party just south of Berlin, to block revolutionary forces that might move on the capital. At the end of July the *New York Times* reported what most observers had concluded: "complete internal anarchy" meant that a revolt which could upend Germany was just "a question of days," but "whether the outbreak will come from the Conservative Right or the Radical Left, no one knows."[15]

On August 11, time had run out for Chancellor Cuno. The Socialist parties passed a resolution of no confidence in his leadership and swung their support to Gustav Stresemann, the leader of the People's Party. Cuno resigned the next day. Stresemann knew what he was stepping into: "We are dancing on a volcano," he said one month earlier. "[W]e stand on the brink of revolution."[16] This was not political grandstanding; it was an honest assessment of the uncontainable civil violence that was tearing across Germany.

Consider just a sample of events in August and early September 1923.

Reports were reaching Berlin about a food crisis that was beyond control. Across the Reich farmers were refusing to sell potatoes, meat, butter, and eggs for a currency that was losing value by the day. In Düsseldorf on the northern Rhine, in Aachen on the far western border with the Netherlands, in Duisburg on the Ruhr, in the town of Werra on the Swiss border, workers were invading the fields to dig up potatoes and dozens were dying as farmers fought back to defend their property. Hundreds of thousands of children had been evacuated from the Ruhr because of malnutrition, which hit this region hardest. German leaders didn't have to look far, however, for evidence of this national disaster. Nearly every retail shop in Berlin was closed; there were no potatoes, no sausages, lard, or eggs to be found. A pound of butter cost one million marks, when a typical store clerk in the capital brought home just six million marks for a month's pay. Striking electrical workers kept much of the city in the dark; streetcars, buses, and subways were idled. Strikes by Berlin newspaper workers meant that Communist and Socialist papers were the only source of news in the city. Police held off Communist bands at bayonet point as they rushed the French embassy. Rioting at industrial plants in Berlin went on for days in a row, while one thousand young Communists ran through the Wilhelmstrasse, the heart of official Berlin, shouting "Death to [President] Ebert and [Chancellor] Cuno" outside their homes.[17] The Reichsbank was printing eight trillion marks a day, but could only supply banks with 60 percent of the currency they needed.

In Upper Silesia, on the far eastern border with Poland, the provincial governor was dragged through the streets and beaten. Martial law was declared in Hamburg, where shipyards had locked out workers to prevent them from seizing the facilities, and three dockworkers died fighting German police. Strikers had closed all factories in Leipzig, and the city's gas and electric supply was cut. Nine Communists died after trying to capture the town of Seitz. Nearly thirty thousand rioted in Aachen; ten died and more than one hundred were wounded attacking the police station. Communists took the town of Dattein, north of Essen, churning out heavy casualties along the way, and they controlled Helmstedt, while nationalists battled Communists in Arnstadt. On the day Stresemann assumed office, thirty-five died in German riots. One month later, one thousand unemployed workers in Dresden attacked police with bricks and clubs; six were killed in the melee, and nationalists and Communists fought each other in Bremen.

From exile in the Netherlands, the former crown prince was warning of an imminent Communist coup,[18] but this was not Stresemann's only problem. There were two other dire crises threatening to swamp the republic: Nazis in Bavaria and separatists in the Rhineland. Gen. Erich Ludendorff, the hero of the 1914 battles of Liège and Tannenberg, the man who held near-dictatorial emergency authority over Imperial Germany with General Hindenburg during the Great War, was now in Munich to throw his support behind Adolf Hitler and his National Socialist movement. The Nazis had been making noise for months in Bavaria, holding rallies and railing against the French occupiers and the weakness of the Weimar Republic. Together, Hitler and Ludendorff were treated as a serious threat by the German government. During a review of goose-stepping shock troops in mid-April, Ludendorff announced that "the time is soon coming when the whole German people will be called on to rise up to free our country from the foe." It was not just the French that he had in mind here, but the republican government of Germany itself. Once the republic was overthrown, Ludendorff saw a day "when we can again serve in the good cause of our old ruling house, which we formerly so loyally and honorably served."[19] In June, before a crowd of twenty-five thousand gathered to memorialize Albert Leo Schlageter, a young German executed by the French for sabotage, Hitler called on true heroes to lead Germany, and for a "fighting front of fanatics" that could avenge Schlageter through another death struggle with France.[20]

On September 2, General Ludendorff presided over a giant nationalist rally that engulfed the city of Nuremberg. Sedan Day demonstrations, to mark Germany's victory over the French Second Empire in 1870, were banned around Berlin and in the regions of Saxony and Thuringia. But in Bavaria, it was cause for championing nationalist revolution. Hundreds of thousands were there, a mixed throng of traditional monarchists, military veterans, and Nazis, joining forces to share in the rally's theme: the celebration of Germany's past glory and a call for the overthrow of the government. They held a giant field mass for the war dead and paraded by the uniformed thousands: youth groups, members of university student dueling corps, gray-shirted Nazis with their swastika banners, and veteran soldiers of 1870 and 1914. While Ludendorff presided, Hitler had the honor of the keynote address, which he used to call for "a new revolution . . . a nationalist revolution today, to restore Germany's might and greatness. We can save Germany from internal and foreign foes," he said, "only through blood and sword."[21]

In the Rhineland, a very different threat to the German state emerged, in the form of separatists working to sever the Rhineland from the Reich for good. Like Cuno, Stresemann saw this as the true goal of the French occupation. It's an impossible objective, he declared. Yet still, Stresemann had to contend with separatist agitation that further rattled Germany's political future. Stresemann's greatest allies in this fight were staunch German nationalists in the Rhineland who were breaking up separatist meetings with swinging fists and clubs over the previous months. But as some observers were warning, the ranks of the separatists seemed to be approaching a critical mass that helped them blunt the nationalists' violent resistance. Thousands were brought by special French trains to Coblenz in July, and to Düsseldorf and Bonn in August, to attend mass separatist meetings. French officials not only provided security, but they had booked the meeting halls as well.[22] Two weeks after the Sedan Day rally in Nuremberg, twelve thousand separatists marched through the streets of Aachen, fending off the attacks that followed. At the end of the month, forty thousand were in the streets of Düsseldorf, mostly simple spectators with their families, watching the fifteen thousand agitators marching for an independent Rhenish republic. Among them were two thousand members of a "separatist police force" that had been brought to the city on twenty-five special trains. Shots were fired, there was a frantic scramble in the streets, and when the gun battle between German police and armed separatists ended, at least twenty were dead and hundreds wounded. Occupation authorities blamed the German police for starting the "Bloody Sunday" fight, so French soldiers arrested every police officer they could find.

AN ACT OF DESPERATION

From the beginning of the Ruhr War, Gustav Stresemann had been an unshakable supporter of Cuno's passive resistance campaign. And, like Cuno, Stresemann's defiance was driven by what he saw as the invasion's goal: as

he put it, "the destruction of Germany."[23] While Stresemann would condemn "senseless" acts of violence when resistance turned active, he could
dismiss the bloody ways in which Germans hit back against the occupiers
by calling France the "intellectual creator of every act of violence" they suffered. France and Belgium "must be made to feel that they have invaded
a hostile country," he said in August.[24] Stresemann blamed Germany's
cascading crises—the runaway inflation, the Communist uprising, the
food riots, the nationalist agitation, and the Rhineland separatists—"in its
entirety" on France. It was a charge he repeated to the British and French
ambassadors, in cabinet meetings, to his People's Party colleagues, and in
public speeches.[25] Breaking Germany, he said, was the route to French
"political hegemony" in Europe.[26]

Despite the defiance they shared, by September 1923 Stresemann came
to a conclusion Cuno never broached publicly. In this battle of political
wills and irreconcilable positions, Germany had finally cracked. "This fight
is for the very existence of the Reich," Stresemann said in early July,[27] but
soon after, he realized that Germany had already lost. One astute foreign
observer, Anne O'Hare McCormick, reported that "Anyone who visits
Germany with the once popular idea that the allied armies should have
marched into Berlin to show the Germans that they lost the war is soon
disabused of his theory that the defeated do not know they are beaten."
McCormick saw that the Germans knew defeat "too well"; they "brood
over it constantly. . . . Just now Germany is fairly wallowing in defeat."[28] In
September Stresemann told the Foreign Committee of the Reichsrat what
defeat meant. "If the Government did not succeed in finding a solution to
the acute problems . . . confronting the country in both home and foreign
affairs, it would be the last constitutional Government in Germany." "In
other words," he said, "if the plans of the Government failed" to bring relief from French pressure, "economic and political chaos and the collapse
of the Reich would be imminent and inevitable."[29] The only way to escape
this fate is to succumb, end passive resistance, and negotiate a reparations
settlement. Passive resistance was valiant, but it was time to admit that "it
is not to the tune of 'Deutschland Uber Alles'"—the muscular German
national anthem—"that France will withdraw her regiments from the
Ruhr," Stresemann said. "Therefore, as long as Germany is weak, we cannot expect anything but a policy of compromise."[30] On September 24, after
a nine-hour cabinet meeting, the German government agreed to abandon
the passive resistance campaign, order full industrial production in the
Ruhr, and negotiate a deal that would get the occupiers' "stranglehold off
our neck."[31]

Germany had met defeat in the Ruhr War. But just like in 1918, defeat in 1923 didn't bring relief from foreign pressure or domestic turmoil. In the months after capitulation, the German crisis got much worse. In mid-October the cost of living spiked 534 percent in just one week; in Berlin a loaf of bread cost 14 cents, while the average worker was paid 20 cents a day. Food riots and looting by "hunger strikers" exploded again across Germany. Back in the United States, Maj. Gen. Henry Allen, who had commanded the American force on the Rhine, was taking charge of an emergency relief effort that would feed up to two million young Germans over the coming winter. "My recent visit there," General Allen said, "convinced me of the necessity of immediate action to prevent the wholesale starvation among German children."[32] Forty-four Germans were dead in Hamburg after a fight between unemployed workers and police over control of the shipyard. In Freiburg thirteen died in a clash with German army units. In Essen, five thousand stormed and seized the Krupp factory at the end of October; seven died in the fight. On October 21, Rhineland separatists declared independence for the "Rhenish Republic" from the government buildings they controlled in Aachen. Separatists were gathering power in Coblenz, Wiesbaden, Bingen, Crefeld, and Duren. In Mainz, separatists were fighting to seize city hall. In Duisburg, they controlled the city for five days until a brawl with Communists and trade unionists broke their hold; fifty Germans died in the struggle. Eighteen Germans were killed in a fight with pistols and hand grenades in a futile effort by local farmers to hold off separatists moving to seize Bonn, which they dominated on October 22. In Berlin, one thousand shops were looted in early November.

As hunger strikers and separatists were fighting their battles through the Ruhr valley, in the Rhineland, and in eastern Germany, in Bavaria the Nazi movement was preparing its own revolutionary uprising to bring down the republic. On the night of November 8, Adolf Hitler staged his Beer Hall Putsch in Munich. His goal was to seize control of the Bavarian state government, which since early October had been run by dissident nationalist leaders who declared emergency rule after Stresemann ended passive resistance in the Ruhr. Bavaria's new rulers refused to acknowledge Berlin's authority, and they were scheming over ways to take this nationalist uprising nationwide. In an interview on October 3, Hitler shared the new Bavarian leaders' disgust with Stresemann's defeatism. I "would never submit to France," he said. "If I had been at the head of the Government, the Ruhr district would have been burned down," just "as Moscow was burned by the Russians" while Napoleon's army was approaching in 1812. "France would never have found a single tree or a bridge there. Since the

Ruhr district no longer belongs to us today, it should vanish from the face of the earth."

But Hitler then scoffed at the idea that the new Bavarian leader, Gustav Ritter von Kahr, "has the strength necessary to carry the Nationalist movement across Bavaria into the rest of Germany."[33] The Beer Hall Putsch was Hitler's answer to these doubts. Once in control of Bavaria, Hitler intended to lead thousands of his Nazi storm troopers, along with thousands of soldiers in Bavaria who had defected from the national army, on a march to Berlin to mount his coup. In Berlin, President Ebert and Chancellor Stresemann proclaimed Hitler and his "crazed" followers to be traitors that had to be crushed. This included General Ludendorff, who joined Hitler that night to assume command of the nationalist military force. In their proclamation, Ebert and Stresemann warned that "The success of this crazy mutiny can only bring a new catastrophe to Germany."[34] The next morning, two thousand Nazis marched through the city toward the Bavarian Defense Ministry, but were challenged by a small contingent of loyal soldiers and state police when they reached Odeonsplatz square. In the gun battle that followed, fourteen Nazis and four German police were killed, the revolutionaries scattered, and the collapse of his coup led to Hitler's arrest two days later.

Just a few weeks after Hitler's defeat in Munich, Stresemann was forced to defend his own leadership in the Reichstag. And once again, he pointed an accusing finger at France for the political extremism tearing at the republic. "Nobody will deny that the development of internal German conditions is driving toward radical tendencies," Stresemann said. "Communism in Germany derives its strongest support from the misery breaking in on us, and the radicalism of the extreme Right builds its support under the National opposition we are now experiencing from France's attitude."[35] French leaders were not going to help Stresemann solve this desperate problem. In fact, French premier Raymond Poincaré decided to leverage this moment of crisis by raising the pressure on Germany even further. French withdrawal from the Ruhr would no longer hinge on German payment of reparations demands, he said. French forces would remain until renewed inspections by the Military Inter-Allied Commission of Control confirmed that Germany was in full compliance with disarmament obligations in the Versailles Treaty. With calamity swirling around the republic, Stresemann lost a Reichstag vote of confidence on November 23, and he resigned from the chancellorship. His successor, Wilhelm Marx, summed up Germany's position in a sad Christmas address: "What has been done through the last year is nothing but war," he said, a war "being continued against the defenseless and disarmed nation in the center of an official but unexisting peace."[36]

In July 1924, French and Belgian soldiers were still in the Ruhr valley, their leaders talking about another two years before the region would be liberated from foreign occupation. In August, when Germany accepted the new Dawes Plan on reparations, France and Belgium agreed to evacuate the Ruhr one year later. For Germany, this seemed like the beginning of the end of this nightmare, until the British government made a shocking announcement in December: British forces would not evacuate the city of Cologne by January 10, 1925, as called for by the terms of the Versailles Treaty. They offered two reasons. First, French and Belgian forces would still be on the far northeastern side of Cologne in the Ruhr valley, so Allied evacuation of the northern Rhine zone was impossible until that operation was complete. Second, the military control commission would not have its report on German disarmament finalized in time to validate this evacuation deadline.

The German government had faithfully followed the reparation requirements of the Dawes Plan for months and felt confident they were on track toward freedom from foreign soldiers. So this announcement was like a kick in the stomach, the most dismaying news the Germans had heard on the Ruhr occupation question since the previous summer. On December 30, 1924, Stresemann, now foreign minister in a new cabinet, gathered foreign correspondents for an address to ensure that the world understood Germany's position. As one reporter wrote after the meeting, "[T]he subject of military control worked Stresemann up to a frenzy of anger. Red in the face and sputtering in his excitement," he glared repeatedly at the French correspondents at the front of the room while he "thundered" about the "fact that Germany is fully disarmed," and the "fairy tales" others spread to the contrary.[37] But Stresemann was painfully aware of the reality he faced; while he could thunder all day long, there was little else he could actually do to bend the Allies' will or undermine the power that gave them the freedom to take whatever steps they chose against Germany. This painful reality brings our story full circle, back to the "remarkable" and "courageous" diplomatic push of early 1925 that led to the celebrations of a new era in Locarno, Switzerland.

Impotence and vulnerability—these were the roots of the Treaty of Mutual Guarantee negotiated at Locarno. Stresemann was desperate to find relief from the persistent dangers of the past few years. As long as the Allies kept boots planted on German soil, Germany would never escape the economic and political turmoil that this occupation generated—an existential threat to the unified German state and its republican government. So Stresemann made his opening offer to Britain and France in January 1925 to start a diplomatic process that might solve this problem. As he explained to the Reichstag, "A straight line of German foreign policy leads through the liquidation of the Ruhr war, to which we were forcibly subjected . . . and the exploitation of the Ruhr, to the . . . Security Pact." This initiative helped clear the way for the final withdrawal of French forces from the Ruhr at the end of July 1925. Stresemann emphasized, however, that liberation of the Ruhr was just the beginning. "Germany has started a peace offensive on the grand scale, and it is the desire of the Reich Government to pursue it to a favorable conclusion."[38]

When the German cabinet developed its negotiating position for Locarno, the top priority was to get the Allies to agree "that the existing system of occupation shall be fundamentally altered." Not only did the Germans want the promised withdrawal from Cologne, they also asked for cuts in the total number of occupation soldiers in the Rhineland, an end to occupation of all German territory before 1935, and freedom from any system of inspections in the Rhineland after evacuation was complete.[39] These demands didn't go over well with the French. In his diary from the Locarno meetings Stresemann recorded that French foreign minister Aristide Briand "had almost fallen off the sofa when he heard what I had said."[40]

But Stresemann pushed these points with a warning: Occupation will not bring peace or security; instead, it will be an "insurmountable obstacle" preventing France and Germany from ever moving past the hostility and vengeance that had gripped this relationship for generations. As long as the Rhineland was held by French forces, he said, this region would hang like an "iron curtain" between our countries and war could once again tear through Europe.[41] Despite the warning, Briand and British foreign minister Austen Chamberlain refused to offer formal guarantees. In the end, they held out mere verbal promises of early evacuation once Germany had fully complied with its disarmament obligations.[42] The three foreign ministers would leave the question there, but Stresemann's Rhineland demilitarization pledge helped open the door to its early freedom from foreign troops in 1930. Unfortunately for Gustav Stresemann, the architect of this change, he would not live to see that day. Stresemann died of a stroke in October 1929, just fifty-one years old.

The "Spirit of Locarno" was justly celebrated in late 1925. The rhetoric that flew about in the afterglow of the conference was perhaps a bit overwrought, but in the shadow of the painful years leading up to 1925, the conviviality of the Locarno meetings seemed to signal that a promising shift in

European politics was under way. This was particularly true for the British, like Foreign Minister Austen Chamberlain, who anguished over the corrosive effects of French policy, while feeling powerless to stop that "devil's merry-go-round" of spiraling conflict that would lead to a more dangerous future. For Chamberlain, the Spirit of Locarno was a decisive break in this trend, something to build on. But a more frank assessment suggests that it's important not to make too much of this conclusion. After all, the animating spirit of Locarno, what drove it forward, was not mutual conciliation among free and equal states trying to move past the fear and hostility that bred the Great War. The animating spirit of Locarno was coercion and desperation, direct by-products of the Ruhr War. With this in mind, as we look ahead to 1936, the key question to consider is this: What was the legacy of the Ruhr War for the evolving European security dilemma of the 1930s?

For France, the short-term legacy of the Ruhr War was a vibrant debate over whether territorial occupation was a useful tool for ensuring that Germany met its obligations. In the spring of 1924, more than a year after French and Belgian forces took control of the Ruhr valley, official statistics on the occupation showed that France ended up paying much more to execute the operation than it ever got back in reparation payments. Raymond Poincaré's political opponents blamed his Ruhr policy for the falling value of the French franc, for higher taxes and government debt, as well as increasing alienation of France from other major states. Poincaré's National Bloc was routed by leftist parties in the election of May 1924, and he was replaced as premier by Edouard Herriot. Its long-term legacy, however, was much more important.

The Ruhr War, it seemed, had finally compelled Germany to accept its subordinate position in the European system, exactly where France expected it to stay. And Germany's submission was symbolized most vividly by the pledge to respect Rhineland demilitarization. As the French would continue to point out, this pledge found its way into the Locarno treaty because Germany itself laid the promise on the table in its original security pact proposals of January 1925. In turn, Germany's initiative cemented French expectations that this Rhineland pledge was indelible, a permanent feature of the European political landscape that was sanctified by international law. France could now point to this "voluntary" act as the legal and political basis for holding Germany accountable in perpetuity, and for holding Britain accountable for enforcement, with military power if necessary.

The legacy of this stinging defeat for Germany was a conundrum. Impotence and vulnerability had indeed compelled German ratification of this new peace treaty. It was a near-term necessity, given the power realities at the time, not a one-sided voluntary sacrifice of national sovereignty on behalf of future peace. From the very beginning, Germans of all political stripes would agree that one day, when it was strong enough to do so, Germany would reclaim its full rights over the Rhineland. The conundrum for a future leader would be to decide how long Germany would abide by the Locarno treaty, and when the challenge came, how it should go about upending the political expectations that the DMZ was supposed to last forever. Gustav Stresemann had predicted this moment in 1925; he knew some future German leader would bring the demilitarized zone to an end. One thing Stresemann never would have predicted, however, is that Adolf Hitler, his most rabid antagonist from that painful year of turmoil in 1923, would be the leader to solve this conundrum.

For Britain, the Ruhr War left a legacy that reverberated heavily into the next decade. By the time the Locarno treaty was signed, British leaders had already concluded that whatever gains France made in the power game against Germany through these preventive military measures, these gains would be short-lived, while the future would be even more dangerous once this temporary advantage passed. Long before Adolf Hitler abruptly challenged Rhineland demilitarization in 1936, British leaders were primed to recognize that preventive military force to push the Germans back out, and down, would not solve the security problems that still gripped Western Europe. Preventive war would blow up in their faces.

7

SOWING DRAGON'S TEETH

Vengeance is a poor thing. It breeds vengeance . . . if we go on . . . there will be another war and we shall have this merry-go-round of the devil forever and forever.

—Former British prime minister David Lloyd George, October 1923

Austen Chamberlain's legacy was in tatters. On March 7, 1936, Adolf Hitler tore it to pieces with his thundering pronouncement that Rhineland demilitarization was over. Thousands of German soldiers were now streaming into the forbidden zone, turning Hitler's words into an accomplished fact. The Locarno treaty was the achievement of a lifetime, the work that defined Chamberlain's career, the diplomatic breakthrough that earned him the Nobel Peace Prize. And, he believed, Locarno had saved civilization from the downward spiral of power politics that could only end in another catastrophic world war. Austen Chamberlain was now on the sidelines of British politics, still a Member of Parliament (MP), but no longer in a leadership role within the British government. This didn't keep him from declaring his outrage over Hitler's defiance, however. In a speech at Cambridge University on March 11, in what the *New York Times* called a "blistering denunciation," Chamberlain railed against this "act of brutal force" that had him "quivering" with dark memories of events that "rendered the great war inevitable."[1]

In a speech in Birmingham three days later, Chamberlain reminded his constituents that Britain could not shrink from its responsibilities during this profound crisis. "Our country's signature is sacred . . . I drink to our country as one who knows the value of its pledged word and who knows that it will make good its obligations."[2] But was the British government living up to its obligations to its Locarno partners? In private, Chamberlain seemed anguished by this question. "I am profoundly unhappy about the developments of the last ten days, and particularly about the hesitations of the Government" in response to Hitler's "hostile act," he told a friend in a letter. "What is the value of England's word," he asked, "if she does not honour it on this occasion?"[3] Writing to his sister Hilda, Chamberlain sounded despondent. He worried that Britain would not "keep its solemn engagement" with France, leading "every other country in Europe [to] feel that England is a broken reed," which could only end in "our own ultimate ruin."[4] But what were Britain's obligations here?

The French government certainly had an answer to this question, and Britain embraced French expectations for the first step in the process: formal condemnation of German actions. From the opening days of the crisis Britain was center stage, playing host in London to the special meetings of the Locarno powers and then the League of Nations Council, where Germany was found in blatant violation of both the Locarno and the Versailles treaties. But for France this guilty verdict was just the beginning; it merely opened the door to the next steps toward France's ultimate goal. The Rhineland must be "liberated" from German jackboots. This indelible feature of the postwar order, this key to French security and European peace, sanctified by international law and accepted by every German government since 1925, must be freed from the Wehrmacht forces that now roamed Rhineland soil and peered across the French border. And as the French saw it, Adolf Hitler's violation was a flagrant act of aggression that gave France every right to resort to war to turn back the threatening power shift it represented. France expected Britain to join it on a ladder of escalating preventive actions, which could ultimately lead to preventive attack against the German army if economic sanctions on the lower rungs failed to achieve this goal.

French foreign minister Pierre-Étienne Flandin was confident in this strategy, and he worked hard to convince his British counterpart, Anthony Eden, that Germany would cave in the early stages of this confrontation. Even if the Allies had to push the Germans to the wall, drive them out of the Rhineland with force, so be it. We have this window of opportunity to stifle the continuing rise of German power and solve the security problem that looms before us, he argued, and we must jump through this window right now. If we fail to take bold action, Flandin warned, we will face war in the next two years, and pay a high price for the delay.[5]

Despite the impassioned warning, British leaders were unmoved. What the French foreign minister did not know is that he had taken on an impossible diplomatic mission. The British cabinet held its first crisis meeting on Monday morning, March 9, and accepted the "no preventive war" position immediately without dissent, debate, or even a respectable discussion of the question. The minutes of the cabinet meeting reveal this glaring void: not a single minister asked for deeper study of the political or military implications of the preventive war option.[6] A week later British officials made this position explicit by refusing to sign a secret French letter promising support for military action if diplomacy failed to pry the Wehrmacht out of the Rhineland.[7] Of course, nothing was standing in the way of independent Franco-Belgian military operations. If French leaders believed their own predictions about this window of opportunity to save themselves from a more-costly future war, there was nothing Great Britain could do to block the preventive war option. But politically, France would not strike out alone; they would not repeat the experience of the Ruhr invasion of a decade earlier, with only the Belgians at their side. The proposal was dead. Flandin, it was said, was "mystified."[8] As we've seen, postwar observers have been mystified as well—more than mystified, in fact, looking back on the British veto with anger and accusations of willful blindness to the threat or cowardly pacifism.

This brings us back to the heavy judgment of history that hangs over this moment in time. Where was Great Britain as the Nazi menace grew? British leaders had been warned by their French partners, they heard the "better now than later" logic at the heart of the preventive war temptation, yet still they refused to take those bold steps that, it is said, might have changed the course of history. So why did British leaders dismiss the preventive war option so abruptly in 1936? A few common answers have been floated over the years, but each fails to account for the deeper strategic perspective that ultimately shaped Britain's choices.

BLINDNESS? COWARDICE? WEAKNESS?

Was it willful blindness to the growing German threat? Winston Churchill, it seems, thought this was a debilitating British pathology in the early years of the Third Reich's rise. And Churchill was quite sensitive to how others treated his persistent efforts to trumpet a warning cry. "I have been mocked and censured as a scare-monger and even a warmonger," criticized as a "hothead and an alarmist," he said in 1936. But by the time the

Rhineland crisis flared, he was saying this with a tone of satisfied vindication, as a strong consensus on the problem of rising German power had already swung behind his alarmism.[9]

It is hard to sustain the claim that Britain avoided preventive war in 1936 because of blindness to future dangers. In early March 1935 the cabinet issued a white paper berating Germany for its continuing rearmament, which was "unabated and uncontrolled"; for stirring up the spirit of militarism among its youth; for whipping up anxiety across the Continent, and putting peace itself in "peril." With the German threat on the rise, the white paper declared, the British government had no choice but to move decisively away from its pursuit of great power disarmament and ramp up its own defense spending. The day after Britain's defense white paper was released, Hitler feigned illness and canceled a conference with British foreign minister John Simon, scheduled for later that week, even though in press photos from Berlin a cheerful Führer appeared healthy enough to visit an auto show that day. It was a subtle protest, but Hitler leveraged this moment to send an even louder retort to Britain's armament plans, and he did so through Hermann Göring, the Reich Air Minister, who then unveiled the new German air force to the world.

Days later Hitler went one step further, announcing that Germany was reintroducing conscription to build a standing army 550,000 strong. The announcement helped the British government make its case on the importance of rebuilding its own armed forces. At the end of the month Hitler met with John Simon as originally planned and proudly shocked the foreign minister by informing him that German airpower was already a match for the Royal Air Force. This further rattled British leaders, who now fixated on the threat of a surprise "knockout blow" from the air and poison gas bombs falling on British cities.[10] In early 1936 Churchill was still raising the alarm, but he was no longer marginalized by this position. In fact, the only prominent political figure to challenge Churchill's threat assessment directly during the Rhineland crisis was former prime minister David Lloyd George, who pointed to what he saw as the overwhelming collective power of the states ranged against Germany that tipped the balance of power decisively in Britain's favor.[11]

The British cabinet, however, did not share Lloyd George's confidence in the military balance of power. In mid-January 1936, two months before Hitler sent the Wehrmacht across the Rhine, Foreign Minister Anthony Eden circulated a set of threat assessments to his colleagues, prepared over the past several years by their ambassador in Berlin. In his cover memo Eden characterized Germany's goals in blunt terms: "the destruction of the peace settlement" from the Great War "and re-establishment of Germany as the dominant Power in Europe."[12] British leaders were still unsure about the details of Germany's plans. Where would Germany make its push? How far did its revisionist ambitions reach? Would it resort primarily to political and economic means to extend its influence, or would it turn to aggressive military action?

Despite the uncertainty, Eden's January 1936 threat assessment was meant to prepare government ministers for Britain's response to the general threat: a massive three-year rearmament financing bill that the cabinet would submit to Parliament in the coming weeks. Three days after German soldiers fanned out across the Rhine zone, over 70 percent of British MPs voted to approve the resolution on the second day of debate. A few months later, in his regular column for the *Evening Standard*, Churchill was reporting with approval that "Britain has begun to rearm on a great scale."[13] A keen awareness of the growing threat pushed British defense spending up by 37 percent from 1935 to 1936, by 87 percent from 1935 to 1937, and it doubled between 1935 and 1938.[14] With this in mind, the "willful blindness" to the threat explanation doesn't account for Britain's rejection of preventive attack in the Rhineland.

Was it cowardice or rampant pacifism? This argument is as old as the "guilty men" thesis rolled out in the spring of 1940, as British soldiers were being pulled off the beaches of Dunkirk in France to escape the German blitzkrieg. Today it remains a popular theme. According to this view, while British leaders recognized the Nazi threat to European security, they were paralyzed by the enduring trauma of the Great War, by personal angst, and by a frightened population still grappling with war weariness born in the trenches of the Western Front. Without the moral courage and political will to take a stand with military counterforce and hold the German menace in check, this argument goes, all Britain had left was appeasement of German desires, this desperate and naive impulse to hide from the threat, hoping it would just go away.

This explanation too is unconvincing. This is not to say that the Great War experience was irrelevant in British decision-making during the 1930s. It had a profound effect on ideas about war, security, and peace, and these ideas are a critical part of the story.[15] We'll explore this subject in greater detail in the next chapter. But a generic claim that British leaders and the public were paralyzed and unable to contemplate war throughout this decade simply does not square with evidence demonstrating the will to confront aggression and risk war at key moments. Two basic examples illustrate this point. In the fall of 1935, the British public was outraged by Fascist Italy's aggressive campaign to crush Ethiopia and pull it into Benito Mussolini's dream of an expanding Italian empire in northern Africa. In the general election of November 1935, the Conservative Party won a parliamentary majority with a platform promising British leadership in the League of Nations to make collective security against international aggression a reality. The Conservatives pointed to the economic sanctions imposed against Italy in October, and British naval reinforcements sent to the Mediterranean as the crisis escalated, as a perfect example of bold British action. But it had an unintended consequence. Containing Italian aggression threatened to shatter the Stresa Front, an initiative in April 1935 linking Italy, France, and Great Britain in a collective effort to block German expansion. To alleviate this stress, in December 1935 British foreign minister Samuel Hoare signed off on a secret proposal with his French counterpart that essentially abandoned Ethiopia and granted Italy the right to annex choice territory in exchange for an end to this ugly war. When news of the proposal leaked in the press, the British public's reaction was explosive. British war minister Duff Cooper recalled, "[T]here arose a howl of indignation from the people . . . During my experience of politics I have never witnessed so devastating a wave of public opinion."[16] Samuel Hoare was forced to resign, the appeasement plan was dropped, and sanctions against Italy continued. Hoare's successor Anthony Eden admitted in July 1936 that war with Italy was a near miss; the government rejected the option not because of pacifist impulses or fear of war in general, but because even victory would simply stir up broader strategic problems elsewhere in Europe.[17] As Churchill observed later, the escalating standoff generated serious threats and counterthreats of military attack through the spring of 1936, and the British public never blanched.

Perhaps the best example challenging the notion of paralyzing pacifism is the rapid shift in British public opinion soon after the 1938 Munich Agreement, which saw an unmistakable spike in support for muscular containment, even at the risk of war, to block further German expansion. As one scholar notes, by October 1938, "The same public that had overwhelmingly supported appeasement" going into the Munich conference "now demanded confrontation," as political leaders across the three main parties and the public came to "see this revisionist state as insatiable, impervious to negotiation, and responsive only to the language of force."[18] It was a reaction to a jarring shift in German rhetoric on the future of Europe. Until late 1938, the Third Reich followed the postwar German tradition of making claims for territorial changes based on notions of equality and justice. After Munich, Germany dropped the pretense and justified its demands merely by pointing to its own military might.

Germany's flagrant coercion and military occupation of the rump Czechoslovakian state in March 1939 cemented this new attitude. Two weeks later the British government reversed its long-standing refusal to ally with Eastern European states and pledged publicly to stand with France and help defend Polish independence against future German aggression.[19] Two days after Germany invaded Poland in September, the Allies declared war. There was no paralyzing pacifism standing in the way of this evolving strategy; the British accepted war in spite of the raw memories of the last conflict and the frank recognition that the next Great War would be even worse. So if the British recognized the growing danger Germany posed, and if general pacifism didn't stand in the way of a muscular response, what else might account for the rejection of preventive war to solve this security problem in 1936?

Was it because of military weakness? The debate over the military balance question endures as scholars continue to puzzle over the 1930s. Some postwar observers, drawing on estimates of relative military strength during the 1930s, suggest that the Western Allies still had enough of a hard power edge against Germany to achieve victory in a fight over the Rhineland, and that war in 1936 was a smarter option than waiting to confront Germany at some point in the future, as it grew stronger each year.[20] With these estimates in mind, and the brutal costs of World War II looming over our retrospective assessment, the postwar lament seems reasonable: Wasn't this the great "lost opportunity" to stop Hitler before he was ready to push his murderous agenda to its awful conclusion? In this debate, some shine a more-sympathetic light on the pressing military conditions the Allies faced and the constraints that they argue made avoiding war the smartest option in 1936. France and Britain had global military commitments to far-flung colonies, and Japanese aggression in Asia and Italian aggression in the Horn of Africa put these commitments at risk. In contrast to the military optimists, these sympathetic pessimists argue that neither France nor Britain had the margin of power necessary to accept the risks of war over the German demilitarized zone. Declassified British government documents clearly show how they worried about a potential armed clash.

The real problem in early 1936 was the festering possibility of armed conflict with Fascist Italy to stop its war of conquest against Ethiopia. The threat of war to the south demanded a heavy British defense commitment in the Mediterranean, from the Strait of Gibraltar in the west to the Suez Canal in the east, through the canal and into the Red Sea to safeguard the sea lanes to India. In a verbal report to the British cabinet on March 16, the Chief of the Imperial General Staff admitted that war with Germany would "be a disaster for which the Services with their existing commitments in the Mediterranean are totally unprepared."[21] And with Parliament's rearmament resolution ready to launch the biggest British defense buildup since the Great War, the most sensible grand strategy according to this alternative view was to delay a fight until the Allies had enough time to rebuild and refocus their armed forces on the German threat. In other words, if war was coming, "better later than now."[22]

While this argument captures a legitimate British concern about military readiness for a fight with Germany, it falls short as an explanation for the decision to reject preventive war in 1936. The problem is that the "better later than now" argument assumes that had British leaders been more confident in their military capabilities and Britain's global strategic position, they would have been more likely to fight to restore the demilitarized zone and preserve its strategic benefits. In other words, implicit in this argument is a claim that the British believed the Rhineland was something worth fighting to protect, as long as the distribution of power made the battlefield prospects of preventive war a reasonable choice. But this is a poor interpretation of the government's assessment of the military risks. While the question was studied carefully, it was not to determine if war now was better than delaying the clash until rearmament improved the odds of battlefield victory. The real goal was to understand the risks of imposing economic sanctions as a mechanism to force the German army out of the Rhineland.

Foreign Minister Flandin wanted the League of Nations to hit Germany with tough international penalties: a boycott of German products and an embargo on financial credits, arms sales, and raw materials that might feed Germany's military production. But in Britain, the Committee of Imperial Defence delivered a stark conclusion to the cabinet: Economic sanctions would fail to compel German withdrawal. The only countries expected to participate in punitive sanctions were three signatories to the Locarno treaty: Britain, France, and Belgium. Italy would refuse, of course, since it was already the target of international sanctions over Ethiopia. And given that Germany's move into the Rhineland was not actually aggression against another state, the League of Nations wouldn't authorize punitive sanctions by all its members. Financial penalties imposed by just three of the Locarno states would have no practical effect. And the only way to tighten a noose around Germany's foreign trade was to launch a maritime blockade, which created a high risk of wider war. In the cabinet discussion of this question, another conclusion was put on the table: Economic sanctions would trigger a retaliatory German attack, quickly pushing the Allies up the escalatory ladder toward preventive war.[23]

And this was the problem, because Britain had no intention of fighting Germany to preserve the Rhineland demilitarized zone. This decision didn't spring from the operational military question, but from a strategic question: Would preventive war solve the political problem that generated the threat of another great power conflict in Europe? Their answer, unsurprisingly, was no. The table was set for this decision a decade earlier, and the sudden rise of the Nazi regime in 1933 did nothing to change the simple conclusion that underpinned it: Preventive war was a strategic dead end. It would not fix the German problem. Even if Western armies forced Germany into retreat from the Rhineland, this victory would be merely temporary. And with the legacy of the Ruhr War hanging over the Rhineland question, over the demilitarization pledge in the Locarno treaty, and over French security policy in general, British leaders reasoned that an invasion of Germany would make the security problem even more dangerous than it already was.

The preventive war paradox loomed over this decision. Like the ancient Greek legend of Cadmus, who sowed the teeth of a slain dragon and brought to life savage warriors that sprouted from the earth, British leaders worried that an invasion of German territory, even with self-defense and the sanctity of international law as its rationale, would churn out such intense hostility and desire for revenge that the second great war Allied leaders wanted to prevent would inevitably spring to life.

To explain this perspective, we need to return to 1925, to the Ruhr War, and to the Locarno treaty. This is where we find the roots and the strategic rationale behind British policy. This is where we discover that Britain didn't shrink from its obligations to its Locarno partners; instead, this period reveals that Britain's choices in 1936 were perfectly consistent with policy set out a decade earlier.

TIME IS AN ALLY

There was one important fact about the 1920s that French and British leaders could agree on: The Great War Allies were passing through a window of opportunity made possible by the European power structure. More specifically, the *current* European power structure. If the Ruhr War demonstrated anything, it was the fact that, as Winston Churchill described it, "Germany is prostrate" in the shadow of domineering French strength. Churchill found great comfort in this fact. The "frightful possibility" of that next Armageddon he was already worrying about in the 1920s "is happily some considerable way off." German weakness and French strength—these were two sides of the same coin that bought the Europeans time. This condition, however, would not last. That too was a fact they agreed on. But within this window of opportunity, British leaders knew that time afforded them a chance to change the political dynamics that could pull the great powers into another total war. "At the worst," Churchill said, "there is a breathing space, measured by decades. Our problem is how to use this breathing space to end the quarrel."[24]

The French did not share this optimistic perspective. For the British time was an ally; for France, it was an adversary. French leaders, even internationalists like Foreign Minister Aristide Briand, fixated on the darker implications of German recovery in the years to come. There was strong support within France for developing alternatives to power politics, but at its core French security strategy depended on holding German power down,[25] through the mechanisms found in the Versailles Treaty, and with an iron girdle of military alliances that would contain Germany's future aggressive potential. Two years into the Ruhr War, British leaders found this haunting sense of insecurity absurd. Lord George Curzon, the chairman of the British Committee of Imperial Defence, reflected cabinet consensus in early 1925 when he mocked France's perspective. This so-called "defenceless condition of the Eastern frontier of France," he said, had no grounding in reality. "There is no defenceless condition there. France is the most powerful military country in Europe. Germany is disarmed. It may be that a danger will grow up in the future . . . But for the moment, surely, there is no danger at all."[26]

The problem with the French view was not simply that they suffered needless psychological stress by exaggerating their vulnerability. As the British saw it, the real problem was that such intense fear of the future was driving France to act in ways that stoked its rivalry with Germany, making the future more dangerous than it otherwise had to be. While the leaders of the three major political parties in Great Britain disagreed sharply on important foreign policy issues like trade and disarmament, on this point they all agreed. The only real difference among the parties was in style. The Conservative governments of Prime Minister Bonar Law and Stanley Baldwin set an enduring precedent for British policy during the Ruhr War, opposing France obliquely from the start with "benevolent neutrality." Austen Chamberlain proudly noted in a memorandum that when French coercion flared most dangerously, Britain held firm. "When our Allies . . . marched into the Ruhr, we refused to march with them," he wrote. "Again, in the Rhineland, we all along disassociated ourselves from the illegal and disreputable practices of the French" that sought to wrench the Rhineland away from Germany through separatist violence and political schemes. "We not only disassociated ourselves, but often drove the French to abandon such practices."[27] But they did so primarily by quietly working to shape French behavior in closed diplomatic settings, avoiding harsh public condemnation.

In January 1924 the Conservatives were replaced by the first Labour Party–led government in British history; the new prime minister, Ramsay MacDonald, took a brash new approach, opposing French policy with unusually frank language to express British grievances. A letter MacDonald sent to French premier Raymond Poincaré on February 21 was leaked to newspapers in both London and Paris a week later, and it nicely captures general British attitudes. The French want freedom from the German "menace," MacDonald wrote, which is understandable. But in the pursuit of "absolute security," they believed the "frontiers of France should be extended to the Rhine." The "view of . . . my countrymen," he said, "is that that policy can only perpetuate the uncertainty and dangers of a condition not of peace, but of war, and that in the end it will destroy whatever temporary security France may gain."[28] A leading figure in the Liberal Party, David Lloyd George, continued to grumble from the sidelines about the dysfunctions of the Versailles system, even though as prime minister he had a direct hand in the 1919 Paris peace talks that produced the document.

While a split in the party sent the Liberals on a downward spiral in British politics, Lloyd George remained highly visible and eminently quotable on the Franco-German problem. When the wartime German leader Field Marshal Paul von Hindenburg was elected president of the Weimar Republic in April 1925, raising fears of surging militant nationalism, Lloyd George simply said, "It is the inevitable result of the French policy of pinpricks, the Rhineland, and the Ruhr. I think France has driven Germany into this mood, which is extraordinarily stupid."[29] German foreign minister Gustav Stresemann had been complaining about this phenomenon for several years—"Every speech made by Poincaré furnishes the extreme Nationalists with another 100,000 votes," he said, a year before Hindenburg's election.[30] British leaders shared this assessment.

The coalition Labour-Liberal government under Ramsay MacDonald was short-lived; the Conservatives won a commanding parliamentary majority in the elections of October 1924, but little changed in the British attitude once the Conservatives were back in power. As the diplomatic wheels leading to Locarno began to turn in early 1925, Lord Arthur Balfour, former Conservative prime minister and foreign secretary in David Lloyd George's wartime coalition cabinet, piped up during a Committee of Imperial Defence meeting in mid-February to vent his exasperation. "I am so cross with the French," he said. "I think their obsession is so intolerably foolish . . . They are so dreadfully afraid of being swallowed up by the tiger, but yet they spend their time poking it." He was rewarded with the hurrahs of colleagues around the table.[31]

But the European power structure provided time, and time created an opportunity to heal the raw political relationship that made the Franco-German power game so dangerous. As foreign minister, Austen Chamberlain would assert time after time that the "first factor" in a strategy to secure Europe against future war was "making the position of Germany tolerable, so that she may lose something of her bitterness and forget something of her humiliation" before it was in a position to wreak havoc once again.[32] While Churchill saw a breathing space of a few decades, Chamberlain imagined a longer window of opportunity to break this perverse cycle, measured in generations. "I have to keep my eyes fixed on a date like 1960 or 1970," he told his colleagues. When that distant era arrives, "Germany will be in a position . . . to attack again if she wants to, and by that time there must have grown up in Germany a new generation who, whatever their feelings of resentment about the Treaty of Versailles . . . will yet say . . . things must have an end." But what did that mean for British policy? "If you are to have a chance of getting that kind of generation in Germany in 1960 or 1970," Chamberlain advised, "you must begin the work of pacification to-morrow."[33]

As conflict in the Ruhr continued to churn, the British War Office weighed in on this strategic problem and came to the same conclusion civilian leaders did. The War Office was the most pessimistic organ of the British government on the question of Germany's future behavior, but it also pointed a finger at France. The French "fear of Germany is profound and universal"; it "infects the leading French soldiers," it is the "dominating psychological military factor in Europe at the moment." If this fear "is not allayed . . . this French obsession will render impossible the development of stability and peace." In 1925 the General Staff saw a ten-year window in which "allied statesmen, the League of Nations, and possibly the moderate elements in Germany itself, will be free to develop the conditions essential to a lasting peace. The development of these conditions is not a military problem. The allied forces can only hold the ring so that statesmen can have a free hand."[34]

Locarno was a key moment in that process. But all the fanfare, the fireworks, the good cheer, and the Nobel Peace Prizes could not paper over the doubts that nagged at British leaders in the weeks that followed the Locarno conference. What had the statesmen actually accomplished on the shores of Lake Maggiore? Had they truly drawn a "veil across the lurid and tragic past," as Churchill hoped they had?

THE RHINELAND IS A TIME BOMB

Locarno was, without question, the most constructive moment since the end of the Great War, and it was worth celebrating. But British enthusiasm was deceptive. Austen Chamberlain's own "peace for our time" moment, when he descended that staircase in Locarno with the precious treaty text held high for the happy crowd, masked an undercurrent of clear-eyed skepticism. With the misery of the Ruhr War and the searing civil conflict it stoked among Germans hanging over the deliberations, British officials knew that in reality the Spirit of Locarno was corrupted by coercion—that the Locarno treaty itself was the product of German impotence and vulnerability. Gustav Stresemann himself signaled this fact in his Nobel Peace Prize lecture in June 1927, when he warned his Locarno partners about the dangers of inequality built into the current system. "It is easier for the victor than for the vanquished to advocate peace," Stresemann said. "For the victor peace means the preservation of the position of power which he has secured. For the vanquished it means resigning himself to the position left him. To walk behind others on the road you are traveling together, to give precedence to others without envy—this is painful for an individual and painful for a nation."[35]

British leaders didn't need this blunt warning to recognize that the Rhineland demilitarization pledge was an act of desperation. In fact, a year and a half before the diplomats met at Locarno, the British General Staff was already warning that the Rhineland was a time bomb. In March 1924, the military's assessment was that "any attempt to alienate" the Rhineland from Germany, "whether by 'Separatist' movements, by occupation or by neutralisation" for the long term, "will only result in converting it into a *terra irredenta*." The dangers of irredentism—that burning desire to recover lost territory—weighed heavily on postwar politics. French anger over Alsace-Lorraine never faded in the years after 1871, which haunted German leaders like Otto von Bismarck, who always knew this grievance could drive France into war to take it back. To British strategists, the Rhineland was no different. "Alienating" the Rhineland would not solve the security problem; it would simply create "an inevitable cause of future wars. Any continuance of France's policy in the Ruhr, or any occupation of the treaty zones beyond the treaty periods, can only result in the creation of an atmosphere more and more dangerous to peace."[36]

Before the treaty was officially signed in London on December 1, 1925, the Committee of Imperial Defence formed a Sub-Committee on Demilitarized Zones in mid-November to explore the potential and the risks of this concept and to figure out what Britain was getting into by signing off on the Rhineland DMZ. A key figure in this effort was Brig. Gen. Edward L. Spears, a British army officer with deep affection for France. Born and raised in Paris, Spears was one of the few British officers fluent in French; he had translated several French military studies into English, and spent the Great War as a liaison officer to the highest levels of the French military command. Reliably pro-French in the years after the war, Spears nonetheless was the first to denounce the DMZ concept officially within the British government. In a detailed memorandum submitted to the subcommittee in late December 1925, he carefully articulated what eventually became the subcommittee's definitively gloomy perspective. His first conclusion was that "no DMZ should be established wholly at the expense of one country." This "is an arrangement no State would freely accept unless adequate compensation were offered it," Spears argued. Drawing implicitly from security paradox logic, he predicted that

> If such a zone be set up by treaty after a war with a view to insuring the safety of the victor, the result might well prove contrary to the expectation. The country on whose territory the zone had been established would in time react against what would be considered a humiliating and permanent reminder of defeat. The DMZ would in that case become a cause of friction instead of a guarantee of security.

"The case of the demilitarized zone established under . . . the Treaty of Versailles," Spears continued, "is a case in point. Once Germany has got rid of the occupying armies, which are her chief concern at the present moment, it is probable that she will react against the unilateral character of this arrangement."

In a prescient assessment of the dilemma Britain would face in 1936, Spears warned not only of the inevitable German reaction against this humiliating unilateral constraint, but he also predicted correctly that "it is absolutely certain that in a period of crisis the French military authorities would put forward the strongest arguments in favor of an advance to the Rhine for reasons of national defence." This inevitability would put Britain in a position Spears euphemistically describes as "extreme embarrassment." Britain would be forced either to accept the reality of the eventual collapse of Rhineland

demilitarization as part of the Locarno treaty, or to support a French punitive response, perhaps even an invasion of the Rhineland, to preserve the
"sanctity of international law" and continued constraints on German power.[37]
Over the next year consensus crystallized on this point within the cabinet,
the Foreign Office, and the War Office: All agreed that demilitarized zones
"cannot prevent war and [are] ineffective as a military barrier" because "any
DMZ depends primarily on the good faith of the parties concerned . . . and
can seldom—if ever—be imposed." The implications of this conclusion were
clear in the DMZ subcommittee's final report: "[T]hough imposed by the
Treaty of Versailles," the Rhineland DMZ "has only been made even partially
acceptable to Germany by the Locarno Treaty."[38]

So what did this mean for British policy when growing German power
made the Rhineland DMZ too fragile to sustain? What were Britain's obligations when in practice the DMZ was no more secure than the quicksand
Woodrow Wilson worried about in the peace talks ending the Great War?
The British government made sure that the answer to this question was
clear from the outset, drawing from one of Austen Chamberlain's guiding
principles. Britain's "continual policy," he said in 1926, is to ensure that
Germany's postwar obligations are "placed upon a common-sense footing."[39] Put another way, Britain's role in the Franco-German rivalry was
"preaching the gospel of reasonableness."[40] Since the Rhineland DMZ did
not rest on common sense, since it wasn't reasonable to treat it as an indelible feature of the European political landscape, Great Britain had *no* obligation to fight to preserve it. As a result, from the start of the Locarno era
British leaders stood ready for that day when Germany issued its challenge,
ready to negotiate the DMZ away to help nurture Germany's willingness to
live in peace with its neighbors.

This did not mean, however, that Britain wouldn't fight to help protect
France and Belgium. Locarno did commit Britain to their defense. But
the treaty language describing when Britain was expected to join the fight
raised its own diplomatic dust storm. The key passage at the heart of this
controversy, found in Article 2, sounds straightforward enough: Parties to
the treaty had the right to resist a "flagrant breach" of the demilitarization rules, and resist with military force, "if such breach constitutes an
unprovoked act of aggression and by reason of the assembly of armed
forces in the demilitarised zone immediate action is necessary." But the
critical terms here were not defined. What exactly constitutes an "act of
aggression"? When is "immediate action" truly necessary for self-defense
when German armed forces assemble in the Rhineland? For the French,
the meaning of this clause was simple: The movement of German forces

across the Rhine River would automatically constitute an act of aggression; military attack in response would automatically qualify as self-defense; and Britain had an obligation to answer the French call to arms to help push the Germans back.

To steer hesitant British leaders toward this same interpretation, the French government quietly fed information to the international press, which European and American newspapers dutifully repeated for weeks during the spring of 1925, suggesting that the British would rally around the French position. In June a report circulated by Havas, the leading French news agency, took things too far. According to the report, not only had Britain agreed to treat even minor violations in the Rhineland as a cause for war, but Britain would also support France if it chose to use "the demilitarized zone as a field of operations" if an unrelated conflict erupted between Germany and France's Polish or Czech allies in the east. According to Lord D'Abernon, the British ambassador in Berlin, the story had a "startling" effect across Europe. Gustav Stresemann was perhaps more rattled than anyone. The ambassador tried to reassure the German foreign minister; London, he told Stresemann, has confirmed that the "Havas telegram put the matter in an entirely false light."[41] So what was London's position on this question? As D'Abernon told Stresemann, Britain would support immediate military action only if the movement of forces in the Rhineland was an *"immediate danger to others.* In such a case, and only in such a case, is an immediate recourse to force contemplated."[42]

For Britain, the cornerstone of the Locarno order was not the DMZ; it was Germany's acceptance of the western borders drawn at Versailles, its consent to Alsace-Lorraine remaining in French hands in particular, and the joint pledge that Germany, France, and Belgium would never launch aggressive attacks against the others' territory. As guarantor powers, both Britain and Italy agreed to defend France, Belgium, *and* Germany against actual attack by any other party to the treaty. Even in its more-limited form, this guarantee was a major breakthrough in the structure of the European security system. In practical terms, it restored that treasured alliance France's wartime partners promised in 1919, but abandoned in 1920, when the United States retreated into isolationism, and in turn, Great Britain backed out. For Austen Chamberlain, this promise was critical to future peace because of its effects on French behavior. Without it, "France will go on provoking and aggravating Germany," he said.[43] Once France relaxes, the window on a stable political relationship will open wide enough for real security.

From the very beginning—when the Committee of Imperial Defence began discussing Germany's proposed security pact in February 1925—British leaders carefully defined the scope of this military commitment. During this meeting, Austen Chamberlain described the British position that future governments would stick to: "[I]f the Germans *entered* Belgium or *crossed the French frontier* aggressively . . . the interest of the British government is the same as the French government."[44] From this point forward we find the same phrases—*flagrant violations, unprovoked aggression, attack across frontiers*—invoked repeatedly to place strict limits on the conditions that would trigger a British military response, and the conditions that would not. Clearly, Britain was "bound to go to war," even without League of Nations approval, if "an attack has been made . . . on France or Belgium by Germany . . . of so flagrant a nature that His Majesty's Government are convinced that it constitutes an unprovoked act of aggression."[45]

But there is a critical caveat embedded in this statement: Not every German violation of the DMZ could be considered a flagrantly aggressive act, so not every violation would demand a military response. Chamberlain had to explain this point to nervous delegates attending the Imperial Conference in October 1926, who wondered whether London would call on members of the British Commonwealth someday, like Canada, Australia, South Africa, and New Zealand, to join in a fight over the Rhineland. This is how Chamberlain explained it. "The Treaty of Versailles entitled France to make war on Germany if Germany violated, even in the smallest particular, the provisions of articles 42 and 43 of that treaty," he said. "The Treaty of Locarno, on the other hand, *limits this right of France* to the case of a flagrant breach of articles 42 and 43, which is defined as" unprovoked aggression that actually threatens French or Belgian territory.[46]

Pulling all of these statements together, we can summarize Britain's interpretation of its obligations this way. *Defense* of Belgium and France against an actual attack across their borders? Absolutely. A *preemptive* attack against a German force assembling in the Rhineland when it appears that it truly poses an immediate danger? Certainly possible, and permissible under Locarno. A *preventive attack* against a violation of the Rhineland DMZ that does not pose an immediate danger? Britain had no obligation, or even the intent, to intervene militarily to constrain German power in this way. And in a future crisis, Britain would not relinquish decisions over using military force to any other country or international body. In all cases, Chamberlain insisted, the "British Government [would be the] absolute judge of whether we should act or not."[47] Just as Austen Chamberlain predicted in February 1925, when the inevitable challenge came in 1936, London refused to let Paris have the final word on their response.

REARM, RECOMMIT, AND SETTLE

They called it another one of Hitler's "Saturday Surprises," like his earlier pronouncement in March 1935 that Germany was officially dropping the pretense of Versailles-mandated disarmament. While the exact timing of a Rhineland coup was never clear, it wasn't a surprise; French and British leaders knew it was on the horizon. A year before the Wehrmacht marched in, French foreign minister Pierre Laval was already advising Anthony Eden, then British minister to the League of Nations, that now was the time to think through how they would respond.[48] Intelligence reports streamed in from diplomats and military attachés posted around Germany about a coming Rhineland move, and newspaper stories repeated the diplomatic buzz.[49]

For his part, Hitler was dismissing this prediction. Two months after he rattled the international system with his rearmament announcement, the Führer insisted that the Nazi regime would remain "scrupulously" faithful to all treaties Germany had voluntarily signed in the past, including Locarno with its Rhineland rules. The DMZ, he said, was Germany's contribution to the "appeasement of Europe." But in this very same speech Hitler issued a subtle warning. The demilitarized zone was "an unheard-of hardness for a sovereign State." So Germany's tolerance for this sacrifice came with a condition: Other parties must remain faithful to Locarno as well. His meaning was clear. Two weeks earlier, on May 2, 1935, Paris had hosted the final meeting with Soviet delegates that sealed the mutual defense pact linking the military power of France and the USSR. This new alliance was a grave threat to German security, Hitler charged, and a blatant violation of Locarno.[50] This was the political opening he was looking for to break his own Locarno promise as 1935 gave way to 1936.

Anthony Eden, now foreign minister, took Laval's earlier advice seriously. As German power surged ahead, as expectations of a Rhineland challenge swelled, he knew he had to get ahead of the problem before it broke around him. When the expected crisis hit, Eden had held this senior leadership position for less than three months, after being pulled into the job abruptly when Foreign Minister Samuel Hoare was sacked over his plan to reward Italian aggression with large chunks of Ethiopia. Despite early signs of the cabinet's guarded confidence—his fellow ministers sent Lord Halifax along as a more-senior chaperone on the young foreign minister's first crisis visit to Paris—Eden drove British policy throughout. Prime Minister Stanley Baldwin was keeping a low public profile, still stinging from the humiliation of the Ethiopian fiasco and the shaken confidence in his leadership this fiasco produced. So Eden remained in the forefront as the public face and the voice of the British government; he crafted the parameters of British policy; and he served from start to finish as Britain's chief interlocutor on the international stage. Most important, Eden was the conduit for the strategic consensus that emerged so firmly from the Ruhr War and Locarno ten years before. The DMZ was unsustainable without a fight. And a fight to suppress German power this way was a strategic dead end. Instead of solving Europe's enduring security problems, it would unleash the preventive war paradox with its perverse spiral into greater future dangers.

Austen Chamberlain's words from 1926 still echoed in 1936. With its preventive invasion of the Ruhr Valley in 1923, France was "sacrificing future advantages for the sake of momentary triumph," he said, "and sowing the seeds of certain retribution in the future."[51] *Certain retribution. Momentary triumph, future catastrophe.* This is exactly how British leaders saw the preventive war option as rumors of a Rhineland coup swirled. So before Hitler himself had settled on a plan for Rhineland remilitarization, Anthony Eden was moving forward with a plan of his own to defuse this time bomb.

Eden's plan had two basic elements, devised months before Hitler launched his fait accompli: *rearm* and *settle*. These two elements were inseparable in Eden's mind. As we have seen, the very first debate in the House of Commons after the Rhineland crisis broke focused on funding the largest rearmament bill passed by the British government since the end of the Great War. Despite the timing of the debate, it was not a direct response to this specific German move. Eden had been preparing this step from his first few weeks in office. As he said in two secret memoranda for the cabinet in January and February, "Parliament is shortly to be asked to foot a formidable bill made inevitable by rearmament elsewhere." But while rearming to counterbalance German power, he said, Britain must explore whether it "could come to some *modus vivendi*," some way of coexisting "with Hitler's Germany, which would be both honourable and safe for this country." Eden insisted on "one indispensable condition" along the way: "that we offer no sops to Germany. There must be no concession merely to keep Germany quiet, for that process only stimulates the appetite it is intended to satisfy."[52]

The first place to look for such an opportunity was in the Rhineland. Eden knew this was no weak sop to German appetites. General Spears's advice in 1925 was to get ahead of the "extreme embarrassment" that a Rhineland fait accompli would create by negotiating it away, before the inevitable happened. This is exactly how Anthony Eden saw the problem over a decade later. On February 11 Eden circulated a memorandum within the cabinet arguing that the time had come to extract concessions in exchange for restoring Germany's full sovereign rights. "Taking one thing with another, it seems undesirable to adopt an attitude where we would either have to fight for the zone or abandon it in the face of a German reoccupation," he said. "It will be preferable for Great Britain and France to enter betimes into negotiations with the German Government for the surrender, on conditions, of our rights in the zone."[53] They were going to lose the benefits of the DMZ anyway, so why not gain something in return before a sudden move robbed them of negotiating leverage? Eden's goal for an agreement reflected what losing the DMZ would mean to Britain: He wanted an Air Pact that would limit Germany's strategic bombing capabilities, the most worrisome emerging threat when combined with the shorter striking distance offered by Rhineland airfields.[54] What he didn't know, of course, was that time to leverage the Rhineland was far shorter than imagined. On March 2, just as Eden was coordinating a memorandum with the Air Ministry and the War Office laying out this concept, the Führer was meeting in the Reich Chancellery with his inner circle. The decision had been made; the Wehrmacht would march at the end of the week.[55]

Eden must have felt like a fool. On Friday, March 6, he invited German ambassador Leopold von Hoesch to join him at the Foreign Office to kick-start immediate discussions that he hoped would lead to a grand bargain. But as Hoesch listened to Eden's pitch that day, he kept silent about the futility of Eden's urgent proposal on the DMZ and German airpower. Hoesch knew what was coming. He knew Hitler was in Berlin preparing for his triumphant announcement in the Kroll Opera House. He knew the General Staff's deployment orders would shoot over the wires that evening. But Hoesch could not break from Hitler's tightly choreographed plan to reveal the fait accompli in a flash as German soldiers were moving into the Rhineland.[56]

The very next morning, the German ambassador was back in Eden's office, with Berlin's diplomatic note in hand. He read the English-language translation out loud so Eden would hear in precise terms that he had already lost whatever diplomatic leverage a Rhineland concession might have produced. It was simply a matter of timing. A Rhineland window of opportunity seemed to open wide for Hitler on February 27, when the French Chamber of Deputies ratified the Franco-Soviet defense agreement. Hitler seized it. To the Führer, this was a meaty propaganda tool that would help him justify calling Locarno obsolete. Unfortunately for Eden, his own political timetable for negotiations just couldn't keep pace with Hitler's timetable for staging this bold drama.

But now that it had happened, what difference did the "Rhineland coup" really make? British leaders, the French government, and the League of Nations Council could agree on one important point: As Austen Chamberlain said repeatedly during the crisis, Nazi Germany was guilty of a "flagrant breach of the public law of Europe," the "tearing up of treaties" that render law no "more than a scrap of paper." In Parliament, Chamberlain declared "the real issue" to be "whether in future the law of force shall prevail or whether there shall be substituted for it the force of law."[57] Chamberlain was echoing the argument French premier Albert Sarraut made to the Chamber of Deputies and that Flandin presented to the League of Nations; international law, the "effective rules of conduct of governments," Flandin said, would "guarantee peace and security" among nations.[58]

What did this mean for Britain's response? Did the fact that Hitler violated international law demand muscular enforcement actions to preserve the "sanctity of treaties"? For the British, the legal implications of this move did nothing to change their long-standing strategic assessment of the problem. The DMZ was a time bomb embedded in both the Versailles and Locarno treaties that did more to jeopardize international security than sustain it. Should their reaction be governed by treaties that perpetuate such dangerous political conditions? In his typically irascible way, David Lloyd George reminded his fellow MPs that the DMZ, like the Versailles Treaty itself, was the result of political compromise among combative allies, reflecting the political conditions of a particular point in time. It was not "Holy Writ," sacred and immutable for all time, to be defended without question.[59] And Germany's DMZ pledge at Locarno was a political decision made in a moment of desperation, the product of coercion and vulnerability, and these conditions were bound to change. Strategic concerns trumped international law.

Eden agreed. What really mattered was *how* Hitler acted, rather than the substantive political content or consequences of his actions. Germany's move, Eden said, did not produce "a result so far as the demilitarization zone itself is concerned, which we were not prepared to contemplate." The only real problem was that it was abrupt and unilateral, so the British government "deplored" the "*manner* of their action." Hitler "might have declared himself no longer bound by Locarno, and asked for negotiations to replace it by another treaty without the demilitarization zone provision.

This would have been plausible," Eden said. As it is now, "by reoccupying the Rhineland he has deprived us of the possibility of making to him a concession which might otherwise have been a useful bargaining counter in our hands."[60]

On March 26, Eden revealed how potent the lessons of 1923 remained on this question. Germany's original Rhineland pledge must be understood in historic context. "I do not think it is very difficult, looking back," Eden noted in the House of Commons, "to see why" Germany included the DMZ in its treaty proposals of 1925. "The Locarno Treaty was signed not very long after the Ruhr, and it would not be astonishing if the German Government of that day reflected that some guarantee from us"—protection from future French coercion, specifically—was worth the price of Rhineland demilitarization.[61] Nothing had changed between 1925 and 1936 in the political character of the DMZ. The only real change was that Germany had finally reached a level of power that made the inevitable challenge possible. The British military attaché in Paris explained his government's position this way: "The average Englishman thought that something of this sort was bound to happen sooner or later . . . The Rhineland was, after all, German territory, and it was, therefore, impossible to refuse permission in perpetuity to a powerful State to do what it liked in its own country."[62] As Anthony Eden saw it, most British citizens shared the view of a taxicab driver who told him, "I suppose Jerry can do what he likes in his own back garden."[63]

Germany had pulled away a central pillar of the Locarno treaty, and Britain let it fall for practical strategic reasons. But no matter how practical this specific decision might have been, French and Belgian leaders had to wonder, Was Locarno dead? Was Great Britain prepared to abandon every article in the treaty, along with the DMZ? The answer to this question could have profound consequences. Abandoning Locarno completely meant one essential thing: abandoning France and Belgium if they once again fell victim to unprovoked aggression. On this question, Eden stood firm. In the House of Commons at the end of March, Eden declared, "I am not prepared to be the first foreign secretary to go back on a British signature." It was an implicit threat. He would resign if the British government pulled away from its Locarno obligations by refusing to join the fight against aggression in Western Europe. Great applause echoed across the chamber. There is nothing revolutionary in this commitment, he said; after all, for hundreds of years Britain was willing to throw its weight into the weaker side of Continental great-power wars to prevent any one of them from dominating the system. Eden pointed to Austen Chamberlain sitting on the Conservative benches: "[A]nd I say with apologies to my right honorable friend . . . there was nothing new in Locarno" either. "Hear, hear!" shouted Chamberlain in reply. Eden continued, "It is a vital interest of this country that the integrity of France and Belgium be maintained," so the opposite shoreline of the narrow English Channel would never serve as a springboard for invasion by hostile powers.[64]

Eden was right, in a way; the Locarno "guarantee" was built on a four-hundred-year tradition. But he was selling Austen Chamberlain short in this speech. Chamberlain's Locarno promise was indeed substantively different, as it was a standing defense commitment in peacetime, not merely an unwritten tradition. The Locarno commitment was concrete—Britain would take up arms against unprovoked aggression—and Eden declared that it was rock solid, made even more salient by Wehrmacht soldiers settling into new Rhineland garrisons.[65] For all those paying attention at the time, the Rhineland crisis was cast in stark contrast to the crisis in the Horn of Africa, where the Italian army had been tearing into Ethiopian forces for the past six months, as the poor Ethiopians were fighting a losing struggle on their own soil to repulse this brutal imperial assault. And this was a story that captivated and infuriated the British public.

Two days after German soldiers began fanning out across the Rhine zone, Eden reported the cabinet's assessment to Parliament. "The course taken by the German government [is] . . . complicating and aggravating the international situation," he observed, and it has "profoundly shaken confidence in any engagement into which the government of Germany may, in the future, enter." The cheers were "loud and universal." "I am thankful to say," however, there is "no reason to suppose that the present German action implies or threatens hostilities."[66] The "unanimous applause" in the chamber grew louder.[67] Jarring? Yes. Illegal? Yes. But flagrant aggression? No. Austen Chamberlain had reassured delegates to the Imperial Conference in 1926 that Britain would never cede judgment in such situations to any other state or organization. In 1936, Eden did the same, reassuring his parliamentary colleagues and anxious British citizens that their sons would never be "tied to the chariot wheels" of France.[68] Britain would not wage a counterproductive preventive fight to "liberate" the Rhineland or follow the French banner into war on behalf of its Polish, Czech, or Soviet allies. Even so, its defense commitment to France and Belgium was solid. To put muscle on the bone, the cabinet took a controversial step, initiating direct coordination between French and British military staffs. It was more symbolic than practical, but it sent an important political signal to Germany and France alike. Military coordination made some British observers nervous; did this mean that Britain might be drawn into future French fights with

Germany that started in Eastern Europe? The cabinet said no, and the military staff talks went on; so did the search for new political arrangements with Germany that might stabilize the new status quo. If pressed, French officials would admit that if forced to choose, Britain's defense commitment had more value than the DMZ.[69]

Rearm, defend western frontiers, seek political settlement. This is a "hedging strategy," common through history and in contemporary world politics, in which states combine elements of counterbalancing and compromise with a potential adversary, hoping to make progress toward a more-stable political relationship while hedging against the potential for future conflict.[70] These were the three pillars of British strategy in 1936, each pillar perfectly consistent with the precedent set a decade earlier. The idea of a preventive fight over an inherently unsustainable relic of an earlier moment of crisis seemed absurd. But time marched on, German power continued to swell, and its demands for territorial change *outside* Germany's Versailles-drawn borders kept pace with its growing military capabilities and confidence. There was the *Anschluss*, the strong-armed political union between the German Reich and Austria in March 1938. There was Hitler's demand for the Sudetenland, the Germanic wedge of Czechoslovakia that Czech leaders surrendered under pressure from the west, ceded through the Munich Agreement in September 1938. Six months later, German forces rolled into the two remaining independent Czech provinces of Bohemia and Moravia, which Hitler anointed as protectorates of the Third Reich.

By late 1938, one point was unmistakably clear: A grand political settlement with Germany that would erase old grievances and usher in stable peace, the strategic goal British leaders had been pursuing since the end of the Great War, was impossible. Urgent, hard power balancing was the only remaining option to contain the German threat. The arms race was on, and Britain's self-imposed limits on Continental defense commitments were brushed away. At the end of March 1939, Britain joined France in its alliance with Poland. And on September 3, as the German Wehrmacht stormed across the Polish plains in the first dazzling demonstration of blitzkrieg attack, the Allies declared war. Night after night, over the five weeks that followed, convoys of troopships carried the first contingent of soldiers from the British Expeditionary Force, 158,000 strong, across the English Channel to help man the defensive line in northern France.

It was too little, too late. Britain and France were powerless to save Poland in the fall of 1939. The following spring, the German blitzkrieg cracked the Allied defense of France, and Hitler had his conqueror's tour of Paris. Looking back, one conclusion is obvious: Britain's strategy had failed. The British Isles held out, under the leadership of the new prime minister, Winston Churchill. But the guilty men thesis, the recriminations of history, the lament for lost opportunities to stop this Armageddon before it was too late, sprang to life as the desperate struggle unfolded. With this in mind, it seems reasonable to float a few propositions. Surely Winston Churchill, with the support of his political allies in the mid-1930s, his fellow hard-liners, the anti-appeasers, were ready to turn back the Nazi juggernaut in 1936. They must have cried out with urgency, demanding decisive preventive military action to stop Hitler. They were the prophets shouting in the wilderness, whose wisdom was tragically ignored, right? A closer look at what the alarmists were saying in real time reveals a very different story. There were no heroes, and there were no goats. *No one* in Great Britain was calling for preventive war in 1936. It's a fact that speaks volumes about the limitations of foresight, the enduring struggle between the preventive war temptation and the preventive war paradox, and the tragic character of the strategic dilemma in the 1930s.

The next chapter will look at this charge more closely.

8

NO HEROES, NO GOATS

Despite the folly of prophecy, we must try to reply to the question: What will Germany do?

—Eric Phipps, British ambassador in Berlin, December 1935

Britain's reaction to the Rhineland challenge was a legacy of the 1920s. And from this vantage point, Britain's strategic perspective made sense. Germany's promise at Locarno *was* a desperate consequence of the Ruhr War, made necessary by impotence and vulnerability. The Rhineland DMZ *was* unsustainable. A German challenge was inevitable. So, British leaders concluded, a preventive fight to preserve the DMZ would be worse than futile; it would magnify the dangers, and intensify the hostility, fear, and uncontrollable passions for revenge that fed the "devil's merry-go-round" of continuing war. The preventive war paradox, British leaders worried, would convert battlefield victory into strategic defeat over the long term, making a second Great War truly unavoidable. But looking back at Britain's DMZ decision, it's fair to raise an obvious objection to this claim: While the strategic problem had changed radically between 1925 and 1936, Britain's perspective on the Rhineland DMZ had not.

Rejecting preventive war in 1936 might have been consistent with a decade-old policy, but didn't the rise of the Nazi regime in Germany completely undermine the logic of this strategic perspective? Hitler changed everything, one might argue, so doesn't rational adaptation to this new problem demand that British leaders throw their Locarno-era perspective overboard? After all, Britain's strategy in the 1930s was a failure; it opened a path to the near ruin of Europe. That earnest search for a political settlement that would resolve Germany's grievances and bring stable peace did nothing to deflect its aggression. And the Allies lost the rearmament race that sped forward from the mid-1930s; the clash on the Western Front proved this point in 1940. Didn't this new era, defined by the Third Reich's unquenchable appetite for expansion and the inevitability of war, demand a new approach? Wasn't preventive war the only viable strategy to snuff out this threat and stop Hitler? Wasn't the Rhineland crisis the perfect opportunity to execute it?

Surely, the Prometheans of the 1930s, like the ancient Greek Titan Prometheus before them, with their clear-eyed foresight into what the future held, must have seen the problem this way. They were the first ones to recognize the terrible reality of the future threat, so soon after Adolf Hitler took command of the German Reich. Those celebrated anti-appeasers are known to history mainly for their courage to speak out against British complacency, for their commitment to decisive action to blunt the threat, for their opposition to the appeasers who thought it was possible to live alongside Nazi Germany in peace. If anyone of that era was willing to climb the preventive war ladder alongside France, it must have been the hardliners. This included leaders such as Winston Churchill, of course, the most celebrated among the Prometheans. There was Robert Vansittart, the permanent under-secretary in the Foreign Office, who, among the members of this small group, exercised the most direct influence over British policy. There was Duff Cooper, war minister in 1936, who quit Prime Minister Neville Chamberlain's cabinet in 1938 to protest the Munich accord. And of course, there was Austen Chamberlain, the great champion of Locarno who railed against Hitler's Rhineland coup and his reckless thrashing of the pillars of international peace. If British ministers had only listened to Churchill and his fellow anti-appeasement heroes, it's tempting to presume, they certainly would have rejected the naiveté of negotiating with Hitler; they would have made the tough choices demanded of the moment, leveraging this crisis to stop Hitler through preventive war, and thus derailing the horrors the future had in store.

The real story, however, is not that simple. In 1936, there were no clear heroes, and no clear goats. The legends built up around the anti-appeasers of 1938 easily lead to counterfactual musings, those heavy "what-ifs" of history. What if Winston Churchill had been prime minister during the Rhineland crisis? Would he have made radically different choices? Would

he have crafted a very different ending to this tragic story? There's no way
to answer this question with certainty, of course. The best we can do is
examine what Churchill, Vansittart, Cooper, and Chamberlain actually said
and did while the crisis boiled. Whatever Churchill and his fellow hard-
liners said about this crisis in retrospect, with the bright light of hindsight
to guide them, has little value for assessing how they would have handled
the crisis in real time. But when we take a hard look at how they behaved
in the moment, it's clear that they too were struggling with the complexity
of the broader dilemma.

This chapter will explore their views in detail. Along the way, it will showcase the fact that 1936 was a turning point in perceptions of the threat. The
year 1936 was a time when the dominant paradigm of the post–Great War
era—the one that saw arms races and alliances as the cause of war—was
being supplanted by an older, resurgent paradigm that saw military power
as the key to deterring war. It was a year of changing policies that reflected
these changing ideas. To be sure, the hard-liners were on the leading edge
of this change; the essence of their position was to "rearm," to deter aggression or defend against it if deterrence failed. But it's just as important to
recognize that preventive war was *not* part of the hard-liners' toolkit.

THE PROMETHEANS IN THE REARVIEW MIRROR

In the early twentieth century, Winston Churchill was a rising force in
British politics, at times while holding formal cabinet posts (he served as
Secretary of State for the Colonies, Home Secretary, First Lord of the
Admiralty, Secretary of State for War, and Secretary of State for Air, all
before his fortieth birthday in 1919), at other times as a Member of Parliament in both the Conservative and the Liberal parties. In the mid-1920s
his early political power peaked when he was named Chancellor of the
Exchequer, the minister responsible for the British treasury. The 1930s,
in contrast, were his "wilderness years." He kept his seat in Parliament,
but through this entire decade his own party leaders denied Churchill a
cabinet post. So from the wilderness, Churchill's self-appointed role was a
familiar one—that of the gadfly. He was the relentless critic who would rail
from the backbenches against his own party leadership; he was the critic
in parliamentary debate, in public speeches, and in his regular columns in
the *Evening Standard*. And what he mainly railed about was the Baldwin
government's failure to recognize the urgency of the German threat. It's no
surprise then that Winston Churchill of the 1930s is remembered primarily

for one thing: that he was a true visionary who saw the future more clearly than common men could, who cried aloud about the dangers and the need for bold action, but who was mocked and ignored until it was too late to avoid the coming disaster. Churchill has been lionized by history, and he certainly did his part to help shape the postwar image of the prophet tragically dismissed.[1] "I saw it all coming," he said in 1946. The Rhineland crisis, Churchill wrote in his memoirs, was the "last chance [for] arresting Hitler's ambitions without a serious war." France alone, he said with exasperation, was powerful enough "to drive the Germans out of the Rhineland."[2]

Churchill seemed to carry the "alarmist" epithet with pride,[3] but it didn't take the Nazi regime to stoke his alarmist impulses. Years before Adolf Hitler seized control of the German Reich, Churchill was already fretting over Europe's future, and he was outspoken about the problems he saw. He worried about the lingering hangover from the Great War, which solved nothing. He worried about the unsettled fears and the hatred, those seeds of another total war that could erupt with even greater ferocity. He worried about technological advancements in chemical weapons and bomber aircraft that would carry the pain of Armageddon into the cities and homes of innocent citizens. He brought a familiar urgency to the problem, and in the mid-1920s, as a senior cabinet minister, Churchill had a seat at the table to shape his government's policy directly. As we've seen, during those early postwar years Churchill was not alone on this question. His fear of the future put him squarely in the mainstream of British political opinion. And like his colleagues, Churchill pointed to coercive French pressure as the source of greatest danger. As Churchill saw it during the year of Locarno, French antagonism "is what is going to shatter the peace of the world."[4] To solve this problem, Churchill proposed a two-track approach. On the German side, he advocated serious changes in the status quo to generate German cooperation: "real peace" was possible, he said during a Committee of Imperial Defence meeting in February 1925, if Germany was granted "not only the immediate evacuation of territories which are being held," like the city of Cologne and the Ruhr Valley, "but a substantial rectification of her Eastern frontiers" as well.[5] On the French side of the problem, he took a position that put him directly at odds with Austen Chamberlain.

Chamberlain and Churchill shared the same goal: to convince France to ease its pressure on Germany to make a new political relationship possible. To get there, Chamberlain was arguing for British defense guarantees, which he believed was the indispensable cure for French anxieties. Once their anxieties were soothed, France's compulsion to suppress German power and interests would follow. Churchill pushed back. This was the wrong approach, he said, because the more confident France feels, the harder it will squeeze. With the backing of Great Britain, France "would feel strong enough to keep the antagonism alive."[6] Churchill's advice was to take a more bluntly coercive tack. Tell the French, "We feel that your relations with Germany are at present too bitter for us to involve ourselves in the quarrel . . . The better friends you are with Germany, the better friends we shall be with you." The French must know, Churchill argued, that Britain's support hinges on whether it could "approach a real state of peace with Germany . . . It rests with you to create that atmosphere in which Germany will have the least possible incentive to renew the war."[7] "If you could get" these two sides of the political problem in line, Churchill said, "then I think the weight of England might well be thrown in to make that solid."[8]

This perspective, clearly, did not survive the radical shift in German politics that began with Hitler's appointment as chancellor in January 1933. The speed of Churchill's reassessment of the European security problem is remarkable. In fact, the day before the Reichstag turned over emergency powers to Hitler's government, Churchill was in the House of Commons raising the alarm about the implications of two key facts: Germany's insistence on equality in the weapons of war, and the "temper" of its incendiary new government, were transforming the threat at a breakneck pace. It was no longer French coercion of a prostrate Germany that could shatter the peace, but the "tumultuous insurgence of ferocity and war spirit" stoked by Adolf Hitler, who now commanded "one of the most gifted, learned, scientific and formidable nations in the world."[9] For the next three years, Churchill never wavered from this dark theme.

As the Rhineland crisis was roiling European politics, Churchill stood in Parliament to render a proud "confession." Ever since the Nazi dictatorship emerged, "I have been occupied with this idea of the great wheels revolving and the great hammers descending day and night in Germany, making the whole industry of that country an arsenal, making the whole of that gifted and valiant population into one great disciplined war machine."[10] Just as worrisome, Germany is the only nation in Europe unafraid of war, he said. And once rearmament pushes the Third Reich to the maximum level of power it can generate, sometime in 1937 or 1938, Churchill predicted, the regime's confidence would peak as well, stirring the temptation to strike out before its relative power begins to decline. The British government, of course, was moving forward with its own rearmament plans to meet this rising danger, and the cabinet seemed satisfied with the large armaments bill introduced on March 10, 1936. Churchill, however, saw it as inadequate, and he dashed cold water on Conservative Party leaders with his own prognosis for the future balance of power. "Germany will be outstripping us more and more even if our new programmes are accepted," he argued, "and we shall be worse off at the end of this year than we are now, in spite of all our exertions."[11] The result, he worried, would be disaster.

This trajectory in relative power is what Churchill focused on in 1936. "This Rhineland business," as he put it on March 26, "is but a step, is but a stage, is but an incident, in this process" that could drive Europe to war. Like many, he recognized that the loss of the Rhineland DMZ would have several troubling strategic effects. First, the loss of the buffer zone naturally "exposes Holland, Belgium and France" to a greater risk. Second, once Germany fortified the Rhineland, there "will be a barrier across Germany's front door, which will leave her free to sally out eastward and southward by the back door."[12] Third, the Rhineland coup was an "enormous triumph" for the prestige and domestic political strength of the Nazi regime. "Let us suppose," Churchill said, "that any one of us were a German and living there, and perhaps entirely discontented with many things that we saw around us, but thinking that here is the Führer" who was "able to bring home once again a trophy." "On patriotic grounds there is many a man who would say 'I cannot indulge my . . . feelings against this regime.'"[13] Churchill saw 1936 as an inflection point in history, a decisive moment to change the direction of shifting power that made the future so dangerous, if the peaceful nations of Europe were willing to seize it. "Five years ago all felt safe," he said, "five years ago all were looking forward to peace . . . Five years ago to talk of war would have been regarded not only as a folly and a crime but almost as a sign of lunacy. The difference in our position now!" Now "there is fear, in every country." And from this fear one question arises: "[W]hat is going to stop this war which seems to be moving towards us in so many ways?" Whatever the answer might be, Churchill exhorted his fellow MPs, "Let us free the world from the approach of a catastrophe, carrying with it calamity and tribulation beyond the tongue of man to tell."[14]

If we look beyond the Churchillian rhetoric, was this an appeal for the kind of brutal, urgent, decisive measures the French foreign minister was calling for as German troops were bringing new garrisons to life across the Rhineland? Was Churchill doing his part to push a reluctant British government toward the promise of preventive war as a solution to the terrible future he saw? Richard Betts, one of the leading American authorities on war and well-known as a critic of the preventive war option, once said that the Rhineland crisis, as part of the larger threat of rising German power, "is the best example imaginable to justify preventive war."[15] Churchill must have come to the same conclusion in 1936. How could he avoid it? He was fixated on the relentless growth of German strength, which would soon overwhelm the Allies once the present window of opportunity slammed closed. He recognized early on that the Third Reich was devoted to an aggressive vision of dominance, that war was inevitable unless drastic action was taken to block this repugnant regime's ambitions. And according to what he wrote in his memoirs, it was the last opportunity the Allies had to stop Hitler before the bloodletting of the Second World War. He must have been shouting from the rooftops and beating the drums in support of the French proposal to start climbing that escalating ladder of preventive action toward war.

During the first parliamentary debate of the Rhineland crisis, before Churchill had even weighed in on the problem publicly, the Labour Party MP Herbert Morrison was bold enough to call him out on the question, implying, like we might today, that Churchill would favor preventive attack against Germany. "The more I listened to the [R]ight [Honourable] Member for Epping," Morrison said, "the more I got the impression . . . that he was anxious for something dramatic to happen in the world in order that we might try out his various doctrines." The Conservative benches erupted in Churchill's defense, with shouts of "No" and "Withdraw." Morrison immediately backtracked from this insult: "I do not mean war," he assured them. "I would not for a moment suggest that. I am sure that no one would regret the outbreak of war more than the [R]ight [Honourable] Gentleman."[16] Morrison was indeed right, once he corrected himself.

Churchill had a plan to confront the danger in 1936, and he was immensely frustrated by British policy in these years. But preventive war was never part of Churchill's strategic vision for the German problem. He never called for economic sanctions. He never urged the French to take independent military action, such as full mobilization of its army or a preventive attack to turn back the Wehrmacht. He never encouraged the French to throw a counterpunch with Allied support; he never spoke out in favor of preventive attack by a larger coalition under the League of Nations banner. In fact, when Churchill stepped forward during his most public moments of the crisis, he praised France for *not* pulling the preventive war trigger.

In the March 13 issue of the *Evening Standard*, Churchill articulated his position on this question clearly: "Instead of retaliating by armed force, as would have been done in a previous generation, France has taken the *proper* and prescribed course of appealing to the League of Nations."[17] The very next day he reinforced this public position during a speech to the Jewelers Association in Birmingham: "[T]he only safe course in an anxious world is to meet this violent act" of Rhineland remilitarization "with the calm, patient but inexorable process of *law*." Despite all the urgency in his security assessment, despite all the muscular postwar talk about this opportunity to stop Hitler, Churchill appealed for calm, patience, and the mechanisms of international law to resolve the crisis. Then he explained what this really meant: "[W]e are not called upon at this moment to judge the ultimate justice of what has happened in the Rhineland . . . If the World Court pronounces that the Franco-Soviet pact violated Locarno"—Hitler's excuse for trampling on the treaty himself in the DMZ—"then clearly the German action, although utterly wrong in method, could not be seriously challenged by the League of Nations."[18] In other words, if legal proceedings find that the German case against France had merit, no one had the right to challenge the ultimate justice of Hitler's fait accompli. Three weeks into the crisis, during a speech in Parliament on March 26, Churchill once again spoke about the value of international law to resolve it: "[N]o one can deny that but for the existence of the League of Nations there might have been war at this moment. France and the nations associated with her might have attempted to rectify this situation by the sword. Instead of that they have appealed to a tribunal."[19] And Churchill was genuinely relieved.

So if he never called for preventive war, what was Churchill's preferred strategy in 1936? When it comes to strategic advice, if Churchill is remembered for anything in the 1930s, it is for one specific, urgent message: *Rearm*. As he said simply on March 10 of that pivotal year, "I am not assuming that war is coming at all, but we ought not to be unprepared." It was a message he repeated in speech after speech, in article after article, both before and after 1936. After just one year of Nazi rule, Churchill recognized that German rearmament was an unavoidable fact. And by this early date in the power shift he was so worried about, he had already dismissed preventive war as a strategy to stifle it. "No one proposes a preventive war to stop Germany breaking the Treaty of Versailles," he said in Parliament in March 1934.[20] Having ruled out preventive war to physically *stop* Nazi Germany from becoming stronger, Churchill argued that Britain and its partners had to *adjust* to this reality. The only sensible response, he concluded, was to turn to traditional balance-of-power tools—arms and alliances—to deter whatever aggressive schemes Hitler might be plotting.

In March 1933 Churchill was in Parliament decrying Prime Minister MacDonald's push for general disarmament in Europe, particularly British pressure on France to cut the size of its army.[21] The following February he called for the reorganization of civilian factories to ensure that British industry could be quickly converted to war production if necessary. He wanted out of the London naval treaty that crippled Britain's freedom to design and build new classes of warships, and he advocated for an air force as strong as the most powerful in Europe. This message continued through 1935.[22] His assessment of the Conservative government's rearmament bill of March 1936 was that they "err seriously on the side of inadequacy." "When they have spent all that they can," he said, "they will have spent much less than we need." So Churchill worried, "Will there be time to make these necessary efforts, or will the awful words 'too late' be recorded?"

Despite his fears, with sufficient determination and haste, Churchill concluded, "I will never despair that we can make ourselves secure. The Royal Navy, especially after the toning up which it has received, is unsurpassed in the world . . . and even at this eleventh hour, if the right measures are taken and if the right spirit prevails in the British nation and the British Empire, we may surround ourselves with other bulwarks equally sure," like airpower, "which will protect us against whatever storms may blow." "All I urge," he said, "is do it now."[23] While Britain had work to do to prepare its own defenses, it could not deter Germany alone. Churchill's answer to this problem was stated bluntly on July 12, 1936, in his "How to Stop War" article for the *Evening Standard*: "[T]here must be a Grand Alliance" under the umbrella of the League of Nations. "Let all the nations and states band themselves together upon a simple, single principle . . . Who attacks any, will be resisted by all, and resisted with such wrath and apparatus . . . that the very prospect may by its formidable majesty perhaps avert the crime."[24]

Raw power was needed to counterbalance the German threat, but arms and collective security were only one part of Churchill's grand strategy. In March 1933, during the debate over general disarmament for Europe, Churchill reminded his fellow MPs of a phrase they had heard before: "[A]s I have been saying for several years, 'Thank God for the French army.'"[25] It's important not to misinterpret this phrase. As Churchill saw it, the problem of European security after the Great War was never about German arms alone. A powerful French army was not for beating back German recovery as it tried to regain its strength. Like Otto von Bismarck before him, he recognized that preventive war—even a successful hammer blow that would knock back the rival's growing power for a while—would not solve the strategic problem. It would merely intensify the danger of burning grievances that would once again bring violent conflict. Churchill shared that general British disposition to see stable peace and sustainable security as a function of political relationships among the major powers. So when Churchill talked about the balance of power after the Great War, he did so with direct reference to the broader strategic-political context. One key question was always on his mind: *Would Germany rebuild its strength while its grievances still smoldered?* If so, then future war was a near certainty. As we've seen, Churchill worried about the danger of European war long before the rise of the Nazi regime. But here is the most important point: Despite the radical changes in the character of the threat and the European security problem from the 1920s through the mid-1930s, Churchill's fundamental strategy for solving the problem did not change. Counterbalancing Germany could "avert the crime" of aggression, but this was a near-term goal. Ultimately, deterrence would serve a deeper strategic objective— providing time to open political space for resolving grievances and building stable relationships among powers that were generally satisfied with the status quo. Satisfied enough, at least, to keep them from seeking further change through war. Negotiating from strength was a key enabler of this strategy. Whether it was Germany under the Weimar Republic or Germany under the Third Reich, a weak Germany or a rapidly strengthening Germany, his goal was the same.

We know that in 1925 Churchill found great comfort in French dominance and German weakness, not merely because German capabilities didn't pose a threat, but because the distribution of power offered "breathing space" for settling the antagonism that would bring Germany and France to blows once again. Seven years later, Churchill was horrified by the proposals for general European disarmament being floated by well-meaning statesmen worried about arms and war. It was too soon, he cried. In November 1932, months before Adolf Hitler was in the Reich Chancellery, Churchill stated his view on the question as a "general principle: *the removal of the just grievances of the vanquished ought to precede the disarmament of the victors.*" Germany's "grievances remain unredressed," he observed, so weakening Allied power now would be like appointing "the day for another European war—to fix it as if it were a prize fight."[26] Four months later, with Hitler's dictatorial powers now secured, Churchill repeated the same vision of "three or four great Powers shaking hands together and endeavoring to procure a rectification of some of the evils arising from the treaties made in the passion of war."[27] In November 1933 he called on the League of Nations to "address Germany collectively, so that there may be some redress of the grievances of the German nation, and that that may be effected before this peril of rearmament reaches a point which may endanger the peace of the world."[28]

In late March 1936, with the world still rattled by the Rhineland coup, Churchill told Parliament what he wanted: "I desire to see the collective forces of the world invested with overwhelming power. If you are going to run this thing on a narrow margin" of armed strength, then "one way or the other, you are going to have war. But if you get five or ten to one on one side, all bound rigorously by the" League of Nations "Covenant and the conventions which they own, then, in my opinion, you have an opportunity of making a settlement which will heal the wounds of the world." Organizing such overwhelming power was not for the purpose of crushing Germany in a devastating preventive attack while it was still relatively weak. Nor was the objective merely to deter the Third Reich. The goal was to "invite Germany to state her grievances, to lay them on the council board and to let us have it out . . . Let us have it out on the basis that we are negotiating from strength and not from weakness; that we are negotiating from unity and not from division and isolation."[29] Two weeks later, in April 1936, Churchill admitted he was cautiously hopeful: "The time available is short," but "I hold that the time is coming for a final and lasting friendly settlement with Germany."[30]

A few other examples from the ranks of the celebrated hard-liners will tell a similar story. Robert Vansittart is among them. As the permanent undersecretary for foreign affairs from 1930 to 1938, Vansittart had a central role in the internal British struggle to understand the character of the Nazi regime and the threat it might pose. He was a professional diplomat, not a politician, but as the senior official among the professional staffers in the Foreign Office, "Van" had more influence over these questions than most cabinet ministers. Since World War II, Vansittart has been hailed as one of the few visionaries in the British government to quickly recognize the menace posed by Nazi Germany, hailed for his persistent demand that Britain rebuild a formidable power base of its own to hold the Third Reich's aggressive intentions in check.[31]

Vansittart didn't wait until the end of the Second World War to publish the *Lessons of My Life*, which appeared in 1943, while the outcome of the terrible struggle was still unknown. The world was suffering enough misery by then for Vansittart to share his reflections on the war's origins, and, most important, to tell his readers just how prescient Vansittart himself had been during the 1930s. By getting out in front of the inevitable postmortems to come, Vansittart could ensure that he was never lumped in with that cast of fools being blamed for the disaster. *Lessons of My Life* goes a long way toward burnishing his reputation as the hard-nosed realist that fought against the tide of complacency and degeneracy that distracted the British people from the dangers that he recognized so clearly. On this topic, he writes with overt disgust. "There were lots of things—sex, money, pleasure, comfort— that" the British people "wanted to talk about more. No generation has ever *talked* more about sex!"[32] What they weren't talking about, to Vansittart's dismay, was the desperate condition of Britain's strategic vulnerabilities.

Vansittart, in contrast, in his telling of the story, was a reliable and persistent voice within the government warning of the dangers that would inevitably appear tomorrow and the critical need for a decisive British response today. Vansittart was indeed among the early alarmists. In just one example among many from the early 1930s, he prepared a memorandum in August 1933 that provided a blunt assessment: "Germany is an exceedingly competent country, and she is visibly being prepared to external aggression," most likely by 1938, he said. "I do not think that anything but evil and danger for the rest of the world can come out of Hitlerism."[33]

So what exactly was Robert Vansittart's advice when the Rhineland crisis exploded a few years later, as the danger was growing ever more severe? In his memoirs, he scoffed at the common British refrain of the time: "My dear fellow, it's German territory," they said.[34] But what Vansittart ignores is that he too held this view at the time. In a memorandum dated February 3, 1936, he agreed with the British consensus that "maintenance of the demilitarized zone was the last surviving example of treating Germany as unequal; it was really more a prestige matter than a military one." He never saw the Rhineland as some golden moment in the inevitable march toward war that the Allies could leverage to stop Hitler before the inevitable happened. Vansittart never advocated preventive war to hold down German power. Instead, he fully supported the cabinet's position: Rhineland demilitarization was unsustainable and should be bargained away. Hitler wouldn't wait long before raising the Rhineland issue officially, Vansittart concluded, so it was "better to reach an agreement with Germany before she decided upon any aggressive or dangerous step," he wrote. "The aim of the agreement should be concrete—an air agreement, for example." The "process of give and take, before Germany took the law into her own hands . . . This policy is still the constructive one."[35]

Beyond this immediate problem, though, he argued that a fervent push on rearmament was essential to counter the long-term German threat. "For rearmament, like the elimination of the demilitarised Zone," Vansittart said, "must form part of *any* policy that we may adopt."[36] Looking back in *Lessons of My Life*, Vansittart stuck to this point in his criticism of the prewar period: "[D]uring the crucial years all the three great political parties were opposed to the only means of restraining the blood-thirsty ambitions of the German nation: massive and timely rearmament."[37] Rearmament to deter German power, rather than preventive war to smash it, was Vansittart's consistent position. And in his 1936 memorandum, Vansittart was hopeful about the long-term possibilities of delaying war. The "essential thing is that we should gain time," he wrote, "and things postponed have a way of not happening."[38]

British war minister Duff Cooper earned a coveted spot on the roster of prewar hard-liners by being the only government minister to quit Prime Minister Neville Chamberlain's cabinet over the Munich Agreement in 1938. He has been held up ever since as another one of the tough anti-appeasers that had the wisdom and courage to oppose any policy that treated Hitler as though he were a reasonable statesman that would accept peaceful settlement of political grievances. Cooper created a bit of a kerfuffle in June 1936, which seems to reinforce his place on the hard-liner roster, by getting too far ahead of government policy on Britain's relationship with France. In a banquet speech in Paris, Cooper defined this relationship as one of "sheer necessity—a matter of life and death for both our countries," because these two great democracies stood together against the centers of oppression and aggression in Europe. The Labour opposition in Parliament said Cooper had to be reined in by the prime minister because he was dangerously undermining the prospects of stable relations with Germany.[39]

It was a tough line for sure, but what about the Rhineland crisis specifically? In his memoirs, Cooper is honest about the limitations of prognosis for those responsible for national policy: "In the light of after-events," he says, "a light that is always denied to us" in the actual stream of history, "this was undoubtedly the moment when Great Britain and France should have taken a firm line and insisted upon the withdrawal of the German troops as a preliminary to any discussion." Despite this important cautionary note about the tension between foresight and hindsight, Cooper then echoes Vansittart by laying heavy criticism on his fellow countrymen in *Old Men Forget*: "[T]he average Englishman was quite unable to appreciate the significance of Hitler's military occupation of the Rhineland. 'Why shouldn't the Germans move soldiers about in their own country?' was the not unnatural reaction of the ignorant," he complained.[40]

Old Men Forget, indeed. What Cooper failed to note in his memoirs is that he took this exact position in 1936. In fact, without the illumination cast by the "light of after-events," he understood the problem exactly as Anthony Eden, and the average Englishman, did at the time. There was no demand from Duff Cooper for Nazi Germany to roll its soldiers back out of the Rhineland, no call for preventive war to enforce the DMZ if Hitler refused—just a mild protest over the jarring manner of Hitler's actions. This was revealed during a meeting with the German military attaché on March 9, two days after the Wehrmacht rolled in. Cooper said he "took a poor view of *how* the Germans had gone about matters. They had unilaterally violated a treaty that they had signed of their own free will." But remilitarization itself, the substance of Hitler's challenge to the status quo, "could have been achieved through negotiations instead," the war minister admitted.[41]

We'll give Austen Chamberlain the final word among this small group of hard-liners. As we saw in the last chapter, Hitler's assault on Chamberlain's legacy in the Rhineland was a terrible blow to the former foreign minister. Chamberlain worried about this flagrant thrashing of international law. He worried that Britain would fail to stand by its commitments to the principles at stake and its partners in peace. But what did Chamberlain think Britain should actually do about Hitler's fait accompli? Would he be the one to encourage the British government to follow France—politically or militarily—up that ladder of preventive action to turn German soldiers back and restore the Locarno order? No. Despite his deepening hostility to the Nazi regime and his support for a vigorous rearmament program to meet a future threat, Austen Chamberlain saw the Rhineland problem the same way he did in 1925. Ten years earlier, Chamberlain conceded that a German challenge over the DMZ was inevitable. So when this prediction became reality in 1936, he publicly and privately vented his genuine dismay, but he never veered from the basic policy set out long before Hitler ruled Germany.

Throughout the crisis, Chamberlain never labeled Hitler's Rhineland move an act of aggression that required an immediate defensive response, nor did he advocate a preventive military attack to preserve the DMZ. Like Eden, Vansittart, and Cooper, Chamberlain said during parliamentary debate that "the real question being tried out in these anxious and critical days is not demilitarization of the Rhineland. That might well have been a subject for discussion" to restore Germany's rights. The question was whether international law would replace brute force in the affairs of great states.[42] He called Eden's March 26 speech in the House of Commons a "first-class performance," and said he was "well satisfied with it." It was this speech that reaffirmed Britain's commitment to stand alongside France and Belgium in a fight only if they faced an actual attack, and it laid out the government's decision to negotiate a broader settlement to maintain European peace. In Parliament Chamberlain pointed to a diplomatic opening: "[T]he German proposals as laid before us," he said, "need a great deal of very careful examination." As Chamberlain put it in a private letter to his sister, "the net result of recent events is to throw us more and more back on the *essence* of the Locarno policy—a definite guarantee of peace in the area where we are vitally interested," the Belgian and French frontier.[43] In the end, Chamberlain's preferred response to the loss of the DMZ was to drop economic sanctions against Italy to draw it back into a common front against Germany, then "to sit down seriously to try to come to terms with Germany if possible, and fortify peace against her if it is not."[44] Austen Chamberlain didn't live to see the next World War; he died of a heart attack in London in March 1937, just a year after Hitler's fait accompli in the Rhineland. It's impossible to know what Chamberlain might have said about the Rhineland question in his memoirs if he had experienced the terrible end to this tragic story. But in the moment, Chamberlain, like Winston Churchill, supported Britain's basic policy: rearm, deter, and seek political settlement.

THE DEVIL'S MERRY-GO-ROUND

When French leaders put the preventive war option on the table in 1936, the British government knocked it off again. Churchill and his allies—the alarmists, the hard-liners—accepted this decision without protest. But there was an alternative. The hard-liners were now on the leading edge of an ongoing shift in British policy, no longer isolated voices in the wilderness, as a growing critical mass came to embrace rearmament and alliance building as a necessary reaction to the expanding German threat. While no one saw preventive war as a viable strategic solution to this problem, many were abandoning the idea, so widespread in earlier years, that great-power disarmament was the road to peace. Opposition to rearmament was concentrated within the Labour Party, but the Conservative-led national government enjoyed a 70 percent parliamentary majority after the elections of November 1935. As Conservatives lined up behind the cause, the most important question being debated by the mid-1930s was not "rearmament: yes or no?" Rather, the question was whether Britain's balancing measures were vigorous enough to keep German power in check. Hindsight seems to offer a crisp answer to that question. The ferocious hammer blows Germany landed against Poland in 1939 and France in 1940 provide enough evidence to conclude that the Western Allies failed the ultimate test of a balance-of-power security strategy. They could not deter German aggression, and could not defend themselves against it, even with eight more months to prepare between the declaration of war in September 1939 and the day blitzkrieg forces were unleashed in May 1940.

From our vantage point, World War II is the most spectacular case we have of a phenomenon political scientists call *underbalancing*. One scholar defines underbalancing as situations in which "threatened countries have failed to recognize a clear and present danger or, more typically, have simply not reacted to it or, more typically still, have responded in paltry and imprudent ways."[45] This definition captures the various postwar critiques of British and French strategy perfectly. They were blind to the threat, some charge. If not blind, then they were paralyzed by fear, others claim, doing "nothing" to push back against direct German challenges when they had the chance. Or if they did take steps to balance German power, many others conclude, these measures were obviously "paltry and imprudent" in the face of the terrible threat that loomed just over the horizon. The dazzling power of the Wehrmacht seems to drive home that simple observation.

We must be humble enough to acknowledge, however, that such a self-assured conclusion is only possible because we know the *outcome* of the story. Today we know in fine detail what Hitler plotted and executed step by step, from his ascension to power in 1933 to his final defeat in 1945. It's nearly impossible to see this history as anything but a logical, ineluctable train of events that could only end with the horrors of the Second World War. With so much information now available on the actors, their motivations, their capabilities, the choices they would make at each point on the timeline, and what these choices produced, comes the temptation to declare with great self-confidence what should have been "obvious" to those living within the stream of events, obvious about the problem and its solutions. Here we have "the tyranny of hindsight bias," that tendency to expect those living in the past to have the same clarity into the problems they faced that those living years in the future have.[46] And in this case, it leads to some harsh conclusions: that British leaders of the 1930s should have recognized early on that they were losing the rearmament race and losing time, and once realizing this fact, they should have gone all in with a policy of confrontation—if not with preventive war, then by embracing hard balancing with the heaviest arms and the tightest alliances, the earlier the better, to deter and defend against German aggression. After all, didn't Churchill and his allies see it this way? Perhaps it was smart to buy time, some might say, to avoid confrontation and delay war until the Allies were better prepared. Even so, the voice of hindsight suggests that British leaders should have embraced the fact that war was inevitable unless they could create a cage of countervailing power around Germany.

Churchill rightfully earns postwar praise for recognizing the dangers of underbalancing and for raising the alarm that helped push his countrymen toward rearmament. But hindsight bias most often leads to caricatures of the British reaction to the German threat, a ready assertion that whatever they were doing, it must have been "paltry and imprudent," which should have been obvious to those alive and aware at the time. But this is a straw-man assessment that ignores how those alive and aware at the time actually understood the situation. A "paltry" counterbalancing effort? Most observers in 1936 would have found this claim absurd. Their policy was "imprudent" in light of the dangers? But what, exactly, is meant by imprudent? Not bal-ancing hard enough, or balancing *too vigorously*? This question was another legacy of the Great War: Do arms and alliances deter war and provide se-curity, or does rampant power competition actually lead to war by stoking fear and the security dilemma? A strong consensus was forming around the shift toward balancing in 1936, but across the political spectrum, observers also worried about the dangers of *overbalancing*. Again, in hindsight this worry sounds odd. Was it possible to overbalance Nazi Germany? But even Churchill and his fellow hard-liners were not immune from this troubling question. This worry is at the heart of a more interesting and complicated story that's routinely lost in the standard accounts of the time, yet it helps to round out the explanation for the decision to reject preventive war. The only way to uncover this story is to showcase contemporary perspectives, to crawl inside the transcripts of parliamentary debates and public speeches, to scour government reports, to review newspaper analysis and editorials. From the vantage point of February and March 1936, how did observers understand the state of play among the great powers? Paltry and imprudent?

In mid-February, the *Boston Globe* captured the dominant view with a pair of sharp headlines: "Seven European Nations in Great Arms Race," the *Globe* declared, as an "'Iron Ring' Closes Round Nazi Germany."[47] The pace of events in early 1936, the momentum behind the rearming and the alliance building, both before and after Hitler's Rhineland dash, gave cre-dence to the Associated Press assessment that a "circle of steel" was being constructed "around Germany."[48] A somber event for the British people, the death of King George V on January 20, seemed to kick-start a flurry of balancing in the new year. Adolf Hitler was the first foreign leader to tele-gram London with his condolences, upstaging the French, whose telegram arrived soon after. Nevertheless, French foreign minister Pierre-Étienne Flandin was determined to leverage the King's funeral to quietly agitate against the Third Reich's growing power. Among the two million people in London to pay their respects were heads of state from around the world.

German foreign minister Konstantin von Neurath had his own private meeting with Anthony Eden on January 29, which he used to disavow all reports of imminent Rhineland remilitarization. Eden had already heard from Flandin the day before that a Rhineland challenge was indeed in the works. Three days later, Flandin hosted an impromptu security conference in Paris that rolled through the first ten days of February. He drew together key Central and Eastern European leaders on their way home from London—the Soviet commissar for foreign affairs Maxim Litvinov, King Carol of Romania, King Boris of Bulgaria, the vice chancellor of Austria, the Czechoslovakian premier, the regent of Yugoslavia, and the foreign ministers of Turkey and Lithuania—all of whom shared French fears of growing German influence and the potential for future aggression. On February 10, the Soviet assistant defense commissar, Marshal Mikhail Tukhachevsky, met with the French war minister to confer on operational details necessary to make the pending Franco-Soviet defense pact work in practice. All of these meetings were covered widely in the press.

By mid-February, Anthony Eden was announcing that British defense policy was about to shift abruptly. In a press interview, he put it bluntly. "We are going to rearm. That's the only thing left for us to do, and it is the only sane conclusion from a diagnosis of the European muddle." No one doubted that Germany was Britain's rearmament target. "We must be so powerful," Eden said, "that no Continental State will dare start a war."[49] On February 24, during debate in the House of Commons, he put his colleagues and the British public on notice that a white paper making the case for rearmament, and a resolution funding it, was coming in a matter of weeks. Two days later, the French Chamber of Deputies ratified their defense pact with the Soviet Union. The Führer railed against the agreement and used it to declare the Locarno treaty dead on March 7. Three days later the House of Commons seemed to answer Hitler's challenge with overwhelming approval of the government's resolution, funding what a report in the *Washington Post* called "the greatest peacetime armament program ever launched in Great Britain."[50]

On March 12, the French Senate followed up with its own ratification of the defense pact with the USSR by a vote of 231 to 53. The Associated Press characterized final ratification as a direct French counterstrike over the Rhineland. This is a fair interpretation. The defense pact troubled many French rightist politicians who had grave concerns about opening more doors for a Bolshevik infection of Central Europe. After the Rhineland, scores of French Senate opponents voted in favor of the defense pact as a patriotic duty. On March 27, Flandin hosted Soviet foreign minister Maxim Litvinov in Paris once again, this time to exchange treaty ratifications, to formalize what one observer called a "massive cable, uniting France and Soviet Russia in military alliance against the Third Reich," a "mighty network of steel . . . along Germany's borders."[51] According to Soviet premier Vyacheslav Molotov, in an interview with the French newspaper *Le Temps*, there were "no limitations" on the kind of military aid the USSR would provide France if attacked.[52] In the meantime, the British government had reaffirmed its own military commitment to defend France and Belgium against unprovoked aggression; by the end of the month, with talks scheduled for initial coordination among Western military staffs, the French government was calling this a de facto alliance.

Looking back over the previous weeks, and considering Hitler's efforts to divide the European states during the crisis, the London *Observer* declared that Hitler's grand political scheme was a flop. The Rhineland coup failed to "smash the Franco-Soviet pact, which he hates, because it is one of the surest instruments of European peace." Germany "has also failed . . . to destroy the Franco-British understanding."[53] "Hitler Is Cornered," the *New York Times* diplomatic correspondent concluded; these alliances are "an assurance of peace on the Continent."[54] Flandin apparently agreed. To the Chamber of Deputies on March 20 he reported that "For us" the British defense commitment "marks the accomplishment of a persistent effort" to forge "solidarity in the face of a threat of war which will enable us better than in 1914 to drive back that hideous specter." There was great applause in the hall. "What danger might lie in German occupation of the Rhineland," he said, "is fully offset by the new promise of the guarantor powers."[55]

For generations, postwar scholars have argued over the relative distribution of power in Europe at the time, and over the efficacy of the rearmament programs on all sides; as one has observed, "a statistical war has been waged since 1940" on these questions, and "this is to be a war in perpetuity."[56] The statistical war continues to this day. But as seen from early 1936, Germany was grossly outweighed by France and its allies. "No need to be alarmist about this situation," said the *Christian Science Monitor*; "Germany is weaker and is virtually isolated."[57] Walter Lippmann, perhaps the most influential American journalist of the twentieth century, had been watching the crisis spiral, and he reported to his huge readership that "Europe is now engaged in a feverish race of armaments."[58] But, he assured them, "There is no doubt that together Britain and France possess military, economic and financial power which no nation and no combination of nations could challenge."[59] J. L. Garvin, the editor of the London *Observer* and an early supporter of Winston Churchill, agreed with this assessment. During the Rhineland crisis Garvin was a vocal critic of the preventive war option. "There is not a shred of sane justification for war to reimpose unique inequality upon the German people on their proper soil," he said. Britain's defense commitment to France and Belgium was "far preferable to any sort of action against Germans in Germany for reasserting their proper right over their own acres." Britain's commitment "is an elementary precaution against the huge uncertainties of the future. And it is necessary in view of the increasing predominance of German strength."[60] The future is uncertain, but balancing will work, he said. "Britain, France and Belgium . . . if they are properly organized for defence . . . need not fear Germany."[61] When he considered this commitment along with the Franco-Soviet pact, Garvin wrote that "Once again Germany found herself enclosed in effect between the iron walls of a gigantic military alliance."[62]

Observers looking at the broader European system were drawing the same basic conclusions, even if their statistics varied a bit. Writing in the *Washington Post*, Livingston Hartley reported that this did not look like a replay of 1914: "[R]ival alliances do not exist today," he said. "We see, instead, Germany standing alone in Europe. Arrayed against Germany is an infinitely stronger group of states—France, Russia and the Little Entente," France's Eastern European allies, "with the probable support of Great Britain—in the event of another war. This line-up is perhaps the strongest bulwark against war in Europe at the present time."[63] In the *Los Angeles Times*, Albin Johnson's analysis was notable for being perhaps the most assertive American voice on the inevitability of another European war. But in 1936 he still reported that "Around Germany is a ring of steel." According to his figures, France, the Little Entente, and the USSR could mobilize twenty-seven million men, while Germany was financially bankrupt and could only count on one million "fighters" and two million reserves.[64] "Hitler did not kill Locarno as he hoped to do," Johnson wrote. "He simply has changed it into a sinister negative military alliance . . . a triple-plated menace on the Reich's western front."[65]

Hanson Baldwin, who was promoted by the *New York Times* in 1937 to serve as its chief military analyst, concluded a week after the Rhineland coup that despite the Third Reich's advances, there is a "ring of steel about Germany." "The strength of France and her allies today, measured against that of Germany, Austria and Hungary, is overwhelming," Baldwin wrote. "The cards of war are overwhelmingly stacked against Hitler's legions. Even without the help of England, France and her ring of steel can put 2,336,607 men in the field almost immediately, and have available trained reserves of more than 25,000,000 to draw upon." In contrast, Germany's regular army at the time had 426,800 men, with 1,850,000 reserves. French government estimates were that 8 million Allied troops could be mobilized within forty-eight hours, and ultimately 40 million were available to fight a total war.[66]

Winston Churchill worried that this "iron ring" was still too flimsy. Most observers, however, would have rejected the underbalancing charge out of hand. As seen from 1936, this was no "paltry" rearmament and alliance-building initiative. But to return to the other component in the definition of underbalancing offered above: Were these balancing measures "prudent"? Putting aside hindsight bias and looking at this question from the vantage point of 1936, we discover a raging debate under way over how to judge the prudence of this policy. The question at the center of this debate was more profound than whether the money being spent, the military force structure being developed, and the defense agreements being negotiated across Europe were powerful enough to meet the German challenge. The real question was whether balancing would actually produce the desired strategic effect. Would balancing contain German aggression?

For Churchill, the answer was obvious: of course. In March 1936 he urged members of the Conservative Party Foreign Affairs Committee to fall back on Britain's balancing tradition. "For four hundred years," Churchill said, "the foreign policy of England has been to oppose the strongest, most aggressive, most dominating Power on the Continent . . . I know of nothing which has occurred to alter or weaken the . . . wisdom . . . and prudence" of meeting power with power.[67] This was a basic statement of support for the "deterrence model" of international security. World War II and the Cold War elevated the deterrence model as a seemingly uncontested, commonsense approach to ward off the threat of potentially aggressive states. The logic of this model is simple. A deterrence policy achieves its goal by generating fear in the target state—specifically, fear that its own aggression will be met with the pain of violent retaliation. The potential aggressor must believe that its opponents have sufficient power and the political will to inflict this pain, and it must fear the costs of retaliation more than it values whatever goals might be pursued through aggression. The common conclusion about World War II is that the Allies simply didn't balance hard enough to deter or contain the Third Reich, while America's containment policy during the Cold War, particularly the threat of conflict escalation to an apocalyptic nuclear exchange, is said to have deterred the Soviet Union from taking the risks of highly aggressive expansion into Western Europe.[68]

While World War II and the Cold War have served as ready models of deterrence logic (or its failure) since the mid-twentieth century, what models did they have in the mid-1930s to think through the relationship between arms and alliances and the likelihood of war? The experience that cast the darkest shadow, of course, was the Great War. And this particular example left behind a very different lesson—what international security scholars call the "spiral model"—and it raised serious questions about the prudence of hard balancing. The deterrence and spiral models of war share one critical assumption: A push for greater arms and tighter alliances generates *fear* in opposing states. The question they then disagree on is what *effect* does this fear have on the rival's behavior?[69]

According to the spiral model, we find the same phenomenon—the security dilemma—discussed throughout this book: Instead of containing the threat, a rival's growing arms and alliances spurs it on. All states, so goes the argument, regardless of differences in their form of government, their ideologies, culture, economy, geography, and leadership are embedded within an anarchic international system, so every state must worry about the hard power others possess to do them harm. As one state's military capabilities grow, a potential rival will likely see this as a rising threat that must be counterbalanced to ward off future dangers. The perverse paradox of this phenomenon is that the "instinct of preservation" leads to a spiraling "vicious circle" of fear and competition, even among states simply wishing to survive, that can spin out of control and trigger war.[70]

For generations of theorists studying international conflict, World War I has served as the inspiration for the spiral model, so it's no surprise that the Great War served this same role for those who lived through this catastrophe and were wrestling with its lessons in the decades that followed. There was wide agreement among those living in its immediate wake, at least in Britain and America, that the mainspring driving war in the early twentieth century was the escalating spiral of fear, arms, and alliances.[71] An excellent example comes from Sir Edward Grey, British foreign minister for a decade before the Great War, as Britain drew closer to the Franco-Russian alliance and Germany frantically built battleships for a High Seas Fleet that could challenge British supremacy in northern European waters. Grey has been criticized for failing to clearly warn the German government in July 1914 that Britain would indeed fight if Germany invaded Belgium as an attack route toward France. This warning, some argue, if delivered early enough, might have deterred Germany's offensive in the west; others present evidence that German leaders fully expected British participation in the war, which had no deterrent effect on the German decision.[72] But when he looked back on the years before the war, Grey saw deeper forces at work that created the conditions for a great-power clash. Hard balancing against a rival is meant to generate strength and security, Grey wrote, but the Great War demonstrated that it "does not produce these effects. On the contrary, it produces a consciousness of the strength of other nations and a sense of fear. Fear begets suspicion and distrust and evil imaginings of all sorts, till each Government feels it would be . . . a betrayal of its own country not to take every precaution, while every Government regards every precaution of every other Government as evidence of hostile intent."[73]

In 1936, much of the press coverage of the evolving security scene saw this cycle starting all over again. The *Chicago Tribune* trumpeted that "Trouble Lies in Endless Chain of Secret Pacts," while the *Boston Globe* decried the "Military Madness of the World." An editorial in the *Washington Post* said "It is not accidental that the growing reliance upon force has coincided with increasing expectations of a second world war."[74] The *Los Angeles Times* reviewed the shifting political landscape a day after Hitler's Rhineland coup, and all its analyst saw was the world "Lining Up for Armageddon." "The new line-up in Europe," John Clayton wrote, "may be carrying all nations to a world war so destructive and bitter as to make us forget the one that closed less than eighteen years ago."[75] A few months later Clayton observed, "[C]atastrophe is just over the horizon . . . For never has the world placed so many of its sons in army barracks; never have such armies been concentrated on frontiers in peace time. . . . [S]o the world heads toward destruction."[76]

Walter Lippmann, in his first column about the Rhineland crisis, struck a humble tone as he studied its complexities. "It is not for Americans to suggest how this momentous issue should be decided nor to judge those who have the awful responsibility." Nevertheless, Lippmann appreciated the British government's efforts to straddle the competing logics of the deterrence and spiral models. Locarno was a good treaty, he wrote; Germany's violation made him cynical about the prospects for a better agreement that might actually maintain peace. But Lippmann worried that if European governments failed to find a reasonable political settlement, "the race of armaments in Europe, already bad enough, would become frantic." Whatever replaced Locarno must be rigorous enough to give France and her allies a sense of security, he advised, but any security scheme must be one that "Germany will not treat as another threat, like the Soviet treaty." For if the Germans see it this way, new security measures will just become an "occasion for another military thrust." If political settlement fails, he warned, European leaders will have to prepare "with a sense of grim desolation for the disaster of European anarchy."[77]

Parliamentary debate over the British government's rearmament bill and military staff talks with France and Belgium stirred up the same warnings. Voting records show that while the majority Conservatives lined up solidly behind the cabinet's rearmament resolution on March 10, opposition to the bill was concentrated in the Liberal and Labour parties. A close review of the debate transcripts explains why. The legacy of the Great War is easy to spot, in speech after speech, but the arguments here don't reflect the raw pacifism said to have sprouted out of the mud of the Western Front. Instead, the arguments reflect serious strategic claims about the causes of war and peace,

230 FROM HITLER'S GERMANY TO SADDAM'S IRAQ

an earnest desire to learn from recent experience about the political effects of balancing, and a willingness to question old assumptions about security. Among British politicians, the spiral model purists were now concentrated in the Labour Party; 71 percent of Labour MPs participating in the debate pointed to spiral logic specifically to justify their vote. Labour's amendment to the rearmament bill made this point up front, saying the party "cannot agree to a policy which . . . seeks security in national armaments alone and intensifies the ruinous arms race between the nations, inevitably leading to war."[78] Clement Attlee, the party leader, repeated this warning in Parliament on March 9: "We do not know at the moment whether we are in 1911 or 1912 or 1913; but we are now on that slope which leads down to another world war."[79] George Lansbury, Attlee's predecessor as party leader, argued that "the more you strengthen these so-called Defence Forces, the more you pile up, the more certain is it that you will have to face the catastrophe of war. Every historical record of Europe proves the truth of that statement."[80] The only alternative, they believed, was to shore up the League of Nations so its collective security mechanisms could hold off the threat of Nazi Germany and the threat of great power war alike.

These were the spiral model purists. The bill's supporters were obviously drawn back to the logic of balancing and deterrence to contain the potential dangers of German power. But the interesting thing about this shift in British policy is that even the strongest champions of balancing could not shake off the lessons of recent history. The year 1936 was a transitional one between these two strategic logics. Even as they rearmed, the cabinet and its parliamentary supporters refused to abandon the insights drawn from the spiral model. In effect, they worried about "overbalancing," the danger that going all in to create a truly suffocating iron ring around the Third Reich would inevitably lead to a catastrophic, and perhaps unnecessary, total war. So their mantra became "Balance, but don't *encircle!*" Encirclement, the perennial fear that bedeviled German leaders since Otto von Bismarck, would spike German anxiety, British leaders believed, and produce the very danger they were trying to avoid.[81]

It's possible to trace this mantra back to Robert Vansittart, the permanent undersecretary in the Foreign Office, one of the alleged Promethean hard-liners celebrated in the postwar years. As we saw in the first part of this chapter, Vansittart played a vital role in preparing the cabinet to make the argument for rearmament with his important memorandum of February 3, 1936. In a bilateral matchup, he wrote, "we are, in the matter of most armaments and all munitions, already dangerously weaker than Germany. Bargains can be better driven when one is strong than when one is weak." Vansittart rejected the blanket claim that armaments lead to war, but he immediately acknowledged that *how* Britain and others went about counterbalancing Germany was a critical question. "There are," he said, "*grave* and *obvious dangers* in a policy of encirclement." If hard balancing "were our only method of dealing with Germany, it would almost certainly provoke the organization by her of a counter block" and the likelihood of a spiral toward war. Vansittart had a solution to this problem: Do not arm within the framework of rival alliances, but support the League of Nations system of collective security. This offered a safe alternative, because as it held German aggression at bay, it could "be combined with an elastic policy of settlement" to resolve German grievances.[82]

Three weeks later, Anthony Eden picked up Vansittart's formula to make the government's case to Parliament. Britain must rearm on behalf of a viable collective security system, he argued, so all potential aggressors will be "convinced that in no circumstances can aggression be made to pay." We will not, however, support a system that replicates the dangerous "pre-war system of alliances," Eden assured his colleagues, nor will this become isolated British rearmament against Germany. Instead, by "reaffirming our attachment to the League and to collective security," Eden said, Britain can rearm without taking any "part in encirclement," and thus avoid the spiral of fear and hostility that flared into world war.[83] On March 26 Eden made the same point when forced to defend the decision to initiate military staff talks in Paris. This is not like 1914, he said, when Britain's commitment to Belgium and France was tightly linked to the conflict in Eastern Europe through France's alliance with Russia. Today, Eden insisted, Britain's coordination with its French and Belgian partners is strictly limited to the defense of the Low Countries and our obligations under the Locarno treaty. Britain will not throw its fortunes in with France's allies to the east, tightening the circle around Germany that might lead to trouble. Rearm, and defend, but don't encircle. From this point forward, his Conservative Party supporters ran with this message; fear of the spiral wasn't a syndrome isolated to Labour Party pacifists still clinging to dreams of peace through disarmament and international law. Fully two-thirds of Conservative MPs participating in the debate—including the hard-liners—warned specifically about the spiral effect and the dangers of encirclement.[84]

It was Liberal MP David Lloyd George, Britain's Great War prime minister, who forced the Conservatives into a testy exchange over the danger of spirals during the March 26 debate. Lloyd George reminded his colleagues of the crisis of 1914, when military timetables and the technical details of crisis mobilization, worked out in advance by general staffs across Europe, took on an autonomous role, driving fear and the imperatives of escalation forward, to the point where political leaders lost the power to put the brakes on the spinning conflict. Hitler is "reckless," no doubt, Lloyd George acknowledged. "[H]e organized a torchlight parade through a powder magazine," and his recklessness demands a response. But if we react by getting our "staffs together to make arrangements, to arrange how many divisions are going, where they are going, to what frontier, what part they will take, how they are to attack the Germans, it is the shortcut to war." "It is the shortest cut that I know of to the ghastly mechanical carnage of modern war, raining fire and destruction upon our cities, raining down from the skies as upon Gomorrah."

Conservative MP Robert Boothby was the first to jump in with a direct reply. Boothby had been an MP since 1924 and a reliable Churchill ally since serving as his private parliamentary secretary when Churchill was Chancellor of the Exchequer in the 1920s. And like his mentor, Boothby was one of the proud rebels of the Conservative Party during the 1930s,[85] remembered for his bitter criticism of the Third Reich and appeasement, and his strong support for bringing the Soviet Union into a closer alliance with Western democracies. In a close review of the transcripts from every parliamentary debate that addressed the German problem between March and December 1936, Boothby pops off the page as the hardest of the hardliners on the certainty of future German aggression. What an "alluring road" the German General Staff has lying before it, he said on March 26, "which begins at Vienna, goes on to Belgrade, and finishes up at Bucharest . . . Prague would be very early on the line . . . the House should face up to the facts," accept that "this is going to happen, it is obvious." In his own review of recent history, Boothby argued that the Allies missed a golden opportunity after the Locarno conference, while Gustav Stresemann was still German foreign minister. That was the moment to pursue a serious settlement of the defects in the Versailles Treaty, and to immediately remove the military occupation in the Rhineland to help this along. But then the Great Depression hit, Boothby said, and the Nazis were swept into power. Like Anthony Eden, like Austen Chamberlain, like Winston Churchill, Robert Boothby said it was not too late to negotiate and stabilize the European political system, and we must do so from a position of strength. But as we rearm to deter and open space for a political settlement, he cautioned, collective security will be the key to saving civilization from the conflict spiral. Britain must "stand by the League and France." If the League breaks up, we will fall back to rival military alliances and the "inevitability of war."

Soon after, Willie Gallacher, the only Communist Party MP in Parliament, picked up on Lloyd George's theme to prod Churchill. "The Right

Honourable Member for Epping," Mr. Churchill, Gallacher reminded his colleagues, "said that the menace is war, and he is correct. It is war that is the menace to civilization." But rearmament and the military staff talks that the Foreign Secretary is proposing "now is suspiciously like a war encircle-ment of Germany," when "he should have said that we do not want to make a war encirclement of Germany," we should have a "peace encirclement" through the League of Nations.

Churchill jumped in. "We hear talk of the encirclement of Germany," he replied. "I thought that the last speaker quite justly said that war encircle-ment would be intolerable." "War encirclement" would be intolerable, Churchill agreed, if by this term we meant encirclement for the purposes of aggression against Germany. But this is not a "case of encirclement of Ger-many but of the encirclement of the potential aggressor," which any state, he said, including Great Britain, should be willing to tolerate if it poses a threat to international peace.[86] "In my view, all the nations and States that are alarmed at the growth of German armaments ought to combine for mu-tual aid, in pacts of mutual assistance, approved by the League of Nations and in accordance with the Covenant of the League."

In typical fashion, Churchill was an outlier among British officials and MPs. Most were still trying to figure out how to generate the right kind of power to deter without tipping the scales into encirclement and a conflict spiral. Churchill, on the other hand, had already made the mental shift to hard balancing to contain the German threat. To be sure, during the 1920s he contributed immensely to the British zeitgeist of the early postwar period; Churchill learned the same lessons about the dangers of spiraling conflict from the Great War that his compatriots did. But when it came to the Third Reich, Churchill no longer seemed troubled by the logic of the spiral model and the risks of encirclement. But only under one very specific condition: as long as Germany faced *massive encirclement* across the Con-tinent. As we've seen, Churchill's view on the deterrent effect of arms and alliances hinged on "the collective forces of the world invested with *over-whelming* power." Trying to balance with a "narrow margin"—now, that would generate a spiral toward war.[87] Achieving this level of countervailing power, however, proved impossible.

While Churchill was an outlier, he was not isolated. He really was on the leading edge of an ongoing policy shift, away from the Great War's heavy legacy and the spiral model of conflict it showcased, toward reluc-tant acceptance of increasingly harder balancing to deter a threat that was becoming less ambiguous, and more certain, over time. And, like his fellow Conservatives and the opposition Labour Party, Churchill looked to the

League of Nations as the best vehicle for amassing power to deter Germany while dodging the dangers of the conflict spiral. The main difference among these leaders is that Churchill wanted Britain to push its own rearmament much faster than it already was, while avoiding "undue prominence" as the "whole of Europe" worked to deter Germany and negotiate fair changes to the system that might keep the peace.

By July 1936, the promise of collective security with overwhelming power had collapsed. As one reporter described it, "diplomats are unable to keep pace with the speed of events," ever since Italy's victory over Ethiopia set in motion new political alignments that, in just a few weeks, seemed to split the system into tightening rival blocs.[88] On May 5, the Italian army rolled into the Ethiopian capital of Addis Ababa as Emperor Haile Selassie steamed north into exile on a British warship. Once Italy declared that Ethiopia was now merged with Eritrea and Italian Somaliland to form Italian East Africa, the League of Nations was forced to concede its failure to restrain Italian aggression. On July 4 the League Council voted to drop economic sanctions. The vote lit a fire under the geopolitical chessboard. On July 11, Germany surprised the world by announcing a new agreement with Austria in which the Third Reich dropped its demand for political unification and promised to respect Austrian independence. While this seemed to extinguish one of the dangerous hot spots on the list of German targets for expansion, it actually swept away the one dispute that kept Fascist Italy from linking arms with Nazi Germany. In July 1934 the Italian army had rushed four divisions into the Brenner Pass, the primary gate through the Alps between Austria and Italy, as a warning to Adolf Hitler that a German invasion would be met with force, and Italy stood united with France and Great Britain in April 1935 as a member of the Stresa Front to declare their joint demand for continuing Austrian independence.

With one quick pen stroke, Hitler pushed the problem aside, opening the door to an entente with Mussolini. Within weeks, Nazi Germany was prodding Italy to join its intervention on behalf of the military revolt that sparked the Spanish Civil War. With diplomatic circles and newspapers abuzz in July about a coming war in the east between Germany and the USSR, the Soviets successfully negotiated rights to sail its fleet from the Black Sea into the Mediterranean through the Turkish Straits, and Romania agreed to the construction of a Soviet rail line over the Carpathian Mountains so the Red Army could rush into Czechoslovakia in case of war with the Third Reich. This helped to shore up the viability of the Franco-Soviet defense pact, while French chief of staff Maurice Gamelin visited

Poland in August so both governments could publicly reaffirm their alliance and work on the logistical challenges posed by Rhineland remilitarization.

Through it all, Anthony Eden remained hopeful that he could pull together a five-power Locarno conference that summer so each of the signatories, including Italy and Germany, could hammer out an agreement to stabilize the new status quo. But the system continued to fracture. There were no more Locarno meetings, and no comprehensive political settlement. On October 14, King Leopold III of Belgium shocked his Western partners when he announced that his small and vulnerable nation was retreating from the whole frightening thing, withdrawing from Locarno and the 1920 defense compact with France, into neutrality. Belgian leaders had decided that it was safer to hide from this tightening balance-of-power system than to trust Belgium's safety to an alliance that would surely drag them into war once again. Two weeks later Mussolini announced in Milan that during his recent visit to Germany a Rome–Berlin Axis was forged, around which the politics of Europe would revolve. Three weeks later, the geographic scale of this system of rival alliances expanded once again, when Japan joined Germany in an anti-Communist pact, promising consultations on common defense interests and benign neutrality if either went to war with the USSR.

Back in March, in the immediate wake of the Rhineland coup, Churchill's protégé Robert Boothby laid this question before his colleagues as a warning: Where are we going to draw the line? Where do we take a stand? "Are we at any stage going to take up a line, and say, 'We are not going to let this happen'?" Boothby asked. "I am sure that a moment will come when the whole of the people of this country unitedly will say to Germany, sooner or later, 'You have got to stop' . . . This country can never in the long run tolerate a Nazi Germany astride the whole of Europe, omnipotent right across the Continent." What he didn't say, but clearly meant, is that British leaders had to determine *where* they were willing to fight to stop the continuing growth of German power. Was the Rhineland the place to make that stand? Would Britain fight to prevent an *Anschluss* uniting Germany and Austria or to defend Czechoslovakia or Poland against German aggression? Would Britain wait until the Wehrmacht was storming across the Belgian and French frontiers? Despite his impeccable hard-liner credentials, Boothby said that the Rhineland was not a cause for war. "I agree" with the cabinet, he said, "that the moment has not come now."[89]

British leaders finally answered Boothby's question in March 1939 with a new alliance commitment to Poland, which Britain backed up in September by declaring war against Germany as the Poles fought for national survival.

By this point, the Third Reich had consumed Austria and Czechoslovakia; Italy and Germany had formalized their alliance through the so-called Pact of Steel; and the Soviet colossus had withdrawn from the anti-German bloc through its nonaggression pact with the Third Reich. While the Allies had been actively balancing before this moment arrived, they were not balancing actively enough. Deterrence failed to hold Hitler in check. The defense of the British Isles was a close-run thing. And final victory over the Axis powers depended on Soviet and American intervention, the two giants on the wings of the European Continent that chewed up Nazi Germany's military machinery, its manpower, and its industry through horrific attrition warfare. So maybe Boothby was wrong. Maybe 1936 was the place to draw the line, to take a stand, and fight against the growing power of the Third Reich. While Churchill wasn't calling for preventive war in 1936, an early draft of his memoirs carries what might be a hint of regret for the decisions not made: "Nothing could have stopped Hitler after the seizure of the Rhineland except a very serious war," he wrote.[90]

One of the main objectives of this book has been to explain why British leaders rejected the preventive war option during the Rhineland crisis. They were constrained by the preventive war paradox—the notion that victory on the battlefield would not deliver strategic success and truly neutralize the German threat. To the contrary, they worried that short-term victory would simply fire up the desire for revenge, adding to the pent-up frustrations that were already pushing Germany to change the terms of Versailles. Taking up arms to suppress German power in the Rhineland would sow the dragon's teeth of spiraling conflict and lead to the Armageddon they all wanted to avoid. The DMZ was a time bomb, they recognized, and international law could never sustain conditions that are nonsensical from a practical point of view. Winston Churchill saw the problem this same way.

But even if we concede that this was a reasonable decision as seen from 1936, we can still indulge our own frustrations over the "lost opportunities" to alter the tragic turns of history. So when it comes to the uniquely threatening character of Nazi Germany, doesn't preventive war remain the only viable option for solving this terrible strategic problem?[91] If Churchill is right—that "serious war" was inevitable after the Rhineland coup—it seems, at least in hindsight, that seizing the initiative and taking the fight to Germany in 1936, before it was ready to unleash Armageddon four years later, was a better option.

Did the Rhineland crisis actually hold the promise of stopping Hitler and the horrors of the Second World War? It's time to revisit this claim.

9

SEARCHING FOR
A SILVER BULLET

War disappoints.

—Sir Lawrence Freedman,
New America Future of War Conference, 2016

"Lost opportunities" haunt our thinking about World War II. The theme runs like a fluorescent thread through countless histories, through the memoirs of those who lived through it, the biographies of those who shaped prewar policies, the questions explored by political scientists studying war, through television documentaries, newspaper editorials, the speeches of American politicians, and casual conversations. In the same breath used to note the horrors of this war comes the familiar recitation of what seems to be an unchallenged postwar consensus: Bold action could have prevented this catastrophe. And once this judgment is in the air, it's natural to search for both culprits and those moments when courage and decisiveness could have altered the tragic story. Throughout this book, we've focused on one of these specific moments in the prewar years—the Rhineland crisis of 1936. And we've done so for an important reason: because war against Germany in 1936 would have been a *preventive war*. This particular crisis has given us a chance to explore the distinctive logic motivating the preventive war temptation, along with the strategic problems inherent to preventive war, enduring problems we find throughout world history and embedded within some of the trickiest foreign policy challenges we face today.

If the Allies had gone to war against Germany in 1938 to aid Czecho-slovakia during the Sudeten crisis, the war would have been fought under very different political conditions than a war launched in 1936. This later conflict, like the war actually declared in 1939 to assist Poland, would have had a simple strategic objective: to help an allied state turn back a neighbor's aggressive attack. In 1936, on the other hand, there was no actual aggression to compel a war of defense. No enemy tanks were storming across borders, no artillery shells were screaming downrange to break apart a defender's fortifications, no dive-bombers swooping in to destroy the victim's armored forces, or enemy infantry rushing in to seize its terrain. But here lies the appeal of preventive war—start the fight before that enemy attack is delivered, before aggression is even made possible by the adversary's growing military power. Why wait until 1938 or 1939, goes the argument, when you can solve the problem of Nazi Germany before the threat swells into an unstoppable force?

We've seen what Winston Churchill, and many others, have had to say about this question—that 1936 was the "last chance" to thwart Hitler's ambitions *without* a serious war. Even though Churchill himself didn't make this argument at the time, we need to return to that big counterfactual question: What if France *had* launched a preventive attack against Germany in 1936? It's the question that so many have found irresistible in the years since the Second World War, a question that continues to ripple into contemporary policy debates over our own power-shift problems. It's time to indulge those enduring frustrations with what might have been. Assuming *battlefield success*—that is, if French forces were able to drive the Wehrmacht into retreat across the Rhine River and restore the DMZ—would this preventive attack have produced *strategic success*? We need to put the insights of Prussian strategist Carl von Clausewitz at the center of this discussion. Strategic victory, he reminds us, cannot be defined by the immediate operational objectives of warfare. Victory on the battlefield can still end in strategic defeat if we fail to achieve the political goals that spark armed conflict. In this case, the political objective can be defined generally, as in "Preventive war would have made France more secure from potential German aggression." Or we can phrase strategic success the way so many have over the years—that restoring the Rhineland DMZ would have "stopped Hitler," or "stopped World War II."

These are bold claims, but as we've seen, belief in the promise of preventive war in this case is ubiquitous, and it continues to shape thinking about preventive war in the twenty-first century. So this counterfactual claim deserves serious consideration. How would preventive war in the Rhineland have produced such an amazing strategic outcome? What are the likely scenarios? Through what logic? This type of counterfactual analysis is by definition speculative. Who knows what alternative futures might have emerged if key details of the past were changed. After all, we cannot treat history like a laboratory experiment. We can't go back in time and rerun events to test how new combinations of variables will alter the outcome. Counterfactual questions are unorthodox in the fields of political science and history. These disciplines have well-established research methods for collecting empirical data and testing propositions about the way the world works or why events occurred the way they did. But as a growing number of scholars have observed, despite the speculative nature of counterfactual analysis, it's the only approach we have for studying certain questions.[1] In fact, the immense literature on the 1930s and World War II is riddled with counterfactual reasoning. Every hint of "what might have been" in a scholar's work is drawing from this alternative approach to thinking through the questions that matter.

With this in mind, this chapter will wade into a counterfactual universe and think through what might have happened if the French had launched a preventive attack in 1936. But before we jump into this thought experiment, it's fair to ask, What's the payoff from rethinking the Rhineland crisis—or any past decision, for that matter? There is nothing we can do to change the past, of course, but raising counterfactual questions can carry high stakes nonetheless. The past is a wellspring of insight into recurring problems, and leaders routinely convert historical cases into analogies that help them to understand their own problems. Whenever we look to history for lessons, it's imperative to have confidence that our conclusions are sound.[2]

For example, the most influential moment from history, in terms of offering up "lessons" that have shaped actual future decisions, is the Munich Agreement of 1938. It's become axiomatic to say Munich serves as an enduring warning about the bankruptcy of "appeasement" and the value of "confrontation" as alternative strategies to deal with states challenging the status quo. If only Britain had confronted Hitler and threatened war over the Sudetenland, choosing the counterfactual option, instead of trying to appease him. If only confrontation . . . then what? Would this show of strength have convinced Hitler that his aggressive ambitions were futile, deterred further Nazi challenges to the European order, stopped World War II? Maybe; maybe not. Simply assuming that this alternative best-case outcome would follow the alternative policy choice does not make it so. Without carefully constructing plausible alternative futures, we have no way to judge which outcome was more or less likely. Would confrontation have deterred all possible forms of future aggression? Would it have forced Hitler to change his tactics and the sequence of events that followed, without actually preventing future aggression? Or would war simply have erupted in 1938 rather than 1939? And would this have been better or worse than the actual sequence of events?

Despite all the "what-if" attention devoted to the Rhineland crisis over the years, there's a shocking lack of actual assessment of how and why a brighter future would likely have emerged following a French attack. The claim that preventive war would have stopped Hitler is thrown about casually, and with great confidence, as if this outcome is so obvious that it doesn't need to be explained. But the case is too important in our thinking about preventive war to be treated so cavalierly. The first step, in the next section, is to lay out some basic guidelines for counterfactual assessment of the question. We'll then turn to a systematic exploration of the "what-might-have-beens" in the Rhineland. Admittedly, the counterfactual story in this chapter remains grim; it won't offer the happy ending pushed by conventional wisdom on the promise of this moment in history to produce a sunnier future if only different decisions were made. To put it bluntly, there's little reason to believe that a militarily successful preventive attack in 1936 would have solved the security problem presented by Nazi Germany. In fact, there is a strong counterfactual argument suggesting that the dynamics of the preventive war paradox could have further undermined European security, as hard as that is to imagine.

In essence, the argument below supports D. C. Watt, one of the great historians of the Second World War, who rejected as "myth" the notion that the Rhineland crisis was "the last great unexploited opportunity to over-throw or 'stop' Hitler without a second world war."[3] Too much hope has been heaped onto this one event as a moment brimming with possibility for radically altering the disasters that followed. British leaders recognized the false promise of preventive war during the Rhineland crisis, and hindsight does little to challenge their conclusion—that rejecting preventive war was a fundamentally sound decision. This conclusion, of course, does nothing to change the thoroughly tragic character of this entire period of history.

AN ALTERNATIVE PAST

To indulge our frustrations with the choices made by earlier generations, to lament the decisions not made, the lost opportunities of the past, is to venture into the world of alternative histories. The list of "what-if" questions we can pose about the past is as diverse and rich as the human imagination. A quick look through the literally thousands of discussion threads on websites devoted to debates over alternative histories will make it clear how compelling this way of thinking about history is. Some alternative storylines quickly spin off into fantasy, with little concern for the real-world viability of the alternative conditions proposed or the logic driving imagined alternative futures. Fantastic storylines might indeed lead to the ruin of Adolf Hitler or the collapse of his murderous plans, but fantasy won't bring us any closer to useful insight into serious questions about alternative paths to peace and security.

To be useful, counterfactual thinking must be disciplined by some basic guidelines. First, we must clearly describe the *alternative initial conditions* in the counterfactual scenario. What, specifically, is different from the real-world experience? To make the scenario as plausible as possible, we must follow the "minimal rewrite of history rule." That is, we'll change the key variables we want to explore in the storyline, while diverting as little as possible from all other actual conditions. The more changes we introduce at the beginning of the scenario, the less plausible it is as an alternative path that could have been selected. Second, we must specify the *expected consequences* of making these changes. How would things be different? This step demands a strong dose of humility. While we must be precise enough with the expected outcomes that the counterfactual scenario says something meaningful, there is still so much uncertainty as to how an alternative future would actually unfold that highly detailed predictions lose their plausibility. A related caution is that the further into the future our predictions run, the more uncertainty and variation is introduced, and the counterfactual predictions become less plausible.

The final, and perhaps most important, guideline is to carefully *explain the logic* linking the alternative initial conditions and the expected outcomes. Why do we expect specific changes in initial conditions to drive alternative outcomes? It has to be more than wishful thinking. What mechanisms produce this change? What theory or evidence supports the logical link between the new starting point and where the scenario ends up? And throughout this exercise, we must think in terms of *probabilities*, not hard certainties. The question is, "What is more or less likely to happen?" rather than "What will happen?" With these guidelines in mind, the first task is to reimagine some key details about March 1936 in order to open a window into further thinking about preventive war.

This counterfactual story opens with one vital change to real-world events: The French government, frightened by Foreign Minister Flandin's predictions about inevitable war, seizes this window of opportunity to launch a preventive attack to drive the Wehrmacht across the Rhine River. Such an attack could include a Belgian force protecting the French army's left flank as it swept north and eastward. And on the battlefield, they achieve victory. It's a limited war, but French officials expect it to pay big strategic dividends by turning back the growing German threat. For anyone who has expressed regret in hindsight that the French let the Rhineland crisis pass without a bold counterstrike, this is the essential starting point for the promise of preventive war. There were multiple operational objectives France could have pursued in a preventive attack, of course. They might have conducted a modest incursion, driving out the border garrisons in the German towns of Saarbrucken, Trier, and Kehl; they might have seized a thin strip along the northern French border, as the French army proposed. Such a limited operation, however, seems to lack sufficient punch to have had the desired political effects on the Nazi regime. To give this counterfactual preventive war a decent chance of stopping Hitler, we need to give it a more-robust battlefield outcome. As postwar research has shown, German battalions on the frontier had standing orders to hold their positions against a French assault, but in full expectation of being overwhelmed, to conduct a fighting retreat while delaying the French advance as long as possible. The German army was then expected to maintain a strong defensive line behind the Rhine River. Hitler himself said in 1938 that his forces would have been pushed back at least sixty kilometers into the Rhine zone, and he hoped to hold the line there.[4] For the sake of analysis, let's assume that Hitler was a bit too optimistic—that German forces fought hard, but French momentum pushed the Wehrmacht across the Rhine. The French then stopped at the river's western bank, mission accomplished.

The viability of this military victory is a debated question. There have been skeptics, beginning with the French war minister and the army chief of staff, who worried in March 1936 that they had neither the numbers nor the force structure necessary to challenge Germany in a clash that escalated to general war. Several scholars looking back at this military question support their pessimistic assessment.[5] This view, however, seems to be a minority opinion. If we limit the conflict to a fight over the Rhineland alone, which doesn't escalate to general war or include a drive to seize the Ruhr Valley, then many contemporary political figures and postwar scholars think this military objective was possible.[6] We don't need to adjudicate this debate on the military capabilities question, but we must assume that France could have pulled it off. Without this basic change in initial conditions, the rest of the thought experiment on the political consequences of preventive war has no purpose.

Keeping to the "minimal rewrite rule," we'll assume that few other important conditions change. Given strong British pessimism over the strategic value and the legitimacy of a preventive fight over the Rhineland, as well as their belief that Italy would attack Egypt and Japan could attack Britain's colony in Singapore in the event of war in Europe,[7] we'll assume the British government adopts the same position it did during the Ruhr War: benevolent neutrality. We must also assume this wouldn't be a replay of 1945: There is no Allied march on Berlin. France and Belgium weren't strong enough to pull off such an audacious offensive. And the only solid ally French leaders thought they could count on if the crisis escalated to war was Czechoslovakia, which saw itself as an early stepping-stone in the Third Reich's future expansion. With good reason, the British military estimated that the Czechs posed little offensive threat to Germany, and at best, could put up a defensive fight against the Wehrmacht for no more than a week.[8]

What about Soviet support with a military offensive from the east? The colossal weight of the Soviet army was decisive when the Allies finally pulverized the Nazi war machine in 1945. But in 1936, even a modest Soviet offensive is beyond plausibility. France did enjoy its strongest political support in the League of Nations from Soviet foreign minister Maxim Litvinov, who declared that the USSR would support "all measures" passed by the League Council to punish Germany for Rhineland remilitarization. This was in no way an expression of support for preventive war, however; Litvinov knew the League would never authorize armed attack unless Germany was actually on the offensive against a neighboring state. Even if Litvinov had argued for Soviet participation in a preventive attack, the assumption that Soviet leader Joseph Stalin would mobilize an offensive against Germany in 1936 is not a viable rewrite of history. Stalin was deeply suspicious of collective security, as was Vyacheslav Molotov, Litvinov's more-influential rival among senior government officials, and Stalin's top priorities were at home. In practical terms, the USSR had no direct access to German borders. Preventive war would depend on Poland granting access rights for Soviet troops to rumble through and fly over its territory, while living with the fear that Soviet forces would never leave once the war was over. And the Polish foreign minister Józef Beck assured the German ambassador that its alliance with France would only be activated if France were the victim of actual aggression. This is the same position taken by Romania and Yugoslavia.[9] Even if Soviet leaders were motivated enough to seek, and then successfully negotiate, transit permission, its military was judged at the time to be seriously deficient in offensive power projection.[10] On the day Hitler announced his Rhineland fait accompli, Soviet marshal

Mikhail Tukhachevsky informed American ambassador William Bullitt that the USSR could offer no military assistance to Czechoslovakia in the event of war.[11]

The crushing Soviet drive on Berlin during World War II was fired by Nazi Germany's opening assault on the USSR in 1941, which brought the horrors of the Siege of Leningrad, the attempt to capture Moscow, and the pounding of Stalingrad. For the Soviets, it was a fight for national survival. The year 1936 was nothing like 1941. The same holds true for the United States, the other behemoth that would be roused into action in 1941 only by Japan's surprise attack and Hitler's declaration of war on America four days later. In 1923 the United States had quickly severed its remaining military ties with its Great War allies and the postwar Rhineland occupation, precisely because of the French invasion of the Ruhr valley. In 1936, American leaders most likely would have stood back and watched in dismay as France pushed into the Rhineland, giving thanks once again for the blessings of the Atlantic Ocean and the wisdom of isolation and neutrality that kept them detached from the continuing turbulence of European affairs.

Given these complications, the most reasonable counterfactual scenario is that successful "liberation" of the Rhineland would remain a Franco-Belgian operation. Once we accept the plausibility of these initial conditions for the alternative storyline, we need to turn to an even more important question: "And then what?"

STRATEGIC VICTORY IN THE RHINELAND?

Success in war, as Clausewitz said, cannot be defined by battlefield victories. What really matters are the political goals war is meant to achieve, and the broader political effects armed conflict spits out. So here is the question before us: If France and Belgium were able to push the German army back across the Rhine River in a counterfactual replay of history, what are the likely political consequences? When postwar observers look back to 1936, they tend to think about the promise of preventive war on a grand strategic scale. Few settle for merely restoring the Rhineland DMZ, that deep buffer zone between the Wehrmacht and the French and Belgian borders, as the ultimate strategic objective. The prize that truly fires the imagination is as grand as they come. Preventive war over the Rhineland, it is said, held the promise of "stopping" Hitler and the horrors of World War II. While still a bit vague when stated this way, this prediction packs a massive counterfactual punch that demands scrutiny.

How might this specific military objective produce such a tremendous strategic outcome? Two explanations dominate the postwar musing. Perhaps the most common, and certainly the most exciting prediction, is that the German military would have overthrown Adolf Hitler for taking this reckless step, replacing the Nazi regime with a cautious conservative government that would have avoided the risks of a great-power war. The second prediction is that even if Hitler had survived the domestic crisis created by a French invasion, the searing experience of this preventive military blow would have rattled Hitler's confidence and tempered his risk-prone personality, while the German military, responding to the deterrent effect of this attack, would have constrained Hitler from taking further risks to advance his expansionist vision on other battlefields. In either case, Hitler's aggressive campaigns are spoiled before he is ready to redraw the European map through mass bloodshed.

These general counterfactual predictions have set the terms for the postwar lament over the Rhineland crisis. It's distressing to discover, however, that despite the widespread repetition of this conclusion, detailed assessments of this claim are nonexistent. Filling the gaps in this counterfactual story is the task ahead. To be sure, had France launched a preventive attack in 1936, the course of events in Europe would certainly have taken a different path. But this doesn't mean that the future would have been *better*. It's just as likely that an even worse outcome would have followed the successful military operations in the Rhineland.

The Downfall of the Nazi Regime?

On Monday, March 9, as German soldiers were still settling in to their makeshift Rhineland garrisons, the French foreign minister made an audacious prediction. If the Locarno powers presented a solid front, if they convinced the German government that this Rhineland venture was a "hopeless escapade" that would lead to economic sanctions, to military mobilization, and war, and if Hitler refused to withdraw the Wehrmacht, the German general staff would step in to reverse Hitler's dangerous decision and the Nazi regime would collapse under the weight of this blow. The German army, the foreign office, and the business community, Flandin told the Belgian ambassador, would cheer the downfall of the thugs and the zealots propping up the Third Reich.[12] It never happened, of course, but this bold counterfactual scenario lives on, with a seductive appeal that many find irresistible.

Winston Churchill popularized the idea through his memoirs. In Churchill's view, this single crisis held the key to the very survival of the

Nazi regime. Once the French government began mobilization of its massive army and its air force, Churchill claimed, "there is *no doubt* that Hitler would have been compelled by his own General Staff to withdraw, and a check would have been given to his pretensions which might well have proved fatal to his rule."[13] William Shirer shared this view. A mere police action in the Rhineland, he said years later, would "bring the Nazi dictatorship" and Hitler's "regime tumbling down."[14] Two main points seem to keep this alternative storyline alive. First, as we saw in chapter 2, there was in fact dissent among senior army leaders over the Führer's decision to remilitarize the Rhineland at that time, led by Gen. Werner von Blomberg, the war minister. Second, there was precedent in recent German history of chancellors being tossed out of office through army intervention in moments of political turmoil. During the Great War General Hindenburg used his emergency authority to dismiss two civilian chancellors, and Gen. Kurt von Schleicher, who saw himself as the ironfisted ruler Germany desperately needed to overturn the dysfunctional Weimar Republic, engineered the ouster of Chancellor Heinrich Brüning in May 1932 and Chancellor Franz von Papen the following December, to assume the chancellorship himself.[15]

The Sudeten crisis of 1938, which sparked a coup plot against Hitler, also seems to provide a compelling analogy. As the Führer was threatening to invade Czechoslovakia and tear away its western rim for the German Reich, a small group of officers from German intelligence and the army devised a plan to storm the Reich Chancellery and kill Hitler once the orders for war were issued, but before the Wehrmacht went into battle. While the British government heard of this scheme, Prime Minister Neville Chamberlain refused to put the question of war or peace in the hands of German conspirators, so he moved ahead with the negotiations that ceded the Sudetenland without a fight. As the postwar assessment of this episode goes, by failing to stand firm and push Hitler into a corner in 1938, Chamberlain fouled the opening the conspirators needed to put their assassination plot into motion.[16] If the Locarno powers had stood firm against the Third Reich during the Rhineland crisis, some might argue, Hitler would have faced a similar backlash that might have been fatal to his regime in 1936.

What a stunning strategic outcome, the ultimate prize in great-power jockeying, achieved at virtually no cost. In this counterfactual scenario, preventive attack serves up a silver-bullet solution, not just for the pain suffered on all sides during World War II, but a solution to the broader brutalities of the Third Reich and the horrors of the Holocaust as well. Few events in history seem to present such an opportunity to radically alter the storyline by simply removing one individual from the narrative. Adolf Hitler, most agree, is what can be called a "chance cause" of huge events.[17] It was his singular political genius, his uncontainable appetite for violent revolution at home and domination of Europe and beyond, and his ferocious personal willpower, which spawned the outrages of this period in time. You remove Hitler, and the process leading to war quickly grinds to a halt. Given the magnitude of the future costs wiped away with this small sum paid in advance, the appeal of the "Hitler deposed" counterfactual is undeniable. Unfortunately, the postwar commentaries that make this enticing prediction provide no insight at all into how it might have actually happened. The claim is treated as a matter of faith, with vague hand waves at the fear and doubts that rippled within the German military during the Rhineland crisis as reason enough to believe that the Nazi regime could have been snuffed out. On close inspection, the idea that the German military would have taken such drastic action in 1936, while the Fatherland was under attack by foreign powers, defies both evidence and reason.

Previous military interventions in domestic politics occurred under profoundly different circumstances. Kaiser Wilhelm II granted General Hindenburg the emergency powers he used to dismiss two German chancellors during the Great War without incident. General Schleicher was able to engineer the peaceful ouster of chancellors Brüning and Papen in the final months of the disintegrating Weimar Republic, while manipulating the grand old war hero, now President Hindenburg, to serve as the official vehicle to force political change. But in 1936, the Führer enjoyed a degree of consolidated power that no twentieth-century German chancellor ever had. And the 1938 analogy can be written off immediately. There was no active coup plotting during the Rhineland crisis, as there would be two years later over Hitler's threat of war with Czechoslovakia.[18] There is good reason for this. Going into the Rhineland venture, Adolf Hitler held unchallenged authority within the Third Reich; the military was enjoying a burst of new life under Hitler's leadership, while the Führer and his propagandists whipped up an explosion of patriotic support for the Rhineland cause with an appeal to stirring themes—freedom, equality, justice, and peace for the German people. Together, these elements insulated Hitler from the kind of internal opposition that might take a dangerous turn, while rallying public support for the risks he was running in the Rhineland, which would help the regime weather whatever international blowback his fait accompli might stoke.

While personal attitudes toward Adolf Hitler and the Nazi movement varied widely within the officer corps, in general terms his relationship with the Wehrmacht in 1936 was on solid ground. This is no surprise. Over the previous three years, Hitler had delivered exactly what the military wanted: He shredded the Versailles Treaty, he invested in rearmament at a furious pace, he showered the Wehrmacht with respect and prestige, and he generated a spike in national pride and a flood of young Germans eager to fill the ranks of the expanding army. As Telford Taylor describes the relationship, the summer of 1934 to the spring of 1937 was a "time almost of honeymoon with Hitler," when "all open and most latent opposition to Hitler . . . was withered at the roots."[19] From much of the testimony during the Nuremberg war crimes trials, when German officers were trying to save their necks from the hangman's noose, it might appear that there was substantial opposition before the war. But General Blomberg, who served as Hitler's defense minister and war minister from 1933 to 1938, provided an honest assessment of this question after the war.

> Until Hitler entered upon the period of aggressive politics, whether one dates it from 1938 or 1939, the German people had no decisive reason for hostility to Hitler, we soldiers least of all. He had not only given us back a position of respect . . . and had freed all Germans from . . . the shame of the Treaty of Versailles, but by the rearmament of Germany, which only Hitler could achieve, he had given the soldiers a larger sphere of influence, promotion and increased respect.

"No general raised any objection then, or offered any resistance," Blomberg reported. "Whoever speaks now of his opposition to Hitler in the years up to 1938–1939 has been betrayed by his memory."[20] All senior leaders supported Rhineland remilitarization, Britain's military attaché reported from Berlin on April 9, after holding quiet conversations with general staff officers. The only question in dispute was its timing, given "the unprepared state of" Germany's "fighting forces." Despite this fear, German officers recognized that France would never agree to restore Germany's full sovereign control in the Rhineland through negotiations, no matter how much British leaders insisted that this was an option. General Staff officers reported "it is obvious that Germany, sooner or later, would make another attempt to obtain equality on the Rhineland and that inevitably France would continue to be distrustful and suspicious." Germany had no choice, officers believed, but to resort to the fait accompli option at some point.[21]

In the summer of 1934, Hitler executed two bold strokes that tightened his relationship with the military and delivered a brutal warning about the consequences of challenging his authority. The first was the sudden butchery of political rivals on June 30, the Night of the Long Knives. The primary target of the purge was the leadership of Hitler's own Brown Shirts, the SA, a paramilitary force of street brawlers and Nazi Party security personnel. Ernst Röhm, who had led the SA since 1931, was getting restless, looking for more independence and power within the Third Reich, and scheming to have the German military absorbed into the SA and placed under his command. Hitler broke Röhm's challenge with a set of concurrent lightning strikes across the Reich. Röhm has been called "perhaps Hitler's closest approximation to an 'intimate friend.'" He was executed on July 1 on Hitler's personal orders.[22] Hitler struck other rivals that night; at least eighty-five, perhaps up to two hundred, were slain during the operation. Among the victims was Gustav von Kahr, the Bavarian nationalist leader who helped to foil Hitler's Munich Beer Hall Putsch in 1923. Kahr was hauled out of his apartment that night, tortured, then shot at the Dachau prison camp. Gregor Strasser, the leader of a Nazi faction that tried to split the Party and undermine Hitler's control in late 1932, bled to death after being shot in a prison cell. And Gen. Kurt von Schleicher, Hitler's immediate predecessor in the chancellor's office—the man who had engineered the fall of chancellors Brüning and Papen in 1932, and who continued to meddle over Hitler's cabinet appointments in 1934—was charged with conspiracy and treason. He was shot in the face that night by Nazi assassins as he stood in the doorway to his home.[23] As the historian Gordon Craig has said, "Hitler's political genius" was at its best "in moments of crisis." General Schleicher had been "hopelessly outclassed by the Führer and his paladins" in the leadership turmoil of 1932, and in 1934 the Führer eliminated this particular threat for good.[24] While the foreign press ran stories predicting Hitler's imminent demise during the Long Knives purge, not a word of protest was heard from the officer corps.[25] In fact, the next day General Blomberg praised Hitler's action in his Order of the Day for its "soldierly decision and exemplary courage" against these "mutineers and traitors."[26]

Within weeks, Hitler struck again. President Hindenburg was dying, which raised profound questions for German politics. What did the passing of the hero of Tannenberg and the Great War mean for the army's loyalty to the regime? Hitler solved this problem with another audacious coup that was accepted without hesitation. After Hindenburg's death on August 2, Hitler consolidated the offices of the presidency and the chancellor into one Führer for the Reich, and from August 20 on, military personnel would swear a personal loyalty oath to Adolf Hitler, rather than to the German state. Up and down the ranks, each pledged "unconditional obedience to Adolf Hitler, the Führer of the German Reich and people, Supreme Commander of the Armed Forces," and to stand "ready as a brave soldier to risk my life at any time for this oath." Its effect was potent, "a seemingly insurmountable obstacle to any decisive opposition to Hitler within the officers' corps."[27]

There were no kingmakers in the military after the Night of the Long Knives and the loyalty oath. General Blomberg became a sycophantic Nazi enthusiast.[28] General Werner von Fritsch, commander in chief of the army in 1936, had no warm devotion to Adolf Hitler. But Fritsch knew that he had originally been on the Long Knives hit list,[29] which may account for how totally he shunned politics and accepted that "Hitler was 'Germany's destiny for good or evil.'"[30] During the Rhineland crisis, he opposed Blomberg's panicky recommendation to withdraw the Wehrmacht battalions on the frontier.[31] Gen. Ludwig Beck, chief of the General Staff of the Army, earned eternal fame as a leading anti-Hitler conspirator during the Sudeten crisis in 1938, and he was executed in 1944 for his part in a botched assassination attempt against the Führer in July of that year.

But in 1935 and 1936, circumstances were very different. In October 1935, at the opening ceremony for the War Academy, which had been closed since 1920, General Beck tore into the Versailles Treaty, which was responsible for the "death of our old magnificent Army," a treaty dictated, he said, by enemies "filled with hatred." He exhorted the young officers to remain faithful to "the duty which they owe to the man who re-created and made strong again the German Wehrmacht and who finally struck off the fetters of Versailles." He was a robust champion of demolishing the hated DMZ and rebuilding German power in the Rhineland. Any dissent he might have expressed during this period was never about the goals, just the timing of the risks Germany would take on as it rebuilt.[32] Reich Marshal Hermann Göring, commander in chief of the air force, was part of Hitler's inner circle.

Hitler's ability to manipulate this strong relationship with the Wehrmacht was reflected in a brilliant political move the day after its soldiers marched across the Rhine River. The timing of remilitarization created a golden propaganda opportunity for the Führer to shine a bright spotlight on the military, and to let the military shine that spotlight right back onto him. March 8 was Heroes' Remembrance Day, a holiday reserved specifically for glorifying those who fought and died for the Fatherland. For the Nazi regime, it was a chance to stage a demonstration of support that left no doubt in the public mind where the military stood. As a reporter for the Associated Press described it, General Blomberg "delivered a knock-out blow to any speculation in foreign quarters that the army someday might [endorse] a change in government."[33]

The setting for the ceremony was the State Opera House on Unter den Linden, Berlin's central thoroughfare. General Blomberg took the podium, as Hitler and the full lineup of senior military leaders looked on from the imperial box above. Thirty-nine soldiers lined up behind the war minister holding battle flags from the Great War; a giant iron cross hung above them on the back wall. In a speech broadcast by radio throughout the Reich, which was enhanced by the recorded sounds of marching boots and bugle calls, General Blomberg praised the justice compelling Germany's assertion of its rights that weekend, along with the Reich's commitment to peace. His most important goal was to hail the Führer and the Nazi Party as liberators, as Germany's greatest hope for the future, while he proclaimed the military's loyalty to the Party's cause. "Today and forever," General Blomberg said,

> the defense force is cognizant of the fact that it owes its freedom and greatness to the struggle and victory of the National Socialist idea . . . To the creator of the Third Reich, who is our supreme commander, the defense force renders thanks from an overflowing heart . . . Today and for all time the defense force feels itself indissolubly bound up with the National Socialist Party and all of its formations. The party and the army are two pillars that carry the new state and that cooperate most intimately in forming the new Germany.

And according to Blomberg, what the Party, the armed forces, and their Führer wanted, through the disruption and the change, was to show that "a strong Germany is a secure support for peace, freedom, and honor."[34]

The "Herald of Peace" Makes His Case

The day before, Adolf Hitler had stood in the Kroll Opera House and shaken his fist at the world, and with a pugnacious, chest-thumping speech, he had torn apart Versailles' final tether on German power. For an hour, Hitler had railed against the injustices of Versailles, the Franco-Soviet defense pact, and the evils of bolshevism. And then he made his surprise announcement. Jackboots were marching into the forbidden zone. It was a defiant move, a military operation, with serious military implications, and bound to provoke. But from the start, Hitler knew that strategic success depended on the *politics* that framed the changes he put in motion and justified the risks he asked the Wehrmacht and the German people to confront. By the end of his speech, Hitler had become an apostle of peace. The French and the British would decry the illegitimacy of the German move, the tearing up of treaties, the display of force that was rattling Europe. But Hitler was determined to win the political battle over the legitimacy question, at least with his own people and the key power centers in German society.

This was about justice and freedom for the German people, Hitler insisted; it was to restore equality for Germany among the nations of the world. Throughout, Hitler played the role of the proud nationalist, confidently, yet merely defending Germany's rights, he nurtured the image of a responsible statesman simply correcting past injustices while serving the larger cause of European peace.[35] And then he laid out a peace offer: a joint demilitarized zone along the entire French-Belgian-German border; a twenty-five-year nonaggression pact with France and Belgium (open to the Netherlands), guaranteed by Great Britain and Italy; a treaty limiting bomber aircraft "to forestall the danger of sudden air attack"; nonaggression pacts with Germany's eastern neighbors; and an offer to rejoin the League of Nations.[36]

Hitler played a surprisingly limited role in the military dimensions of the Rhineland operation once he gave the order to execute.[37] The opposite was true on the political side. Jubilant crowds greeted their returning soldiers with spontaneous outbursts of pride in garrison towns across the Rhineland. But Hitler wouldn't rely on spontaneous enthusiasm alone to anchor public support. Soon after the Führer's message of his "purely defensive" intent was sent traveling across the airwaves and placed in the hands of foreign governments, the Reich's interior minister, Wilhelm Frick, launched the next phase of the operation. The German people would weigh in on this great question through a nationwide referendum: On March 29, he announced, they would cast ballots on the Führer's Rhineland decision. The regime had three weeks until the vote—three weeks to whip the German people into a patriotic frenzy. So on Tuesday night, March 10, Hitler's propaganda minister, Joseph Goebbels, kicked off a barnstorming political campaign with a giant rally at Deutschland Hall, built to host the 1936 Berlin Summer Olympics. And from the very first day, the people responded exactly as Goebbels intended. Thousands of Nazi Party canvassers went door to door across the city that night, instructing residents to listen in by radio to the rally broadcast, while tens of thousands of office and factory workers, under orders from employers, joined marches to two hundred additional meeting halls to listen to the speech. Every single day, until the morning of the vote, hundreds of Party supporters, from high-ranking officials like Goebbels and Hermann Göring, to neighborhood Nazi block captains, rallied the public in large and small meetings across the Reich, repeating the same message: justice, equality, freedom, and peace.[38]

The star of the campaign, of course, was Adolf Hitler. Five days after German troops moved into the Rhineland, Hitler began his propaganda tour in the Rhine River city of Karlsruhe, less than six miles from the

French border, where forty thousand "wildly" cheering citizens listened to his carefully balanced pitch. The Locarno pact, he said, "was concluded at a bad time. It demanded from us a very heavy sacrifice" that no nation should tolerate, leaving over fourteen million Germans "unprotected on the open border of the Reich . . . Nothing in the world can make us renounce" the sovereignty we have reclaimed here. "Not because we desire unrest," Hitler asserted. "I do not want to deprive others of their rights. I want to find a synthesis between the rights of both peoples . . . Germany has neither the intention nor the will to attack France, neither the intention nor the will to attack Czechoslovakia nor to attack Poland . . . Germany has but one desire," he said: "to be happy according to their own liking."[39] One hundred thousand Bavarians flooded into Munich on March 14 for the Führer's next rally; forty-five thousand came on special Strength through Joy tourist trains, while others enjoyed reduced fares on regional rail lines to join the festivities. Only six thousand could pack into the exhibition hall to see the Führer in person, so three hundred thousand filled Theresa's meadow (Theresienwiese) like it was Oktoberfest to listen to his speech on loudspeakers. They cheered "frantically" when they heard him condemn the "principle of violence" at the heart of Versailles, when he swore that other nations would not "treat us as slaves," and asked for the "thunder of your approval."[40]

March 16 was Army Day, a new holiday commemorating the anniversary of the March 1935 conscription announcement, and in every garrison across Germany soldiers were parading with the Third Reich's War Flag, designed by Hitler himself just a few months before, with its swastika and iron cross melding Party with army. Hitler was in Frankfurt that day for his third campaign speech in the Rhineland, the city "virtually blanketed in swastika flags." Several hundred thousand "frantically acclaimed" the Führer as he traveled from the train station to Festhalle, where twenty thousand awaited his arrival. Sitting dutifully behind Hitler on the stage were General Blomberg and the commanders in chief of each of the Wehrmacht's armed services. Loudspeakers in the streets and in Nazi Party meetings around Frankfurt carried his desire "to bury the hatchet" with France. Radios in every café and restaurant, where the waiters had been ordered to serve their patrons in silence, heard the Führer declare that "no might in the world" could overcome Germany's demand for justice and sovereignty, particularly when the people are "united like one man," a people who are "masters in their own house."[41]

On March 18, the self-proclaimed "herald of peace in Europe" was in Königsberg, in far East Prussia, where one eyewitness said his "audience

cheered rhythmically and vociferously like well-trained football rooters."
On March 22 Hitler was in Breslau, where the "frenzied" crowd heard him
declare that Germany was opening a new era in which the reigning themes
will be "reason, logic, understanding and mutual respect," and he asked
other nations "if their people want hatred to be sown or if they do not wish
for this mad war of all against all to come to an end."[42] On March 24 his
motorcade rolled past a million and a half Germans in Berlin as he traveled
to Deutschland Hall for another giant rally. The five-mile route was lined
by one hundred loudspeakers for the crowds that were ordered to remain
in place until Hitler's motorcade roared through again after the speech later
that night.[43]

On Friday, March 27, two days before the referendum vote, Hitler's
propagandists pulled off a master feat. The Führer was in the Ruhr Valley,
in the industrial city of Essen, standing in front of a locomotive chassis at
the Krupp Works for his next speech. At exactly 3:45 that afternoon, Joseph
Goebbels's voice rang out over loudspeakers across Germany: "Hoist flags,"
he shouted, and swastika flags snapped up flagpoles all over the Reich. At
four o'clock, the Krupp factory siren wailed for one minute, joined by the
sirens, horns, and whistles of factories, trains, and ships nationwide. The
sirens and horns stopped, there was a minute of silence, all vehicle traffic
came to a standstill, and an estimated twenty million listened in by loud-
speaker or radio to the Führer's message. "Our generation surrendered
Germany; our generation must make good its crime," he told them. "I have
done nothing to other people. I have not placed my foot on foreign soil. I
have taken nothing from other people . . . and I will not tolerate anybody
who makes himself judge of a matter that concerns only me and my German people."[44] In the largest campaign rally of all, in Cologne the day before the vote, the crowd was reported as five hundred thousand strong and
"delirious" as Hitler spoke in the central square, swastika flags flying from
the cathedral gallery high overhead, while over two million were reported
in the streets to support Rhineland enthusiasm, wearing "The Rhineland is
Free" buttons with pride.[45]

According to the official electoral count, 98.79 percent of voters approved of Hitler's Rhineland venture on March 29. Of course, this is the
kind of vote tally that earns a skeptical eye-roll in similar cases in which
corrupt regimes send their subjects to the polls. The only option on the
ballot was "yes." Nazi thugs were active throughout the campaign and on
the day of the vote to enforce participation, and the foreign press reported
voting irregularities.[46] But foreign reporters also unanimously agreed that
public enthusiasm for Rhineland control was genuine. Anne O'Hare Mc-

Cormick was amazed by what she called "Hitler evangelism." "Nobody who did not witness in recent weeks his power to stir people . . . can imagine the intense patriotism he arouses," she wrote soon after the referendum. "His audience is firmly convinced that the Führer is a prophet of peace and that the Hitler peace plan is the way to a new equilibrium in Europe . . . The new mood of Germany reflects with extraordinary fidelity the mood of Hitler. The land echoes like a sounding board the phrases he has been pouring into the oddly absorbent air in the last three weeks."[47] American ambassador William Dodd reported that 90 percent of the German public honestly believed in the justice of Hitler's Rhineland initiative, while the British consul in Frankfurt reported "that he had not yet met a German who believed that the remilitarization could have been achieved through" any other means, such as negotiations.[48]

Hitler as the "herald of peace" was bald propaganda, of course. His words ring today as tragic farce. But in March 1936, within Germany at least, he was clearly convincing. The Nazi regime electrified the political atmosphere with its message of justice, freedom, and equality. The crowds thrilled to the Führer's nationalist cry for German rights, and they were soothed by his statesmanlike appeal for peace across Europe, his careful emphasis on the limits to his objectives, his assurances that he had no aggressive plans to take the fight to Germany's neighbors. Hitler fawned over the Wehrmacht and its leaders and they pledged fealty, trotting alongside the Führer at every step in this stage-managed display of national dignity.

If we throw a counterfactual French preventive attack into the storyline, Hitler might not have had three full weeks to shape the domestic politics of Rhineland remilitarization. Considering the decision-making in Paris, it's still reasonable to assume that Hitler had a political window that would have stayed open until sometime between March 16 and 20, at the earliest, before French forces had rolled across the border. Gen. Maurice Gamelin, the chief of staff of the French Army, insisted that he needed time to mobilize the full *couverture* force of 1.2 million men before launching any offensive operations. This would take at least eight days, he said.[49] If the decision were made during that Sunday-morning cabinet meeting and if the orders were issued the following day, the covering force would be in place on March 16.

Given the French government's sensitivity to international political support, we might also assume the cabinet would have sought League of Nations censure of Germany before launching a preventive attack. The League Council took this vote of censure on March 19, so we can assume the French might have rolled on March 20. So what could the regime's political campaign have accomplished during this window? This would have given Hitler time to stage the Heroes' Remembrance Day events, to rally the crowds in Karlsruhe, in Munich, in Frankfurt, and perhaps in Königsberg. If France had invaded on March 16, they would have hit the Wehrmacht on its Army Day.

Even if the political campaign ended here, under pressure of foreign invasion, it's fair to say that few Germans would have missed the excitement whipped up by the Führer's previous rallies, those broadcasts exhorting his countrymen to stand tall in defense of their rights and freedom. And every day the invasion was delayed, the regime would have had one more day to push this message, one more day to tighten its bonds with the army. It's nearly impossible to imagine a military coup against Hitler in the midst of this political milieu. As we've seen, there were no coup plotters quietly planning to take down the Führer if the French rolled in. And in the face of actual attack, the intense national spirit that quickly rallied German society behind the regime would have further insulated the Führer from violent internal opposition. Reporting from Berlin in the fall of 1935, British ambassador Eric Phipps offered this prognosis: "If war were to break out to-day, I have little doubt that the order to march would be received with infinite joy" among the Germans, just like in 1914.[50] With French and Belgian soldiers advancing into the Rhineland, with German units falling back in retreat, what would the Wehrmacht most likely have done in response? Overthrow the Führer in the middle of an international crisis, knowing this move would unleash an inevitable wave of domestic violence by the regime's fanatical supporters and defy strong public opinion? Or turn its energies toward a defense of the Fatherland during a time of national emergency? Under the military and political conditions of 1936, it's hard to conceive of any other response than a rally around the Third Reich's flag against the foreign invaders.

Hitler Deterred?

Let's assume the silver-bullet solution would have failed to dislodge Hitler from power after a French invasion. Then what? This is clearly a moment ripe with strategic implications, but what might the new future have held? A number of observers have proposed an alternative to the military coup as a strategic mechanism for "stopping Hitler." Preventive attack in the Rhineland, they say, would have been a potent demonstration of Allied power and the political will to safeguard the status quo with military force. In turn, this demonstration might have *deterred* Hitler from pursuing the expansionist ambitions that fueled his march to war in later years.

The logic of deterrence depends on two essential claims. First, that a potential aggressor faces a credible threat of military retaliation as a response to its aggressive acts. Second, if the aggressor calculates that the gains it hopes to achieve are not worth the pain suffered in the aftermath, then it will likely choose wisely and tame its aggressive inclinations. In the language of deterrence theory, a preventive attack into the Rhineland might be called a "costly signal" of French resolve to contain German expansion.[51] Words are cheap. When faced with real danger, mere verbal threats of retaliation for aggressive acts, issued during calmer moments, can collapse. But action in the face of a challenge, assuming risk during a crisis, can reinforce the credibility of a deterrent threat going into the future. Bold French action in 1936, it is said, would have done what Allied rearmament, alliance formation, and the threat of war in 1939 failed to do: convince Hitler that there was a high price to pay for his aggression, forcing him into reluctant acceptance of the status quo.

This is a terribly weak case for general deterrence. Much of the research on the likelihood of deterrence among rival states looks for insight from two different levels in this relationship. There is the power structure of the international system—that is, how power is distributed among the major players—and there is the level of individual motives, leadership calculations, and internal decision-making. After looking at both of these levels, there is little reason for confidence that a French preventive attack would have deterred Nazi Germany into the future. It's much more likely that battlefield success in the Rhineland would have inflicted no more than a temporary setback to Hitler's schemes, followed by a renewed drive to secure the Führer's expansionist goals through war.

As scholars are quick to point out, a balance of power among major states is not sufficient to deter aggression or the escalation of conflict toward war. World War I is the classic example. In 1914 there was general parity in power between the two rival alliances, but this did not keep the Russians from mobilizing for war in defense of their Serbian allies, who were under threat from the Austro-Hungarian empire, nor did it stop the Austro-Hungarians from issuing an ultimatum to the Serbians even though they recognized this move would likely bring conflict with Russia. German leaders recognized there would be a heavy price to pay in the coming clash, but they believed it was a price worth paying to break the looming threat of growing Russian power and continental encirclement between Russia and its French ally. Despite the expected pain, leaders across the Continent were confident that war would work in their favor, so they accepted the risks as the crisis escalated.[52]

During the Cold War, the American and Soviet alliance blocs maintained relative parity in the balance of power for several decades, yet they managed to avoid a Third World War. It was the advent of nuclear weapons, of course, spawned by the Second World War, that made the world-shattering costs of great-power conflict much easier to calculate, and the logic of deterrence much easier to recognize and respect. As President John F. Kennedy intoned during his inaugural address in 1961, it's the "balance of terror that stays the hand of mankind's final war." The bipolar distribution of power during the Cold War, with just two great states dominating the system, also meant that it was simpler for each side to follow its rival's maneuvering, to calculate the likely costs of conflict, and to block the other's potential aggression.[53]

During the 1930s, Adolf Hitler did not face the terrifying simplicity of nuclear weapons in a bipolar system. A French military operation to restore the Rhineland DMZ would have done nothing to slow down the pace of German rearmament. It's reasonable to assume Germany would have continued to outpace its rivals for the next several years, achieving parity, and then perhaps dominance, enhanced by the development of blitzkrieg doctrine that would have boosted Hitler's confidence in taking the offensive. This condition would have been fatal to whatever deterrent effect counterbalancing might have had to check German adventurism. Even if Germany simply maintained parity with France and its partners, the multipolar character of the European system, with its multiple major states tied in loose and shifting defense commitments, would have made it easier for Nazi Germany to pick off its targets. Stable and credible alliances are harder to establish and maintain in a multipolar system, with partners tempted to free-ride on the costs others are willing to pay for security against a common threat.[54] Buck-passing among its adversaries would have lowered the costs Germany would likely have paid for aggression, driving up Hitler's willingness to take the risks of war even after a setback in the Rhineland.

At the individual level, Adolf Hitler is perhaps the worst case imaginable for the logic of deterrence. Three basic factors are at work neutralizing a deterrent effect. The first factor is the intensity of his commitment to territorial expansion for the German Reich. Expansion defined his worldview, which included both material and ideological motives for going down this path: his belief in the racial supremacy of the Aryan people; his fear that unless the German Reich seized territory in the east, it would suffocate from the lack of *lebensraum*, sufficient living space for its growing population; he saw bolshevism in the Soviet Union as an insidious force that could drown the German people; and he shared that long-standing fear of encirclement, which could only be broken through continent-wide wars of conquest.

Second, Hitler was willing to accept high costs to achieve his expansionist vision. His military leaders were naturally risk-averse at key turning points in the 1930s, warning the Führer about his plans for the Rhineland in 1936, Czechoslovakia in 1938, Poland in 1939, and the USSR in 1941. But Hitler demonstrated time after time that when it came to ordering his armed forces into a fight, he had a high tolerance for pain. His perseverance was buoyed by immense confidence in his own judgment and leadership, which he saw as the key to victory despite the inherent risks. Finally, Hitler *wanted war* in a way that no other leader in modern history has. He had a passion for mass violence as the mechanism to secure German greatness; war was not just an instrument to achieve the Reich's strategic goals, it was a moral force that would ennoble and invigorate the German people and the Third Reich. There is nothing about a limited war over the Rhineland that would have changed these fundamental variables driving German aggression under his leadership, yet the claim that Hitler could have been tamed by modest preventive action persists.

Hitler certainly would have had to make tactical changes and adjust to the Rhineland setback; it might have altered the timeline of his decisions. He would remain, nonetheless, among the most risk-acceptant and ravenous revisionists in history. Unfortunately, a French preventive attack in 1936 would have helped him to mask this fact going forward. Consider what a perverted strategic effect preventive war would have had within German society. Instead of serving as a demonstration of French resolve that pointed to the dangers of adventurism and the need for restraint, it would have been seen as another signal of its unrelenting hostility. If a Franco-Belgian force had rolled into the Rhineland after Hitler had already framed remilitarization as an act of justice, freedom, equality, and peace, the move would have had an explosive domestic political effect, firing passionate nationalist outrage over what would have almost universally been seen as French aggression. France would have been feeding Hitler's characterization of Germany as besieged by hostile forces conspiring to keep it weak and suppressed.

Most insidiously, the Nazi regime would have skillfully manipulated this event to build broad support for an urgent defensive war when the nation was ready, to reclaim German rights, to break its enemies on all fronts, and to open up *lebensraum* for the vulnerable German people. This is how British ambassador Eric Phipps saw the future at the time: "[T]he German people would 'rally like one man to the clarion call' of their Führer," he wrote from Berlin; the army and its leaders would "fight to the finish" in this defensive war.[55] During the crisis, Anthony Eden pointed out the paradoxical futility of success on the Rhineland battlefield to his French counterpart. "Even if Hitler were . . . defeated, what would the world have gained? 'Was it thought that Germany could be taught a lesson by such means?' Eden asked."[56] He might have added, What lessons did the Ruhr War teach Germany? The Germans were forced into a temporary surrender in 1923, made essential by weakness, but they certainly didn't learn the enduring lessons France intended. The historian A. J. P. Taylor probably has the best prediction: "[T]he French army could march into Germany; it could exact promises of good behavior . . . and then it would go away. The situation would remain the same as before, or, if anything, worse—the Germans more resentful and restless than ever."[57] And as German power continued to grow, Hitler would have been in an even stronger political position to carry his aggressive plans forward, facing less resistance, and more enthusiastic support, from the Wehrmacht leadership.[58]

On one key point, Winston Churchill is probably right. Perhaps "nothing except war could have stopped Hitler after we had submitted to the seizure of the Rhineland."[59] But it also seems that *after* a preventive attack, the most likely alternative future would have led to the same basic outcome: German aggression driving Europe into a major war. There was probably no escape from the ultimate solution to the unique strategic problem presented by Germany under Adolf Hitler: total war and unconditional surrender, the decimation of the German military machine, and the destruction of the ideological movement that fed its violence. A temporary push in the Rhineland would just not have been enough to deliver the strategic outcome necessary to solve this problem. If there's any solace to be found in the failure to stop Hitler before he launched the Second World War, it has to be found in the war's aftermath—in the progressive turn in world politics, at least in the West, that the aggressive character of this terrible war made possible.

SOLVING THE STRATEGIC PROBLEM

In January 1943, President Franklin Roosevelt was in Casablanca, Morocco, meeting with Prime Minister Churchill to begin the long-range planning for the end of the war. It had been only two months since the Allies had launched their first major assault on Axis forces, in North Africa, and they would remain locked in combat with Nazi Germany for nearly two and half

more years. But Roosevelt and Churchill were already looking ahead to the
strategic end state, the character of the peace that would follow battlefield
victory. Roosevelt wanted much more out of this war than the physical
destruction of the Third Reich's war machine and the Nazi regime. He
wanted to destroy the animating spirit of militarism in Europe. In his own
words, he sought "the destruction of the philosophies in those countries
which are based on conquest and the subjugation of other people." This was
an offshoot of the Atlantic Charter, signed by Roosevelt and Churchill in
August 1941, which called for a postwar order free from the fear of runaway
arms races and wars of aggression.

To achieve this strategic end, Roosevelt made a bold pronouncement
during this summit meeting: The Allies would accept nothing less than
"unconditional surrender." It was a controversial decision. Some worried
that it would toughen German resistance, lengthen the war, increase its
brutality, and raise the costs to both sides. Others argued that rolling back
German forces all the way to Berlin would open much of Eastern Europe
to Soviet domination. But President Roosevelt was determined to salvage
something worthy out of all the suffering of the early twentieth century. He
wanted to break the notion that conquest is a viable path to both national
greatness and security in a potentially threatening world. And to do this, the
Allies needed to prove this point on the battlefield and then open as much
political space as possible to create a new international order when victory
was secured.[60]

While unconditional surrender might open up political space for grand
strategic ends, there was one vital prerequisite for the outcome Roosevelt
wanted: crystal-clear German aggression as the cause of total war in Europe. Unambiguous aggression mobilized an otherwise reluctant America
to fight a total war against Nazi Germany; it sustained the country through
the fight, and helped to justify America's commitment to building a new
political system in Western Europe when the fight was finished. Joseph
Stalin was content to sit on the sidelines while Nazi Germany crushed Poland, subdued France, and battered Great Britain by air. It took a desperate fight for survival against Hitler's ferocious assault on the USSR itself
to bring Stalin around. Germans paid a terrible price in return. But just as
important, it was acceptance of unambiguous guilt within German society
that destroyed the *spirit* of militarism. Looking back to the end of the First
World War, the eminent German historian Ludwig Dehio said that what
kept militarism alive was the Germans' fixation on the injustice of one-sided
war guilt imposed at Versailles. What Germany needed most after World
War I, he argued, was "insight into the much greater threat." It was "war for

supremacy, so pregnant with disaster," that Germans ignored in the years after 1918. But clarity on the war guilt question in the Second World War fixed this problem by forcing Germans into "unconditional recognition of the terrible role that we have played in this period. We were the last and the most demonic power," Dehio wrote, when other powers had given up on European wars of conquest.[61]

The German philosopher Karl Jaspers pointed to the same problem. The Versailles war guilt clause was a political judgment rendered by the victors, he argued, and not a fact that the Germans themselves would acknowledge. "Today," he wrote in 1947, "things are altogether different."

> This time the war-guilt question . . . is very clear. The war was unleashed by Hitler Germany. Germany is guilty of the war through its regime, which started the war at its own chosen moment, when none of the rest wanted it . . . This time there can be no doubt that Germany planned and prepared this war and started it without provocation from any other side . . . The consciousness of national disgrace is inescapable for every German.[62]

Friedrich Meinecke, for decades a proud German nationalist historian who had gleefully cheered on the invasion of Poland in 1939, was rattled by what he called the "German catastrophe." Militarism was to blame; "the desire to become a world power has proven to be a false idol for us." After living through this catastrophe, he wrote in 1950, a catastrophe Germany itself was responsible for, "we stand at the main turning-point in the evolution of the German people." Germany could only be secured through European integration, not through dominance, through a system in which Germany is "a member of a future federation, voluntarily concluded, of the central and western European states."[63] The immediate postwar generation of Germans cast responsibility for the Reich's aggression and its consequences onto the Nazi regime. The most common theme in the public sphere was that all Germans were victims—victims of Nazi terror and victims of the Allied bombing and invasion brought on by Nazi aggression. This narrative might too easily excuse many Germans who were overtly complicit in the crimes of the Nazi era, or at least passively supportive of what the regime was doing. But the fact that clear responsibility for this war was beyond dispute served as a necessary condition leading Germans to accept democratization and integration with their former enemies in the West as the best way forward.[64]

The philosopher Michael Walzer, the most prominent modern voice on the question of the "just war," once wrote about what made World War II different among all wars through history. It was Nazism, Walzer said, "evil objectified in the world, and in a form so *potent* and *apparent* that there could never have been anything to do but to fight it."[65] Today, we treat this observation as self-evident. As a set of ideas, as a worldview with aspirations, Nazism is repugnant. But it was Nazism *in practice*, at home and on the international stage, that made its evils apparent, that demonstrated its potency, and that galvanizes such unquestioning condemnation, then and today. Adolf Hitler's worldview in practice was really put into motion in 1938, when he turned from purely internal measures to restore German strength—rearmament and Rhineland remilitarization—to aggressive expansion outside the Reich, as he picked off his targets one by one: Austria, Czechoslovakia, Poland, Denmark, Norway, the Netherlands, Luxembourg, Belgium, France, Yugoslavia, Greece, and the USSR. It was this train of brutality that lit the fire of total war and brought Nazi Germany crushing defeat. It was this unambiguous evil that compelled German political leaders and their citizens to accept a heavy burden in the years that followed, and that provided an enduring incentive to salvage something of value out of pure tragedy. Which raises another disturbing counterfactual question: If great-power war had spiraled out of a French preventive attack in the Rhineland in 1936, would the same progressive path have opened up for postwar generations? Or, would a French attack have muddied the postwar assessment of how much blame Germany should actually carry? Would France carry a stain for feeding the spirit of militarism? Would France earn praise for a valiant and farsighted effort to snuff out a madman before it was too late, or would it be tarred for launching a reckless and unnecessary drive to maintain French security through dominance, an act seen as inherently dangerous and bound to lead to another large-scale war?

It's impossible to answer this counterfactual question with high confidence. But we must recognize that 1936 is not 1938. As A. J. P. Taylor wrote, 1936 marked the end of the post–Great War period, when the last of the Versailles restrictions on German power were abandoned. The year 1938 is the beginning of the pre–World War II period, when Nazi Germany began to push hard against the territorial status quo, with its sights set on Austria and Czechoslovakia, and with a penchant for coercion to build the Greater German Reich.[66] By contrast, 1936 was a year of uncertainty over what the cascade of events meant for the future. It was a year of nagging ambiguity over how far and how aggressively German leaders would push their revisionist goals, a year hobbled by lingering fears that hard balancing would actually tip the system toward war rather than deter it.

Given this level of persistent ambiguity, a preventive attack by France in the middle of the Rhineland crisis would not be wrapped in that same shroud of moral clarity that made such a critical difference in the war that was actually fought. The historian James Emmerson is certainly right to argue that "only a clear act of aggression or blatant intimidation could cause a significant hardening against the Third Reich."[67] And with Hitler leading a rousing campaign to paint his Rhineland decision as an issue of justice and equality, the contemporary judgment against any violence that exploded out of this event would likely recoil against France. The future would have been different, but not necessarily any better, and potentially worse than the actual tragic storyline is.

THE STRATEGIC PROBLEM ENDURES

In the summer of 1950, the wars of aggression launched by Nazi Germany and Imperial Japan had been over for five years; the threat had been decimated on the battlefield, in the enemies' cities, and in their industrial centers. The deeper strategic problem of militarism and cycles of armed conflict among historic rivals was being resolved through new forms of political, economic, and security integration, a process made possible by the stain of aggression Germany and Japan carried into the postwar order. While this conflict was becoming a relic of history, the more-general problem of shifting power and fear of the future was not. It endured beyond this war, on a grand new scale, between the two giant powers that had been mobilized so thoroughly by the Second World War. On the evening of August 25, 1950, the US Secretary of the Navy stood before a crowd of more than one hundred thousand at the Boston Naval Shipyard. They were there to celebrate the historic site's one hundred and fiftieth anniversary, but Secretary Francis Matthews's speech that night delivered an unexpected punch. The time had come, he said, for a decisive showdown with the Soviet Union to prevent the further erosion of American power.

Matthews didn't need to provide his audience with evidence of this new enemy's growing military strength, nor did he have to convince them of the growing dangers they all faced. In the five years since the war, the Soviets had consolidated control over Eastern Europe, they were squeezing the American position in West Berlin, Communist forces won a decisive victory in the Chinese civil war, and American soldiers were falling back to the southern tip of the Korean peninsula in what seemed to be a losing defensive fight against the Soviets' North Korean ally. The most frightening development, of course, was America's loss of its atomic monopoly in August 1949, when the Soviets exploded their first bomb. Just a few months before

Matthews's speech, the official government assessment of the problem was developed in a top-secret study, National Security Council Memorandum 68, or NSC 68, the most influential analysis of the Soviet threat and American strategy of the early Cold War.

According to NSC 68, the stakes and the risks were literally existential. The Soviet Union was "animated by a new fanatic faith" driving the USSR to "impose its absolute authority over the rest of the world." Along the way, the Soviets would subvert or destroy the "integrity and vitality" of the United States, which meant the "destruction not only of this Republic but of civilization itself." NSC 68 leaves no doubt that the United States had a maximum of four years to deal with the enemy's growing capabilities; 1954 was the critical date, when the Soviet atomic arsenal and its long-range bomber force were expected to be large enough to execute a "decisive initial attack" against "vital centers of the United States, provided it strikes a surprise blow." And while NSC 68 ultimately argues for a deterrence and containment strategy to keep the threat in check, it also delivered a stark warning about the risks of this option.

> When it calculates that it has sufficient atomic capability to make a surprise attack on us, nullifying our atomic superiority and creating a military situation decisively in its favor, the Kremlin might be tempted to strike swiftly and with stealth. The existence of two large atomic capabilities in such a relationship might well act, therefore, not as a deterrent, but as an incitement to war.[68]

With this assessment of the terrifying future in hand, with the nightmare of total war against Nazi Germany still fresh, and in the "shadow of Pearl Harbor,"[69] it should be no surprise that someone like Secretary Matthews would call out for preventive war before it was too late to stop World War III. Matthews came up with a nice catchphrase for this alternative to deterrence; America, he said, should become the world's "first aggressors for peace."[70] "It is a role which, in my opinion, we cannot escape . . . we should first get ready to ward off any possible attack . . . and we should boldly proclaim our undeniable objective to be a world at peace. To have peace we should be willing to pay, and declare our intentions to pay, any price—even the price of instituting a war to compel cooperation for peace."[71]

Days later, the commandant of the US Air War College, Maj. Gen. Orvil Anderson, created a firestorm by repeating this brash proposal during an interview that was picked up by newspapers across the country. While Anderson started his career flying hot-air balloons during World War I, he now worried about the dawn of the nuclear age, and the dangers turned him into a champion of decisive preventive action. "To assume that the

Russians won't use their A-bombs if we sit by and watch them build them is a dangerous assumption. Joe Stalin is a realist. We've got to wake up and be realists, too," General Anderson insisted. The solution, he believed, was obvious. "Give me the orders to do it and I can break up Russia's five A-bomb nests in a week." For General Anderson, this was preventive self-defense that even God would endorse. "And when I went up to Christ," Anderson told reporters, "I think I could explain to him why I wanted to do it—now—before it's too late. I think I could explain to him that I had saved civilization."[72] While this kind of colorful language was rare, Anderson was not alone; as historian Marc Trachtenberg has observed, support for preventive war was not restricted to a "lunatic fringe." A parade of strategic thinkers in the military, in academia, and among pundits joined him in urging preventive war to save America from this horrible future while there was still time.[73]

Winston Churchill, perhaps unsurprisingly, was among this broader community of anti-Soviet preventive war champions. As we've seen, while Churchill did "cry aloud" about the rising Nazi threat, he never openly called for preventive attack during the Rhineland crisis or at any other time before World War II. But in the new era unfolding after 1945, it seems that Churchill was determined not to make that mistake again. In the immediate wake of victory over the Axis powers, Churchill was once again in the opposition after the Labour Party won a huge upset victory at home in the elections of July 1945. As was true in 1936, he was no longer in a position to direct British policy, but Churchill continued to agitate about the postwar problems at hand. What did Prometheus see when he looked to the future? A situation far more dangerous than what the world had just come through. He warned in a 1949 speech in Manhattan that "We are now confronted with something which is quite as wicked but much more formidable than Hitler." Churchill had been predicting that the Soviets would have the atomic bomb by about 1954, and as he said to both the American ambassador and to Anthony Eden in 1948, when that day comes, "nothing can stop the greatest of all world catastrophes," because "war will become a certainty."[74]

The Soviets were far more dangerous than the Nazis, war was a certainty given enough time, and the Western powers had a window of opportunity for action before this terrible moment arrived. What to do? According to Churchill, the answer was clear: leverage America's nuclear monopoly to the hilt, force Joseph Stalin to roll back his growing empire in Eastern Europe under threat of massive attack, and if he refused, "bring things to a head" and hit them hard with an atomic preventive strike to eliminate the problem while they still could.[75] In July 1948, Churchill wrote to Gen. Dwight Eisenhower to push this argument, and he made the same pitch during a Conservative Party conference in October, predicting confidently that Stalin would back down.

In a 1947 meeting with US senator Styles Bridges, who was traveling in Europe that summer, Churchill made an urgent appeal for Bridges to take the case for preventive war to President Truman. According to an FBI memo that captured Bridges's notes from the meeting, Churchill said "that the only salvation for the civilization of the world would be if the President of the United States would declare Russia to be imperiling world peace and attack Russia." An atomic bomb "could be dropped on the Kremlin," Churchill explained, "wiping it out," which would make it "a very easy problem to handle the balance of Russia, which would be without direction." If the United States failed to take decisive action, Churchill told Bridges, "Russia will attack the United States in the next two or three years when she gets the atomic bomb and civilization will be wiped out, or set back many years."[76] In 1953, when Churchill was back in the prime minister's office, he was still encouraging Eisenhower, now president, to consider using America's strategic superiority before the Soviet atomic arsenal was a match for the United States.[77]

Against Churchill's advice and the warning cries in America, both presidents Truman and Eisenhower refused to turn to the preventive war option.[78] As we know, there was no preventive attack on the USSR, just like there was no preventive attack on Nazi Germany. But in stark contrast to the way we remember the 1930s, no one today calls this decision in the early Cold War *a mistake*. There are certainly grounds for such a charge. We might argue that Truman and Eisenhower were moral failures, like British and French leaders before them, because they would not take decisive action to eliminate the existential risks created by this evil regime, a greater threat to Western civilization than the Third Reich ever was. The great political scientist Samuel Huntington made this point in 1957: "[T]he government which did not engage in preventive action" to stop a "serious reduction in relative military strength" while a "clearly hostile" state developed crushing levels of power, Huntington said, "would be morally guilty of gross dereliction of duty to its citizens."[79] And with World War I and World War II available as ready examples of deterrence failure leading to great-power war, with NSC 68 warning about atomic arms provoking rather than deterring conflict, we might say Truman and Eisenhower foolishly placed their hopes in a faulty strategy against what they saw as a "fanatic" regime with plans for violent subjugation of the globe.

So was rejecting preventive war against the USSR a mistake? The question sounds absurd on its face. Following Churchill's advice in the early Cold War would have been both horribly tragic and unnecessary to safeguard the West against Soviet aggression. But we can only confidently say that because of what British war minister Duff Cooper once called the "light of after-events," through hindsight knowledge of the fact that the Cold War ended peacefully after forty-five dangerous years when the Soviet Union collapsed internally. In a counterfactual world in which deterrence failed, or if one of the many superpower crises, like the Cuban Missile Crisis of 1962, had spun out of control and escalated to World War III, then we can be sure that those who survived to pass judgment would condemn Truman and Eisenhower in the most scorching terms. The lament would be familiar: Didn't they realize that preventive war was the only viable strategy for eliminating the threat in its early stages? To a future post-apocalyptic generation, evidence of the inevitability of World War III, evidence available in the early Cold War, would scream out as so tragically obvious. How could they have ignored it? How could they have failed to act on it? Major General Anderson was fired from his War College position and forced into early retirement from the Air Force in 1950 because of his preventive war interview. In this alternative future he would be revered as a martyred prophet unfairly disgraced for crying aloud about the dangers of Joseph Stalin's Communist colossus and its plans for global conquest. But in the real world, hindsight bias makes his advice sound like the kind of reckless paranoia so brilliantly satirized in *Dr. Strangelove*.

These two cases, Nazi Germany in the mid-1930s and the Soviet Union in the early Cold War, stand as valuable counterpoints for contemplating the timeless dilemma—finding security in an often dangerous world—at the heart of this book. Placing them side by side forces us to confront the enduring strategic problems each showcases: shifting power, fear of the future, and the preventive war temptation to eliminate rising threats; the inherent uncertainty of the future, the limited human capacity for predicting with precision, the fractured lenses that distort those predictions with ambiguous evidence, faulty assumptions, fear and biases; the security paradox that can turn battlefield victory into strategic defeat when bold action to eliminate a potential threat sets in motion an even more dangerous cycle of hostility, fear, and violence. In 1950, the future was no clearer than it was in 1936. Leaders in both periods struggled with uncertainties, with ambiguities, with rival assessments of the dangers inherent to both action and inaction. In other words, they struggled with the problem at the heart of the preventive war temptation. Preventive war promises deliverance today from a more-threatening tomorrow, through physical destruction of the rival's growing capabilities. But it's impossible to know what it is we're saving ourselves from by pulling the preventive war trigger.

The ultimate irony of preventive war is that the act itself wipes away knowledge of what the future might have held, thus wiping away our ability to judge whether it was actually necessary to avoid an even worse course of events than what preventive attack itself produces. There are die-hard champions of the 2003 war against Iraq that still defend the wisdom of its preventive logic, even though the invasion revealed that there were no weapons of mass destruction programs or viable stockpiles, along with revealing the pathetic state of the Iraqi military more generally. The decision to topple the Saddam Hussein regime was a smart move, they say, because it forever eliminated the potential for this regime to threaten the United States and its allies with weapons of mass destruction. Technically speaking, this is correct. Saddam Hussein is dead. But how likely was this future scenario? What would have happened if Saddam Hussein were left in power? Was war to eliminate this question worth its immense costs and the general havoc it unleashed in the postwar vacuum?

The strategic problem endures, and with it, many more counterfactual questions about the preventive war dilemma. Was it a mistake for President Lyndon Johnson to reject the preventive attack option, contemplated at the time, to destroy China's nuclear development facilities before its first successful atomic test in 1964? There were plenty of good reasons to be drawn into the preventive war temptation in the 1960s. Chinese leader Mao Tsetung had scoffed at Soviet fears of a nuclear war with America and the Soviets' willingness to be deterred, while millions of Chinese were murdered by Mao's regime or died in grand social engineering schemes. American leaders saw a future of expanding Communist power that could push the United States out of Asia, and there was great fear that a Chinese nuclear test would set off a cascade of nuclear proliferation in the region and around the world. As Americans watch the continuing growth of Chinese power in the twenty-first century, should they look at 1964 as a lost opportunity to blunt Chinese power? Or would preventive attack merely have delayed a Chinese bomb, while planting the seeds of enduring hostility that would make the future more dangerous than it otherwise will be? Was it a mistake for President Clinton to reject his defense secretary's advice to destroy North Korea's nuclear facilities in 1994? Did President George W. Bush make a mistake by failing to set back North Korea's long-range missile capabilities by destroying test missiles on the launchpad? Did President Bush make a mistake when he refused Israel's request for a green light to attack Iranian nuclear facilities in 2007? Did President Trump waste a precious window of opportunity to neutralize the North Korean threat with preventive attack in 2017, as each month brought it closer to a robust intercontinental nuclear missile capable of threatening the United States directly?

These are not hypothetical questions. They reflect real temptations and real options for policymakers. They reflect the way we judge history and the counterfactual stories we tell about what went right and what went wrong. They reflect opportunities for learning about the security problems earlier generations faced that echo into our own time, and what we carry forward to answer our own questions. The power-shift problem endures, despite the countless ways in which the world has changed since Thucydides told the tale of the devastating preventive war among the ancient Greeks. The history of preventive war—preventive wars fought and preventive wars avoided—has enduring value in the continuing effort to understand this phenomenon. But the very nature of the problem means that this history falls short of offering crystal-clear policy advice.

And ultimately, that's the point of this book. The power-shift problem and fear of the future produce the preventive war temptation, but the wisdom or folly of preventive war hinges on a certain level of confidence in your predictions of what the future holds. But the future is inherently uncertain. Humility, therefore, is key. Humility when we judge the choices made by those who came before us, struggling to separate smart options from foolish, but without the bright light of hindsight to guide them. And humility when we are tempted by ultimate solutions that promise to elimi-nate our future problems; solutions like preventive war, which are seductive precisely because they offer a clean break from what frightens us about the months and years to come. Preventive war is not a silver bullet for solving the enduring problem of security in an anarchic system. Preventive war can backfire strategically, even in the glow of battlefield victory. Each genera-tion of strategic leaders must be prepared to contemplate these challenges whenever the preventive war temptation spikes.

NOTES

CHAPTER I: THE FALSE PROMISE OF LOST OPPORTUNITIES

1. William Shirer, *The Rise and Fall of the Third Reich* (New York: Simon & Schuster, 1960).

2. Albert Speer, *Inside the Third Reich* (New York: Macmillan, 1970).

3. John Ellis, *World War II: A Statistical Survey* (New York: Facts on File, 1993); Encyclopedia Britannica; Melvin Small and J. David Singer, *Resort to Arms: International and Civil Wars 1816–1965* (Ann Arbor: University of Michigan Press, 1982).

4. Winston S. Churchill, *Gathering Storm* (Boston: Houghton Mifflin, 1948), iv.

5. Cato, *The Guilty Men* (New York: Frederick A. Stokes, 1940).

6. Flandin's Address to the League of Nations Council, *New York Times* (March 15, 1936).

7. Robert Gilpin, *War and Change in World Politics* (Cambridge: Cambridge University Press, 1981), 191.

8. B. H. Liddell Hart, *Strategy* (New York: Frederick A. Praeger, 1954), 223.

9. Winston Churchill, House of Commons, May 29, 1936, Hansard Series 5, vol. 312.

10. National Security Council Memorandum No. 68: "United States Objectives and Programs for National Security, April 7, 1950," *Foreign Relations of the United States 1950*, vol. I (Washington, DC: US Government Printing Office, 1977), sections I and V.C.

11. Scott A. Silverstone, *Preventive War and American Democracy* (New York: Routledge, 2007).

12. President Bush Addresses the Nation, March 19, 2003; Remarks by the President at 2002 Graduation Exercise of the United States Military Academy, June 1, 2002.

13. Joel S. Wit, Daniel B. Poneman, and Robert L. Gallucci, *Going Critical* (Washington, DC: Brookings Institution Press, 2004), 204.

14. Jason Le Miere, "U.S. Prepared to Launch 'Preventive War' Against North Korea, Says H. R. McMaster," *Newsweek* (August 5, 2017).

15. "Beyond Baghdad," *Newsweek* (August 18, 2002).

16. Dennis Ross, *Doomed to Succeed* (New York: Farrar, Straus and Giroux, 2015), 369.

17. Hillary Clinton Addresses the Iran Nuclear Deal, The Brookings Institution, Washington, DC, September 9, 2015.

18. Yuen Foong Khong, *Analogies at War* (Princeton, NJ: Princeton University Press, 1992), chaps. 1 and 2; Robert Jervis, *Perception and Misperception in International Politics* (Princeton, NJ: Princeton University Press, 1976); Ernest May, *"Lessons" of the Past: The Use and Misuse of History in American Foreign Policy* (New York: Oxford University Press, 1973).

19. Conan Fischer, *The Ruhr Crisis, 1923–1924* (London: Oxford University Press, 2003), 15.

20. Quoted in Etienne Mantoux, *The Carthaginian Peace* (London: Oxford, 1946), 23.

21. William R. Keylor, *The Legacy of the Great War* (Boston: Houghton Mifflin, 1998), 34.

22. Versailles Treaty, Part III, Section III.

23. Churchill, *Gathering Storm*, 194–95.

24. Churchill, *Gathering Storm*, 194. Emphasis added.

25. Shirer, *The Rise and Fall of the Third Reich*, 295.

26. Telford Taylor, *Munich: The Price of Peace* (Garden City, NY: Doubleday and Co., 1979), 141.

27. James T. Emmerson, *The Rhineland Crisis* (Ames: Iowa State University Press, 1977), 151.

28. Paul Schmidt, *Hitler's Interpreter* (New York: Macmillan, 1951), 41.

29. "Why Wasn't Hitler Stopped?" *Der Spiegel* (September 1, 2009).

30. Søren Kierkegaard, *Journalen* JJ: 167 (1843), vol. 18 (Copenhagen: Søren Kierkegaard Research Center, 1997), 306.

31. Philip Tetlock, *Expert Political Judgment* (Princeton, NJ: Princeton University Press, 2005).

CHAPTER 2: ANOTHER FAIT ACCOMPLI

1. Details of the events covered in this chapter were drawn from a comprehensive review of contemporary news reports filed by the *New York Times*, *Manchester Guardian*, *Observer*, *Chicago Tribune*, *Christian Science Monitor*, *Times* of London, *Boston Globe*, and *Los Angeles Times*.

2. Sigrid Schultz, "Hitler Speaks Today; Alarm Sweeps Europe," *Chicago Tribune* (March 7, 1936).

3. "Hitler Memorandum to Ambassadors," *New York Times* (March 8, 1936).

4. William E. Dodd, *Ambassador Dodd's Diary, 1933–1938* (New York: Harcourt Brace, 1941), 318–19.

5. William L. Shirer, *Berlin Diary* (New York: A. A. Knopf, 1941), 50–52.

6. "Text of Chancellor Hitler's Speech to Reichstag," *New York Times* (March 8, 1936).

7. "Text of Hitler's Speech," *Times* of London (March 13, 1936).

8. Shirer, *Berlin Diary*, 53.

9. James T. Emmerson, *The Rhineland Crisis* (Ames: Iowa State University Press, 1977), 102.

10. Eva Harazsti, *The Invaders: Hitler Occupies the Rhineland* (Budapest: Akadémiai Kiadó, 1983), 112; Emmerson, *The Rhineland Crisis*, 102.

11. Ian Kershaw, *Hitler, 1889–1936: Hubris* (New York: W. W. Norton, 1999), 588, fn. 35.

12. Zach Shore, "Hitler, Intelligence and the Decision to Remilitarize the Rhine," *Journal of Contemporary History* 34, no. 1 (January 1999), 5–18.

13. Shirer, *Berlin Diary*, 54.

14. Emmerson, *The Rhineland Crisis*, 82–83; Stephen A. Schuker, "France and the Remilitarization of the Rhineland, 1936," *French Historical Studies* 14, no. 3 (Spring 1986), 307.

15. Emmerson, *The Rhineland Crisis*, 98, 162–63; John W. Wheeler-Bennett, *The Nemesis of Power: The German Army in Politics, 1918–1945* (London: Macmillan and Co., 1964), 352.

16. The French government estimated 30,000 *Landespolizei* in the Rhineland, postwar scholarship puts the number at 15,000–22,000. R. A. C. Parker, "The First Capitulation: France and the Rhineland Crisis of 1936," *World Politics* 8, no. 3 (April 1956), 365; Donald Cameron Watt, "German Plans for the Reoccupation of the Rhineland: A Note," *Journal of Contemporary History* 1, no. 4 (October 1966), 195; Schuker, "France and the Remilitarization of the Rhineland, 1936," 308.

17. Emmerson, *The Rhineland Crisis*, 96.

18. Schuker, "France and the Remilitarization of the Rhineland, 1936," 307, fn. 23.

19. Emmerson, *The Rhineland Crisis*, 101.

20. Dirk Forster letter to the *Wiener Library Bulletin*, no. 5, 1956, Archives of the Wiener Library.

21. Schuker, "France and the Remilitarization of the Rhineland, 1936," 309.

22. "The War Minister and Commander-in-Chief of the Armed Forces Operations Order WA No. 380/36, March 2, 1936." Printed in Office of United States Chief of Counsel for Prosecution of Axis Criminality, *Nazi Conspiracy and Aggression*, vol. VI (Washington, DC: US Government Printing Office, 1946), C-159.

23. Kershaw, *Hitler, 1889–1936*, 586; Emmerson, *The Rhineland Crisis*, 101–2.

24. "Rhine Occupation Is in First Stage," *New York Times* (March 9, 1936).

25. General Werner von Blomberg Orders of March 2, 1936; Emmerson, *The Rhineland Crisis*, 97; Harazsti, *The Invaders*, 12–13; Parker, "The First Capitulation," 364–67.

26. Emmerson, *The Rhineland Crisis*, 97.

27. Anne O'Hare McCormick, "Rhineland Expects Backing of Britain," *New York Times* (March 20, 1936).

28. Watt, "German Plans for the Reoccupation of the Rhineland," 196; Emmerson, *The Rhineland Crisis*, 98.

29. Anne O'Hare McCormick, "War Ghosts Meet at the Rhine," *New York Times* (March 22, 1936).

30. "Rejoicings in the Rhineland," *The Observer* (March 8, 1936).

31. Emmerson, *The Rhineland Crisis*, 158.

32. "Rhineland Border is at High Tension," *New York Times* (March 10, 1936).

33. Judith M. Hughes, *To the Maginot Line* (Cambridge: Harvard University Press, 1971); J. E. Kaufmann and H. W. Kaufmann, *Fortress France: The Maginot Line and French Defenses in World War II* (London: Praeger Security International, 2006); A. F. Kovacs, "Military Origins of the Fall of France," *Military Affairs* 7 (Spring 1943), 32.

34. McCormick, "War Ghosts Meet at the Rhine."

35. "Rhinelanders and the Army," *The Observer* (March 15, 1936). British intelligence estimated France had a two-to-one advantage across the frontier zone. French intelligence put German armed strength at 300,000 in the Rhineland, including 90,000 regular Wehrmacht troops and security and labor forces with enough military training to join the fight. To British intelligence, these numbers were far too high. Robert J. Young, *In Command of France* (Cambridge, MA: Harvard University, 1978), 284, fn. 78.

36. Young, *In Command of France*, 13.

37. Kovacs, "Military Origins of the Fall of France," 28–29.

38. Jon Jacobson, *Locarno Diplomacy: Germany and the West 1925–1929* (Princeton, NJ: Princeton University Press, 1972), 107.

39. Maxim Weygand, "How France Is Defended," *International Affairs* 18, no. 4 (July–August 1939), 459–77; Enno Kraehe, "The Motives Behind the Maginot Line," *Military Affairs* 8, no. 2 (Summer 1944), 109–12; Barry R. Posen, *The Sources of Military Doctrine* (Ithaca: Cornell University Press, 1984), chap. 4.

40. "Locarno on the Screen," *Manchester Guardian* (March 14, 1936).

41. Weygand, "How France Is Defended," 461.

42. Telford Taylor, *Munich: The Price of Peace* (Garden City, NY: Doubleday, 1979), 98.

43. James S. Corum, *The Roots of Blitzkrieg* (Lawrence: University Press of Kansas, 1992), 170–71.

44. Young, *In Command of France*, 8–9.

45. Young, *In Command of France*, 88–106; Martin S. Alexander, *The Republic in Danger: General Maurice Gamelin and the Politics of French Defense, 1933–1940* (Cambridge: Cambridge University Press, 1992), 51–53; Nicole Jordan, "The Cut Price War on the Peripheries," in eds. Robert Boyce and Esmonde M. Robertson, *Paths to War: New Essays on the Origins of the Second World War* (New York: St. Martins, 1989); George Sakwa, "The Franco-Polish Alliance and the Remilitarization of the Rhineland," *The Historical Journal* 16 (1973), 125–46.

46. Young, *In Command of France*, 119.

47. "France Moves to Oust Nazis," *Boston Globe* (March 8, 1936); "France Puts Her Army on War Footing," *Los Angeles Times* (March 8, 1936); "France Moving to Combat Hitler," *New York Times* (March 9, 1936); "French Talk Preventive War," *Boston Globe* (March 12, 1936); "British Agree to Back Paris with Army," *Atlanta Constitution* (March 10, 1936).

48. "Speech Received Calmly in Paris," *New York Times* (March 8, 1936); Emmerson, *The Rhineland Crisis*, 116–17.

49. "Parisians Fear War," *Chicago Tribune* (March 14, 1936); "Odds 9½ to 1 Against War in Six Months," *Washington Post* (March 14, 1936); "War Scare Passes— Era of Abundance Is Predicted," *Boston Globe* (March 11, 1936).

50. Emmerson, *The Rhineland Crisis*, 161–163.

51. "Premier Sarraut's Radio Talk," *New York Times* (March 9, 1936).

52. "Flandin's Address to Council of League," *New York Times* (March 15, 1936).

53. "Troops Near Frontier," *Manchester Guardian* (March 13, 1936).

54. John M. Sherwood, *Georges Mandel and the Third Republic* (Stanford, CA: Stanford University Press, 1970), 176.

55. Sherwood, *Georges Mandel and the Third Republic*, 111–13.

56. Young, *In Command of France*, 122–23.

57. Young, *In Command of France*, 30, 121.

58. Emmerson, *The Rhineland Crisis*, 104–5, 111–14. This was not a new question to the cabinet; in January ministers agreed that any punitive action against Germany had to be channeled through the League and France's Locarno partners. Emmerson, *The Rhineland Crisis*, 48.

59. Emmerson, *The Rhineland Crisis*, 180–81.

60. "Litvinov Flays Hitler; Charges Nazis Plan War," *Chicago Tribune* (March 18, 1936).

61. Cabinet Meeting Minutes, March 11, 1936, Cabinet Papers 18 (36); Cabinet Meeting Minutes, March 16, 1936, Cabinet Papers 20 (36). All cabinet papers (abbreviated CAB) are available through the British National Archives at http://www .nationalarchives.gov.uk/cabinetpapers.

62. Emmerson, *The Rhineland Crisis*, 124–27; Schuker, "France and the Remilitarization of the Rhineland, 1936," 329; Parker, "The First Capitulation," 356–58, 361–64, 366; Earl of Avon, *The Memoirs of Anthony Eden: Facing the Dictators, 1923–1938* (Boston: Houghton Mifflin, 1962), 390–93; Harazsti, *The Invaders*, 94–95.

63. Cabinet Meeting Minutes, March 11, 1936; Cabinet Meeting Minutes, March 16, 1936.

64. Cabinet Meeting Minutes, March 11, 1936; Cabinet Meeting Minutes March 16, 1936; Report of the Chiefs of Staff Sub-Committee of the Committee of Imperial Defense, "Possible Dispatch of an International Force to the Rhineland," March 17, 1936; Cabinet Meeting Minutes, March 25, 1936, CAB 24 (36); Memorandum by the Secretary of State for Foreign Affairs, "Germany and the Locarno Treaty," March 1936, CAB 86 (36).

65. Memorandum by the Secretary of State for Foreign Affairs, April 28, 1936, CAB 123 (36); Questions to Be Addressed to the German Government, May 1, 1936, CAB 125 (36); Questions to Be Addressed to the German Government, May 5, 1936, CAB 127 (36).

66. Sigrid Schultz, "Hitler Rejects Rhine Peace Terms," *Chicago Tribune* (March 25, 1936).

67. "'Won't Retreat a Centimeter,' Hitler Declares," *Washington Post* (March 20, 1936).

68. Foreign Office Memorandum, "Preparations for the Proposed Five-Power Conference," August 19, 1936, CAB 220 (36); see also Emmerson, *The Rhineland Crisis*, 232–36.

69. "Military Service in Germany to Be Doubled," *Manchester Guardian* (August 25, 1936); "8 New Divisions to Bolster Nazi Army; 6 to Guard Rhineland," *Chicago Tribune* (September 29, 1936); "Reich Organizes 12 Corps of Army," *New York Times* (October 3, 1936).

70. Alistair Horne, *To Lose a Battle* (New York: Penguin Books, 2007), 261.

71. Horne, *To Lose a Battle*, 207–8, 229–33; Guy Chapman, *Why France Fell* (New York: Holt, Rinehart and Winston, 1968), 346–47; Alexander Swanston, *The Historical Atlas of World War II* (Edison, NJ: Chartwell Books, 2007); John Keegan, ed., *Collins Atlas of World War II* (New York: Collins, 2006); David Jordan, *Atlas of World War II* (New York: Barnes and Noble, 2004).

72. Bradford A. Lee, "Strategy, Arms and the Collapse of France, 1930–40," in *Diplomacy and Intelligence during the Second World War*, ed. Richard Langhorne (Cambridge: Cambridge University Press, 1988), 48–50.

73. Horne, *To Lose a Battle*, 292.

74. Theodore Draper, *The Six Weeks' War* (New York: Viking Press, 1944), 5; Bevin Alexander, *Inside the Nazi War Machine* (New York: NAL Caliber, 2010), 24–35, 48–49, 65–67; Horne, *To Lose a Battle*, 241–47.

CHAPTER 3: THE PREVENTIVE WAR TEMPTATION MEETS THE PREVENTIVE WAR PARADOX

1. Thomas Hobbes, *Leviathan* (New York: Penguin, 1968), chap. 13.

2. Paul Kennedy, *The Rise and Fall of the Great Powers* (New York: Random House, 1987).

3. Condoleezza Rice interview with CNN, September 8, 2002; President George W. Bush, The President's State of the Union Address, January 29, 2002. Emphasis added. Also see President George W. Bush, "The Iraqi Threat," speech delivered in Cincinnati, Ohio, October 7, 2002. "The National Security Strategy of the United States," September 2002, 15.

4. Dan Reiter, "Exploding the Powder Keg Myth: Preemptive Wars Almost Never Happen," *International Security* 20, no. 2 (Fall 1995), 5–34.

5. Report to the President of the United States by Robert H. Jackson, Chief of Counsel for the United States, June 7, 1945, in Robert H. Jackson, *The Nurnberg Case* (New York: Alfred A. Knopf, 1947).

6. Richard Ned Lebow, "Windows of Opportunity: Do States Jump through Them?," *International Security* 9 (Summer 1984), 150, 160, 164. See also Stephen Van Evera, *The Causes of War* (Ithaca: Cornell University Press, 2001), 79. Jack S. Levy, "Preferences, Constraints and Choices in July 1914," *International Security* 15, no. 3 (Winter 1990–1991), 151–86.

7. Dale C. Copeland, *The Origins of Major War* (Ithaca: Cornell University Press, 2000).

8. Lebow, "Windows of Opportunity," 160–68; Barbara Tuchman, *The Guns of August* (New York: Ballantine Books, 1962), 75, 120.

9. Scott D. Sagan, "The Origins of the Pacific War," *Journal of Interdisciplinary History* 18, no. 4 (Spring 1988), 912. See also Dale C. Copeland, "A Tragic Choice: Japanese Preventive Motivations and the Origins of the Pacific War," *International Interactions* 37 (January–March 2011), 116–26.

10. Jack S. Levy, "Declining Power and the Preventive Motivation for War," *World Politics* 40 (October 1987), 99. This is a seminal article on the logic of preventive war. For a review essay on the broader literature, see Scott A. Silverstone, "Preemption and Preventive War," in Oxford Bibliographies—International Relations, Oxford University Press online (http://www.oxfordbibliographies.com/view/document/obo-9780199743292/obo-9780199743292-0053.xml).

11. Harry G. Summers, *On Strategy: A Critical Analysis of the Vietnam War* (New York: Dell Publishing, 1982), 21.

12. Carl von Clausewitz, *Two Letters on Strategy*, eds. Peter Paret and Daniel Moran (Carlisle Barracks, PA: US Army War College, 1984), 9.

13. Colin S. Gray, "How Has War Changed Since the End of the Cold War?," *Parameters* (Spring 2005), 25.

14. B. H. Liddell Hart, *Strategy* (New York: Praeger, 1967), 351.

NOTES

15. Thomas Carothers, "Promoting Democracy and Fighting Terror," *Foreign Affairs* (January/February 2003); Bush, "The Iraqi Threat."

16. James A. Baker III and Lee H. Hamilton, "Iraq Study Group Report," December 2006, 41.

17. Amy Belasco, "The Cost of Iraq, Afghanistan, and Other Global War on Terror Operations Since 9/11," Congressional Research Service, March 29, 2011; Joseph E. Stiglitz, *The Three Trillion Dollar War* (New York: W. W. Norton, 2008).

18. Charles Duelfer, "Comprehensive Report of Special Advisor to the Director of Central Intelligence on Iraq's WMD," September 2004.

19. Kevin Woods, James Lacey, and Williamson Murray, "Saddam's Delusions: The View from the Inside," *Foreign Affairs* 85, no. 3 (May–June 2006), 2–26.

20. Carl von Clausewitz, *On War*, eds. Peter Paret and Michael Howard (New York: Alfred A. Knopf, 1993), 89. Emphasis added.

21. Seth Johnston, "What Is Strategy? Its Meaning in History, Tactics, and Policy." Paper presented at the 2014 Midwest Political Science Association Conference.

22. Robert Jervis, "Cooperation Under the Security Dilemma," *World Politics* 30, no. 2 (January 1978), 167–214; Stephen M. Walt, *The Origins of Alliances* (Ithaca: Cornell University Press, 1990); G. John Ikenberry, *After Victory* (Princeton, NJ: Princeton University Press, 2000).

23. Kenneth N. Waltz, *Theory of International Politics* (Reading, MA: Addison-Wesley, 1979), 173–75.

24. Ken Booth and Nicholas J. Wheeler, *The Security Dilemma* (New York: Palgrave Macmillan, 2008).

25. Charles L. Glaser, "The Security Dilemma Revisited," *World Politics* 50, no. 1 (October 1997), 174–75.

26. Waltz, *Theory of International Politics*, 113–14.

27. John H. Herz, "Idealist Internationalism and the Security Dilemma," *World Politics* 2, no. 2 (January 1950), 179–80.

28. Stephen Walt, "Alliance Formation and the Balance of World Power," *International Security* 9, no. 4 (Spring 1985), 13. For other Defensive Realist sources, see Charles L. Glaser, "Political Consequences of Military Strategy: Expanding and Refining the Spiral and Deterrence Models," *World Politics* 44, no. 4 (July 1992), 497–538; Glaser, "The Security Dilemma Revisited." For a Neoclassical Realist perspective, see Randall L. Schweller, "Neorealism's Status-Quo Bias: What Security Dilemma?," *Security Studies* 5, no. 3 (1996), 90–121. For a Constructivist perspective, see Alexander Wendt, "Anarchy Is What States Make of It: The Social Construction of Power Politics," *International Organization* 46, no. 2 (Spring 1992), 391–425 and "Constructing International Politics," *International Security* 20, no. 1 (Summer 1995), 71–81. Among the various schools of thought, Offensive Realism is quickest to dismiss this claim. John Mearsheimer's solution to the security dilemma is to dominate it by pursuing maximum relative power. *Tragedy of Great Power Politics* (New York: W. W. Norton, 2014), 30–31, 35–36.

29. For a critique, see Michael W. Doyle, *Striking First: Preemption and Prevention in International Conflict* (Princeton, NJ: Princeton University Press, 2008).

30. Clausewitz does not weigh in specifically on the strategic pros and cons of the preventive motive for war. Jon Sumida, "On Defence as the Stronger Form of War," in *Clausewitz in the Twenty-First Century*, eds. Hew Strachan and Andreas Herberg-Rothe (Oxford: Oxford University Press, 2007), 172. See Clausewitz, *On War*, 455. Also see Janeen Klinger, "The Social Science of Carl von Clausewitz," *Parameters* 36, no. 1 (Spring 2006), 79–89; Hew Strachan, "Preemption and Prevention in Historical Perspective," in *Preemption: Military Action and Moral Justification*, eds. Henry Shue and David Rodin (Oxford: Oxford University Press, 2007), 24–25.

31. Scott A. Silverstone, *Preventive War and American Democracy* (New York: Routledge, 2007).

32. Paul Hensel, "An Evolutionary Approach to the Study of Interstate Rivalry," *Conflict Management and Peace Science* 17 (1999), 175–206.

33. Thucydides, *History of the Peloponnesian War* (New York: Penguin Classics, 1972), 35.

34. Thucydides, *History of the Peloponnesian War*, 48.

35. Thucydides, *History of the Peloponnesian War*, 49. Emphasis added.

36. Thucydides, *History of the Peloponnesian War*, 55.

37. Thucydides, *History of the Peloponnesian War*, 62.

38. Thucydides, *History of the Peloponnesian War*, 65.

39. Thucydides, *History of the Peloponnesian War*, 67–68.

40. Thucydides, *History of the Peloponnesian War*, 103.

41. Thucydides, *History of the Peloponnesian War*, 108.

42. Thucydides, *History of the Peloponnesian War*, 48.

43. Robert L. O'Connell, *The Ghosts of Cannae* (New York: Random House, 2010).

44. For the most detailed account of the military dimensions of the raid, see Rodger W. Claire, *Raid on the Sun* (New York: Broadway Books, 2004).

45. Transcript of the President's News Conference on Foreign and Domestic Matters, *New York Times* (June 17, 1981).

46. "U.S., Citing Possible Violations of Arms Agreement, Suspends Shipment of 4 Jets to Israel," *New York Times* (June 11, 1981).

47. Text of the UN Draft Resolution, *New York Times* (June 19, 1981). For background on the joint US–Iraqi endeavor to develop the resolution, see "U.S. Consults Iraqis on Israeli Raid," *New York Times* (June 18, 1981); "U.S. and Iraq Agree on UN Resolution to 'Condemn' Raid," *New York Times* (June 18, 1981); "Israelis Condemned by Security Council for Attack on Iraq," *New York Times* (June 20, 1981).

48. "Mrs. Kirkpatrick's Speech Before the Security Council Vote," *New York Times* (June 20, 1981). See also Shai Feldman, "The Bombing of Osiraq—Revisited," *International Security* 7, no. 2 (Fall 1982), 114–42.

49. "Reagan Ends Ban on Sending Israel 16 Jet Warplanes," *New York Times* (August 18, 1981).

50. Feldman, "The Bombing of Osiraq—Revisited," 116–18; Shlomo Nakdimon, *First Strike* (New York: Summit Books, 1987).

51. Nakdimon, *First Strike*, 163.

52. "Begin Defends Raid, Pledges to Thwart a New 'Holocaust,'" *New York Times* (June 10, 1981); "Israeli and Iraqi Statements on Raid on Nuclear Plant," *New York Times* (June 9, 1981); "Israeli Jets Destroy Iraqi Atomic Reactor," *New York Times* (June 9, 1981).

53. "Mushy-Mindedness," *Wall Street Journal* (June 19, 1981).

54. Alan Cranston, "Condemn Israel? Didn't We Plan to Hit Cuba?," *New York Times* (June 10, 1981); William Safire, "Hail to the Nuclear Entebbe," *New York Times* (June 11, 1981); "Senators Open Hearing to Examine Whether Iraq Raid Broke U.S. Law," *New York Times* (June 19, 1981); "Kennedy Calls U.S. Vote on Israeli Raid 'Disastrous,'" *New York Times* (June 23, 1981).

55. "Reagan Ends Ban on Sending Israel 16 Jet Warplanes," *New York Times* (August 18, 1981).

56. Avner Cohen, "A New Nuclear Reaction," *Haaretz* (November 13, 2011); Nakdimon, *First Strike*, 191–93, 197–98, 205, 333.

57. Nakdimon, *First Strike*, 165.

58. Claire, *Raid on the Sun*, 145–46; Nakdimon, *First Strike*, 160, 165, 194.

59. Malfrid Braut-Hegghammer, "Revisiting Osirak: Preventive Attacks and Nuclear Proliferation Risks," *International Security* 36, no. 1 (Summer 2011), 122; Cohen, "A New Nuclear Reaction."

60. Braut-Hegghammer, "Revisiting Osirak," 103.

61. Nakdimon, *First Strike*, 59.

62. Braut-Hegghammer, "Revisiting Osirak," 106–10.

63. Braut-Hegghammer, "Revisiting Osirak," 110; Anthony Fainberg, "Osirak and International Security," *Bulletin of the Atomic Scientists* (October 1981); Dan Reiter, "Preventive Attacks Against Nuclear Programs and the 'Success' at Osiraq," *The Nonproliferation Review*, 12, no. 2 (2005), 356, 358–61; Joshua Kirshenbaum, "Operation Opera: An Ambiguous Success," *Journal of Strategic Security* 3, no. 4 (2010), 49–62; David Albright and Mark Hibbs, "Iraq and the Bomb: Were They Even Close?" *Bulletin of the Atomic Scientists* 47, no. 2 (March 1991).

64. Braut-Hegghammer, "Revisiting Osirak," 116.

65. Reiter, "Preventive Attacks Against Nuclear Programs and the 'Success' at Osiraq," 361–62. See also Richard Stone, "Profile: Jafar Dhia Jafar," *Science* (September 2005).

66. Braut-Hegghammer, "Revisiting Osirak," 116; Reiter, "Preventive Attacks Against Nuclear Programs," 362.

67. Robert M. Gates, *Duty: Memoirs of a Secretary at War* (New York: Alfred A. Knopf, 2014), 192. For an extended analysis of the preventive war paradox in the

case of an attack on Iran, see Kenneth M. Pollack, *Unthinkable: Iran, the Bomb, and American Strategy* (New York: Simon & Schuster, 2013), chaps. 8 and 9.

68. "Ex-Defense Chief Says Hit on Iran Would Be Disastrous," *Virginia-Pilot* (October 4, 2012).

69. Josh Rogin, "Bush's CIA Director: We Determined Attacking Iran Was a Bad Idea," *Foreign Policy* (January 19, 2012).

CHAPTER 4: HAUNTED BY THE PREVENTIVE WAR PARADOX

1. Arden Bucholz, *Moltke and the German Wars, 1864–1871* (New York: Palgrave, 2001), 8, 34, 103; Geoffrey Wawro, *The Franco-Prussian War* (Cambridge: Cambridge University Press, 2005), 3, 16–23; Dennis E. Showalter, *The Wars of German Unification* (London: Arnold, 2004), 195–96.

2. Edward Crankshaw, *Bismarck* (New York: Viking Press, 1981).

3. Alfred Vagts, *Defense and Diplomacy* (New York: King's Crown Press, 1956), 272.

4. Otto von Bismarck, *Bismarck: The Memoirs* (New York: H. Fertig, 1966), 103.

5. Vagts, *Defense and Diplomacy*, 286.

6. Otto Pflanze, *Bismarck and the Development of Germany*, vol. I (Princeton, NJ: Princeton University Press, 1990), 470, fn. 1.

7. Carl von Clausewitz, *On War*, eds. Peter Paret and Michael Howard (New York: Alfred A. Knopf, 1993), Book I, chap. 2, Book II, chap. 1; C. Grant Robertson, *Makers of the Nineteenth Century: Bismarck* (New York: Henry Holt and Company, 1919), 40.

8. von Bismarck, *Bismarck: The Memoirs*, 106–7.

9. "Occupied Paris," *New York Times* (March 3, 1871); "Evacuation of the French Capital by the Germans," *New York Times* (March 4, 1871); Michael Howard, *The Franco-Prussian War* (New York: Macmillan, 1961), 450.

10. von Bismarck, *Bismarck: The Memoirs*, 50, 106, 42–43; Crankshaw, *Bismarck*, 217.

11. Crankshaw, *Bismarck*, 268–69.

12. W. N. Medlicott and Dorothy K. Coveney, *Bismarck and Europe* (New York: St. Martin's Press, 1971), 59; William L. Langer, *European Alliances and Alignments, 1871–1890* (New York: Alfred A. Knopf, 1950), 8; A. J. P. Taylor, *Bismarck: The Man and the Statesman* (New York: Vintage Books, 1955), 103.

13. Taylor, *Bismarck*, 118, 202. See also David Wetzel, "A Reply to Josef Becker's Response," *Central European History* 41 (2008), 113; Emil Ludwig, *Bismarck* (Boston: Little, Brown and Co., 1927), 338.

14. Wetzel, "A Reply to Josef Becker's Response," 117. See also Ludwig, *Bismarck*, 341.

15. Howard, *The Franco-Prussian War*, 51–54.

16. Crankshaw, *Bismarck*, 266–67.

17. von Bismarck, *Bismarck: The Memoirs*, 94–97.

18. Wawro, *The Franco-Prussian War*, 52, 65–66; Howard, *The Franco-Prussian War*, 77.

19. Wawro, *The Franco-Prussian War*, 2, 17, 19, 41–43; Geoffrey Wawro, *The Austro-Prussian War* (Cambridge: Cambridge University Press, 1997), 16–17, 277, 282–83; Showalter, *The Wars of German Unification*, 204.

20. Wawro, *The Franco-Prussian War*, 304.

21. von Bismarck, *Bismarck: The Memoirs*, 101.

22. Josef Becker, "The Franco-Prussian Conflict of 1870 and Bismarck's Concept of a 'Provoked Defensive War': A Response to David Wetzel," *Central European History* 41 (2008), 99.

23. Ludwig, *Bismarck*, 349.

24. A. J. P. Taylor, *Struggle for Mastery in Europe, 1848–1918* (Oxford: Clarendon Press, 1954), 210; Becker, "The Franco-Prussian Conflict of 1870," 100–101; Wetzel, 122.

25. Medlicott and Coveney, *Bismarck and Europe*, 63.

26. W. E. Mosse, *The European Powers and the German Question, 1848–71* (New York: Octagon Books, 1969), 358.

27. Taylor, *Struggle for Mastery in Europe*, 205–6; Howard, *The Franco-Prussian War*, 40; Showalter, *The Wars of German Unification*, 231; David Wetzel, "Was the Franco-Prussian War a Preventive War?" Paper presented at the 2008 International Studies Association conference, 8–9.

28. Louis L. Snyder, *The Blood and Iron Chancellor: A Documentary Biography of Otto von Bismarck* (New York: D. Van Nostrand Co., 1967), 198; Crankshaw, *Bismarck*, 280.

29. Mosse, *The European Powers and the German Question*, 323–26; 335–36.

30. Taylor, *Bismarck*, 107.

31. Ludwig, *Bismarck*, 309.

32. Chancellor Otto von Bismarck speech to the German Reichstag, May 2, 1871, in *Bismarck*, ed. Frederic B. M. Hollyday (Englewood Cliffs, NJ: Prentice Hall, 1970), 35–36.

33. *Bismarck*, ed. Hollyday, 37.

34. Bismarck to Henry Reusz, Dispatch no. 95, February 28, 1874, in Medlicott and Coveney, *Bismarck and Europe*, 88.

35. James Stone, *The War Scare of 1875* (Stuttgart: Franz Steiner Verlag, 2010), 208. Moltke also worried that a stronger France would be better able to attract allies. Stone, *The War Scare of 1875*, 237.

36. Medlicott and Coveney, *Bismarck and Europe*, 77.

37. Stone, *The War Scare of 1875*, 199, 207; Gordon Craig, *Germany, 1866–1945* (New York: Oxford University Press, 1978), 107.

38. State Secretary Bernhard von Bulow reported Bismarck's agreement with this view to Prince Hohenlohe, Germany's ambassador in France, on May 3, 1875. Pflanze, *Bismarck and the Development of Germany*, vol. II, 269.

39. Letter from Chancellor Otto von Bismarck to Prince Hohenlohe, German ambassador to Paris, February 26, 1875, in Medlicott and Coveney, *Bismarck and Europe*, 88.

40. Stone, *The War Scare of 1875*, 202–8. See also Craig, *Germany*, 107. Moltke had encouraged Bismarck to attack France in 1867, an earlier period of French military reforms, during a crisis over French demands for the annexation of Luxembourg. Hew Strachan, "Preemption and Prevention in Historical Perspective," in *Preemption: Military Action and Moral Justification,* eds. Henry Shue and David Rodin (Oxford: Oxford University Press, 2007), 26. See also Pflanze, *Bismarck and the Development of Germany*, vol. II, 261, 268.

41. Vagts, *Defense and Diplomacy*, 288; Craig, *Germany*, 107. See also dispatch from British ambassador Odo Russell to Foreign Minister Lord Derby, April 27, 1875, in Medlicott and Coveney, *Bismarck and Europe*, 89.

42. Craig, *Germany*, 108. See also William Mulligan, "Restraints on Preventive War Before 1914," in *The Outbreak of the First World War*, eds. Jack S. Levy and John A. Vasquez (Cambridge: Cambridge University Press, 2014), 123.

43. Holstein asserted Bismarck had this story published, and recent scholarship on the crisis supports the contention. Friedrich von Holstein, *The Holstein Papers: The Memoirs, Diaries and Correspondence of Friedrich von Holstein 1837–1909* (Cambridge: Cambridge University Press, 2011), 94; Stone, *The War Scare of 1875*, 216.

44. von Holstein, *Holstein Papers*, 118; Pflanze, *Bismarck and the Development of Germany*, vol. II, 264.

45. Stone, *The War Scare of 1875*, 223–33.

46. Dispatch from Ambassador Élie de Gontaut-Biron to French Foreign Minister Louis, duc Decazes, dispatch April 21, 1875, in Medlicott and Coveney, *Bismarck and Europe*, 88–89.

47. Stone, *The War Scare of 1875*, 67, 70, 182; Vagts, *Defense and Diplomacy*, 287; Pflanze, *Bismarck and the Development of Germany*, vol. II, 261.

48. Pflanze, *Bismarck and the Development of Germany*, vol. II, 237–38.

49. French Foreign Minister Louis, duc Decazes to Ambassador Élie de Gontaut-Biron, Dispatch no. 34, April 29, 1875, in Medlicott and Coveney, *Bismarck and Europe*, 90; Stone, *The War Scare of 1875*, 252–54; Pflanze, *Bismarck and the Development of Germany*, vol. II, 269; Craig, *Germany*, 108.

50. "A French Scare," *Times* of London (May 6, 1875).

51. William L. Langer, *European Alliances and Alignments, 1871–1890* (New York: Knopf, 1950), 41.

52. Langer, *European Alliances and Alignments*, 51.

53. Langer, *European Alliances and Alignments*, 48.

54. Lord Derby letter to Queen Victoria, *The Letters of Queen Victoria*, Second Series, vol. II, ed. G. E. Buckle (New York: Longmans, Green, 1907), 389. Emphasis added.

55. Crankshaw, *Bismarck*, 328–29; Langer, *European Alliances and Alignments*, 50–51.

56. von Bismarck, *Bismarck: The Memoirs*, 252.

57. Stone, *The War Scare of 1875*, 313.

58. von Bismarck, *Bismarck: The Memoirs*, 192. See also 253–54. Kaiser Wilhelm, in a meeting with the Russian tsar on May 11, 1875, also argued against the utility of preventive war by predicting that Germany would lose the "benevolent neutrality of the other great powers." Stone, *The War Scare of 1875*, 277.

59. "Unrest Again in France," *New York Times* (July 18, 1886).

60. Langer, *European Alliances and Alignments*, 373–75; "General Boulanger's Reforms," *Hartford Courant* (July 17, 1886); "The Insult to Boulanger," *New York Times* (July 17, 1886); "A French Duel," *Atlanta Constitution* (July 18, 1886); "Parisian Portraits," *New York Tribune* (August 8, 1886); "Midsummer Paris Talk," *New York Times* (August 11, 1886).

61. "General Boulanger's Compliments," *Washington Post* (September 18, 1886).

62. "France and Boulanger," *New York Times* (July 29, 1886).

63. Otto von Bismarck speech to the German Reichstag, January 11, 1887, in Medlicott and Coveney, *Bismarck and Europe*, 160. See also Langer, *European Alliances and Alignments*, 379–82; Craig, *Germany*, 129.

64. "European War Talk," *New York Times* (February 1, 1887).

65. Langer, *European Alliances and Alignments*, 379.

66. Interview with British journalist W. Beatty-Kingston, September 22, 1867, in Snyder, *The Blood and Iron Chancellor*, 164.

67. Pflanze, *Bismarck and the Development of Germany*, vol. III, 218.

68. "War Rumors," *Manchester Guardian* (December 22, 1886); "They All Expect War," *Chicago Tribune* (December 26, 1886); "Russian Preparations," *Chicago Tribune* (January 14, 1887).

69. "Paris Talking of War," *New York Times* (August 15, 1886).

70. Langer, *European Alliances and Alignments*, 425–26.

71. Otto von Bismarck letter to Lord Salisbury, November 22, 1887, in Medlicott and Coveney, *Bismarck and Europe*, 166.

72. Holstein diary entry December 27, 1886, 327, and March 27, 1888, 366. See also Walter Goerlitz, *History of the German General Staff, 1657–1945* (New York: Praeger, 1953), 112–13.

73. Waldersee diary, October 15, 1885, Alfred von Waldersee, *A Field Marshal's Memoirs* (London: Hutchison & Co., 1925), 122–23.

74. Waldersee diary, July 10, 1888, 148.

75. Gordon Craig, *Politics of the Prussian Army, 1640–1945* (Oxford: Oxford University Press, 1964), 275.

76. Langer, *European Alliances and Alignments*, 444, emphasis added; Craig, *Politics of the Prussian Army*, 268.

77. Ambassador Reuss to Holstein, December 8, 1887, *Holstein Papers*, 233; Pflanze, *Bismarck and the Development of Germany*, vol. III, 272.

78. Norman Rich, *Friedrich von Holstein: Politics and Diplomacy in the Era of Bismarck and Wilhelm II* (Cambridge: Cambridge University Press, 1965), 218.

79. Rich, *Friedrich von Holstein*, 219.

80. Otto von Bismarck speech to the German Reichstag, February 6, 1888, in Snyder, *The Blood and Iron Chancellor*, 314–15.

81. Langer, *European Alliances and Alignments*, 485. Emphasis added.

82. Bulow letter to Holstein, December 10, 1887, *Holstein Papers*, 236–37.

83. Bismarck speech to the Reichstag, February 6, 1888, in Snyder, *The Blood and Iron Chancellor*, 313–14.

84. Text of the Reinsurance Treaty, signed June 18, 1887, in Medlicott and Coveney, *Bismarck and Europe*, 163–64.

85. Medlicott and Coveney, *Bismarck and Europe*, 361.

86. Crankshaw, *Bismarck*, 404.

87. Wolfgang J. Mommsen, *Imperial Germany, 1867–1918* (London: Arnold, 1995), 43, 51–54, 77–84; Edgar Feuchtwanger, *Imperial Germany, 1850–1918* (London: Routledge, 2001), 116–17; Richard F. Hamilton and Holger H. Herwig, *The Origins of World War I* (Cambridge: Cambridge University Press, 2003), 37.

88. Mommsen, *Imperial Germany*, 75, 93, 174–76; Hew Strachan, *The First World War*, vol. I (Oxford: Oxford University Press, 2001), 9–25; William Harbutt Dawson, *The German Empire, 1867–1914* (Hamden, CT: Archon Books, 1966), 495.

89. Craig, *Politics of the Prussian Army*, 230, 232.

90. Mommsen, *Imperial Germany*, 93; Dawson, *The German Empire*, 376, 459; Hamilton and Herwig, *The Origins of World War I*, 82–86, 197–213, 241, 272; Strachan, *The First World War*, 11, 16–25; Craig, *Politics of the Prussian Army*, 239, 312, 331.

91. Craig, *Politics of the Prussian Army*, 325; Mommsen, *Imperial* Germany, 185–86.

92. Mommsen, *Imperial* Germany, 170, 183; Hamilton and Herwig, *The Origins of World War I*, 165–66, 197–201, 212–14, 241; Niall Ferguson, *The Pity of War* (New York: Basic Books, 1999), 91–96, 100.

93. Stephen Van Evera, "The Cult of the Offensive and the Origins of the First World War," *International Security* (Summer 1984), 80–81.

CHAPTER 5: THE ROOTS OF A BITTER PEACE

1. Martin Gilbert, *The First World War* (New York: Henry Holt, 1994), 513.

2. Jon Jacobson, "Locarno, Britain and the Security of Europe," in *Locarno Revisited: European Diplomacy, 1920–1929*, ed. Gaynor Johnson (London: Routledge, 2004), 12.

3. Robert B. Asprey, *The German High Command at War* (New York: William Morrow and Co., 1991), 11; Roger Parkinson, *Tormented Warrior* (London: Hodder & Stoughton, 1978), 148–52.

4. Parkinson, *Tormented Warrior*, 168.

5. Asprey, *The German High Command at War*, 64, 433.

6. Parkinson, *Tormented Warrior*, 176; Asprey, *The German High Command at War*, 463–64.

7. David Stevenson, *With Our Backs to the Wall: Victory and Defeat in 1918* (Cambridge, MA: Harvard University Press, 2011), 392.

8. Carl von Clausewitz, *On War*, eds. Peter Paret and Michael Howard (New York: Alfred A. Knopf, 1993), chap. 1, emphasis added.

9. Asprey, *The German High Command at War*, 473. See also Harold I. Nelson, *Land and Power: British and Allied Policy on Germany's Frontiers, 1916–19* (London: Routledge and Kegan Paul, 1963), 55; Gilbert, *The First World War*, 478, 482.

10. Henry T. Allen, *The Rhineland Occupation* (Indianapolis: The Bobbs-Merrill Co., 1927), 62–63; Zara Steiner, *The Lights That Failed: European International History, 1919–1933* (Oxford: Oxford University Press, 2005), 29; Gilbert, *The First World War*, 500.

11. Jere Clemens King, *Foch versus Clemenceau* (Cambridge: Harvard University Press, 1960), 22.

12. Harold I. Nelson, *Land and Power*, 74.

13. Keith L. Nelson, *Victors Divided: America and the Allies in Germany, 1918–1923* (Berkeley: University of California Press, 1975), 22, 11, 20–21; Harold I. Nelson, *Land and Power*, 55, 72–73, 82–83; Gilbert, *The First World War*, 486; Stevenson, *With Our Backs to the Wall*, 390.

14. "American Military Government of Occupied Germany 1918–1920," Report of the Officer in Charge of Civil Affairs, Third Army and American Forces in Germany (Washington, DC: US Government Printing Office, 1943), v, 4, 6, 27, 35; Johnson Hagood, *Caissons Go Rolling Along*, ed. Larry A. Grant (Columbia: University of South Carolina Press, 2010), 40, 176; Margaret Pawley, *The Watch on the Rhine* (London: I. B. Tauris, 2007), 4; Allen, *The Rhineland Occupation*, 2; Keith L. Nelson, *Victors Divided*, 30–31, 34–35.

15. King, *Foch versus Clemenceau*, 57.

16. John Keegan, *The First World War* (New York: Vintage Books, 2000), 342.

17. German chancellor Theobald von Bethmann Hollweg address to the Reichstag, January 31, 1917. See also German ambassador Johann von Bernstorff letter to US Secretary of State Robert Lansing, January 31, 1917. *Source Records of the Great War*, vol. V, ed. Charles F. Horne (US: National Alumni, 1923).

18. Andre Tardieu, *The Truth About the Treaty* (Indianapolis: The Bobbs-Merrill Company, 1921), chap. IV.

19. King, *Foch versus Clemenceau*, 22.

20. Walter A. McDougall, *France's Rhineland Diplomacy, 1914–1924* (Princeton, NJ: Princeton University Press, 1978), chaps. 1 and 2; Stephen A. Schuker, "The Rhineland Question: West European Security at the Paris Peace Conference of 1919," in *The Treaty of Versailles: A Reassessment After 75 Years*, ed. Manfred F. Boemeke, Gerald D. Feldman, and Elisabeth Glaser (New York: Cambridge University Press, 1998), 279.

21. King, *Foch versus Clemenceau*, 12, 16–19; Harold I. Nelson, *Land and Power*, 28, 199, 204; Keith L. Nelson, *Victors Divided*, 75.

22. Allen, *The Rhineland Occupation*, x, 202.

23. The clearest statement of this position is the Fontainebleau memorandum written by Prime Minister David Lloyd George in late March 1919. Keith L. Nelson, *Victors Divided*, 83; Harold I. Nelson, *Land and Power*, 28, 200, 203, 206, 209, 224, 226; King, 19, 66; Steiner, *The Lights That Failed*, 29.

24. Harold I. Nelson, *Land and Power*, 223.

25. Harold I. Nelson, *Land and Power*, 211.

26. David Lloyd George, *The Truth About the Peace Treaties* (London: V. Gollancz, 1938), 402–3.

27. Harold I. Nelson, *Land and Power*, 207, 220–21, 225; Keith L. Nelson, *Victors Divided*, 79–81, 86–87; King, *Foch versus Clemenceau*, 47; Steiner, *The Lights That Failed*, 48.

28. Winston Churchill, Memorandum by the Chancellor of the Exchequer, February 24, 1925, Cabinet Papers, CAB 4/12/590-B, 276–77.

29. "Mr. Chamberlain in Paris," *Times* of London (October 20, 1925); Arnold Wolfers, *Britain and France Between the Wars* (New York: Harcourt, Brace, 1940), 13–14; Martin Gilbert, *Roots of Appeasement* (London: Weidenfeld and Nicolson, 1966), 47; Patrick O. Cohrs, "The Quest for a New Concert of Europe," in *Locarno Revisited*, 34–38; Jacobson, "Locarno, Britain and the Security of Europe," 16–17.

30. Robert C. Self, ed., *The Austen Chamberlain Diary Letters*, vol. 5 (Cambridge: Cambridge University Press, 1995), 265.

31. Minutes of the 195th Meeting of the Committee of Imperial Defence, February 13, 1925, Cabinet Papers 2/4/195, 108.

32. Peter Jackson, *Beyond the Balance of Power* (Cambridge: Cambridge University Press, 2013), chap. 13.

33. "Locarno," *Times* of London (October 17, 1925).

34. Brigadier General J. H. Morgan, "First Thoughts on the Security Pact," *English Review* (November 1925), 622n.

35. William J. Newman, *The Balance of Power in the Interwar Years, 1919–1939* (New York: Random House, 1968), 205–27; F. J. Berber, *Locarno: A Collection of Documents* (Edinburgh: William Hodge and Co., 1936), 48–61.

36. Minutes of the 195th Meeting of the Committee of Imperial Defence, 115.

37. "Locarno Success Hangs on Germany," *New York Times* (October 4, 1925); "Locarno," *Observer* (October 4, 1925).

38. "Locarno." See also Austen Chamberlain to Ida Chamberlain, November 28, 1925, in *Austen Chamberlain Diary Letters*, 284–86.

39. "The Road to Peace," *Times* of London (November 6, 1925), 9.

40. "Mr. Churchill on Locarno," *Times* of London (October 20, 1925), 16.

41. "Locarno Conference," *Times* of London (October 6, 1925). Emphasis added.

42. Gustav Stresemann letter to former Crown Prince, September 7, 1925, in Eric Sutton, ed., *Gustav Stresemann: His Diaries, Letters and Papers*, vol. I (New York: Macmillan, 1935), 505.

CHAPTER 6: THE RUHR WAR

1. Many of the details of the Ruhr War and the domestic crisis it created in Germany are drawn from 873 contemporary news articles published in Europe and the United States from the *Observer, Times* of London, *Manchester Guardian, New York Times, Chicago Daily Tribune, Christian Science Monitor, Los Angeles Times, Baltimore Sun,* and the *Boston Globe*.

2. Royal J. Schmidt, *Versailles and the Ruhr* (The Hague: Martinus Nijhoff, 1968), 10.

3. Conan Fischer, *The Ruhr Crisis, 1923–1924* (Oxford: Oxford University Press, 2003), 40.

4. Arnold Wolfers, *Britain and France Between the Wars* (New York: Harcourt, Brace, 1940), 23, 40–44; Fischer, *The Ruhr Crisis*, 43; Walter A. McDougall, *France's Rhineland Diplomacy, 1914–1924* (Princeton, NJ: Princeton University Press, 1978), 214–49.

5. "Paris Applauds Movies of Invasion of Essen," *Chicago Tribune* (January 15, 1923).

6. "Germany Refuses to Pay Further Sums to France," *Christian Science Monitor* (January 11, 1923).

7. "Germans Vote to Back 'Moral War' on French," *Chicago Tribune* (January 14, 1923); Wolfers, *Britain and France Between the Wars*, 43; Fischer, *The Ruhr Crisis*, 40–41.

8. Fischer, *The Ruhr Crisis*, 101.

9. "Cuno at Meeting Hears Plea of Hate," *New York Times* (March 15, 1923).

10. "Ruhr, Losing Hope of Ousting French, Awaits New Lead," *New York Times* (February 24, 1923).

11. "Germans Cut Off Lights in Essen," *Christian Science Monitor* (February 14, 1923).

12. "Germans Resent Plan to Separate Ruhr from Reich," *Christian Science Monitor* (February 26, 1923).

13. "Cuno Defies France as Reds Assail Him," *New York Times* (August 9, 1923).

14. "Stresemann's Foes Threaten His Fall," *New York Times* (August 31, 1923).

15. "Revolt a Question of Days," *New York Times* (July 28, 1923).

16. "Stresemann Sees Ruin Looming for Germany," *New York Times* (July 10, 1923).

17. "400 Fall as Germans Riot," *Chicago Tribune* (August 12, 1923).

18. "Ex-Crown Prince Declares Fascisti Will Fight Reds," *Chicago Tribune* (August 14, 1923).

19. "Bavaria Monarchists Defy Reich Court," *New York Times* (April 15, 1923).

20. "Cuno Embittered, Will Still Resist," *New York Times* (June 13, 1923).

21. "Thousands Hoch Der Kaiser in Bavarian Mass," *Chicago Daily Tribune* (September 3, 1923).

22. McDougall, *France's Rhineland Diplomacy*, 299–300.

23. For example, see Gustav Stresemann speech in Berlin, April 22, 1923, in Eric Sutton, ed., *Gustav Stresemann: His Diaries, Letters and Papers*, vol. I (New York: Macmillan, 1935), 63–64; Gustav Stresemann statement on French invasion of Ruhr, January 13, 1923, in Sutton, ed., *Gustav Stresemann*, 35–36.

24. Text of speech by Gustav Stresemann in *New York Times* (August 26, 1923).

25. Gustav Stresemann to British Ambassador Lord D'Abernon, November 2, 1923, 191–92; Minutes of German People's Party Meeting, November 3, 1923, 194–96; Cabinet Meeting November 8, 1923, 199–200; Note by Gustav Stresemann on Meeting with French Ambassador, November 9, 1923, 201–3; Gustav Stresemann speech at Halle, Germany, November 11, 1923, 203–7, in Sutton, ed., *Gustav Stresemann*.

26. Fischer, *The Ruhr Crisis*, 225.

27. "Stresemann Sees Ruin Looming for Germany."

28. Anne O'Hare McCormick, "Germany, Seeking a Moses, Turned to Dr. Stresemann," *New York Times* (October 14, 1923).

29. Gustav Stresemann Notes for a Speech to the Foreign Committee of the Reichsrat, September 7, 1923, 107–10; Note by Gustav Stresemann, September 27, 1923, 129–30; Cabinet Meeting Minutes, October 26, 1923, 180–81; Note by Gustav Stresemann, November 8, 1923, 198–200, in Sutton, ed., *Gustav Stresemann*.

30. "The German Shift to Stresemann," *Christian Science Monitor* (August 14, 1923).

31. Gustav Stresemann letter to former Crown Prince, September 7, 1925, in Sutton, ed., *Gustav Stresemann*, 505.

32. "Open Drive to Feed German Children," *New York Times* (November 1, 1923).

33. "Ruhr Should Vanish from the Earth," *Christian Science Monitor* (October 3, 1923).

34. "On to Berlin!" *Chicago Tribune* (November 9, 1923).

35. "Defying His Foes, Stresemann Offers to Resign at Once," *New York Times* (November 23, 1923).

36. Sigrid Schultz, "Give Us Chance to Work," *Chicago Tribune* (December 25, 1923).

37. "Stresemann, Angry, Says Allies Menace Whole Dawes Plan," *New York Times* (December 31, 1924).

38. Gustav Stresemann speech to Reichstag, July 22, 1925, in Eric Sutton, ed., *Gustav Stresemann: His Diaries, Letters and Papers*, vol. II (New York: Macmillan, 1937), 149. See also Zara Steiner, *The Lights That Failed: European International History, 1919–1933* (Oxford: Oxford University Press, 2005), 411.

39. Note by Gustav Stresemann, August 3, 1925, 151; Gustav Stresemann's diary, September 23, 1925, 165–66; Note by Gustav Stresemann, September 26, 1925, 169; Gustav Stresemann Locarno diary, October 12, 1925, 179–80; Gustav Stresemann letter to the American Ambassador, June 4, 1925, 246–47, Sutton, ed., *Gustav Stresemann*, vol. II.

40. Gustav Stresemann Locarno diary, October 13, 1925, in Sutton, ed., *Gustav Stresemann*, vol. II, 180.

41. Jon Jacobson, *Locarno Diplomacy: Germany and the West, 1925–1929* (Princeton, NJ: Princeton University Press, 2014), 147–48.

42. Gustav Stresemann Locarno diary, October 18, 1925, 187–88.

CHAPTER 7: SOWING DRAGON'S TEETH

1. "Chamberlain Scores Violations by Reich," *New York Times* (March 12, 1936).

2. "Mr. Churchill on Britain's Duty," *The Observer* (March 15, 1936).

3. Austen Chamberlain letter, March 16, 1936, in Robert C. Self, ed., *The Austen Chamberlain Diary Letters*, vol. 5 (Cambridge: Cambridge University Press, 1995).

4. Austen Chamberlain to Hilda Chamberlain, March 15, 1936, Self, ed., *The Austen Chamberlain Diary Letters*, vol. 5, 502.

5. Cabinet Meeting Minutes, March 11, 1936, Cabinet Papers CAB 18 (36); Cabinet Meeting Minutes, March 16, 1936, CAB 20 (36).

6. Cabinet Meeting Minutes, March 9, 1936, CAB 16 (36).

7. Cabinet Meeting Minutes, March 18, 1936, CAB 21 (36).

8. "France Mystified by British Stand," *New York Times* (March 14, 1936).

9. Winston Churchill, text for a speech at Chingford, May 8, 1936, Churchill Archives, CHAR 9/120; Winston Churchill, text for a speech at Rolls Park, Chigwell, June 20, 1936, CHAR 9/120.

10. Robert Paul Shay Jr., *British Rearmament in the Thirties* (Princeton, NJ: Princeton University Press, 1977), 48–56. For British assessments of German rearmament, see Foreign Office to British Ambassador at Berlin, October 11, 1934; Information received by the British Embassy at Paris, October 24, 1934; Memoranda on German Rearmament, prepared by British military attachés at Berlin for the Foreign Office, November 21, 1934; Memorandum on German Rearmament prepared by the Foreign Office for the Secretary of State, November 24, 1934, all in E. L. Woodward, et al., *Documents on British Foreign Policy, 1919–1939* (H.M.S.O.), 2nd series, XII.

11. House of Commons Debate, March 10, 1936, Hansard Series 5, vol. 309.

12. "The German Danger," Memorandum to the Cabinet, January 17, 1936, CAB/24/259. See also "Germany," Memorandum by the Secretary of State for Foreign Affairs, February 11, 1936, CAB/24/260; and Cabinet Meeting Notes, February 25, 1936, CAB/23/83.

13. Winston Churchill, draft text of *Evening Standard* article, November 10, 1936, CHAR 8/543.

14. Shay, *British Rearmament in the Thirties*, 297.

15. John Mueller, *Retreat from Doomsday* (New York: Basic Books, 1989).

16. Duff Cooper, *Old Men Forget* (London: Rupert Hart-Davis, 1953), 192–93.

17. "Eden Tells How Close England Came to a War," *Chicago Tribune* (July 19, 1936).

18. Stacie E. Goddard, "The Rhetoric of Appeasement: Hitler's Legitimation and British Foreign Policy, 1938–39," *Security Studies*, 24, no. 1 (2015), 98, 106.

19. Foreign Office Memorandum, Central Department, November 19, 1925, Foreign Office Archives F.O. 371/10746; Cabinet Minutes, August 13, 1925, CAB/23/50/45 (25).

20. For a useful summary of the debate, see Norrin M. Ripsman and Jack S. Levy, "The Preventive War That Never Happened: Britain, France, and the Rise of Germany in the 1930s," *Security Studies* (January–March 2007), 38, fn. 23; and Stephen A. Schuker, "France and the Remilitarization of the Rhineland, 1936," *French Historical Studies* (Spring 1986), 299–338. Also see A. J. P. Taylor, *The Origins of the Second World War* (New York: Atheneum, 1962), 97; James T. Emmerson, *The Rhineland Crisis* (Ames: Iowa State University Press, 1977), 239.

21. Committee of Imperial Defence, Chiefs of Staff Sub-Committee Report on Possible Despatch of an International Force to the Rhineland, March 17, 1936, CAB/24/261. See also Chiefs of Staff report, "The Condition of Our Forces to Meet the Possibility of War with Germany," in Eva H. Haraszti, *The Invaders: Hitler Occupies the Rhineland* (Budapest: Akademiai Kiado, 1983), 172–83.

22. Ripsman and Levy, "The Preventive War That Never Happened," 32–67; Norrin M. Ripsman and Jack S. Levy, "Wishful Thinking or Buying Time? The Logic of British Appeasement in the 1930s," *International Security* 33, no. 2 (Fall 2008), 148–81; Schuker, "France and the Remilitarization of the Rhineland, 1936," 299–338; Anthony Adamthwaite, *The Making of the Second World War* (London: George, Allen and Unwin, 1979).

23. Economic Pressure on Germany Without There Being a State of War, Committee of Imperial Defence, March 19, 1936, CAB 24/261; Germany and the Locarno Treaty, CAB 23 (36), March 19, 1936, CAB/23/83.

24. Winston Churchill, Memorandum by the Chancellor of the Exchequer, February 24, 1925, CAB 4/12/590-B, 276–77.

25. Peter Jackson, *Beyond the Balance of Power* (Cambridge: Cambridge University Press, 2013).

26. Minutes of the 195th Meeting of the Committee of Imperial Defence, February 13, 1925, CAB 2/4/195, 108.

27. Austen Chamberlain, Memorandum: The Foreign Policy of His Majesty's Government, April 15, 1926, Foreign Office Archives 371/11848, 81.

28. "Air Fleet Worries British," *New York Times* (March 3, 1924).

29. "British Are Calm Over the Situation," *New York Times* (April 28, 1925).

30. "Germany Willing to Accept Findings Without Reservation," *Christian Science Monitor* (April 18, 1924).

31. Minutes of the 195th Meeting of the Committee of Imperial Defence, 108–9.

32. Minutes of the 196th Meeting of the Committee of Imperial Defence, February 19, 1925, CAB 2/4/196(1), 117.

33. Minutes of the 195th Meeting of the Committee of Imperial Defence, 108. See also Foreign Office Memorandum on French Security, July 8, 1924, CAB 4/11/513-B, 211.

34. Memorandum by the Secretary of State for War, February 26, 1925, CAB 4/12/597-B, 313-314.

35. Gustav Stresemann, 1926 Nobel Peace Prize Lecture, delivered June 29, 1927.

36. General Staff Memorandum on the Military Aspects of the Future Status of the Rhineland, March 28, 1924, CAB 4/11/516-B, 229–30.

37. Memorandum by Brig.-Gen. E. L. Spears for the Committee of Imperial Defence, December 31, 1925, CAB 16/68/D.Z.-2, 15–16.

38. General Staff Note on DMZs, June 11, 1926, CAB 16/68/D.Z.-8; Memorandum by the Foreign Office, February 16, 1926, CAB 16/68/D.Z.-6; Committee of Imperial Defence, Report of Sub-Committee on DMZs, December 9, 1926, CAB 16/68/743-B; Memorandum by the General Staff, December 14, 1925, CAB 16/68/D.Z.-3.

39. Memorandum: The Foreign Policy of His Majesty's Government, 81.

40. Self, ed., *The Austen Chamberlain Diary Letters*, vol. 5, 265.

41. Viscount D'Abernon, *The Diary of an Ambassador: Dawes to Locarno, 1924–1926* (Garden City, NY: Doubleday, Doran, and Co., 1931), 167–69.

42. D'Abernon, *The Diary of an Ambassador*, August 11, 1925, 186.

43. Minutes of the 196th Meeting of the Committee of Imperial Defence, February 19, 1925, 118.

44. Minutes of the 195th Meeting of the Committee of Imperial Defence, 18, emphasis added.

45. Memorandum by Central Department, Foreign Office, "British Obligations under Locarno Treaty and under the Covenant of the League of Nations," November 13, 1925, Foreign Office Archives 371/10746 C14807/459/18, 19.

46. Statement by Sir Austen Chamberlain to the Imperial Conference, October 30, 1926, Foreign Office 371, 4. See also Foreign Policy of His Majesty's Government, April 15, 1926, 3–4.

47. Minutes of the 195th Meeting of the Committee of Imperial Defence, 114. See also General Staff Note on DMZs, June 11, 1926, CAB 16/68/D.Z.-8; Memorandum by the Foreign Office, February 16, 1926, CAB 16/68/D.Z.-6; Committee of Imperial Defence, Report of Sub-Committee on DMZs, p. 3; Memorandum by the General Staff, December 14, 1925, CAB 16/68/D.Z.-3.

48. Martin S. Alexander, *The Republic in Danger: General Maurice Gamelin and the Politics of French Defense, 1933–1940* (Cambridge: Cambridge University Press, 1992), 49–50.

49. See the intelligence reports described in Haraszti, *The Invaders*, 36–46; Emmerson, *The Rhineland Crisis*, 67.

50. Hitler speech to the Reichstag, May 21, 1935, in F. J. Berber, *Locarno: A Collection of Documents* (London: William Hodge and Co., 1936), 152.

51. Statement made by Sir Austen Chamberlain to the Imperial Conference, October 20, 1926, 371.

52. "The German Danger," Memorandum for the Cabinet, January 17, 1936; "Germany," Memorandum by the Secretary of State for Foreign Affairs, February 11, 1936. See also Gaines Post Jr., *Dilemmas of Appeasement* (Ithaca: Cornell University Press, 1993), 193–229.

53. Eden Memorandum of February 14, 1936, quoted in Memorandum by the Secretary of State for Foreign Affairs, March 8, 1936, CAB 73 (36), 144–45.

54. Eden Memorandum of February 14, 1936, 145. See also Emmerson, *The Rhineland Crisis*, 62, 65; Post, *Dilemmas of Appeasement*, 196–206.

55. Post, *Dilemmas of Appeasement*, 194.

56. Ian Colvin, *None So Blind* (New York: Harcourt, Brace and World, Inc., 1965), 96.

57. Austen Chamberlain letter, March 16, 1936; "Germany and Locarno," *Times* of London (March 12, 1936); Austen Chamberlain, "Right of Last Defence," *Times* of London (March 19, 1936); House of Commons Debate, March 26, 1936, Hansard Series 5, vol. 310.

58. Text of Flandin's Address to Council of League, *New York Times* (March 15, 1936); Text of Sarraut's Attack on Germany in French Chamber of Deputies, *New York Times* (March 11, 1936).

59. House of Commons Debate, March 26, 1936.

60. Memorandum by the Secretary of State for Foreign Affairs, in Haraszti, 145. Emphasis added. See also Lt.-Col. Beaumont-Nesbitt to Sir G. Clark, "Notes on a Conversation with Commandant Petibon," March 20, 1936, in Haraszti, *The Invaders*, 224.

61. Address by Foreign Secretary Eden, March 26, 1936, in Haraszti, *The Invaders*, 365.

62. Lt.-Col. Beaumont-Nesbitt in Haraszti, *The Invaders*, 224.

63. Anthony Eden, *The Memoirs of Anthony Eden: Facing the Dictators, 1923–1938* (Boston: Houghton Mifflin, 1962), 389.

64. House of Commons Debates, March 26, 1936.

65. House of Commons Debate, March 26, 1936. See also Memorandum by Secretary of State for Foreign Affairs, March 15, 1936, CAB/24/261; Cabinet Meeting Minutes, March 19, 1936, CAB/23/83; Cabinet Meeting Minutes, April 1, 1936, CAB/23/83.

66. House of Commons Debates, March 9, 1936, Hansard Series 5, vol. 309.

67. "Britain Sees No 'Attack,'" *New York Times* (March 10, 1936).

68. Extracts from Eden's Speech on Germany, *New York Times* (March 27, 1936).

69. House of Commons Debates, March 26, 1936; Memorandum by Secretary of Foreign Affairs, March 15, 1936, CAB/24/261; Minutes of Cabinet Meeting, March 19, 1936, CAB/23/83; Minutes of Cabinet Meeting, April 1, 1936, CAB/23/83; Emmerson, *The Rhineland Crisis*, 48, 50–51.

70. Goddard, "The Rhetoric of Appeasement," 122; Robert J. Art, "Europe Hedges Its Security Bets," in *Balance of Power: Theory and Practice in the 21st Century*, eds. T. V. Paul, James J. Wirtz, and Michel Fortmann (Stanford, CA: Stanford University Press, 2004).

CHAPTER 8: NO HEROES, NO GOATS

1. David Reynolds, *In Command of History* (New York: Basic Books, 2007).
2. Winston S. Churchill, *Gathering Storm* (Boston: Houghton Mifflin Co., 1948), 194–95.
3. Churchill, *Gathering Storm*, 180.
4. Minutes of the 195th Meeting of the Committee of Imperial Defence, February 13, 1925, Cabinet Papers, CAB 2/4/195, 113.
5. Minutes of the 195th Meeting of the Committee of Imperial Defence, 113–14.
6. Minutes of the 195th Meeting of the Committee of Imperial Defence, 113–14.
7. Winston Churchill, Memorandum by the Chancellor of the Exchequer, February 24, 1925, CAB 4/12/590-B, 276–77.
8. Minutes of the 195th Meeting of the Committee of Imperial Defence, 113.
9. Winston S. Churchill, "The MacDonald Disarmament Plan," March 23, 1933, and "The Darkening Scene," April 13, 1933, in *While England Slept: A Survey of World Affairs, 1932–1938* (New York: G. P. Putnam's Sons, 1938), 48–65.
10. House of Commons Debate, March 26, 1936, Hansard Series 5, vol. 310.
11. House of Commons Debate, March 10, 1936, Hansard Series 5, vol. 309.
12. House of Commons Debate, March 26, 1936, and April 6, 1936, Hansard Series 5, vol. 310.
13. House of Commons Debate, March 26, 1936.
14. House of Commons Debate, March 26, 1936.
15. Richard K. Betts, "Striking First: A History of Thankfully Lost Opportunities," *Ethics and International Affairs* 17, no. 1 (Spring 2003), 17–24.
16. House of Commons Debate, March 10, 1936.
17. Winston Churchill, "Britain, Germany and Locarno," *Evening Standard* (March 13, 1936), emphasis added.
18. Winston Churchill speech to Jewelers Association annual dinner, March 14, 1936, notes in Churchill Archives CHAR 9/120.
19. House of Commons Debate, March 26, 1936.
20. Churchill, "The Need for Air Parity," March 8, 1934, *While England Slept*, 101.
21. Churchill, "The MacDonald Disarmament Plan."
22. Winston Churchill, "Prepare!" House of Commons Debate, February 7, 1934, and additional speeches of March 8, 1934, July 30, 1934, November 28, 1934, March 19, 1935, May 2, 1935, May 22, 1935, May 31, 1935, July 22, 1935, *While England Slept*, 90, 95–221.

23. House of Commons Debate, March 10, 1936.

24. Churchill, "How to Stop War," *Evening Standard* (June 12, 1936). Also see "The Value of the League," July 13, 1934, *While England Slept*, 122.

25. Churchill, "MacDonald Disarmament Plan," 48.

26. Churchill, "European Dangers," *While England Slept*, 31–32.

27. Churchill, "MacDonald's Disarmament Plan," 53.

28. Churchill, "The League and Germany," November 7, 1933, 82.

29. House of Commons Debate, March 26, 1936.

30. House of Commons Debate, April 6, 1936. Also see Winston Churchill, "Stop It Now," *Evening Standard* (April 3, 1936); Winston Churchill speech at Rhodes House, Oxford University, May 22, 1936, in CHAR 9/120.

31. For example, see Ian Colvin, *None So Blind* (New York: Harcourt, Brace and World, Inc., 1965).

32. Robert Vansittart, *Lessons of My Life* (New York: Alfred A. Knopf, 1943), xiv.

33. Colvin, *None So Blind*, 26–27.

34. Vansittart, *Lessons of My Life*, xvii.

35. Robert Vansittart, "Britain, France and Germany," February 3, 1936, enclosure to Memorandum by the Secretary of State for Foreign Affairs, February 11, 1936, Cabinet Papers CAB 42 (36). See also Colvin, *None So Blind*, 52–55; Gaines Post Jr., *Dilemmas of Appeasement* (Ithaca: Cornell University Press, 1993), 195–96.

36. Vansittart, "Britain, France and Germany."

37. Vansittart, *Lessons of My Life*, 123.

38. Vansittart, "Britain, France and Germany."

39. House of Commons Debate, June 29, 1936, Hansard Series 5, vol. 313.

40. Duff Cooper, *Old Men Forget* (New York: E. P. Dutton & Co., Inc., 1954), 196.

41. Quoted in Eva H. Haraszti, *The Invaders: Hitler Occupies the Rhineland* (Budapest: Akademiai Kiado, 1983), 121.

42. House of Commons Debate, March 26, 1936.

43. Austen Chamberlain to Hilda Chamberlain, March 28, 1936, in Robert C. Self, ed., *The Austen Chamberlain Diary Letters*, vol. 5 (Cambridge: Cambridge University Press), 503.

44. House of Commons Debate, March 26, 1936; Austen Chamberlain to Hilda Chamberlain, May 10, 1936, in Self, ed., *The Austen Chamberlain Diary Letters*, vol. 5, 507.

45. Randall L. Schweller, "Unanswered Threats: A Neoclassical Theory of Underbalancing," *International Security* 29, no. 2 (Fall 2004), 159.

46. Philip E. Tetlock, Richard Ned Lebow, and Geoffrey Parker, eds., *Unmaking the West: "What-if" Scenarios That Rewrite History* (Ann Arbor: University of Michigan Press, 2006), 15.

47. "Seven European Nations in Great Arms Race," and James H. Powers, "'Iron Ring' Closes Round Nazi Germany," *Boston Globe* (February 16, 1936).

48. "Franco-Soviet Pact Effective," *Boston Globe* (March 28, 1936).

49. "Britain Shifts Her Plans," *New York Times* (February 16, 1936).

50. "British Public Studying Costs of Arms Plan," *Washington Post* (March 5, 1936).

51. Powers, "'Iron Ring' Closes Round Nazi Germany."

52. "War Aid to France Pledged by Soviet," *New York Times* (March 24, 1936).

53. "France and the White Paper," *Observer* (March 22, 1936).

54. "Hitler Is Cornered in Rhineland Plans," *New York Times* (March 22, 1936).

55. "France Is Pleased by British Pledge," *New York Times* (March 21, 1936).

56. Robert J. Young, *In Command of France: French Foreign Policy and Military Planning, 1933–1940* (Cambridge: Harvard University Press, 1978), 172.

57. "History Need Not Repeat," *Christian Science Monitor* (April 4, 1936).

58. Walter Lippmann, "The Four Pillars of Peace," *Boston Globe* (May 30, 1936). On Lippmann's influence, see Ronald Steel, *Walter Lippmann and the American Century* (Piscataway, NJ: Transaction Publishers, 1999).

59. Walter Lippmann, "The Pivot of Europe," *Boston Globe* (April 2, 1936).

60. J. L. Garvin, "Not Now—But . . . ," *Observer* (March 22, 1936).

61. J. L. Garvin, "Bedrock," *Observer* (March 29, 1936).

62. J. L. Garvin, "Settle or Fight," *Observer* (March 15, 1936).

63. Livingston Hartley, "Europe: 1914 and 1936," *Washington Post* (April 9, 1936).

64. Albin E. Johnson, "Long-Heralded War Declared Under Way," *Los Angeles Times* (March 15, 1936).

65. Albin E. Johnson, "Locarno Peace Pact Now Military Alliance," *Los Angeles Times* (April 26, 1936).

66. Hanson W. Baldwin, "Europe's Battalions Greater than in 1914," *New York Times* (March 15, 1936); "French Ratify Soviet Treaty," *Boston Globe* (March 13, 1936). For an authoritative postwar source on the military balance, see Williamson Murray, *The Change in the European Balance of Power, 1938–39: The Path to Ruin* (Princeton, NJ: Princeton University Press, 1984).

67. Churchill, *Gathering Storm*, 207–8.

68. Thomas C. Schelling, *Arms and Influence* (New Haven: Yale University Press, 1966).

69. Robert Jervis, *Perception and Misperception in International Politics* (Princeton, NJ: Princeton University Press, 1976), 78; Charles Glaser, "Political Consequences of Military Strategy," *World Politics* 44, no. 4 (July 1992), 497–538.

70. John Herz, *Political Realism and Political Idealism* (Chicago: University of Chicago Press, 1951), 4.

71. For an assessment of the evolving debate on the causes of World War I, see Kier A. Lieber, "The New History of World War I and What It Means for International Relations Theory," *International Security* 32, no. 2 (Fall 2007), 155–91. It's important to note that even if modern scholars are now challenging the spiral model and defensive realist theory to explain the First World War, the dominant view in

the 1920s and 1930s was that encirclement and spiral dynamics were the deeper problems driving toward war, and that this logic still had relevance after the war.

72. Lieber, "The New History of World War I," 185.

73. Jervis, *Perception and Misperception in International Politics*, 65.

74. "Trouble Lies in Endless Chain of Secret Pacts," *Chicago Tribune* (March 22, 1936); James H. Powers, "Military Madness of the World," *Boston Globe* (April 26, 1936); "Time for a Peace Conference," *Washington Post* (March 10, 1936).

75. John Clayton, "Lining Up for Armageddon," *Los Angeles Times* (March 8, 1936).

76. John Clayton, "Cannon Fodder—Ready for War!" *Los Angeles Times* (July 19, 1936).

77. Walter Lippmann, "The Fateful Hour," *Los Angeles Times* (March 11, 1936); "The Issue," *Boston Globe* (March 12, 1936); "The Crucial Difficulty," *Boston Globe* (March 17, 1936); "The German Peace Plan," *Boston Globe* (April 9, 1936).

78. "To-Day's Rearmament Debate," *Manchester Guardian* (March 9, 1936).

79. House of Commons Debate, March 9, 1936, Hansard Series 5, vol. 309.

80. House of Commons Debate, March 10, 1936.

81. Jervis defines encirclement as a general phenomenon in which hard balancing leads a rival to overestimate your degree of hostility, raising its own security fears with dangerous consequences.

82. Vansittart, "Britain, France and Germany," emphasis added.

83. House of Commons Debate, February 24, 1936, Hansard Series 5, vol. 309.

84. During debate on March 9, March 10, and March 26, which focused on rearmament and the commitment to France and Belgium, the following Conservative Party members spoke out about the dangers of encirclement spiraling toward war: Anthony Eden, Leopold Amery, Robert Boothby, Ian Hannah, Stanley Baldwin, Samuel Hoare, Edward Grigg, Philip Sassoon, Austen Chamberlain, Paul Emrys-Evans, and Winston Churchill.

85. Robert John Graham Boothby, *Boothby: Recollections of a Rebel* (London: Hutchison, 1978).

86. House of Commons Debate, March 26, 1936.

87. House of Commons Debates, March 26 and April 6, 1936.

88. "Helpless Pawns," *Washington Post* (July 30, 1936).

89. House of Commons Debate, March 26, 1936.

90. Reynolds, *In Command of History*, 94.

91. Randall L. Schweller, *Unanswered Threats: Political Constraints on the Balance of Power* (Princeton, NJ: Princeton University Press, 2008), 33.

CHAPTER 9: SEARCHING FOR A SILVER BULLET

1. Gary Goertz and Jack S. Levy, eds., *Explaining War and Peace* (New York: Routledge, 2007); Philip Tetlock, Richard Ned Lebow, and Geoffrey Parker, eds.,

Unmaking the West (Ann Arbor: University of Michigan Press, 2006); Philip E. Tetlock and Aaron Belkin, *Counterfactual Thought Experiments in World Politics* (Princeton, NJ: Princeton University Press, 1996); Niall Ferguson, ed., *Virtual History* (New York: Basic Books, 1999); David Sylvan and Stephen Majeski, "A Methodology for the Study of Historical Counterfactuals," *International Studies Quarterly* 42, no. 1 (March 1998), 79–108; Richard K. Herrmann and Richard Ned Lebow, *Ending the Cold War* (New York: Palgrave, 2004), chap. 7; George G. S. Murphy, "On Counterfactual Propositions," *History and Theory* 9, no. 9 (1969), 14–38; Stuart J. Thorson and Donald A. Sylvan, "Counterfactuals and the Cuban Missile Crisis," *International Studies Quarterly* 26, no. 4 (December 1982), 539–71.

2. Richard E. Neustadt and Ernest R. May, *Thinking in Time* (New York: Free Press, 1986); Yuen Foong Khong, *Analogies at War* (Princeton, NJ: Princeton University Press, 1992).

3. Donald Cameron Watt, "Introduction," in James T. Emmerson, *The Rhineland Crisis* (Ames: Iowa State University Press, 1977), 11.

4. Donald Cameron Watt, "German Plans for the Reoccupation of the Rhineland: A Note," *Journal of Contemporary History* 1 (October 1966), 193–99; Emmerson, *The Rhineland Crisis*, 7, 98–100.

5. Emmerson, *The Rhineland Crisis*, 105–10; Stephen A. Schuker, "France and the Remilitarization of the Rhineland, 1936," *French Historical Studies* 14 (Spring 1986), 299–338; Anthony Adamthwaite, *France and the Coming of the Second World War, 1936–1939* (London: Frank Cass, 1977). The decisive question for many scholars is the date they estimate German power surpassed French and British power. For a useful review, see Norrin M. Ripsman and Jack S. Levy, "The Preventive War That Never Happened: Britain, France, and the Rise of Germany in the 1930s," *Security Studies* (January–March 2007).

6. Among French officials we find Premier Albert Sarraut, League delegate Joseph Paul-Boncour, and Georges Mandel; it was also supported by a postwar French parliamentary investigative committee. Germans in this group include war minister General Blomberg, Army Chief of Staff General Fritsch, General Beck, and General Jodl. See Emmerson, *The Rhineland Crisis*, chaps. 3, 4, and 6. See also: Telford Taylor, *Munich: The Price of Peace* (Garden City, NY: Doubleday and Co., 1979); Zach Shore, "Hitler, Intelligence and the Decision to Remilitarize the Rhine," *Journal of Contemporary History* 34, no. 1 (1999), 5; E. M. Robertson, *Hitler's Pre-War Policy and Military Plans, 1933–1939* (New York: Citadel Press, 1963), 79–81; Williamson Murray, *The Change in the European Balance of Power, 1938–39* (Princeton, NJ: Princeton University Press, 1984); Gerhard Weinberg, *The Foreign Policy of Hitler's Germany* (Chicago: University of Chicago Press, 1970); A. J. P. Taylor, *The Origins of the Second World War* (New York: Atheneum, 1962), 97, 101; Nicholas Henderson, "Hitler and the Rhineland: A Decisive Turning-Point," *History Today* (October 1992), 15.

7. Emmerson, *The Rhineland Crisis*, 139–42.

8. Emmerson, *The Rhineland Crisis*, 119, 141, 157.

9. Emmerson, *The Rhineland Crisis*, 119, 158–59. Polish leaders were intrigued by the preventive war option during Hitler's first year in power, but by 1934 Poland had a nonaggression pact with the Third Reich. Jameson W. Crockett, "The Polish Blitz, More than a Mere Footnote to History: Poland and Preventive War with Germany, 1933," *Diplomacy & Statecraft* 20 (2009), 561–79.

10. Jonathan Haslam, *The Soviet Union and the Struggle for Collective Security in Europe, 1933–39* (New York: St. Martin's Press, 1984); Jiri Hochman, *The Soviet Union and the Failure of Collective Security, 1934–1938* (Ithaca: Cornell University Press, 1984); Gabriel Gorodetsky, ed., *Soviet Foreign Policy, 1917–1919* (London: Routledge, 1994); Hugh D. Phillips, *Between the Revolution and the West: A Political Biography of Maxim M. Litvinov* (Boulder, CO: Westview Press, 1992); Emmerson, *The Rhineland Crisis*, 157–58.

11. Emmerson, *The Rhineland Crisis*, 141–42.

12. Emmerson, *The Rhineland Crisis*, 126–27.

13. Winston S. Churchill, *Gathering Storm* (Boston: Houghton Mifflin Co., 1948), 194.

14. William L. Shirer, *The Rise and Fall of the Third Reich* (New York: Simon & Schuster, 1960), 295.

15. Telford Taylor, *Sword and Swastika* (New York: Simon & Schuster, 1952), 58–63

16. Patricia Meehan, *The Unnecessary War, Whitehall and the German Resistance to Hitler* (London: Sinclair-Stevenson, 1992); Terry Parssinen, *The Oster Conspiracy of 1938* (New York: HarperCollins, 2003).

17. Scott A. Hawkins and Reid Hastie, "Hindsight: Biased Judgments of Past Events After the Outcomes Are Known," *Psychological Bulletin* 107, no. 3 (1990), 313; John Mueller, "Changing Attitudes towards War: The Impact of the First World War," *British Journal of Political Science* 21, no. 1 (January 1991), 1–28.

18. John W. Wheeler-Bennett, *The Nemesis of Power: The German Army in Politics, 1918–1945* (London: Macmillan, 1954), 358.

19. Taylor, *Sword and Swastika*, 83, 88. See also Ian Kershaw, *Hitler, 1889–1936: Hubris* (New York: W. W. Norton & Company, 1999), xxxvii–xxxviii.

20. Quoted in Taylor, *Sword and Swastika*, 114.

21. Memorandum Respecting the Views of the German General Staff, April 6, 1936, Attachment to Foreign Office memorandum, April 25, 1936, Cabinet Papers 121 (36), 4.

22. Taylor, *Sword and Swastika*, 75. Richard Evans, *The Third Reich in Power* (New York: Penguin, 2005), 39; Kershaw, *Hitler, 1889–1936*, 514–17.

23. Wheeler-Bennett, *The Nemesis of Power*, 315.

24. Gordon A. Craig, *The Politics of the Prussian Army, 1640–1945* (London: Oxford University Press, 1956), 461–62, 467.

25. Taylor, *Sword and Swastika*, 79.

26. Craig, *The Politics of the Prussian Army*, 477–79.

27. Taylor, *Sword and Swastika*, 80–82. See also Craig, *The Politics of the Prussian Army*, 481; Wheeler-Bennett, *The Nemesis of Power*, 393–94.

28. Craig, *The Politics of the Prussian Army*, 472; Taylor, *Sword and Swastika*, 73–74; Wheeler-Bennett, *The Nemesis of Power*, 300.

29. Schuker, "France and the Remilitarization of the Rhineland, 1936," 306, fn. 20.

30. Craig, *The Politics of the Prussian Army*, 490. See also Wheeler-Bennett, *The Nemesis of Power*, 358.

31. Taylor, *Sword and Swastika*, 91.

32. Taylor, *Sword and Swastika*, 90, 111; Wheeler-Bennett, *The Nemesis of Power*, 387.

33. "Germany's Militarists Rally to Support of Hitler in His Rhineland Venture," *Los Angeles Times* (March 9, 1936).

34. "Pledges Loyalty to Nazis," *New York Times* (March 9, 1936); Sigrid Schultz, "German Army Gives Fealty Pledge to Nazi Dictator," *Chicago Tribune* (March 9, 1936).

35. Emmerson, *The Rhineland Crisis*, 93–95; "Hitler Voices Plea for French Amity," *New York Times* (March 13, 1936); "Assures Neighbor Nations," *New York Times* (March 13, 1936); "Bid for Conciliation Seen," *New York Times* (March 13, 1936).

36. Text of Hitler's Memorandum, *Christian Science Monitor* (March 7, 1936).

37. Watt, "Introduction," 15.

38. "Nazi Election Campaign," *Manchester Guardian* (March 11, 1936); "Reich Now United, Göring Asserts," *New York Times* (March 13, 1936).

39. Excerpts from Hitler's Speech Opening Campaign, *New York Times* (March 13, 1936).

40. "Führer Tells 300,000 at Munich He Spurns Role of 'Accused,'" *Washington Post* (March 15, 1936); "Assumes All Responsibility," *New York Times* (March 15, 1936); "Cannon Boom Salutes," *New York Times* (March 15, 1936).

41. "Thousands Cheer a Defiant Hitler," *New York Times* (March 17, 1936); "Hitler Says Reich Is Unyielding," *New York Times* (March 17, 1936); "Berlin Sees Skirmishing," *New York Times* (March 17, 1936).

42. Sigrid Schultz, "Hitler Pictures Self as Europe's Herald of Peace," *Chicago Tribune* (March 19, 1936); "Hitler's Breslau Remarks on Foreign Relations," *New York Times* (March 23, 1936).

43. "Cheered Six Minutes on Entering," *New York Times* (March 25, 1936); "Nazis Open Drive to Bring Out Vote," *New York Times* (March 24, 1936).

44. "Hitler Ridicules Powers' Demand in Plea to Nation," *New York Times* (March 28, 1936); "Nazi Campaign at Its Highest Pitch," *Manchester Guardian* (March 28, 1936).

45. Anne O'Hare McCormick, "Cologne Delirious as Hitler Speaks," *New York Times* (March 29, 1936).

46. "Hitler Gets Biggest Vote," *New York Times* (March 30, 1936).

47. Anne O'Hare McCormick, "German Mood Responds to Hitler's Appeal," *New York Times* (April 5, 1936).

48. Emmerson, *The Rhineland Crisis*, 150. See also Kershaw, *Hitler, 1889–1936*, xxxix–xl.

49. Emmerson, *The Rhineland Crisis*, 106.

50. Sir Eric Phipps to Sir Samuel Hoare, November 13, 1935, included among the documents in Eden's Cabinet Memorandum of January 17, 1936.

51. James Fearon, "Signaling Foreign Policy Interests: Tying Hands versus Sinking Costs," *Journal of Conflict Resolution* 41, no. 1 (1997), 68–90.

52. Jack S. Levy and John A. Vasquez, eds., *The Outbreak of the First World War* (Cambridge: Cambridge University Press, 2014); John Maurer, *The Outbreak of the First World War* (Westport, CT: Praeger, 1995); Keir A. Lieber, "The New History of World War I and What It Means for International Relations Theory," *International Security* 32, no. 2 (Fall 2007), 155–91.

53. Kenneth N. Waltz, *Theory of International Politics* (Reading, MA: Addison-Wesley, 1979); Scott Sagan and Kenneth Waltz, *The Spread of Nuclear Weapons: An Enduring Debate* (New York: W. W. Norton, 2012); John Lewis Gaddis, *The Long Peace: Inquiries into the History of the Cold War* (Oxford: Oxford University Press, 1989).

54. Thomas J. Christensen and Jack Snyder, "Chain Gangs and Passed Bucks: Predicting Alliance Patterns in Multipolarity," *International Organization* 44, no. 2 (1990), 137–68.

55. Emmerson, *The Rhineland Crisis*, 134–35.

56. Emmerson, *The Rhineland Crisis*, 179.

57. Taylor, *Origins of the Second World War*, 101.

58. Military commanders were surprised and unnerved when first briefed on Hitler's specific territorial goals, which was not until November 1937. Taylor, *Origins of the Second World War*, 131–34; Craig, *The Politics of the Prussian Army*, 488–89.

59. Churchill, *Gathering Storm*, 186.

60. Wheeler-Bennett, *The Nemesis of Power*, 559; US Department of State, Office of the Historian, https://history.state.gov/milestones/1937-1945/casablanca.

61. Ludwig Dehio, *Germany and World Politics in the Twentieth Century* (New York: Knopf, 1959), 37, 70.

62. Karl Jaspers, *The Question of German Guilt* (New York: Capricorn Books, 1947), 47–48, 53, 54.

63. Friedrich Meinecke, *The German Catastrophe* (Cambridge, MA: Harvard University Press, 1950), 107, 109–10.

64. Thomas U. Berger, "Norms, Identity, and National Security in Germany and Japan," in *The Culture of National Security*, ed. Peter J. Katzenstein (New York: Columbia University Press, 1996). There is a large literature on how successive generations of Germans have confronted their painful history. For a sample, see Siobhan Kattago, *Ambiguous Memory: The Nazi Past and German National*

Identity (Westport, CT: Praeger, 2001); Bill Niven, *Facing the Nazi Past* (London: Routledge, 2002); Michael Burleigh, ed., *Confronting the Nazi Past* (New York: St. Martin's Press, 1996); Bill Niven, ed., *Germans as Victims: Remembering the Past in Contemporary Germany* (New York: Palgrave Macmillan, 2006); Norbert Frei, *Adenauer's Germany and the Nazi Past* (New York: Columbia University Press, 2002).

65. Michael Walzer, "World War II: Why Was This War Different?" *Philosophy and Public Affairs* (Fall 1971), 4, emphasis added.

66. Taylor, *Origins of the Second World War*, 131.

67. Emmerson, *The Rhineland Crisis*, 241. Some have pointed to the blueprint for aggression contained in Hitler's *Mein Kampf* as clear evidence of what was to come. A common claim at the time was that it was written under profoundly different conditions for Hitler—at a time of revolutionary fervor in the immediate years after World War I, while Hitler stewed in prison—and now that Hitler was in power, his behavior would be modified by the heavy responsibilities of governing. Taylor, *Munich*, 94. The British ambassador to Germany noted that if *Mein Kampf* were taken seriously as the basis of British policy, there would be no choice but to launch a preventive war. For Ambassador Phipps, basing a decision for war on this early political rant was too flimsy. Edward E. Bennett, *German Rearmament and the West, 1932–1933* (Princeton, NJ: Princeton University Press, 2015), 105. Austen Chamberlain shared this view. Austen Chamberlain to Hilda Chamberlain, November 11, 1933, in Robert C. Self, ed., *The Austen Chamberlain Diary Letters*, vol. 5 (Cambridge: Cambridge University Press), 453.

68. NSC 68: United States Objectives and Programs for National Security, April 7, 1950, *Foreign Relations of the United States 1950*, vol. 1 (Washington, DC: US Government Printing Office, 1977), 228, 251, 266.

69. Michael S. Sherry, *Preparing for the Next War* (New Haven: Yale University Press, 1977), 27, 209.

70. "Aggression for Peace," *Chicago Tribune* (August 28, 1950), emphasis added.

71. "Instituting a War," *Time* (September 4, 1950).

72. "Curb General Who Offered to Bomb Russia," *Chicago Tribune* (September 2, 1950); "Air College Head Suspended for 'Preventive War' Remarks," *Washington Post* (September 2, 1950).

73. Marc Trachtenberg, "A 'Wasting Asset': American Strategy and the Shifting Nuclear Balance, 1949–1954," *International Security* 13, no. 3 (Winter 1988–89), 5, 7. Also see Russell D. Buhite and William Christopher Hamel, "War for Peace: The Question of an American Preventive War Against the Soviet Union, 1945–1955," *Diplomatic History* 14 (Summer 1990), 367.

74. David Carlton, "Churchill and the Two Evil Empires," *Transactions of the Royal Historical Society* 1 (2001), 346–48.

75. Trachtenberg, "A 'Wasting Asset,'" 9.

76. Thomas Maier, *When Lions Roar* (New York: Broadway Books, 2015), 412.

77. Trachtenberg, "A 'Wasting Asset,'" 39.

78. See Scott A. Silverstone, *Preventive War and American Democracy* (New York: Routledge, 2007).

79. Samuel P. Huntington, "To Choose Peace or War: Is There a Place for Preventive War in American Policy?" *United States Naval Institute Proceedings* 83 (April 1957), 362.

SELECTED BIBLIOGRAPHY

Adamthwaite, Anthony. *The Making of the Second World War*. London: George, Allen and Unwin, 1979.

Albright, David, and Mark Hibbs. "Iraq and the Bomb: Were They Even Close?" *Bulletin of the Atomic Scientists* 47, no. 2 (March 1991).

Alexander, Bevin. *Inside the Nazi War Machine*. New York: NAL Caliber, 2010.

Alexander, Martin S. *The Republic in Danger: General Maurice Gamelin and the Politics of French Defense, 1933–1940*. Cambridge: Cambridge University Press, 1992.

Allen, Henry T. *The Rhineland Occupation*. Indianapolis: The Bobbs-Merrill Co., 1927.

Art, Robert J. "Europe Hedges Its Security Bets." In *Balance of Power: Theory and Practice in the 21st Century*, edited by T. V. Paul, James J. Wirtz, and Michel Fortmann. Stanford, CA: Stanford University Press, 2004.

Asprey, Robert B. *The German High Command at War*. New York: William Morrow and Co., 1991.

Baker, James A., III, and Lee H. Hamilton. Iraq Study Group Report. December 2006.

Bennett, Edward E. *German Rearmament and the West, 1932–1933*. Princeton, NJ: Princeton University Press, 2015.

Berber, F. J. *Locarno: A Collection of Documents*. Edinburgh: William Hodge and Co., 1936.

Berger, Thomas U. "Norms, Identity, and National Security in Germany and Japan." In *The Culture of National Security*, edited by Peter J. Katzenstein. New York: Columbia University Press, 1996.

Betts, Richard K. "Striking First: A History of Thankfully Lost Opportunities." *Ethics and International Affairs* 17, no. 1 (Spring 2003): 17–24.

Bismarck, Otto von. *Bismarck: The Memoirs*. New York: H. Fertig, 1966.

Booth, Ken, and Nicholas J. Wheeler. *The Security Dilemma*. New York: Palgrave Macmillan, 2008.

Boothby, Robert John Graham. *Boothby: Recollections of a Rebel*. London: Hutchison, 1978.

Boyce, Robert, and Esmonde M. Robertson, eds. *Paths to War: New Essays on the Origins of the Second World War*. New York: St. Martins, 1989.

Braut-Hegghammer, Malfrid. "Revisiting Osirak: Preventive Attacks and Nuclear Proliferation Risks." *International Security* 36, no. 1 (Summer 2011): 101–32.

Bucholz, Arden. *Moltke and the German Wars, 1864–1871*. New York: Palgrave, 2001.

Buckle, G. E., ed. *The Letters of Queen Victoria*. Second Series, vol. II. New York: Longmans, Green, 1907.

Buhite, Russell D., and William Christopher Hamel. "War for Peace: The Question of an American Preventive War Against the Soviet Union, 1945–1955." *Diplomatic History* 14 (Summer 1990): 367–84.

Burleigh, Michael, ed. *Confronting the Nazi Past*. New York: St. Martin's Press, 1996.

Cabinet Papers, British National Archives, http://www.nationalarchives.gov.uk/cabinetpapers.

Carlton, David. "Churchill and the Two Evil Empires." *Transactions of the Royal Historical Society* 1 (2001): 331–51.

Cato. *The Guilty Men*. New York: Frederick A. Stokes, 1940.

Chapman, Guy. *Why France Fell*. New York: Holt, Rinehart and Winston, 1968.

Christensen, Thomas J., and Jack Snyder. "Chain Gangs and Passed Bucks: Predicting Alliance Patterns in Multipolarity." *International Organization* 44, no. 2 (1990): 137–68.

Churchill Archives, available at http://www.churchillarchive.com.

Churchill, Winston S. *While England Slept: A Survey of World Affairs, 1932–1938*. New York: G. P. Putnam's Sons, 1938.

———. *Gathering Storm*. Boston: Houghton Mifflin Co., 1948.

Claire, Rodger W. *Raid on the Sun*. New York: Broadway Books, 2004.

Clausewitz, Carl von. *On War*, edited by Peter Paret and Michael Howard. New York: Alfred A. Knopf, [1976] 1993.

———. *Two Letters on Strategy*, edited by Peter Paret and Daniel Moran. Carlisle Barracks, PA: US Army War College, 1984.

Colvin, Ian. *None So Blind*. New York: Harcourt, Brace and World, Inc., 1965.

Cooper, Duff. *Old Men Forget*. London: Rupert Hart-Davis, 1953.

Copeland, Dale C. *The Origins of Major War*. Ithaca: Cornell University Press, 2000.

———. "A Tragic Choice: Japanese Preventive Motivations and the Origins of the Pacific War." *International Interactions* 37 (January–March 2011): 116–26.

Corum, James S. *The Roots of Blitzkrieg*. Lawrence: University Press of Kansas, 1992.

Craig, Gordon A. *The Politics of the Prussian Army, 1640–1945*. London: Oxford University Press, 1956.

———. *Germany, 1866–1945*. New York: Oxford University Press, 1978.

Crankshaw, Edward. *Bismarck*. New York: Viking Press, 1981.

Crockett, Jameson W. "The Polish Blitz, More than a Mere Footnote to History: Poland and Preventive War with Germany, 1933." *Diplomacy & Statecraft* 20 (2009): 561–79.

D'Abernon, Viscount. *The Diary of an Ambassador: Dawes to Locarno, 1924–1926*. Garden City, NY: Doubleday, Doran, and Co., 1931.

Dawson, William Harbutt. *The German Empire, 1867–1914*. Hamden, CT: Archon Books, 1966.

Dehio, Ludwig. *Germany and World Politics in the Twentieth Century*. New York: Knopf, 1959.

Dodd, William E. *Ambassador Dodd's Diary, 1933–1938*. New York: Harcourt Brace, 1941.

Doyle, Michael W. *Striking First: Preemption and Prevention in International Conflict*. Princeton, NJ: Princeton University Press, 2008.

Draper, Theodore. *The Six Weeks' War*. New York: Viking Press, 1944.

Duelfer, Charles. Comprehensive Report of Special Advisor to the Director of Central Intelligence on Iraq's WMD. September 2004.

Eden, Anthony. *The Memoirs of Anthony Eden: Facing the Dictators, 1923–1938*. Boston: Houghton Mifflin, 1962.

Ellis, John. *World War II: A Statistical Survey*. New York: Facts on File, 1993.

Emmerson, James T. *The Rhineland Crisis*. Ames: Iowa State University Press, 1977.

Evans, Richard. *The Third Reich in Power*. New York: Penguin, 2005.

Fainberg, Anthony. "Osirak and International Security." *Bulletin of the Atomic Scientists* (October 1981).

Fearon, James. "Signaling Foreign Policy Interests: Tying Hands versus Sinking Costs." *Journal of Conflict Resolution* 41, no. 1 (1997): 68–90.

Feldman, Shai. "The Bombing of Osiraq—Revisited." *International Security* 7, no. 2 (Fall 1982): 114–42.

Ferguson, Niall. *The Pity of War*. New York: Basic Books, 1999.

———, ed. *Virtual History*. New York: Basic Books, 1999.

Feuchtwanger, Edgar. *Imperial Germany, 1850–1918*. London: Routledge, 2001.

Fischer, Conan. *The Ruhr Crisis, 1923–1924*. London: Oxford University Press, 2003.

Foreign Office Archives of the United Kingdom, available at http://www.national archives.gov.uk.

Frei, Norbert. *Adenauer's Germany and the Nazi Past*. New York: Columbia University Press, 2002.

Gaddis, John Lewis. *The Long Peace: Inquiries into the History of the Cold War.* Oxford: Oxford University Press, 1989.

Gates, Robert M. *Duty: Memoirs of a Secretary at War.* New York: Alfred A. Knopf, 2014.

Gilbert, Martin. *Roots of Appeasement.* London: Weidenfeld & Nicolson, 1966.

———. *The First World War.* New York: Henry Holt, 1994.

Gilpin, Robert. *War and Change in World Politics.* Cambridge: Cambridge University Press, 1981.

Glaser, Charles L. "Political Consequences of Military Strategy: Expanding and Refining the Spiral and Deterrence Models." *World Politics* 44, no. 4 (July 1992): 497–538.

———. "The Security Dilemma Revisited." *World Politics* 50, no. 1 (October 1997): 171–201.

Goddard, Stacie E. "The Rhetoric of Appeasement: Hitler's Legitimation and British Foreign Policy, 1938–39." *Security Studies* 24, 1 (2015): 95–130.

Goerlitz, Walter. *History of the German General Staff, 1657–1945.* New York: Praeger, 1953.

Goertz, Gary, and Jack S. Levy, eds. *Explaining War and Peace.* New York: Routledge, 2007.

Gorodetsky, Gabriel, ed. *Soviet Foreign Policy, 1917–1919.* London: Routledge, 1994.

Gray, Colin S. "How Has War Changed Since the End of the Cold War?" *Parameters* (Spring 2005): 14–26.

Hagood, Johnson. *Caissons Go Rolling Along*, edited by Larry A. Grant. Columbia: University of South Carolina Press, 2010.

Hamilton, Richard F., and Holger H. Herwig. *The Origins of World War I.* Cambridge: Cambridge University Press, 2003.

Harazsti, Eva. *The Invaders: Hitler Occupies the Rhineland.* Budapest: Akadémiai Kiadó, 1983.

Haslam, Jonathan. *The Soviet Union and the Struggle for Collective Security in Europe, 1933–39.* New York: St. Martin's Press, 1984.

Hawkins, Scott A., and Reid Hastie. "Hindsight: Biased Judgments of Past Events After the Outcomes Are Known." *Psychological Bulletin* 107, no. 3 (1990): 311–27.

Henderson, Nicholas. "Hitler and the Rhineland: A Decisive Turning-Point." *History Today* (October 1992).

Hensel, Paul. "An Evolutionary Approach to the Study of Interstate Rivalry." *Conflict Management and Peace Science* 17 (1999): 175–206.

Herrmann, Richard K., and Richard Ned Lebow. *Ending the Cold War.* New York: Palgrave, 2004.

Herz, John H. "Idealist Internationalism and the Security Dilemma." *World Politics* 2, no. 2 (January 1950): 157–80.

———. *Political Realism and Political Idealism*. Chicago: University of Chicago Press, 1951.

Hobbes, Thomas. *Leviathan*. New York: Penguin, 1968.

Hochman, Jiri. *The Soviet Union and the Failure of Collective Security, 1934–1938*. Ithaca: Cornell University Press, 1984.

Holstein, Friedrich von. *The Holstein Papers: The Memoirs, Diaries and Correspondence of Friedrich von Holstein, 1837–1909*. Cambridge: Cambridge University Press, 2011.

Horne, Alistair. *To Lose a Battle*. New York: Penguin Books, 2007.

Horne, Charles F., ed. *Source Records of the Great War*, vol. V. London: National Alumni, 1923.

House of Commons and House of Lords Debates, Hansard Series, available at http://loc.gov/rr/main/parliamentarypapers/ParliamentaryDebates.html.

Howard, Michael. *The Franco-Prussian War*. New York: Macmillan, 1961.

Hughes, Judith M. *To the Maginot Line*. Cambridge, MA: Harvard University Press, 1971.

Huntington, Samuel P. "To Choose Peace or War: Is There a Place for Preventive War in American Policy?" *United States Naval Institute Proceedings* 83 (April 1957).

Ikenberry, G. John. *After Victory*. Princeton, NJ: Princeton University Press, 2000.

Jackson, Peter. *Beyond the Balance of Power*. Cambridge: Cambridge University Press, 2013.

Jacobson, Jon. *Locarno Diplomacy: Germany and the West, 1925–1929*. Princeton, NJ: Princeton University Press, 1972.

———. "Locarno, Britain and the Security of Europe." In *Locarno Revisited: European Diplomacy, 1920–1929*, edited by Gaynor Johnson. London: Routledge, 2004.

Jaspers, Karl. *The Question of German Guilt*. New York: Capricorn Books, 1947.

Jervis, Robert. *Perception and Misperception in International Politics*. Princeton, NJ: Princeton University Press, 1976.

———. "Cooperation Under the Security Dilemma." *World Politics* 30, no. 2 (January 1978): 167–214.

Jordan, David. *Atlas of World War II*. New York: Barnes and Noble, 2004.

Jordan, Nicole. "The Cut Price War on the Peripheries." In *Paths to War: New Essays on the Origins of the Second World War*, edited by Robert Boyce and Esmonde M. Robertson. London: Palgrave Macmillan, 1989.

Kattago, Siobhan. *Ambiguous Memory: The Nazi Past and German National Identity*. Westport, CT: Praeger, 2001.

Kaufmann, J. E., and H. W. Kaufmann. *Fortress France: The Maginot Line and French Defenses in World War II*. London: Praeger Security International, 2006.

Keegan, John. *The First World War*. New York: Vintage Books, 2000.

———. *Collins Atlas of World War II*. New York: Collins, 2006.

Kennedy, Paul. *The Rise and Fall of the Great Powers.* New York: Random House, 1987.

Kershaw, Ian. *Hitler, 1889–1936: Hubris.* New York: W. W. Norton, 1999.

Keylor, William R. *The Legacy of the Great War.* Boston: Houghton, Mifflin, 1998.

Khong, Yuen Foong. *Analogies at War.* Princeton, NJ: Princeton University Press, 1992.

King, Jere Clemens. *Foch versus Clemenceau.* Cambridge, MA: Harvard University Press, 1960.

Kirshenbaum, Joshua. "Operation Opera: An Ambiguous Success." *Journal of Strategic Security* 3, no. 4 (2010): 49–62.

Kovacs, A. F. "Military Origins of the Fall of France." *Military Affairs* 7 (Spring 1943).

Kraehe, Enno. "The Motives Behind the Maginot Line." *Military Affairs* 8, no. 2 (Summer 1944): 109–12.

Langer, William L. *European Alliances and Alignments, 1871–1890.* New York: Alfred A. Knopf, 1950.

Lebow, Richard Ned. "Windows of Opportunity: Do States Jump through Them?" *International Security* 9 (Summer 1984): 147–86.

Lee, Bradford A. "Strategy, Arms and the Collapse of France, 1930–40." In *Diplomacy and Intelligence during the Second World War*, edited by Richard Langhorne. Cambridge: Cambridge University Press, 1988.

Levy, Jack S. "Declining Power and the Preventive Motivation for War." *World Politics* 40 (October 1987): 82–107.

———. "Preferences, Constraints and Choices in July 1914." *International Security* 15, no. 3 (Winter 1990–1991): 151–86.

Liddell Hart, Basil H. *Strategy.* New York: Praeger, 1967.

Lieber, Keir A. "The New History of World War I and What It Means for International Relations Theory." *International Security* 32, no. 2 (Fall 2007): 155–91.

Lloyd George, David. *The Truth About the Peace Treaties.* London: V. Gollancz, 1938.

Maier, Thomas. *When Lions Roar.* New York: Broadway Books, 2015.

Mantoux, Etienne. *The Carthaginian Peace.* London: Oxford, 1946.

Maurer, John. *The Outbreak of the First World War.* Westport, CT: Praeger, 1995.

May, Ernest. *"Lessons" of the Past: The Use and Misuse of History in American Foreign Policy.* New York: Oxford University Press, 1973.

McDougall, Walter A. *France's Rhineland Diplomacy, 1914–1924.* Princeton, NJ: Princeton University Press, 1978.

Mearsheimer, John. *The Tragedy of Great Power Politics.* New York: W. W. Norton, 2014.

Medlicott, W. N., and Dorothy K. Coveney. *Bismarck and Europe.* New York: St. Martin's Press, 1971.

Meehan, Patricia. *The Unnecessary War, Whitehall and the German Resistance to Hitler.* London: Sinclair-Stevenson, 1992.

Meinecke, Friedrich. *The German Catastrophe*. Cambridge, MA: Harvard University Press, 1950.

Mommsen, Wolfgang J. *Imperial Germany, 1867–1918*. London: Arnold, 1995.

Mosse, W. E. *The European Powers and the German Question, 1848–71*. New York: Octagon Books, 1969.

Mueller, John. *Retreat from Doomsday*. New York: Basic Books, 1989.

———. "Changing Attitudes towards War: The Impact of the First World War." *British Journal of Political Science* 21, no. 1 (January 1991): 1–28.

Mulligan, William. "Restraints on Preventive War Before 1914." In *The Outbreak of the First World War*, edited by Jack S. Levy and John A. Vasquez. Cambridge: Cambridge University Press, 2014.

Murphy, George G. S. "On Counterfactual Propositions." *History and Theory* 9, no. 9 (1969): 14–38.

Murray, Williamson. *The Change in the European Balance of Power, 1938–39: The Path to Ruin*. Princeton, NJ: Princeton University Press, 1984.

Nakdimon, Shlomo. *First Strike*. New York: Summit Books, 1987.

Nelson, Harold I. *Land and Power: British and Allied Policy on Germany's Frontiers, 1916–19*. London: Routledge and Kegan Paul, 1963.

Nelson, Keith L. *Victors Divided: America and the Allies in Germany, 1918–1923*. Berkeley: University of California Press, 1975.

Neustadt, Richard E., and Ernest R. May. *Thinking in Time*. New York: Free Press, 1986.

Newman, William J. *The Balance of Power in the Interwar Years, 1919–1939*. New York: Random House, 1968.

Niven, Bill. *Facing the Nazi Past*. London: Routledge, 2002.

———, ed. *Germans as Victims: Remembering the Past in Contemporary Germany*. New York: Palgrave Macmillan, 2006.

O'Connell, Robert L. *The Ghosts of Cannae*. New York: Random House, 2010.

Parker, R. A. C. "The First Capitulation: France and the Rhineland Crisis of 1936." *World Politics* 8, no. 3 (April 1956).

Parkinson, Roger. *Tormented Warrior*. London: Hodder & Stoughton, 1978.

Parssinen, Terry. *The Oster Conspiracy of 1938*. New York: HarperCollins, 2003.

Pawley, Margaret. *The Watch on the Rhine*. London: I. B. Tauris, 2007.

Pflanze, Otto. *Bismarck and the Development of Germany*, vol. I. Princeton, NJ: Princeton University Press, 1990.

———. *Bismarck and the Development of Germany*, vol. II. Princeton, NJ: Princeton University Press, 2014.

———. *Bismarck and the Development of Germany*, vol. III. Princeton, NJ: Princeton University Press, 2014.

Phillips, Hugh D. *Between the Revolution and the West: A Political Biography of Maxim M. Litvinov*. Boulder, CO: Westview Press, 1992.

Pollack, Kenneth M. *Unthinkable: Iran, the Bomb, and American Strategy*. New York: Simon & Schuster, 2013.

Posen, Barry R. *The Sources of Military Doctrine*. Ithaca: Cornell University Press, 1984.

Post, Gaines, Jr., *Dilemmas of Appeasement*. Ithaca: Cornell University Press, 1993.

Reiter, Dan. "Exploding the Powder Keg Myth: Preemptive Wars Almost Never Happen." *International Security* 20, no. 2 (Fall 1995): 5–34.

———. "Preventive Attacks Against Nuclear Programs and the 'Success' at Osiraq." *The Nonproliferation Review* 12, no. 2 (2005): 355–71.

Report of the Officer in Charge of Civil Affairs, Third Army and American Forces in Germany. "American Military Government of Occupied Germany 1918–1920." Washington, DC: US Government Printing Office, 1943.

Reynolds, David. *In Command of History*. New York: Basic Books, 2007.

Rich, Norman. *Friedrich von Holstein: Politics and Diplomacy in the Era of Bismarck and Wilhelm II*. Cambridge: Cambridge University Press, 1965.

Ripsman, Norrin M., and Jack S. Levy. "The Preventive War That Never Happened: Britain, France, and the Rise of Germany in the 1930s." *Security Studies* (January–March 2007): 32–67.

———. "Wishful Thinking or Buying Time? The Logic of British Appeasement in the 1930s." *International Security* 33, no. 2 (Fall 2008): 148–81.

Robertson, E. M. *Hitler's Pre-War Policy and Military Plans, 1933–1939*. New York: Citadel Press, 1963.

Ross, Dennis, *Doomed to Succeed*. New York: Farrar, Straus and Giroux, 2015.

Sagan, Scott D. "The Origins of the Pacific War." *Journal of Interdisciplinary History* 18, no. 4 (Spring 1988).

Sagan, Scott, and Kenneth Waltz. *The Spread of Nuclear Weapons: An Enduring Debate*. New York: W. W. Norton, 2012.

Sakwa, George. "The Franco-Polish Alliance and the Remilitarization of the Rhineland." *The Historical Journal* 16 (1973): 125–46.

Schelling, Thomas C. *Arms and Influence*. New Haven: Yale University Press, 1966.

Schmidt, Royal J. *Versailles and the Ruhr*. The Hague: Martinus Nijhoff, 1968.

Schuker, Stephen A. "France and the Remilitarization of the Rhineland, 1936." *French Historical Studies* (Spring 1986): 299–338.

———. "The Rhineland Question: West European Security at the Paris Peace Conference of 1919." In *The Treaty of Versailles: A Reassessment After 75 Years*, edited by Manfred F. Boemeke, Gerald D. Feldman, and Elisabeth Glaser. New York: Cambridge University Press, 1998.

Schweller, Randall L. "Neorealism's Status-Quo Bias: What Security Dilemma?" *Security Studies* 5, no. 3 (1996): 90–121.

———. *Unanswered Threats: Political Constraints on the Balance of Power*. Princeton, NJ: Princeton University Press, 2008.

Self, Robert C., ed. *The Austen Chamberlain Diary Letters*, vol. 5. Cambridge: Cambridge University Press, 1995.

Shay, Robert Paul, Jr., *British Rearmament in the Thirties*. Princeton, NJ: Princeton University Press, 1977.

Sherry, Michael S. *Preparing for the Next War*. New Haven: Yale University Press, 1977.

Sherwood, John M. *Georges Mandel and the Third Republic*. Stanford, CA: Stanford University Press, 1970.

Shirer, William L. *Berlin Diary*. New York: A. A. Knopf, 1941.

———. *The Rise and Fall of the Third Reich*. New York: Simon & Schuster, 1960.

Shore, Zach. "Hitler, Intelligence and the Decision to Remilitarize the Rhine." *Journal of Contemporary History* 34, no. 1 (January 1999): 5–18.

Showalter, Dennis E. *The Wars of German Unification*. London: Arnold, 2004.

Silverstone, Scott A. *Preventive War and American Democracy*. New York: Routledge, 2007.

———. "Preemption and Preventive War." *Oxford Bibliographies—International Relations*. Oxford University Press online (http://www.oxfordbibliographies.com/view/document/obo-9780199743292/obo-9780199743292-0053.xml), 2013.

Small, Melvin, and J. David Singer. *Resort to Arms: International and Civil Wars, 1816–1965*. Ann Arbor: University of Michigan Press, 1982.

Snyder, Louis L. *The Blood and Iron Chancellor: A Documentary-Biography of Otto von Bismarck*. Princeton, NJ: Van Nostrand Co., 1967.

Speer, Albert. *Inside the Third Reich*. New York: Macmillan, 1970.

Steiner, Zara. *The Lights That Failed: European International History, 1919–1933*. Oxford: Oxford University Press, 2005.

Stevenson, David. *With Our Backs to the Wall: Victory and Defeat in 1918*. Cambridge, MA: Harvard University Press, 2011.

Stiglitz, Joseph E. *The Three Trillion Dollar War*. New York: W. W. Norton, 2008.

Stone, James. *The War Scare of 1875*. Stuttgart: Franz Steiner Verlag, 2010.

Strachan, Hew. *The First World War*, vol. I. Oxford: Oxford University Press, 2001.

———. "Preemption and Prevention in Historical Perspective." In *Preemption: Military Action and Moral Justification*, edited by Henry Shue and David Rodin. Oxford: Oxford University Press, 2007.

Sutton, Eric, ed. *Gustav Stresemann: His Diaries, Letters and Papers*, vol. I. New York: Macmillan, 1935.

———. *Gustav Stresemann: His Diaries, Letters and Papers*, vol. II. New York: Macmillan, 1937.

Swanston, Alexander. *The Historical Atlas of World War II*. Edison, NJ: Chartwell Books, 2007.

Sylvan, David, and Stephen Majeski. "A Methodology for the Study of Historical Counterfactuals." *International Studies Quarterly* 42, no. 1 (March 1998): 79–108.

Tardieu, Andre. *The Truth About the Treaty*. Indianapolis: The Bobbs-Merrill Company, 1921.

Taylor, A. J. P. *Struggle for Mastery in Europe, 1848–1918*. Oxford: Clarendon Press, 1954.

———. *Bismarck: The Man and the Statesman*. New York: Vintage Books, 1955.

———. *The Origins of the Second World War*. New York: Atheneum, 1962.

Taylor, Telford. *Sword and Swastika*. New York: Simon & Schuster, 1952.

———. *Munich: The Price of Peace*. Garden City, NY: Doubleday and Co., 1979.

Tetlock, Philip E. *Expert Political Judgment*. Princeton, NJ: Princeton University Press, 2005.

Tetlock, Philip E., and Aaron Belkin. *Counterfactual Thought Experiments in World Politics*. Princeton, NJ: Princeton University Press, 1996.

Tetlock, Philip E., Richard Ned Lebow, and Geoffrey Parker, eds. *Unmaking the West: "What-if" Scenarios That Rewrite History*. Ann Arbor: University of Michigan Press, 2006.

Thorson, Stuart J., and Donald A. Sylvan. "Counterfactuals and the Cuban Missile Crisis." *International Studies Quarterly* 26, no. 4 (December 1982): 539–71.

Thucydides. *History of the Peloponnesian War*. New York: Penguin Classics, 1972.

Trachtenberg, Marc. "A 'Wasting Asset': American Strategy and the Shifting Nuclear Balance, 1949–1954." *International Security* 13, no. 3 (Winter 1988–1989): 5–49.

Tuchman, Barbara. *The Guns of August*. New York: Ballantine Books, 1962.

Vagts, Alfred. *Defense and Diplomacy*. New York: King's Crown Press, 1956.

Van Evera, Stephen. "The Cult of the Offensive and the Origins of the First World War." *International Security* (Summer 1984): 58–107.

———. *The Causes of War*. Ithaca: Cornell University Press, 2001.

Vansittart, Robert. *Lessons of My Life*. New York: Alfred A. Knopf, 1943.

Waldersee, Alfred von. *A Field Marshal's Memoirs*. London: Hutchison & Co., 1925.

Walt, Stephen M. *The Origins of Alliances*. Ithaca: Cornell University Press, 1990.

Waltz, Kenneth N. *Theory of International Politics*. Reading, MA: Addison-Wesley, 1979.

Walzer, Michael. "World War II: Why Was this War Different?" *Philosophy and Public Affairs* (Fall 1971).

Watt, Donald Cameron. "German Plans for the Reoccupation of the Rhineland: A Note." *Journal of Contemporary History* 1, no. 4 (October 1966): 193–99.

———. Introduction to James T. Emmerson, *The Rhineland Crisis*. Ames: Iowa State University Press, 1977.

Wawro, Geoffrey. *The Austro-Prussian War*. Cambridge: Cambridge University Press, 1997.

———. *The Franco-Prussian War*. Cambridge: Cambridge University Press, 2005.

Weinberg, Gerhard. *The Foreign Policy of Hitler's Germany*. Chicago: University of Chicago Press, 1970.

Wendt, Alexander. "Anarchy Is What States Make of It: The Social Construction of Power Politics." *International Organization* 46, no. 2 (Spring 1992): 391–425.

———. "Constructing International Politics." *International Security* 20, no. 1 (Summer 1995): 71–81.

Weygand, Maxim. "How France Is Defended." *International Affairs* 18, no. 4 (July–August 1939): 459–77.

Wheeler-Bennett, John W. *The Nemesis of Power: The German Army in Politics, 1918–1945*. London: Macmillan and Co., 1954.

Wit, Joel S., Daniel B. Poneman, and Robert L. Gallucci. *Going Critical*. Washington, DC: Brookings Institution Press, 2004.

Wolfers, Arnold. *Britain and France Between the Wars*. New York: Harcourt, Brace, 1940.

Woods, Kevin, James Lacey, and Williamson Murray. "Saddam's Delusions: The View from the Inside." *Foreign Affairs* 85, no. 3 (May–June 2006): 2–26.

Woodward, E. L., ed. *Documents on British Foreign Policy, 1919–1939*. London: H.M.S.O., 1973.

Young, Robert J. *In Command of France*. Cambridge, MA: Harvard University, 1978.

INDEX

ABOUT THE AUTHOR

Scott A. Silverstone is professor of international relations at the United States Military Academy at West Point, where he is the deputy head of the Department of Social Sciences. He is an ASU Future of War Senior Fellow at New America, a Washington, DC, think tank, which has supported his most recent work on preventive war. After receiving a BA in political science from the University of New Hampshire in 1985, Silverstone received a commission as a US naval officer and flew P-3 Orions for the US Navy, conducting antisubmarine and maritime reconnaissance operations in the Pacific and Indian Oceans and the Persian Gulf during the final years of the Cold War. From 1990 to 1993 he served as a crisis staff officer for the chief of naval operations in the Pentagon, working issues ranging from the Defense Department's nuclear survivability program to the 1991 Gulf War and the humanitarian intervention in Somalia in 1992. After leaving active duty, Silverstone received a PhD in political science from the University of Pennsylvania, and taught at the University of Pennsylvania and Williams College before joining the faculty at West Point in 2001. Silverstone is also an adjunct professor with Bard College's Globalization and International Affairs program in New York City, and he has been a fellow with the Carnegie Council for Ethics in International Affairs. His previous books include *Preventive War and American Democracy* and *Divided Union: The Politics of War in the Early American Republic*.